The Glannon Guide
to Criminal Procedure

The Glannon Guide to Criminal Procedure

Learning Criminal Procedure Through Multiple-Choice Questions and Analysis

Fifth Edition

John Kip Cornwell
Professor of Law
Seton Hall University School of Law

Wolters Kluwer

Published by Wolters Kluwer in New York.

Wolters Kluwer Legal & Regulatory U.S. serves customers worldwide with CCH, Aspen Publishers, and Kluwer Law International products. (www.WKLegaledu.com)

Cover image: Photographee.eu/Shutterstock.com

To contact Customer Service, e-mail customer.service@wolterskluwer.com, call 1-800-234-1660, fax 1-800-901-9075, or mail correspondence to:

> Wolters Kluwer
> Attn: Order Department
> PO Box 990
> Frederick, MD 21705

Printed in the United States of America.

1 2 3 4 5 6 7 8 9 0

ISBN 978-1-5438-4119-0

Library of Congress Cataloging-in-Publication Data

Names: Cornwell, John Kip, 1961- author.
Title: The Glannon guide to criminal procedure : learning criminal
  procedure through multiple-choice questions and analysis / John Kip
  Cornwell, Professor of Law, Seton Hall University School of Law.
Other titles: Guide to criminal procedure
Description: Fifth edition. | New York : Wolters Kluwer, 2021. | Includes
  index.
Identifiers: LCCN 2021023185 | ISBN 9781543841190 (paperback) | ISBN
  9781543847703 (epub)
Subjects: LCSH: Criminal procedure—United States—Problems, exercises,
  etc.
Classification: LCC KF9619.85 .C67 2021 | DDC 345.73/05026—dc23
LC record available at https://lccn.loc.gov/2021023185

About Wolters Kluwer Legal & Regulatory U.S.

Wolters Kluwer Legal & Regulatory U.S. delivers expert content and solutions in the areas of law, corporate compliance, health compliance, reimbursement, and legal education. Its practical solutions help customers successfully navigate the demands of a changing environment to drive their daily activities, enhance decision quality and inspire confident outcomes.

Serving customers worldwide, its legal and regulatory portfolio includes products under the Aspen Publishers, CCH Incorporated, Kluwer Law International, ftwilliam.com, and MediRegs names. They are regarded as exceptional and trusted resources for general legal and practice-specific knowledge, compliance and risk management, dynamic workflow solutions, and expert commentary.

Contents

1

A Very Short Introduction

This Glannon Guide reviews the Fourth, Fifth, Sixth, and Fourteenth Amendment cases and principles typically covered in law school criminal procedure classes. The format is similar to that of other books in the series, in which carefully designed multiple-choice questions help students apply, reinforce, and ultimately master each concept. Each section of each chapter provides a brief summary of the governing U.S. Supreme Court case law necessary to understand the concept at issue and to answer the question that follows. In responding to the questions, students choose from among four or five proposed answers. Each choice is then discussed, explaining why one is correct and the others, wrong. A final question, called a "closer," incorporates all issues presented in that chapter. In the book's last chapter, each of twenty "closing closers" combines principles from a number of chapters, allowing students to test their understanding of all aspects of constitutional criminal procedure.

The book begins with the Fourth Amendment, the single largest topic in criminal procedure courses due to the wealth of U.S. Supreme Court case law interpreting its provisions. The text of the Fourth Amendment provides:

> The right of the people to be secure in their persons, houses, papers, and effects, against unreasonable searches and seizures, shall not be violated, and no Warrants shall issue, but upon probable cause, supported by Oath or affirmation, and particularly describing the place to be searched, and the persons or things to be seized.

Reading the language of the Amendment, you can understand why its provisions have been so susceptible to interpretive controversy. For example, while the Framers make reference to warrants, they do not clearly delineate the circumstances in which warrants are necessary to justify a search. Are they always necessary, or merely presumptively necessary, or necessary only in certain circumstances? This ambiguity has produced a wide range of opinion from the justices, particularly in the latter half of the twentieth century, as an increasingly conservative Court recognized an ever greater number of exceptions to the warrant requirement. In the view of the Court's more liberal members, this philosophical realignment of the Fourth Amendment has eviscerated the spirit, if not the letter, of constitutional protections against unreasonable searches and seizures by law enforcement officers.

The Amendment's ambiguity is not limited to the need for a warrant. The Framers also failed to define with precision the standards governing searches. While they clearly require "probable cause" for the issuance of a warrant, that standard is left undefined, as is the further requirement of particularity in the description of the place to be searched and the items to be seized. Moreover, if a warrant is deemed unnecessary, does the probable cause standard continue to inform the reasonableness of the search, or is that level of proof relevant only for warranted searches?

We begin with important threshold issues, such as the Fourth Amendment's analytical framework and the areas in which one may reasonably expect constitutional protection in his or her person, houses, papers, or effects. After addressing the Amendment's scope, we will focus next on the need for a warrant, including the meaning of the procedural requirements of probable cause and particularity. The chapters that follow change gears, identifying those circumstances in which obtaining a warrant is not necessary to validate a search under the Fourth Amendment. You will notice that this topic occupies much more space than all other Fourth Amendment issues. There is a simple reason for this: In the last twenty to thirty years, the U.S. Supreme Court has devoted far more attention to addressing and refining the exceptions to the warrant requirement than to the warrant clause itself. We will be analyzing each exception, starting with exigent circumstances. Remember, when answering a question implicating a warrant clause exception, *always* be sure to identify the underlying rationale for the exception, the showing necessary to rely on it, and its scope and corresponding limitations.

After completing this section, you will understand when the Fourth Amendment applies to a search or seizure and, if it does, whether a warrant is necessary to satisfy constitutional requirements. We must now turn to the ways in which a defendant who believes that his or her constitutional rights have been violated through an unlawful search or seizure may have the illegally obtained evidence excluded from criminal prosecution. As we will see, the admissibility of "tainted" evidence is an issue separate from the determination of unconstitutional conduct by government officials.

We begin this inquiry by examining the origins of the "exclusionary rule," its parameters, and how a defendant gains "standing" to invoke it in a given case. We will then apply the rule in the context of defective search warrants, with attention to the applicable standards and the relevance of an officer's "good faith" in avoiding evidentiary exclusion. As we will see, officer "good faith" is not the only tool in the prosecution's arsenal; we next explore three additional doctrines — independent source, inevitable discovery, and attenuation—that also serve to limit the availability to criminal defendants of the exclusionary rule.

Our discussion of evidentiary exclusion finishes with the defense of entrapment and related doctrines. In pleading entrapment, a defendant seeks to exclude evidence based on the government's allegedly overzealous involvement in the criminal enterprise in question, typically through a "sting" operation. While not constitutionally based, the entrapment defense is available by statute or case law in all fifty states, as well as under the federal criminal code.

After the Fourth Amendment, confessions are the next most important topic in constitutional criminal procedure, and they are the focus of most of the remaining chapters of this book. There are three constitutional provisions that criminal defendants can invoke when seeking to exclude incriminating statements: the Due Process Clause of the Fourteenth Amendment, the Fifth Amendment *Miranda* doctrine, and the Sixth Amendment right to counsel. We address each in turn, beginning with the due process standard and its focus on voluntariness—that is, whether the police have compromised a suspect's free will.

The Due Process Clause remained the sole constitutional avenue available to defendants charged with violating state law until the mid-1960s. When the Court issued its watershed decision in *Miranda v. Arizona*, 384 U.S. 436 (1966), the Fifth Amendment privilege against self-incrimination became the primary vehicle used by defendants to challenge the admissibility of incriminating statements made prior to the formal initiation of adversarial proceedings. While subsequent case law has diminished the force of the *Miranda* doctrine in certain respects, it remains the principal constitutional basis for testimonial exclusion.

Miranda responded to abuses in custodial interrogation that led defendants to incriminate themselves. We begin this section by identifying the specific protections provided by *Miranda* and when they apply. What, for example, is the meaning of "custody" and "interrogation" in the context of *Miranda*? If *Miranda* applies, an officer can interrogate a suspect only after obtaining a valid waiver; therefore, we next evaluate the standard for a valid *Miranda* waiver. Of course, a suspect may instead "invoke" his or her *Miranda* rights by refusing to speak to the police or by asking for a lawyer. We next identify the rules that govern both the defendant's assertion of these rights and the response of law enforcement to the assertion.

Our review of the Fourth Amendment addressed the exclusionary rule as applied to searches and seizures. We now turn to the additional restrictions on exclusion that apply to evidence obtained in violation of *Miranda*. As we will see, these exceptions to the exclusionary rule may concern testimonial evidence, such as confessions obtained in violation of *Miranda*, or *physical* evidence discovered through statements that fail to comport with the doctrine's requirements.

A violation of the Sixth Amendment right to counsel is the third, and final, constitutional means by which a defendant may suppress incriminating testimony. While in many respects a more powerful right to counsel than that provided by *Miranda*, the Sixth Amendment has its own rules and restrictions. Thus, we begin our discussion by defining when indigent persons are entitled to counsel and at what stage(s) of the criminal process the Amendment's protections are available. As with *Miranda*, terms such as "interrogation" have their own specific meaning in the Sixth Amendment context. We turn to this issue next, with special attention to the covert, pretrial interrogation of jailed defendants by government informants.

Pretrial identifications—line-ups, "show-ups," and photo arrays—are our final topic. In identifications cases, defendants have two goals: to preclude the introduction at trial of an unconstitutional pretrial identification *and* to prevent the witness who made that identification from making an in-court identification. We will address the scope of the protection provided in the identifications context by the Self-Incrimination Clause of the Fifth Amendment, the Sixth Amendment right to counsel, and the Due Process Clause of the Fourteenth Amendment.

2

The Analytical Framework of the Fourth Amendment

CHAPTER OVERVIEW
A. The Traditional Approach: Trespass
B. The *Katz* Revolution
C. The Return of Trespass
D. The Closer
✦ Cornwell's Picks

A. The Traditional Approach: Trespass

Historically, courts looked to property law to frame Fourth Amendment principles. Thus, in the 1928 case of *Olmstead v. United States*, 277 U.S. 438 (1928), the U.S. Supreme Court held that wiretapping from outside a building did not constitute a search because there was no physical invasion of the building and, hence, no trespass upon a protected location. Had the device been placed inside the building, an unlawful trespass would have occurred. Likewise, trespass would have resulted if a law enforcement officer had entered the building, or any part of it not commonly accessed by tenants, to place the listening device.

Later cases followed *Olmstead*'s reasoning. For example, in *Goldman v. United States*, 316 U.S. 129 (1942), the U.S. Supreme Court found that the Fourth Amendment was not implicated where government agents placed a "detectaphone" against an outer wall of a building to listen to conversations occurring within. In *On Lee v. United States*, 343 U.S. 747 (1952), the justices found that the electronic transmission of statements from an informant to a nearby law enforcement officer did not constitute a search because the speaker's consent to the presence of the informant precluded a trespass.

QUESTION 1. Private ears. Ashley lives in a ground-floor apartment in a large apartment building. Her phone is located next to a window that looks out onto the street. Officer Rick, believing Ashley is using her apartment to sell drugs, places an electronic listening device just underneath Ashley's window on the outside of the building to enable him to eavesdrop on her conversations. Through the listening device, Ashley is heard arranging a sale of cocaine to Sally.

To collect further information, Rick places the apartment building under surveillance. Whenever he sees Ashley enter the foyer, Rick enters the foyer in plainclothes and hides behind a large plant located next to Ashley's mailbox in the hope of overhearing conversations with potential buyers. On one such occasion, Rick hears Erin arranging to purchase some "stash" from Ashley.

Would Rick's conduct implicate the Fourth Amendment under the standards used in *Olmstead* and its progeny?

A. Yes, as to Ashley's conversations with both Sally and Erin.
B. Yes, but only as to Ashley's conversation with Sally.
C. Yes, but only as to Ashley's conversation with Erin.
D. No, as to both conversations.

ANALYSIS. Under *Olmstead* and its progeny, Fourth Amendment analysis revolves around the property-based concept of trespass. In this problem, Rick gathers incriminating information in two ways: first, by listening through an electronic device placed underneath a window to a conversation between Ashley and Sally concerning the sale of cocaine; and, second, by eavesdropping on a conversation between Ashley and Erin in the foyer of Ashley's apartment building concerning additional drug transactions. Turning first to the conversation between Ashley and Sally, we must determine whether the placement of the listening device underneath Ashley's window is trespassory.

Ashley undoubtedly has a property interest in her home that would be invaded by an unwarranted police entry. The facts do not indicate, however, that any such entry occurred. Because the listening device was placed on the outside of the building, Rick did not cross the "threshold" of Ashley's apartment. He was in a common area, open to all. Since no trespass occurred, the Fourth Amendment was not offended under the standard of *Olmstead v. United States*.

The second conversation took place in the foyer of the building in the vicinity of Ashley's mailbox. While Rick was not a tenant of the building, his entry into this area cannot be considered a trespass. Nothing in the facts indicates that the foyer is a restricted area. Rick readily accessed it from the street, and, in doing so, he did not violate any posted sign or warning suggesting that he was not authorized to enter. Indeed, the area was likely accessed daily by mail carriers and others doing business in the building. It is irrelevant that Rick was dressed in plainclothes and was hiding behind a plant when he overheard the conversation. This clandestine conduct does not convert a lawful entry into a trespass. Therefore, the conversation he overheard did not violate the two women's constitutional rights.

For the foregoing reasons, all of the evidence gathered by Rick would be admissible at trial against Ashley, Sally, and Erin under the *Olmstead* standard. The correct answer is **D**.

B. The *Katz* Revolution

By the 1960s, however, the justices began questioning *Olmstead*'s reliance on trespass as the touchstone of the Fourth Amendment analysis. For example, in 1961, the justices found a Fourth Amendment violation where law enforcement officers inserted a "spike mike" into a "party wall" to pick up conversations through the heating ducts, even though the device did not effect a technical trespass. *Silverman v. United States*, 365 U.S. 505 (1961). Six years later, the U.S. Supreme Court accelerated the retreat from property-based principles in the seminal case of *Katz v. United States*, 389 U.S. 347 (1967), and, in so doing, fundamentally altered our understanding of the Fourth Amendment protections.

In *Katz*, the law enforcement officials placed a listening device on the outside of a phone booth to record conversations occurring inside. Relying on *Olmstead*, the government claimed that the Fourth Amendment did not require a warrant, since the device did not physically invade any protected space. The Court disagreed, noting that the Fourth Amendment protects people, not places. Because the listening device infringed the caller's reasonable expectation of privacy in the phone booth, the device violated the Fourth Amendment, whether it was placed inside or outside the booth.

In his concurrence, Justice Harlan refined the majority's privacy analysis, arguing that, in evaluating a Fourth Amendment claim on this basis, courts should use a two-prong test. Part one asks whether the search in question violated the defendant's subjective, or actual, expectation of privacy. If it did, courts must next determine whether that expectation of privacy is one that society would consider to be reasonable. Applying this test to the case at hand, Justice Harlan concluded that the government's actions violated the Fourth Amendment. "The point is not," he stated, "that the booth is 'accessible to the public' at other times, but that it is a temporary private place whose momentary occupants' expectations of freedom from intrusion are recognized as reasonable."

QUESTION 2. Go ask Alice.   Before non-personnel enter public build-ings in the State of Setonia, security officers routinely require them to walk through a metal detector. In addition, all bags, including women's purses, are subject to an external scan designed to detect the presence of weapons. Concerned that the scan is not sufficiently sensitive to detect a well-hidden weapon, security officers in many buildings have taken to removing the contents of all bags as part of the screening process. After numerous complaints from women objecting to the public exposure of private items in their purses, the Setonia legislature enacted a law permit-ting an invasive search of bags only where the initial scan suggested the presence of a weapon.

The month after the law went into effect, Alice went to the state courthouse in the hope of watching a high-profile trial taking place that day. When she entered, security officers scanned her purse and, after doing so, required her to empty its contents for further inspection. "Why?" Alice asked. "Did you see something suspicious on the scan?" "No," the guard replied. "We just thought you looked kinda shifty." "No problem," Alice replied. "People look through my purse all the time. I don't care. There is nothing personal in there. Knock yourself out." The guards then searched the purse thoroughly, finding a razor blade in a side pocket. They seized it and charged Alice with attempting to carry a concealed weapon into a public building. Did the guards' search violate the Fourth Amendment under *Katz*?

A. Yes, because the guards did not believe that the purse contained a weapon.

B. Yes, because the legislature has recognized women's privacy rights in their purses.

C. No, because the guards found a razor blade inside the purse.

D. No, because Alice did not care if the guards searched her purse.

ANALYSIS.   This problem not only applies the *Katz* test, it underscores the importance of reading the facts of each question carefully. While women clearly have a privacy right in their purses, they surrender some of that right in the interest of security when they enter public space. Here, the legislature has clearly defined the scope of that privacy interest by passing a law allowing security officers to perform an invasive search, *provided* they have reason to suspect from an initial screening that the purse contains a weapon. Because the scan did not suggest the presence of a weapon in Alice's purse, the offi-cers lacked the authority to search it. However, this statutory violation does not necessarily implicate the Fourth Amendment. The misconduct rises to the constitutional level only if it infringes Alice's subjective and objectively reason-able expectation of privacy.

Answer **C** can be eliminated since it does not comport with the language of the Setonia law. That the officers actually found a weapon cannot justify an otherwise illegal search. Were this so, the finding of contraband would effectively "cure" constitutional defects and reduce Fourth Amendment protection to a nullity. Thus, the officers' failure to suspect that Alice was carrying a weapon precludes their ability to search further, irrespective of what they subsequently find.

Answers **A** and **B** are better than **C**, inasmuch as both are accurate statements of law. The legislature did recognize privacy rights in women's purses, and the guards did not believe that Alice's purse contained a weapon before searching it. However, as discussed above, the fact that the guards contravened Setonia law is relevant to the Fourth Amendment *only* if their actions violated Alice's expectation of privacy. Alice's invitation to the officers to look through her purse, coupled with her comments that it contained nothing personal and that people routinely look through it, indicate that she lacked a subjective expectation of privacy in the purse's contents. As such, she fails to satisfy the first prong of the *Katz* test.

It is important to remember that both parts of the *Katz* test must be satisfied to implicate the Fourth Amendment in a search or seizure. It is not enough, therefore, that law enforcement officials unlawfully searched an item that society would regard as private. The defendant herself must also have a sincere expectation of privacy. If, as here, she does not, there is no Fourth Amendment violation under *Katz*.

Answer **D** is correct.

C.   The Return of Trespass

In the years following the Supreme Court's 1967 decision in *Katz*, Justice Harlan's test gained broad acceptance as the proper framework for analyzing Fourth Amendment claims on both the state and federal level. Recently, however, the Court breathed new life into trespass. In *United States v. Jones*, 565 U.S. 400 (2012), a five-justice majority held that the government's attachment of a Global-Positioning-System (GPS) tracking device on an individual's vehicle and the subsequent monitoring of that vehicle's movements for 28 days was a Fourth Amendment search, since the device physically intruded on a protected area (the car) for the purpose of obtaining information.

The majority found it unnecessary to determine whether the government unreasonably violated the defendant's expectation of privacy, noting that Jones's constitutional rights "do not rise or fall with the *Katz* formulation." That is, the expectation-of-privacy test simply "enlarged" the Fourth Amendment's analytical framework; it did not replace it. Thus, if designed to obtain information, either a trespass or a "*Katz* invasion of privacy" is a Fourth Amendment search.

Concurring in the judgment, four justices agreed that monitoring the defendant's movements for an extended period of time constituted a Fourth Amendment "search," reasoning that such intrusive government surveillance violated the defendant's reasonable expectation of privacy. Writing for all four justices, Justice Alito sharply criticized the majority's reliance on trespass, an analytical approach he believed the Court had abandoned in *Katz*. The majority's decision to rely on "18th century tort law," Alito opined, is "highly artificial" and "has little if any support in current Fourth Amendment case law."

Notwithstanding these objections, the Court reaffirmed the vitality of trespass the following year in *Florida v. Jardines*, 569 U.S. 1 (2013). In that case, a police officer brought a drug-sniffing dog to the front porch of a homeowner's residence. Because this conduct constituted a physical intrusion on a constitutionally protected area for evidence-gathering purposes, the majority deemed it a Fourth Amendment search. Likewise, in *Grady v. North Carolina*, 135 S. Ct. 1368 (2015), the Court found that subjecting recidivist sex offenders to satellite-based monitoring implicated the Fourth Amendment; forcing offenders to wear a tracking device at all times physically intruded on their bodies in order to obtain information about their movements.

QUESTION 3. A sticky situation. Mary was being questioned at the police station by Detective Dave about the murder of her roommate. One hour into the interrogation, Mary asked to use the restroom and Dave consented. While she was gone, Dave decided to get rid of his chewing gum but, after wrapping the gum in a napkin, Dave discovered that there was no trash can in the room. Eager to dispose of the gum, Dave noticed Mary's backpack on the table and decided to deposit the gum inside it. He unzipped the outside pouch of the backpack, placed the gum inside and zipped it back up.

The following day, police found the murder weapon inside a backpack thrown in a dumpster down the block from Mary's apartment. While the backpack looked very similar to Mary's, she claimed it was not hers. Upon closer inspection, officers discovered the napkin-wrapped chewing gum with Dave's DNA. Arrested for her roommate's murder, Mary moves to suppress the gum, claiming that its placement in her backpack violated her Fourth Amendment rights. Her claim will likely:

A. Succeed, because Dave violated Mary's expectation of privacy in her backpack.
B. Succeed, because Dave's placement of the gum in Mary's backpack constituted an unlawful trespass.
C. Succeed, if Dave's placement of the gum in Mary's backpack violated her expectation of privacy *and* constituted an unlawful trespass.
D. Fail.

ANALYSIS.   This problem gauges the impact of the Supreme Court's recent decisions in *Jones, Jardines,* and *Grady* on Fourth Amendment analysis. Detective Dave is questioning Mary at the police station regarding the murder of her roommate. When Mary steps out of the room to "powder her nose," Dave discards his chewing gum in her backpack upon discovering that the interrogation room has no trash can. The following day, the police find the murder weapon inside a backpack and use the presence of the gum inside it to link the backpack—and, thus, the murder weapon—to Mary. We must evaluate Mary's claim that the placement of the gum in her backpack, an "effect" protected under the Fourth Amendment, was unlawful.

Jones, Jardines, and *Grady* specify that, for the Fourth Amendment to apply to a search or seizure, government agents must *either* physically intrude on a protected area *or* otherwise frustrate an individual's reasonable expectation of privacy in that area. Because a defendant does not need to satisfy both standards, **C** is incorrect.

Addressing the trespass standard, the installation of a tracking device on the defendant's car in *Jones* and the defendant's person in *Grady* constituted a physical intrusion on a constitutionally protected areas, as did the presence of the "K-9" officer on the homeowner's property in *Jardines*. These trespasses were insufficient in and of themselves, however, to vindicate the defendants' claims. To implicate the Fourth Amendment, the Court required that the physical intrusions be "conjoined with . . . an attempt to find something or obtain information," which the tracking devices and drug-sniffing dog clearly were. In our problem, by contrast, Detective Dave did not place the gum in Mary's backpack for informational purposes; he was simply using the backpack as a waste receptacle, since there was no garbage can in the room. Because this trespass did not satisfy the Fourth Amendment standard of *Jones, Jardines,* and *Gray,* **B** is wrong.

The majority in *Jones* noted that this informational requirement applied in the privacy context as well. That is, to implicate the Fourth Amendment, a government agent must have invaded an individual's reasonable expectation of privacy for the purpose of obtaining information. To the extent that Detective Dave violated Mary's expectation of privacy in her backpack, his purpose was not to obtain information, as discussed above. Thus, **A** is incorrect.

The correct answer is **D.**

D.   The Closer

QUESTION 4. The constant gardener.   Lucinda has noticed that her neighbor, Rob, is constantly carrying gardening tools and supplies, such as soil and fertilizer, into a shed located inside a fence in his back yard adjacent to Lucinda's property line. After disappearing inside the shed for a period of time, Rob emerges. Curious as to why Rob would be growing plants inside a shed, Lucinda asks him what he's cultivating. "Can't tell you," Rob replied, winking. "It might get me into trouble." Alarmed, Lucinda called the police to tell them that she believed that her neighbor was growing marijuana inside a shed in his back yard. Officer Larry took the call and drove to Lucinda's house. If Larry does not have a warrant to search Rob's property, which of the following is an unlawful means of gathering information about the contents of the shed?

A. Climbing a tree in Lucinda's yard to peer into shed.
B. While standing in Lucinda's yard, opening the window to the shed to peer inside.
C. Looking into the shed from Lucinda's bedroom window.
D. Sending Lucinda to Rob's house to ask questions about the shed while wearing a listening device that transmits Rob's responses to Larry.

ANALYSIS. This question addresses the two analytical approaches of the Fourth Amendment: the trespass-based standard of *Olmstead/Jones/Jardines/Gray* and the expectation-of-privacy test introduced by *Katz* and used pervasively by state and federal courts ever since.

The trespass standard focuses on physical intrusion on protected areas for information-gathering purposes. Because Larry did not have a warrant, any invasion of Rob's property without consent, either actual or implied, would violate the Fourth Amendment. *Katz*, by contrast, asks whether the conduct in question invades the defendant's subjective and objectively reasonable expectation of privacy.

We can first eliminate **D**. While Rob was unaware that Lucinda was wearing a recording device that transmitted their conversation to Larry, the U.S. Supreme Court held in *On Lee* that this practice does not violate the Fourth Amendment. As in *On Lee*, there is no trespass because Rob welcomed Lucinda onto his property, notwithstanding his lack of knowledge of her cooperation with the police in an effort to incriminate him. Lucinda's conduct is also permissible under the *Katz* test, since her consent to the recording of the conversation eliminates any reasonable privacy expectation Rob may have in it. The consent of only one party to the conversation eliminates Fourth Amendment protection for *both* in the content of the communication. See Chapter 5, part B, *infra*.

A and **C** are similar. In both, Larry views the shed from somewhere on Lucinda's property. In **A**, he climbs a tree in Lucinda's yard; in **C**, he looks out of her bedroom window. Neither action compromises Fourth Amendment principles under trespass principles because neither requires physical invasion of Rob's property to visually access the shed and its contents. Rob cannot, moreover, have a reasonable expectation of privacy in whatever Lucinda can plainly see from her bedroom window. Climbing a tree to obtain visual access is more likely to invade a protected privacy interest, but courts that have considered this are split on the issue.

B is different. While Larry's feet are planted in Lucinda's yard, he reaches into the shed, located on Rob's property, and opens the window. Because part of Larry's body enters Rob's property, Larry physically intrudes on a protected area and does so for the purpose of obtaining incriminating evidence against Rob. Thus, Larry violated Rob's Fourth Amendment rights under the Supreme Court's modern trespass cases. It would likewise violate *Katz*, since Rob has a reasonable expectation of privacy in the contents of the shed that cannot be seen through the closed window.[1]

B is the correct answer.

✦ Cornwell's Picks

1. Private ears	**D**
2. Go ask Alice	**D**
3. A sticky situation	**D**
4. The constant gardener	**B**

---

1. If a court finds a government agent's search physically intrudes on a protected area to obtain information, the Fourth Amendment applies. Therefore, as in *Jones*, *Jardines*, and *Grady*, it does not need to address the alternative, expectation-of-privacy test.

3

The Sanctity of the Home

CHAPTER OVERVIEW

A. The Meaning of "Houses"

B. Moving Outside the House: Curtilage Versus Open Fields

C. "Commercial" Curtilage

D. The Closer

✧ Cornwell's Picks

While conservative and liberal justices on the U.S. Supreme Court have disagreed sharply over many Fourth Amendment issues, all believe that an individual's home merits strong constitutional protection. This reverence for home-based privacy has its roots in American colonial history and events that influenced the Framers' adoption of the Fourth Amendment.

In the latter half of the eighteenth century, customs agents of the English government obtained "writs of assistance" authorizing them to search colonists' homes for taxable goods, without specifying the areas to be searched or the items to be seized. These writs were enforceable indefinitely and would expire only upon the death of the king. Outraged citizens challenged the king's authority to issue these writs, arguing that they violated the sanctity of the home. In one now-famous case, attorney James Otis contended unsuccessfully that the writs annihilated individual liberty by allowing government officials unfettered entry into citizens' homes without cause:

> [W]e are commanded to permit their entry—their menial servants may enter—may break locks, bars and everything in their way—and whether they break through malice or revenge, no man, no court can inquire—bare suspicion without oath is sufficient.[1]

---

1. 2 *Legal Papers of John Adams* 113, 142 (L. Wroth and H. Zobel eds., 1965).

While frustration over the general failure of efforts to nullify these writs contributed to the decision to include "houses" expressly in the text of the Fourth Amendment, the Framers could not have anticipated the challenges posed by the noncorporeal invasion of private spaces through modern technology. Nor did their concerns focus on areas adjacent to but outside the interior of the home. Such issues have engaged, and divided, the justices over the last several decades as shifting majorities have searched for principled ways in which to draw constitutional lines.

A.   The Meaning of "Houses"

While the Framers inserted the word "house" into the text of the Fourth Amendment, the U.S. Supreme Court has not understood that term to be limited to the small residential structures that predominated in colonial America. For example, apartments have been considered "houses," a result that seems compelled by fairness and logic, lest only those who choose, or are able, to live in freestanding houses be able to claim Fourth Amendment protections. Temporary residences also qualify. Guests may claim privacy protection in their hotel rooms, and overnight guests may challenge government searches of private residences where they are staying temporarily whether or not they have complete control of the premises.

The justices have also subsumed within "houses" a variety of buildings that are used for nonresidential purposes. For example, in *Taylor v. United States*, 286 U.S. 1 (1932), the U.S. Supreme Court required a warrant to search a garage adjacent to the defendant's home, noting that "[t]he two houses are part of the same residential premises." Commercial buildings have also merited Fourth Amendment protection. Accordingly, the Court has invalidated warrantless searches of stores, offices, and warehouses. "The businessman," the justices commented, "like the occupant of a residence, has a constitutional right to go about his business free from unreasonable official entries upon his private commercial property." *See v. City of Seattle*, 387 U.S. 541 (1967).

The scope of Fourth Amendment protection available to social guests and those engaging in commercial activity in private residences is not without limits, however. In *Minnesota v. Carter*, 525 U.S. 83 (1998), the defendants challenged the warrantless search of an apartment into which they had been invited for the purpose of bagging cocaine for a two- to three-hour period. In rejecting their claim, the U.S. Supreme Court pointed to three factors: the purely commercial nature of the transaction; the relatively short period of time on the premises; and the lack of a close personal relationship between the defendants and the householder.

QUESTION 1. **Lines through the blinds.**   Sue is vice president for marketing for a large computer software company. Her best friend, Ramona, is the vice president for finance and occupies the office next door. Sue knows that Ramona leaves the office every day at 2:00 P.M. for one hour to exercise at the company fitness center. Sue asks Ramona if she can use her office during that time to "lie down," since Ramona has a sofa. Ramona agrees. Actually, Sue is not using the office merely to rest. She is also using it to snort cocaine and, on occasion, to sell drugs to other office employees. Al is curious when he sees Marty exit the office one day when Sue is inside. He peeks through the slats in the blinds and sees Sue snorting some "lines." He calls the police who burst into the office and seize Sue's stash of cocaine. Sue claims that the entry into the office and subsequent seizure of the cocaine violated her Fourth Amendment rights. Which of the following is LEAST relevant in evaluating her claim?

A. She used the office every day.
B. Ramona gave her permission to use the office.
C. She closed the blinds after entering the office.
D. She sometimes sold drugs in the office.
E. She lied to Ramona about her activities in the office.

ANALYSIS.   In answering this question, you must focus on the key analytical question: Did Sue have a legitimate expectation of privacy in Ramona's office? We know that offices do merit Fourth Amendment protection and that social guests can claim a constitutional right to privacy in protected areas owned or occupied by others. Sue's entitlement is not, however, as clear as that of an overnight guest, nor is it as illegitimate as that of the defendants in *Carter* who were using the apartment of a relative stranger for purely business purposes. Remember, though, we do not need to resolve this ambiguity in answering the question; we must merely identify the factor that is least relevant among the four choices in evaluating Sue's privacy claim.

Answer **A** focuses on the frequency of Sue's use of Ramona's office. This is clearly relevant, since the amount and regularity of time Sue spent in the office informs both her subjective expectation of privacy and its objective reasonableness. Moreover, in *Carter*, the U.S. Supreme Court expressly referenced the limited nature of the defendants' contact with a third-party residence in rejecting their privacy claims.

Ramona's grant of permission to Sue to use the office is likewise important since it affirms the legitimacy of her privacy expectation there. If Sue had used a passkey to enter without first obtaining consent, she might subjectively consider the space to be private, but her misconduct would erode the reasonableness of this belief. Lying to Ramona to obtain permission to use the office is relevant for similar reasons. It is questionable, at the very least, that society would regard a privacy expectation in the protected area of a third party to be reasonable where an individual lied to gain access in the first place. **B** and **E** are wrong.

Answer **C** states that Sue closes the blinds when she enters the office. This conduct is significant because it demonstrates efforts made by Sue to create privacy in the space. The degree to which outsiders could see inside the office through the slats may also be relevant in evaluating the strength of the privacy claim; this fact does not, however, negate the importance of Sue's actions in establishing a Fourth Amendment right to privacy as a threshold matter.

We are left, therefore, with **D**. At first blush, you might conclude that it must be relevant since illegal activity is involved and people cannot have a legitimate privacy expectation in unlawful conduct. However, the question is not whether there is a privacy right in dealing drugs but, rather, whether Sue may reasonably expect privacy in the protected space of a third party that she uses to deal drugs. In *Carter*, the Court opined that the defendants' unlawful commercial activity was relevant since it was the *only* activity the defendants conducted in the apartment. Here, Sue uses the office principally for non-commercial, private activity. The fact that, on occasion, she deals drugs in the office does not negate this. Thus, **D** is the least relevant factor in evaluating Sue's claim.

B.   Moving Outside the House: Curtilage Versus Open Fields

While the foregoing suggests a fairly expansive view of "houses," it does not address the application of the Fourth Amendment to areas outside of, but adjacent to, the home. The U.S. Supreme Court has considered this area, referred to as the "curtilage," an extension of the house and, as such, meriting constitutional protection. Beyond the curtilage lie "open fields," to which the Fourth Amendment does not apply. In any given case, you may be called upon to determine where curtilage stops and the open fields begin.

Unlike open fields, the curtilage harbors "intimate activities associated with the sanctity of a man's home and the privacies of life." *Oliver v. United States*, 466 U.S. 170 (1984) (quoting *Boyd v. United States*, 116 U.S. 616 (1886)). In determining whether an area falls within the curtilage, courts must balance four factors: proximity to the home; whether the area in question is within an enclosure surrounding the home; the nature of the uses to which the area is put; and steps taken to protect the area from observation by passersby.

Applying these factors in *United States v. Dunn*, 480 U.S. 294 (1987), the U.S. Supreme Court's leading case on curtilage, the majority concluded that a barn used to manufacture methamphetamine was outside the curtilage of the defendant's home. First, the barn was located a substantial distance (60 yards) from the home. Second, while a fence surrounded the defendant's home, the barn was outside this enclosure. Third, police surveillance of the barn and the area around it suggested that the structure was not being used for "intimate activities of the home." For example, officers witnessed a large truck whose contents were unloaded into the barn, coupled with sounds of motors running and the strong odor of phenylactic acid, an ingredient used to make methamphetamine. Finally, while a number of perimeter and interior fences enclosed the defendant's 198-acre property, including the barn, the fences were designed to corral livestock. They did little to shield the barn from the view of passersby.

QUESTION 2. Curious George. Police Officer George was walking down a dirt road looking for a stolen vehicle that he believed may have been hidden there. In the distance, he spotted a small shack standing alone in a field. He crossed over a barbed-wire fence and approached the shack, suspicious that it might be used to manufacture drugs. He entered the shack and did not find any drug paraphernalia, but he did find a box of coins with the name "McShane" on it. Remembering that Amber McShane had reported her collection of rare coins as stolen, George seized the box. On his way back to the station, George noticed that the barbed-wire fence also enclosed a house, located 50 yards away. Later that day, he arrested the occupants of the house and charged them with the theft of the coins. The occupants challenge the warrantless search of the shack, claiming it violated their Fourth Amendment rights. This claim:

A. Has merit, because the same fence enclosed both the shack and the house.
B. Has merit, if the owners did not expect anyone to enter whom they did not authorize to do so.
C. Has merit, because George trespassed onto private land.
D. Lacks merit, because the shack appeared to be in an unoccupied, undeveloped area.
E. Lacks merit, because George believed that the shack was being used for unlawful purposes.

ANALYSIS. This problem explores the line dividing curtilage from the open fields. In making this determination, we must reference the four factors listed above. The shack is not used for domestic activities of the home, and it is not in the home's immediate vicinity. In addition, there appears to be no effort to protect the shack from the observation of others; it is, however, within an enclosure surrounding the home. Is this enough to make the shack part of the curtilage? No. No single factor, or combination of factors, is dispositive. On balance, this falls short.

Prior precedent supports this conclusion. The shack is slightly closer (50 versus 60 yards) to the house than was the barn in *Dunn*. However, the shack does not appear to be used for domestic activities and is not enclosed by nearly as many fences as in *Dunn*. The one fence that does exist, moreover, is barbed wire, as was the livestock-corralling fence in *Dunn*.

In accordance with the foregoing, **A** and **B** are wrong. The fact that a fence enclosed both the shack and the house supports a curtilage theory, but it is not enough on its own. In addition, the shack's owners may have subjectively expected that no one would enter it, but this is not enough to occasion Fourth Amendment protection; under the *Katz* test, discussed in Chapter 2, the expectation must also be one that society considers reasonable.

C relies on trespass to invalidate the search. While the Court's recent decisions in *Jones* and *Jardines* reaffirmed this doctrine's vitality in the Fourth Amendment context, it requires physical intrusion on a "protected area." The fact that noncommercial land is privately owned does not mean that it is constitutionally protected; it merits Fourth Amendment protection only if it is located within the curtilage of someone's home.

E is also wrong. George's belief that illegal activity was afoot in the shack does not give him the unilateral right to enter it without a warrant. He may do so only if the building does not merit any constitutional protection.

D tracks the definition of an open field. In thinking about open fields, it is useful to remember that an area might be regarded as such, even if it does not conform to the traditional image of an open field. For example, courts have found a variety of disparate areas to be open fields, including beaches, reservoirs, woods, and lands fenced in with "No Trespassing" signs. As the U.S. Supreme Court noted in *Oliver v. United States*, open fields "may include any unoccupied or undeveloped area that is neither 'open' nor a 'field' as those terms are used in common speech."

D is the correct answer.

C.   "Commercial" Curtilage

Constitutional protection of the curtilage derives from the privacy inherent in the home. Does the Fourth Amendment privacy also reach areas adjacent to commercial buildings in light of the U.S. Supreme Court's vindication of an individual's right "to go about his business free from unreasonable official entries upon his private commercial property"? *See v. City of Seattle, supra.* The U.S. Supreme Court addressed this notion of "commercial curtilage" in *Dow Chemical v. United States*, 476 U.S. 227 (1986), where law enforcement officers, without first obtaining a warrant, used an aerial mapping camera to take photographs of the defendant's business complex at altitudes ranging from 1,200 to 12,000 feet. The defendant claimed that the government had violated its Fourth Amendment rights since the company had gone to tremendous lengths to ensure the privacy of its premises from all ground-level views.

In rejecting this claim, the Court differentiated the curtilage of a home from "outdoor areas or spaces between structures and buildings of a manufacturing plant." At the same time, the majority opined that the areas in question lie somewhere between curtilage and open fields; as such, Dow Chemical's position would have been different if the police had *physically entered* the premises, as opposed to photographing it from above. This conclusion, while technically dicta, imports that "commercial curtilage" merits some Fourth Amendment protection, though clearly less than that available in the context of a private residence.

Lower court opinions have largely supported this interpretation of *Dow Chemical.* While mindful of the fact that the U.S. Supreme Court did not expressly decide the issue, they have recognized "industrial" curtilage claims where police have physically invaded the property surrounding a commercial building and the business entity had taken steps to enclose and protect the grounds from observation by passersby. For example, in *Commonwealth v. Lutz,* 516 A.2d 339 (Pa. 1986), the Pennsylvania Supreme Court distinguished *Dow Chemical* where the state Department of Environmental Resources physically intruded upon enclosed indoor and outdoor areas within the defendant's business premises that were not visible from any public area.

QUESTION 3. College savings plan.   The Smiths own the Everbloom Flower shop, located in the middle of the block on Main Street, between Mary's Excellent Edibles and Terry's Sandwich Shoppe. While they generally buy their "cut" flowers from private vendors, they grow all the plants they sell in a greenhouse behind the store. Alarmed at the rising cost of college, Rita and Travis realize that they need to start saving quickly to pay tuition for their son, who is presently a high-school junior. They decide to build a second, smaller greenhouse near the main one and dedicate it entirely to the cultivation of marijuana. To access the second greenhouse, you need to exit through the back door of the first, walk 20 yards, and open its door, which they keep closed during business hours. A six-foot, opaque fence encloses the entire business premises, including both greenhouses.

Police Officer Brianna learns of the Smiths' illicit activities and decides to investigate. She enters the store and asks to see flowering plants. Mrs. Smith takes her into the main greenhouse where the plants are kept. When Mrs. Smith leaves to attend to another customer, Brianna runs out the back door to the small greenhouse. She finds the door locked but peers through the window and sees the marijuana plants. She then places the Smiths under arrest. Will the Smiths succeed in arguing that their Fourth Amendment rights have been violated?

A. Yes, because Brianna entered the larger greenhouse to access the smaller one.

B. Yes, because customers would have no reason to enter the area behind the store.

C. Yes, because the Smiths erected six-foot-high, opaque fences.

D. No, because the store is surrounded by other commercial buildings.

E. No, because Brianna did not enter the second greenhouse.

ANALYSIS.   Answering this question correctly requires careful consideration of *Dow Chemical*. While it does not affirmatively embrace commercial curtilage, it allows for the possibility where businesses endeavor to conceal their premises from view *and* law enforcement officers physically invade the protected area.

Answer **A** posits that Brianna's use of the larger greenhouse as a pass-through to the smaller one violated the Smiths' Fourth Amendment rights. This is clearly wrong, since the larger facility was open to the public. The Smiths could not, therefore, have had a subjective or an objective expectation of privacy in it during regular business hours since customers routinely accessed the area.

Answer **B** states that customers would generally have no reason to enter the area behind the store. While true, this fact is not dispositive of the defendants' reasonable expectation of privacy in this area. Because it misses the analytical mark, it is wrong.

Answer **D** emphasizes the location of the flower shop, noting that it is surrounded by other commercial buildings. While this would no doubt make it more difficult for the Smiths to shield the area behind the store from the view of other merchants, it is not impossible to do so. While the facts provide no information indicating what efforts may have been taken in this regard, the fact that commercial buildings surround the flower shop is insufficient in and of itself to evaluate the Smiths' Fourth Amendment claim. **D** is wrong.

Answer **C** provides important information of the sort lacking in answer **D**. The presence of six-foot-high, opaque fences indicates that the Smiths have taken significant steps to gain privacy in the area behind the shop from neighboring commercial establishments and others who may otherwise be able to see into the area from the ground. The fences do little, however, to protect the area from the view of those, like Brianna, who enter from the store itself through the larger greenhouse.

Once behind the store, however, the locked, smaller greenhouse arguably retains Fourth Amendment protection as commercial curtilage. As such, Brianna may not enter it without a warrant. She does not, however, do so.

E is, therefore, the correct answer.

D.   The Closer

QUESTION 4. **Shedding problems.**   Despite their numerous protests to town officials, Thomas and Arlene were unsuccessful in their efforts to prevent a dry-cleaning business, owned by Jake, from moving into the building next door. One month after Thomas and Arlene arrived, Jake noticed that clothes were disappearing from his store. Suspicious, Jake set up security cameras that showed two adults breaking into the store, grabbing clothes and carrying them toward a shed located 100 feet from Jake's store on property owned by Thomas and Arlene and situated 100 feet from their home. Jake sent the tape to the police.

After viewing it, Officer Carl approached the shed from the area behind Jake's store. Carl moved a large rock hindering access to the door and then entered the shed, seizing clothes taken from Jake's store. As he left the property, Carl passed by a second shed, located adjacent to Jake's store. Finding it locked, Carl peered inside and saw containers of dry-cleaning solvent, forbidden under state environmental laws. He used this information to obtain a warrant to seize the solvents. Arlene and Thomas challenge the first search and Jake, the second. Which of the following is TRUE?

A. Carl's entry into the shed violated Thomas and Arlene's Fourth Amendment rights in the curtilage of their residence because the shed was located 100 feet from their home.

B. Carl's entry into the shed violated Thomas and Arlene's Fourth Amendment rights in the curtilage of their residence because the shed was located 100 feet from their home and a rock hindered access to the shed door.

C. Carl's actions with respect to the second shed did not implicate Jake's constitutional rights because dry-cleaning stores are not "houses" under the Fourth Amendment.

D. Carl's actions with respect to the second shed did not violate Jake's constitutional rights because Carl merely peered into the shed.

E. Carl's actions with respect to the second shed violated Jake's Fourth Amendment rights.

ANALYSIS.   In focusing on home-based privacy protections, this chapter considered three topics: the meaning of "houses" under the Fourth Amendment, the concept of "curtilage" as an extension of the home, and the availability of curtilage protection in commercial areas. This closer question contains aspects of each.

Concerned that Thomas and Arlene are stealing from his business, Jake sends Carl a videotape that confirms that two adults are taking clothes from his store and are absconding with them in the direction of a nearby shed. Carl's subsequent entry into the shed implicates Thomas and Arlene's constitutional rights only if the shed is within the curtilage of their home. We are told that it is located 100 feet from the residence and that a large rock impedes entry into it. These details are relevant under the *Dunn* curtilage factors, which include proximity to the home and steps taken to shield the shed from outside observation.

One hundred feet is some distance from the residence, a problem compounded by the lack of any fence enclosing the house and shed. As such, anyone may access the shed from neighboring properties, as Carl and the clothes thieves did. Moreover, while the rock makes entry more difficult, it is not equivalent to a lock, which frustrates entry more completely and clearly indicates a desire for privacy. The heavy rock may be designed merely to keep the door closed. We also have no indication that the shed is being used for "intimate activities of the home." On balance, the curtilage argument is weak.

The second shed is, by contrast, located far closer to Jake's business, and it is locked. However, *Dow Chemical* recognized curtilage in the industrial context where the business entity had taken steps to enclose and protect the grounds from observation by passersby *and* police officers physically invaded the property surrounding a commercial building. Here, Carl did not enter the shed but merely peered inside. As such, he is similarly situated to the law enforcement agents in *Dunn* who only looked inside the barn with the aid of a flashlight. As the U.S. Supreme Court noted, this conduct does not implicate an individual's Fourth Amendment rights under a theory of commercial curtilage.

Based on the foregoing discussion, **A** and **B** incorrectly provide that Carl violated Thomas and Arlene's Fourth Amendment rights. Note, in addition, that **A** further misconstrues curtilage analysis by suggesting that proximity to the residence alone is dispositive. As *Dunn* makes clear, courts must use a multifactor analysis; no single factor is sufficient, standing alone, to convey curtilage protection.

Answer **C** states an incorrect principle of law. Commercial structures can constitute "houses" under the Fourth Amendment, as *Dow Chemical* indicates. **E** is likewise wrong, since Carl's conduct did not, in fact, violate Jake's Fourth Amendment rights.

The correct answer is **D**.

Cornwell's Picks

1. Lines through the blinds   **D**
2. Curious George   **D**
3. College savings plan   **E**
4. Shedding problems   **D**

4

Technological Incursions on Private Spaces

CHAPTER OVERVIEW
A. The View from Above
B. Ground-Level Views: From Flashlights to Beepers
C. Technology in the Twenty-First Century
D. Dogs: A Cop's Best Friend
E. The Closer
✧ Cornwell's Picks

As the march of technology gives the government ever greater and more sophisticated means of surveillance, it challenges the Fourth Amendment by redefining the limits of privacy in a modern society. What privacy expectations are reasonable necessarily changes with the times; whereas the Framers may have legitimately expected privacy in any area that could not be visually accessed by the naked eye, mechanical enhancement of our natural senses suggests a different understanding today. At the same time, courts have struggled to identify the proper role of technology in evaluating Fourth Amendment claims, mindful of the potential to read its protections out of existence by linking societal expectations of privacy too closely to technological progress.

To understand the way in which technology has influenced the U.S. Supreme Court's understanding of privacy, it is useful to divide the inquiry into two pieces. We will begin with those cases analyzing intrusions on privacy from above, most notably from airplanes. We will then consider modern devices used by law enforcement on the ground.

A. The View from Above

The U.S. Supreme Court first addressed technology in *United States v. Lee*, 274 U.S. 559 (1927), where the Coast Guard seized contraband from a motorboat sailing on the high seas. The defendant claimed, *inter alia*, that his Fourth Amendment rights were violated by the use of a searchlight to determine the contents of the boat. The Court rejected the challenge, reasoning that the searchlight was no different from "a marine glass or a field glass."

By the 1980s, searchlights had given way to airplanes, which law enforcement officers used to detect criminal activity occurring below. The U.S. Supreme Court was not troubled by the use of aerial surveillance in and of itself; in *Oliver v. United States*, 466 U.S. 170 (1984) (see Chapter 3, *supra*), the Court recognized that the police "lawfully may survey lands from the air." This conclusion does not, however, suggest that all uses of aerial surveillance pass constitutional muster.

In *California v. Ciraolo*, 476 U.S. 207 (1986), police officers received an anonymous tip that the defendant was growing marijuana in his back yard. Unable to observe the yard from the ground, the officers flew over the house in a helicopter. From an altitude of 1,000 feet, the officers identified and photographed marijuana plants, using a standard 35-millimeter camera. The U.S. Supreme Court found this warrantless search to be constitutional, reasoning that the officers were in public, navigable airspace; they did not physically intrude onto the defendant's property; and the plants were visible to the naked eye. The use of a camera to record their observations did not alter the Fourth Amendment analysis.

Three years later, the Court extended *Ciraolo* by rejecting a Fourth Amendment challenge to a warrantless search of a greenhouse in the defendant's back yard from a helicopter flying 400 feet above the residence. A four-justice plurality emphasized the fly-over's compliance with Federal Aviation Administration (FAA) regulations, adding that the lower court record did not indicate "that helicopters flying at 400 feet are sufficiently rare that respondent could have reasonably anticipated that his greenhouse would not be observed from that altitude." *Florida v. Riley*, 488 U.S. 445 (1989). Concurring in the judgment, Justice O'Connor disputed the plurality's focus on FAA regulations. Instead, she reasoned that, in light of evidence suggesting considerable public use of airspace at 400 feet, it was not reasonable for the defendants to expect privacy in areas that could be viewed from that altitude.

Finally, *Dow Chemical*, decided in 1987 and discussed in Chapter 3, addressed aerial surveillance through the use of a commercial camera more technologically advanced than the 35-millimeter model used by the officers in *Ciraolo*. The justices acknowledged that this device augmented human vision "somewhat," but did not find the enhancement to be constitutionally significant. Their conclusion might have been different, however, had the device enabled the police "to penetrate walls or windows so as to hear and record confidential discussions of chemical formulae or other trade secrets."

QUESTION 1. **Shroom with a view.** Andrew, a police officer in Setonia, is convinced John is growing hallucinogenic mushrooms in a greenhouse located adjacent to his home. The greenhouse is not visible from the road, by virtue of an eight-foot-high fence enclosing both it and John's residence. John has also placed a tarp over the top of the greenhouse. Luckily, Andrew finds out that people use a small mountain near John's property for hang gliding. Andrew takes lessons until, one day, he makes his first "flight," choosing to fly directly over John's property. Looking down through holes in the tarp, Andrew sees mushrooms growing below. Relying on this information, he obtains a warrant to seize them. Andrew's search of John's greenhouse is:

A. Lawful, if people routinely hang glide in and over the area where it is located.
B. Lawful, because it is illegal to grow hallucinogenic mushrooms.
C. Unlawful, because Andrew could not have seen into the greenhouse from a ground-level viewpoint.
D. Unlawful, because the greenhouse is adjacent to John's home.
E. Unlawful, if no other police officer in Setonia has ever engaged in hang gliding to obtain criminal information.

ANALYSIS. This problem explores the limits of the Fourth Amendment's protection of private areas from aerial surveillance. While John may reasonably expect privacy in a greenhouse positioned close to his home, the extent of the protection afforded by the Fourth Amendment is a function of the degree to which John has shielded the area from public view. The fence he has erected effectively precludes any ability to see into the greenhouse from the ground level. This has little bearing, however, on the legitimacy of views from other vantage points.

Prior case law instructs that individuals have no reasonable expectation of privacy from aerial surveillance, provided the contraband in question is viewed while the aircraft is traveling lawfully in commonly navigated airspace. Analogizing to our case, Andrew is not infringing John's Fourth Amendment rights if hang gliders regularly and lawfully fly over the greenhouse. If they do, John cannot reasonably expect privacy in whatever may be viewed from such vantage points.

Answer **C** is wrong because the fact that Andrew could not have seen into the greenhouse from the street is unavailing where the contraband is viewed from a different location. **D** is wrong because the greenhouse's location within the curtilage of the home likewise does not suggest blanket privacy protection from all views.

On the other hand, the illegal nature of John's activity does not import that John has no Fourth Amendment protection in the area where the activity occurs. If that were true, the police could invade any protected area and justify the invasion *post hoc* by noting that they found evidence of criminal activity after doing so. **B** is wrong.

Both **A** and **E** focus on the frequency with which the airspace Andrew accessed was used by third parties. This consideration is important, since routine traffic would extinguish John's reasonable privacy expectation in areas within the curtilage of his home that could be viewed from this vantage point.

E limits this inquiry to the conduct of police officers. **A** is broader, suggesting that John's Fourth Amendment rights would be compromised even if individuals other than law enforcement personnel regularly flew in this area. The reasonableness of one's expectation of privacy does not depend on who has visual access to the target area.

A is correct.

B.   Ground-Level Views: From Flashlights to Beepers

In the 1980s, the U.S. Supreme Court decided a series of cases that addressed enhanced technology used to uncover criminal evidence or activity from ground-level views. In *Texas v. Brown*, 460 U.S. 730 (1983), the majority held that the officers' use of a flashlight to illuminate the interior of a car did not implicate Fourth Amendment concerns. Likewise, in *United States v. Dunn*, discussed in Chapter 3, the Court held that police officers' use of a flashlight to peer into the defendant's barn from the open fields "did not transform their observations into an unreasonable search within the meaning of the Fourth Amendment."

While the use of flashlights did not trouble the Court, beepers introduced different concerns. In *United States v. Knotts*, 460 U.S. 276 (1983), police officers attached a beeper to a drum of chloroform, a chemical used to make methamphetamine. They used the beeper to monitor the movements of the car in which it traveled when they lost visual contact with it. In this way, they were able to locate the laboratory where the defendants unlawfully manufactured the drug. The U.S. Supreme Court found no constitutional violation, reasoning that "[a] person traveling in an automobile on public thoroughfares has no reasonable expectation of privacy in his movements from one place to another."

The following year, the justices revisited beepers in *United States v. Karo*, 468 U.S. 705 (1984). *Karo* also involved the placement of a tracking device in the drum of a chemical necessary to an illegal drug operation;[1] but, unlike

---

1. In both *Knotts* and *Karo*, the government's placement of the beeper was not trespassory, since it was placed in the drum with the consent of its original owner.

Knotts, the drum was manually transferred to the defendant and was subsequently used to monitor movements inside the house. While the transfer to the defendant did not trouble the U.S. Supreme Court, monitoring movement inside the home was a different matter altogether. The justices held that the police could not use a beeper for this purpose without a warrant, since the device revealed information about the interior of the home that they could not have gleaned from observation outside of the curtilage.

QUESTION 2. Beeper bust.   Police Officer Matt wanted to know the location of a hideout where gang members manufactured methamphetamine. He had been unable to determine this through ordinary surveillance. To find the location, Matt attached a tiny beeper to the outside strap of Shannon's purse. Matt knew Shannon consorted with gang members and figured that, by placing the beeper there, it would lead him to the gang's secret laboratory.

Matt monitored the beeper as it moved from Shannon's place of work, through public roads, and ultimately to a private residence. From his position on the road, Matt observed Shannon walk to the side of the house where she walked through a gate and entered a detached building, resembling a shed, located ten feet from the residence. The beeper registered no further movement after Shannon reached the gate. Using this and other information, Matt obtained a warrant to search the premises, which turned up a wealth of incriminating evidence against Shannon and her cohorts. If Shannon challenges the use of the beeper to justify the search, she will likely:

A. Prevail, because Matt could not have acquired critical information without electronic surveillance.
B. Prevail, because women have a reasonable expectation of privacy in their purses.
C. Fail, because Matt was located in a public area when he obtained the information.
D. Fail, because Matt obtained no information about the interior of the home.
E. Fail, because Matt acquired no information about activity inside the shedlike building.

ANALYSIS.   In answering this question, we need to address two separate issues: the placement of the beeper, and the movement of the beeper once placed. Women clearly have an expectation of privacy in their purses; the question is whether Matt's conduct violated that expectation. The facts indicate that he placed the beeper on the strap of the purse. This cannot infringe any privacy expectation since the strap is on the outside of the purse and thus is plainly visible to everyone. The strap is not used — indeed, cannot be used — to secrete private items or information. Had Matt entered Shannon's purse and placed the beeper there without her consent, the Fourth Amendment would surely be implicated, but that did not happen here. Therefore, because Matt's conduct did not violate Shannon's expectation of privacy in her purse, **B** is wrong.

Answer **C** posits that Shannon's claim will fail because Matt is located in a public area when he acquires the information from the beeper. This proposition is clearly wrong, inasmuch as it suggests that police officers can lawfully obtain whatever information they want provided they position themselves in a public area when they do so. This contravenes the lesson of *Karo*, where the U.S. Supreme Court deemed certain evidence inadmissible, even though the police were situated in open fields when they acquired it.

By the same token, not all information concerning private residences is inadmissible where police officers could not have acquired it without electronic surveillance. This was, in fact, the factual predicate of *Knotts*; the police used a beeper precisely because they could not otherwise locate the defendant's drug laboratory. This did not compromise the admissibility of the evidence, because the information the beeper provided stopped at the threshold of the residence. **A** is wrong.

This leaves us with **D** and **E**, which are clearly the two best choices. Think carefully before choosing. Students are likely to be drawn to **D** since it is an accurate statement of law and is relevant to the case at hand. Unlike *Knotts*, the beeper does not monitor the movements inside the defendant's home. Instead, the facts appear similar to *Karo*, where the beeper reveals only the location of the lab.

E is, however, the *better* answer. Remember that the curtilage is an extension of the residence that merits equal constitutional protection. While the facts do not resolve the question of whether the "shedlike" structure is within the curtilage, they provide enough information to raise the possibility. Even if it is, however, the beeper did not contravene Shannon's Fourth Amendment rights. Because it stopped at the gate, the beeper provided no information about Shannon's activities inside the curtilage of her home. It did not monitor Shannon's movements inside the shed, just as the beeper in *Karo* did not reveal details about the interior of the defendant's residence.

For these reasons, **E** is a more complete answer than **D**.

C.   Technology in the Twenty-First Century

Unsurprisingly, by the turn of the century, more sophisticated technology of the type referenced in *Dow Chemical* had become available to law enforcement. In *Kyllo v. United States*, 533 U.S. 27 (2001), federal agents used a thermal-imaging device to detect relative amounts of heat radiating from a private residence to detect the presence of high-intensity lamps commonly used to grow marijuana indoors. The device required no physical invasion of the home; officers needed only to aim it at the residence from a public street to obtain a "reading."

The U.S. Supreme Court acknowledged that, to decide *Kyllo*, it must confront the larger question of the extent to which advancing technology "shrink[s] the realm of guaranteed privacy." In upholding the defendant's challenge, the majority emphasized the sanctity of the home, noting that the right to retreat into one's home free from unreasonable government intrusion is "[a]t the very core of the Fourth Amendment." Moreover, unlike the devices considered previously, the thermal-imaging scanner is a device not generally available to the public that has the ability to disclose "intimate" details of the home without physical intrusion. As such, its use in the instant case violated the Fourth Amendment.

Relying on the reasoning of *Kyllo*, lower courts have questioned the constitutionality of using thermal-imaging devices in aerial surveillance of residences or to measure heat emissions in back yards while standing in the open fields. Conversely, the use of a video camera without enhanced magnification has been upheld, as has the retention of a blood sample for possible future testing based on developing technologies. Storing blood samples involves no physical invasion and, unlike the thermal-imaging device, blood testing is commonplace.

QUESTION 3. Joint relief. Law enforcement officials in the Township of Serenity received an anonymous tip that marijuana was being sold out of one of the houses on Weed Lane. Unfortunately, the tipster failed to disclose which of the eight houses on the street was involved. To overcome this problem, the chief of police ordered a scanner he saw in a popular magazine. If pointed at an individual from a distance of up to 100 feet, the scanner is able to detect the presence of marijuana carried on the person targeted. If marijuana is present, the lights on the scanner begin to flash; if not, the scanner remains dark.

The day the scanner arrived at the station, the chief ordered Deputy Dan to use it to conduct surveillance on Weed Lane. Dan spent the day pointing the device at everyone exiting the eight houses there. Finally, after four hours, the scanner began to flash when pointed at Mabel Miller, aged 70, as she exited 18 Weed Lane. Mabel explained that she was using marijuana to alleviate chronic pain in her joints. While she knew this was illegal, her doctor recommended it. If Mabel challenges the use of the scanner, which of the following is LEAST relevant in evaluating her claim?

A. The scanner cannot take account of Mabel's medical authorization to use marijuana.

B. The chief purchased the scanner from a magazine.
C. The scanner was pointed at Mabel after she exited a residence.
D. The scanner revealed information that Dan could not otherwise have discovered without searching Mabel.

ANALYSIS. This problem applies the reasoning of *Kyllo* to a novel technology: a hypothetical marijuana body scanner. Mindful of the inevitability of differing types of technological innovation in law enforcement, the justices intended the reasoning of *Kyllo* to be used by lower courts in resolving future controversies such as this. To determine which of the four choices is the least relevant, we must identify the analytical benchmarks relied on by the majority in upholding Mr. Kyllo's challenge to the thermal-imaging device used to measure heat emissions in his residence.

Answer **B** references the chief's purchase of the scanner from a magazine. In *Kyllo*, the U.S. Supreme Court relied in part on the fact that the thermal-imaging device used by the police was not commonly available to the public; as such, residents would reasonably expect privacy in protected areas into which it alone could invade. Here, the scanner's purchase from a popular magazine suggests that many citizens would have been aware of it and, presumably, could have purchased it for themselves. While we do not have enough information to determine how widespread the distribution of the item may have been, or for how long it had been marketed, its availability to the public through a popular publication is clearly relevant.

Answer **C** notes Mabel's location outside the home when Deputy Dan conducted the scan. This is a relevant consideration, since, in *Kyllo*, the Court emphasized repeatedly that the device's constitutional infirmity was in part a function of its ability to reveal "intimate details of the home." Because the "sanctity of the home" figured so prominently in the Court's analysis, the failure of this device to invade the home is significant.

In *Kyllo*, the Court found that a Fourth Amendment search had occurred based, in part, on the fact that the thermal-imaging device revealed information that the police officers could not otherwise have gleaned without physically invading the defendant's home. Likewise, in this instance, without the scanner, Deputy Dan could only have found the marijuana carried by Mabel if he had searched her body—conduct that certainly constitutes a physical intrusion. Therefore, answer **D** states a consideration that is clearly relevant to Mabel's claim.

This leaves us with **A**. While Mabel may have felt justified in using marijuana because her doctor recommended it to her to alleviate her chronic pain, this belief has no bearing on the constitutionality of Deputy Dan's use of the device to ferret out criminal misconduct. The Fourth Amendment's privacy test asks whether Mabel's expectation of privacy is both genuine and reasonable. Even if she honestly considered her acquisition of marijuana to be a private matter, society would not find this expectation to be reasonable in light of its criminal nature.

A is the correct answer.

D.   Dogs: A Cop's Best Friend

Police dogs merit special treatment because they present a unique type of technological enhancement. The U.S. Supreme Court recognized as much in *United States v. Place*, 462 U.S. 699 (1983), declaring canine sniffs to be *sui generis* by virtue of the limited manner in which information is obtained and the limited scope of the information obtained from the sniff. In *Place*, law enforcement officers brought a narcotics detection dog to an airport concourse and "introduced" it to a closed suitcase believed to contain contraband. The dog "alerted" to the suitcase almost immediately, without the necessity of opening the luggage or otherwise compromising the owner's privacy in its contents. Under these circumstances, canine sniff was held not to be a "search" under the Fourth Amendment.

While it sanctioned the use of police dogs in airport drug interdiction, *Place* did not consider the constitutionality of using canines in other law enforcement contexts. The U.S. Supreme Court first addressed this larger issue in *Illinois v. Caballes*, 543 U.S. 405 (2005), where a state trooper used a narcotics detection dog during a routine traffic stop to detect the presence of narcotics inside the vehicle in the absence of any facts suggesting that either the car or the driver was carrying drugs. The majority held that the use of the canine did not raise Fourth Amendment concerns for two reasons. First, the "sniff" did not infringe any protected interest since it detected only the presence of contraband, and one cannot have a legitimate expectation of privacy in contraband. See also *United States v. Jacobsen*, 466 U.S. 109 (1984). Second, because the ten-minute duration of the stop "was entirely justified by the traffic offense and the ordinary inquiries incident to such a stop," the use of a narcotics dog did not prolong the length of the traffic stop. However, had the K-9 officer's conduct extended the stop beyond the time necessary to investigate the alleged motor vehicle infraction, the Fourth Amendment would be violated. *Rodriguez v. United States*, 135 S. Ct. 1609 (2015). Not all uses of drug-sniffing dogs are shielded, however, from Fourth Amendment scrutiny. In *Florida v. Jardines*, 133 S. Ct. 1409 (2013), the Court held that the Fourth Amendment applied when an officer took a drug-sniffing dog to the defendant's front porch. Because this conduct created an "unlicensed physical intrusion" into a constitutionally protected area (the curtilage) to gather criminal evidence against the homeowner, the officer's trespassory conduct implicated the Fourth Amendment. As such, the majority opinion did not address *Katz'* alternative expectation-of-privacy test.

QUESTION 4. Canine crimestopper.   Myra was pulled over by Officer Adam for speeding on the interstate. When Adam asked Myra for her license and registration, Myra replied, "Sure, Mr. Blue," and started laughing inappropriately. Adam then noticed that her eyes were bloodshot. He asked if she had been smoking marijuana, to which she replied, "You'll never know, will you?" Adam then asked if he could search her car. Myra declined. After Adam finished writing Myra's speeding ticket in the squad car, he called police headquarters and told them to send the canine unit.

Seven minutes later, a narcotics dog arrived. As Adam handed the ticket to Myra, a fellow officer quickly led the dog around the outside of the car, and it alerted to the trunk. Knowing he did not need a warrant to search the trunk, Adam opened it. As he did, Myra told him that the trunk contained an overnight bag that she had brought from home, as she was planning to visit a friend out of state. Myra told Adam not to touch the bag, since it contained "private stuff." He disregarded her request and, searching the bag, found a crack pipe hidden among Myra's undergarments. He seized the pipe and placed Myra under arrest. From start to finish, the stop lasted eleven minutes. If Myra challenges the seizure of the pipe, she will likely:

A. Prevail, because the canine sniff prolonged the traffic stop.
B. Prevail, because the canine sniff revealed items brought from home.
C. Fail, because the narcotics dog was standing in a public area when it alerted.
D. Fail, because the stop was completed in eleven minutes.

ANALYSIS.   Remember that, in answering multiple-choice questions, it is important to keep in mind the relevant legal standard, since the correct answer typically references it. In finding that the canine sniff was not a Fourth Amendment search, *Caballes* focused on two considerations: the failure to prolong the traffic stop unreasonably and the lack of infringement of any protected interest. These factors must, therefore, frame our discussion.

The facts specify that Adam radioed for the dog after Myra refused consent to search and the dog arrived seven minutes later. It alerted to the trunk. Opening the trunk, Adam discovered contraband in an overnight bag. He seized it.

In many respects, the facts of this case mirror those of *Caballes* and *Rodriguez* In all three cases, a canine alerted to the presence of drugs in the vehicle, leading to their seizure. In our problem, however, the contraband was located in a piece of luggage containing personal items of clothing. We must determine, therefore, whether this distinction makes Adam's conduct a search under the Fourth Amendment.

Answer **B** would exclude the contraband because it was found in an overnight bag brought from the defendant's home. While bringing a drug-sniffing dog to the front porch of a residence implicates the Fourth Amendment under *Jardines*, the canine never entered the home or its curtilage in our fact pattern. Because there was no physical intrusion into these areas by law enforcement personnel, *Jardines* does not apply here. **B** is wrong.

Answer **C**'s emphasis on the dog's location in the open fields is a necessary but not sufficient consideration in answering the problem. For example, a dog sniff may violate the Fourth Amendment even if the canine is standing in the open fields if its use created an unreasonable delay in the length of the detention. It is the diligence with which the officer completes his investigation into the alleged traffic violation that is dispositive.

Answer **D** would permit the seizure, since the entire stop—including the canine sniff and the subsequent search and seizure lasted eleven minutes, only one minute more than in *Caballes*. In *Caballes* and *Rodriguez*, however, the U.S. Supreme Court's focus was not on the number of minutes but, rather, on whether the use of a canine officer extended the stop beyond the time necessary to resolve the alleged motor vehicle violation that initially prompted it. Here, unlike in *Caballes*, the officer requested the dog after he had written the ticket for the speeding violation. As such, the canine sniff delayed the stop unreasonably. The fact that Adam waited until the dog arrived to give Myra the ticket is beside the point.

A is the correct answer.

E.   The Closer

QUESTION 5. **Look, I'm flying!** Believing that Paige was growing marijuana plants inside her home, Officer Taylor flew a helicopter over Paige's house to inspect the property. When the helicopter was flying at an altitude of 400 feet, Taylor's colleague, Officer Ross, looked down and could detect nothing. As a result, Ross devised another plan. Wearing a 100-foot cord attached to the helicopter, Ross jumped out of the helicopter and, while suspended 300 feet above Paige's house, viewed the marijuana plants through an open window with a professional quality 35-millimeter camera. If FAA regulations permit flying at altitudes of 400 feet and higher, does the search comply with Fourth Amendment requirements?

A. Yes, because the helicopter was traveling within navigable airspace.
B. Yes, because there was no physical intrusion into Paige's home.
C. No, because aircraft are not permitted to fly at altitudes of 300 feet.
D. No, because Ross used a professional quality camera.

ANALYSIS. This problem revisits the impact of modern technology on Fourth Amendment privacy in a twist on *Ciraolo* and *Riley*. In *Ciraolo*, the U.S. Supreme Court found that the defendant's expectation of privacy was not violated where marijuana plants growing in his back yard were viewed by police officers from an aircraft flying 1,000 feet above his home. In reaching this conclusion, the justices reasoned that Ciraolo could not reasonably expect privacy in his yard under these circumstances, since planes routinely fly at this altitude and the plants were visible to the naked eye from this vantage point. *Riley* permitted a fly-over at 400 feet, with four justices emphasizing the flight's compliance with FAA regulations and a fifth justice reasoning, instead, that any expectation of privacy from this vantage point is unreasonable since there is significant use of public airspace at this altitude.

In this problem, Ross is not viewing the plants from a helicopter; instead, he sees them from the bottom of a 100-foot cord hanging *below* a helicopter flying at 400 feet. This difference changes the constitutional dimension of the case. While the police can argue that they satisfied the plurality in *Riley* by ensuring that the aircraft remained at 400 feet in compliance with FAA regulations, the actual search was conducted from a lower vantage point where aircraft are not permitted to fly. As such, the search would not satisfy the standard embraced by Justice O'Connor, who provided the crucial fifth vote in *Riley*, since there is no evidence that public use of airspace within this prohibited area is sufficiently common to render unreasonable a homeowner's expectation of privacy in areas that can be viewed from 300 feet above the home. See also *Ciraolo*. Therefore, by peering into Paige's house while suspended from a cord 300 feet above it, Ross violated her Fourth Amendment rights.

As explained above, answer **A** misses the point. While it is true that the helicopter was traveling within navigable airspace, Ross viewed the plants from a lower, unlawful altitude. In *Ciraolo* and *Riley*, the U.S. Supreme Court's reference to the aircraft's altitude made sense because the officer viewed the defendants' back yards from the aircraft; here, Ross did not.

Answer **B** is incorrect as a matter of law. A visual search or seizure of an item can be unlawful, even if a police officer never physically invades the home. To that end, we must ask whether law enforcement has intruded upon a protected privacy interest, either physically *or* visually. Ross's conduct satisfies this standard. **B** is wrong.

Answer **D** would invalidate the search because Ross used a professional quality camera. While the U.S. Supreme Court has not decided the extent to which the Fourth Amendment permits police officers to augment their sensory faculties, the device used here clearly does not raise constitutional concerns. While the camera may be of "professional quality," the facts do not indicate that Ross magnified the images he saw through a zoom lens or its equivalent. As such, his conduct is not more invasive than that of the law enforcement personnel in *Dow Chemical*. **D** is wrong.

As discussed above, Ross's descent to 300 feet placed him below the altitude at which aircraft may lawfully travel. Because aircraft are forbidden from entering this area, it was reasonable for Paige to expect privacy in protected areas that could be viewed from this vantage point, including the inside of her home. Ross's conduct, therefore, violated the Fourth Amendment.

The correct answer is **C**.

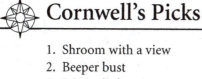

Cornwell's Picks

1. Shroom with a view	**A**
2. Beeper bust	**E**
3. Joint relief	**A**
4. Canine crimestopper	**A**
5. Look, I'm flying!	**C**

5

Private Information

P rivacy protection is not necessarily limited to physical spaces. The U.S. Supreme Court has also considered the extent to which the Fourth Amendment limits the ability of law enforcement to gather potentially incriminating personal information. This information comes in many forms, characterized here as personal characteristics, conversations, and public versus private records.

A.   Personal Characteristics

In *United States v. Dionisio*, 410 U.S. 1 (1973), the defendant was required to furnish a voice exemplar to federal investigators for comparison to recorded voices discussing alleged criminal activity. The justices rejected Dionisio's claim that this procedure violated his Fourth Amendment rights, finding that an individual cannot have a reasonable expectation of privacy in the tone and manner of his or her voice since they are "repeatedly produced for others to hear." That same year, in *United States v. Mara*, 410 U.S. 19 (1973), the U.S. Supreme Court likewise found that Fourth Amendment protections did not apply to handwriting samples compelled by law enforcement. The justices reasoned that because handwriting "is repeatedly shown to the public, . . . there is no more expectation of privacy in the physical characteristics of a person's script than there is in the tone of his voice."

The fact that a bodily characteristic is publicly visible is not always sufficient, however, to extinguish Fourth Amendment protection. In *Cupp v. Murphy*, 412 U.S. 291 (1973), decided the same year as *Dionisio*, police investigators detained a suspect to take fingernail scrapings from him against his will, believing that they would provide DNA evidence linking him to his wife's death by strangulation. Addressing the Fourth Amendment challenge, the U.S. Supreme Court distinguished *Dionisio*, noting that "the search of the respondent's fingernails went beyond mere 'physical characteristics . . . constantly exposed to the public.'" It constituted instead "the type of 'severe, though brief, intrusion upon cherished personal security' that is subject to constitutional scrutiny." *Cupp v. Murphy* (quoting *Terry v. Ohio*, 392 U.S. 1 (1968)). Nonetheless, the Court deemed the fingernail evidence admissible, noting the existence of probable cause, the "very limited intrusion" incident to the suspect's detention and the "ready destructibility of the evidence."

QUESTION 1. Caught in the crosshairs.   Marcie was a bank teller at Fawn Lake Savings & Loan. One afternoon, a man wearing a face mask entered the bank. He approached Marcie's window and demanded all the cash in her drawer. She complied with the demand, after which the man exited the bank. While Marcie could not see the robber's face, she told the police he had platinum blond hair, a strand of which was found at the crime scene. Suspicion focused on Scott, a disgruntled former bank employee, whose hair was platinum blond. Scott agreed to come to the police station to answer questions, but he refused an officer's request to take a sample of his hair. When Scott turned his back, the officer snipped a lock of it anyway. Angry, Scott demanded that the officer return the sample, but the officer refused. The sample was tested that same day to see if it matched the strand found at the crime scene. It did. Scott claims that the introduction of the hair as evidence at his trial violated his Fourth Amendment rights. Which of the following arguments in support of the admission of the hair sample most closely follows the reasoning of *Dionisio* and *Cupp*?

A. Scott's hair is constantly exposed to public view.
B. The hair sample was tested soon after it was obtained.
C. An eyewitness reported that the robber's hair was platinum blond, the same as Scott's.
D. Scott was present at the station house voluntarily when the officer obtained the sample.

ANALYSIS. This problem explores the U.S. Supreme Court's reasoning in *Dionisio* and *Cupp* as applied to a hair sample. Like facial characteristics, fingerprints, and a voice exemplar, the color of an individual's hair can be readily ascertained by anyone who comes into contact with that person. As such, the Fourth Amendment would not be implicated if police officers simply visually observed or photographed someone's hair. In this case, however, the police do more: They take the sample furtively from an unwilling suspect and test it later that day to see if it matches that of the robber. The key question is, therefore, whether any of the police actions compromise Scott's Fourth Amendment rights.

Let us first consider the length of time the police "detained" the sample before testing it. The amount of time the police held the sample to test it is irrelevant, since the violation, if any, occurred the moment the police took the lock of hair against Scott's will. Retaining the sample for a greater or lesser amount of time does not affect the privacy infringement in any way. It is not restricting Scott's movement, as detaining his person would. **B** is, therefore, wrong.

Answer **C** emphasizes Marcie's eyewitness testimony identifying the color of the robber's hair. Such evidence, while important to the prosecution's overall case, is less critical in the Fourth Amendment context of *Dionisio* and *Cupp*. Those cases import that it is not the characteristic's visibility to the *witness* that is dispositive but, rather, its overall public nature.

Thus, we are left with a choice between **A** and **D**. **D** notes that Scott was present at the station voluntarily at the time the officer surreptitiously took a sample of his hair. In this regard, our facts differ from those of *Cupp*, where the defendant was involuntarily detained at the station house for investigatory purposes. This distinction was not, however, the basis of the U.S. Supreme Court's decision, which found that the scraping of the defendant's fingernails, *not* the detention of his person, raised a constitutional flag.

A, by contrast, reflects the Court's primary focus of the Fourth Amendment inquiry in *Dionisio* and *Cupp*: whether the evidence in question is or is not constantly exposed to public view. Accordingly, the prosecution will endeavor to liken the hair sample to a voice exemplar, "static" evidence that is easily discerned by anyone who encounters Scott. The defense may counter that subjecting the hair to forensic analysis distinguishes *Dionisio*. We need not assess the merit of this contention, however, since whoever prevails, **A** identifies the appropriate analytical framework.

A is the correct answer.

B.   "Private" Conversations

In a series of cases decided over an eight-year period, the U.S. Supreme Court considered the extent to which individuals may reasonably expect privacy with respect to information relayed in conversations with friends or confidantes. In the first, *Lopez v. United States*, 373 U.S. 427 (1963), the defendant attempted, in a series of meetings, to bribe an agent of the Internal Revenue Service. In the final encounter, the agent recorded their conversation in the defendant's business office with an electronic device carried in the agent's pocket. The U.S. Supreme Court rejected Lopez's claim that the admission of his recorded statements violated his Fourth Amendment rights. Since the agent himself was constitutionally permitted to testify as to the substance of the conversations, the justices saw no difference, under the Fourth Amendment, between this testimony and a recording of the same. If the placement of the device had created an unlawful physical invasion, the result might have been different but, in this case, with the device in the agent's pocket, the recording device "neither saw nor heard more than the agent himself."

In *Hoffa v. United States*, 385 U.S. 293 (1966), the defendant's incriminating statements were made in a hotel suite to one Partin, who was a business associate, not a government agent. While Hoffa acknowledged that he consented to Partin's entry into the suite, Hoffa claimed that the consent was invalid because he was unaware of Partin's role as a government agent. As such, Partin's conduct amounted to an illegal search for criminal evidence.

The U.S. Supreme Court rejected Hoffa's argument. While Hoffa had a right to privacy in his hotel room, just as Lopez did in his business premises, Partin's conduct did not violate that right. Like the agent in *Lopez*, Partin was invited into the private space by the defendant. All that is left, then, is the conversation itself. The Fourth Amendment is unavailing in this context as well since it does not protect "a wrongdoer's misplaced belief that a person to whom he voluntarily confides his wrongdoing will not reveal it."

The Fourth Amendment analysis is no different if the government agent is someone previously unknown to the defendant who lies about his identity to gain access to the defendant's home. In *Lewis v. United States*, 385 U.S. 206 (1966), the defendant invited an undercover government agent into his home, believing that he was an ordinary citizen looking to purchase narcotics. Lewis's subsequent arrest for the sale made to the agent did not compromise Fourth Amendment protections since one assumes the risk that individuals with whom one converses or transacts business may be law enforcement agents or people working with them.

The final case, *United States v. White*, 401 U.S. 745 (1971), is similar in certain respects to *Lopez* and *Hoffa*. In all three cases, the defendant, believing he was speaking in confidence to a friend, made incriminating statements that were recorded electronically. In *White*, however, the conversations were also simultaneously transmitted via a radio receiver to a government agent located outside the residence. The U.S. Supreme Court did not view this distinction between "probable informers" and "probable informers with transmitters" as raising constitutional concerns, reasoning that a defendant's sense of privacy was not infringed to a greater degree by the possibility that a friend or business associate is "wired for sound."

QUESTION 2. **A third ear.** The police arrested Zack for the murder of his business partner. Zack claimed that he committed the murder at the behest of Ian, a business competitor, who paid Zack $100,000 for the "hit." The district attorney told Zack, who was released on bail, that she would recommend lenient sentencing if he helped garner evidence against Ian about Ian's participation in the crime. Zack agreed to visit Ian at his home, where Zack would introduce topics of conversation designed to elicit incriminating information against Ian.

When he went to Ian's house, Zack carried a tape recorder in his front shirt pocket. When Ian turned his back, Zack secretly placed the recorder under the sofa where Ian was sitting. The device recorded their entire conversation, including incriminating remarks Ian made to his wife while Zack was out of the room. The conversation was also transmitted simultaneously to Officer Bruce, who was sitting in a police van across the street. Before he left, Zack surreptitiously removed the recorder from under the sofa and took it with him. Because Zack was unavailable at trial, the entirety of Ian's remarks was introduced at his trial through the testimony of Bruce. Which of the following is Ian's best argument that the introduction of the tape recording of his conversation with Zack violated his Fourth Amendment rights?

A. Bruce could not witness Ian's facial expression and other nuanced aspects of his conversation with Zack.

B. Zack placed the tape recorder under the sofa where Ian was sitting.

C. Zack was not present when Ian spoke to his wife.

D. The conversation took place in Ian's home.

ANALYSIS. We know from the foregoing discussion of the case law that the U.S. Supreme Court has been largely dismissive of Fourth Amendment claims based on misplaced trust in conversational privacy with friends or business associates — the so-called "unreliable ear" or "false friend." His best argument must, therefore, uncover the type of police or informer conduct that has not yet received judicial approval.

Answer **D** is perhaps the most easily eliminated. The incriminating statements in the leading cases were made in a variety of locations, including a hotel, a business office, and the informant's residence. In *Lewis*, however, the defendant's purchase of illegal narcotics from an undercover agent occurred in the defendant's home, a fact that did not alter the Court's view that one assumes the risk that a person with whom one converses or transacts business may betray one's trust. **D** is, therefore, incorrect.

Answer **B** focuses on the location of the recording device. In the cases discussed, the device was usually a wire attached to the informant's body or a tape recorder carried on his person. Here, Zack removes the recorder and hides it under the sofa. This distinction should not matter under the Fourth Amendment. The analytical focus is the infringement of Ian's privacy. Whether the recording device is secreted on Zack's person or somewhere in the room, the privacy incursion is the same. **B** is wrong.

Answer **A** makes a fine point: The officer listening to the conversation outside the room cannot see Ian's face and thus would be unable to discern any nuance that Ian's facial expression may disclose. Consider, for example, the information an individual can convey by a rolling of the eyes, a hand gesture, or other nonverbal cues. While Zack will have witnessed any such occurrences, Bruce would not. This introduces a risk that Bruce's testimony may mislead the jury since it cannot appreciate the full context of Ian's statements.

This possibility troubled some members of the U.S. Supreme Court in *White*, influencing their decision to dissent. The majority felt, however, that any testimonial infirmity created by the absence of the officer is counterbalanced by the benefit of having a complete and accurate transcript of the dialogue. The tape recording eliminates, that is, the possibility that the informer may recall certain parts of the conversation inaccurately and to the detriment of the defendant. **A** is wrong.

The remaining answer, **C**, is Ian's best argument. In rejecting the defendant's challenge in *Lopez*, the U.S. Supreme Court reasoned that the recording device "neither saw nor heard more than the agent himself." In this case, that is not true. The device recorded the conversation between Ian and his wife, which took place when Zack was out of the room. This distinction may or may not rise to the constitutional level; however, of the four choices, it is the only one not precluded by existing U.S. Supreme Court precedent.

The correct answer is **C**.

C.   Public Versus Private Records

The text of the Fourth Amendment expressly shields "papers" from unlawful search and seizure. Originally, the U.S. Supreme Court interpreted this provision as disallowing the seizure of any private papers that were not instrumentalities of crime. In *Warden v. Hayden*, 387 U.S. 294 (1967), the Court abandoned this "mere evidence" rule, reasoning that an individual's privacy was no more infringed "by a search directed to a purely evidentiary object than it is by a search directed to an instrumentality, fruit or contraband." Thus, the justices found that evidence discovered during a search of the defendant's residence was admissible, whether it was of purely evidentiary value or an instrumentality of crime itself.

The protection afforded to papers does not apply to documentary evidence that is public in nature since seizure of such papers cannot, by definition, infringe any privacy expectation in them. The question is, then, when is information sufficiently public in nature to avoid Fourth Amendment scrutiny?

1. General Principles: The "Third-Party" Doctrine

The U.S. Supreme Court explored this question in *United States v. Miller*, 425 U.S. 435 (1976), where the defendants claimed that law enforcement officials violated their Fourth Amendment rights by issuing a subpoena requiring banks to produce myriad documents concerning financial transactions conducted by the defendants and their companies. The Court rejected the claim, finding that there is no reasonable expectation of privacy in bank records inasmuch as the information kept in them is "voluntarily conveyed to the banks and exposed to their employees in the ordinary course of business." In addition, "a depositor takes the risk, in revealing his affairs to another, that the information will be conveyed by that person to the government."

Applying similar reasoning, the U.S. Supreme Court held, three years later, that the Fourth Amendment is not implicated by police use of a "pen register," a device that records all telephone numbers dialed from a particular phone. As with bank records, customers voluntarily transmit numerical information to a business entity aware that the third party's equipment will view this information in the ordinary course of business. As such, the defendant, like other customers, "assumed the risk that the [third party] would reveal to police the numbers he dialed." *Smith v. Maryland*, 442 U.S. 735 (1979).

QUESTION 3. Teaming with trouble. Police officers believed that Luke was running an illegal fantasy baseball league via e-mail at work. They contacted the president of the company, Morgan, and asked if she would permit them to monitor Luke's e-mail account to determine the extent of participation in the illegal operation. Noting that the use of e-mail for this purpose would violate company policy, Morgan readily consented, and she referred them to Justin, the head of the company's IT department. Justin informed the officers that all employees must sign a form acknowledging the authority of the IT department to access employee e-mail accounts for "care, maintenance and to ensure compliance with company policies and procedures relating to their use." "To be honest, though," Justin told the officers, "I have never really spent any time enforcing this policy."

Using Justin's ID, the police were able to access Luke's account to obtain a list of all recipients of e-mails sent by Luke that referenced fantasy baseball in the title. In so doing, they identified a co-worker, Marcus, who received an e-mail from Luke titled "are you still in the fantasy baseball league?" Luke and Marcus were arrested. Based on these facts, which of the following statements provides the best defense?

A. Marcus's Fourth Amendment rights were violated because Morgan did not consent to police monitoring of Marcus's e-mail.

B. Luke's Fourth Amendment rights were violated because the police viewed the titles of his e-mail transmissions.

C. Luke and Marcus's Fourth Amendment rights were violated because Justin did not routinely monitor employee e-mails.

D. Luke and Marcus's Fourth Amendment rights were violated because there is a greater expectation of privacy in e-mail than bank records or telephone numbers.

ANALYSIS. This problem requires us to apply the reasoning of the 1970s-era cases of *Miller* and *Smith* in a very modern context: e-mail. While the U.S. Supreme Court has yet to address electronic transmissions directly, the *Miller/Smith* framework works nicely with the facts provided.

Answer **A** states that Marcus's Fourth Amendment rights were violated by Morgan's nonconsent to the monitoring of his (Marcus's) e-mail account. There are several problems with this argument. First, it is unclear that the police actually accessed Marcus's account; they could have seen the e-mail sent to Marcus simply by monitoring the "outbox" in Luke's account. Second, even if they did view Marcus's "inbox," the grant of permission to monitor Luke's e-mail would logically permit the police to access the e-mail of other employees for the purpose of determining who received suspicious transmissions. Finally, even if the police exceeded the scope of consent provided by Morgan, their conduct does not necessarily violate Marcus's constitutional rights. While the police may have acted improperly, their actions will not implicate the Fourth Amendment if they nonetheless viewed only what others in the company would have seen in the routine course of business.

Answer **C** relies on Justin's lack of routine monitoring of employee e-mails. This is not a strong defense for two principal reasons. First, all employees must sign a form that expressly acknowledges the company's right to access their accounts. Second, even if Justin has not been fulfilling her oversight responsibilities, there is no indication that either Marcus or Luke knew this.

This leaves us with **B** and **D**. In *Miller* and *Smith*, the police recorded only nonverbal data: financial statements, deposit slips, and phone numbers. Here, they also monitored the titles of the e-mails, which included words conveying the subject matter of the transmission. While this is arguably a greater privacy infringement, Justin, the head of the company's IT department, already had access to this information. Thus, because Marcus and Luke voluntarily exposed the titles of e-mail and their recipients to a representative of the company in the ordinary course of business, the third-party doctrine suggests delivering this same information to the police would not violate their Fourth Amendment rights. Marcus and Luke assumed the risk that this would happen.

On the other hand, e-mail is fundamentally different from bank records or telephone numbers. For most people today, it is a pervasive and routine part of daily life, and the court has been extremely mindful of the heightened privacy expectations that accompany modern technologies. See *Riley v. California*, discussed in Chapter 12, *infra*, and *Carpenter v. United States*, below. While we do not know whether the court would liken the accessing of e-mail titles in this problem to the digital data at issue in those cases, **D** is the best answer since it tracks the court's reasoning and analytical framework most closely in the context of the third party doctrine.

2. *Contemporary Reflections*

The Court revisited the third-party doctrine in *Carpenter v. United States*, 138 S. Ct. 2206 (2018), which addressed government access to an individual's "cellsite location information" (CSLI). In that case, while investigating a series of robberies, police arrested a suspect who subsequently identified 15 accomplices, including Carpenter. Under a federal statute in force at the time, the government could compel wireless carriers to release CSLI and other telecommunications records for many individuals at once, as long as the government demonstrated that there were reasonable grounds to believe that the records sought were "relevant and material to an ongoing criminal investigation." Accordingly, the government demanded and received CSLI showing the whereabouts of Carpenter's cell phone over 127 days at 12,898 locations.

In refusing to extend the third-party doctrine to the government's acquisition of this information, the Court noted that CSLI implicates privacy concerns far beyond those at issue in *Miller* and *Smith*. First, cell phones have become "indispensable to participation in modern society." Second, the location data at issue is automatically generated and cannot be avoided without disconnecting the device from the cellular network. In no meaningful sense, therefore, "does the user voluntarily assume the risk of turning over a comprehensive dossier of his physical movements." Under these circumstances, a warrant based on probable cause is necessary if the government wants to subpoena a carrier's CSLI for a subscriber over a lengthy period of time under non-exigent circumstances, even though the subscriber theoretically entrusted the CSLI to the carrier "voluntarily."

QUESTION 4. Off the grid. After experiencing increased power outages throughout the city during inclement weather, Setonia decided to upgrade its energy grid. As part of the city-wide upgrade, Setonia replaced all residential, analog energy meters with digital "smart meters." Residents could not "opt out" of meter replacement; digital meters were mandatory for all households to sync with the new grid. Analog and smart meters record energy consumption differently. Whereas analog meters provide a monthly, "lump sum" amount of energy use per household, smart meters record consumption much more frequently, often collecting thousands of readings every month. These repeated readings collect data at a granular level that reveal when and where energy is used, based on each appliance's distinct energy-consumption pattern or "load signature."

> After months of police surveillance and interviews with Russel's neighbors, the Setonia Police Department strongly suspects that Russel is using the three-car garage behind his house to grow marijuana. They subpoena the electric company that services Russel's home for digital data about Russel's energy use for the last three months, suspecting that the data will disclose the "load signature" of lamps used in indoor grow operations in the garage. The electric company complies and provides data that supports the police department's theory. Russel argues that the police department's failure to obtain a warrant to secure this information violated his Fourth Amendment rights under *Carpenter*. Does his claim have merit?
>
> A. Yes, because he was not aware that the digital data would be used for this purpose.
> B. Yes, because he did not assume the risk of such pervasive monitoring of electricity usage in his home.
> C. No, because data about electricity usage is far less private than cell-site location information.
> D. No, since the police have credible evidence that Russel is using his property for illegal purposes.

ANALYSIS. This fact pattern is based on *Naperville Smart Meter Awareness v. City of Naperville*, 900 F.3d 521 (7th Cir. 2018). In that case, the court held that the third-party doctrine did not apply to the smart-meter data collected by the utility. The court likened the smart-meter data to the CSLI provided by the cell phone carrier in *Carpenter* noting that, since electricity is necessary to operate one's home, "a choice to share data imposed by fiat is no choice at all."

The court's reasoning eliminates **C** and **D**. The fact that the police have gathered evidence that supports their belief that Russel is conducting illegal activity inside his home merely provides the factual foundation for obtaining a warrant; it does not excuse the necessity of obtaining one. The need to obtain a warrant would be excused only if the information at issue did not implicate Russel's reasonable expectation of privacy. In *Carpenter*, the Court found that tracking an individual's movements for a nearly four-month period invaded a cognizable privacy interest since "[m]apping a cellphone's location over the course of 127 days provides an all-encompassing record of the holder's whereabouts." In our fact pattern, the load consumption data likewise reveals private information about the homeowner, such as "when people are home, when people are away, when people eat and sleep, what types of appliances are in the home, and when those appliance are used." 900 F.3d at 526. Moreover, employing a device that is not in public use to reveal details of home-based activity otherwise unknowable without physical entry also supports the application of the Fourth Amendment to Setonia's conduct. See *Kyllo*, Chapter 4, part C, *supra*.

A would vindicate Russel's claim based on his lack of awareness of the use to which the load signature data would be put. In third party doctrine cases, the defendants typically do not expect the information in question to be used in the manner in which it was employed. This subjective expectation of privacy is not enough, however, to create a Fourth Amendment interest, as was the case with the financial records in *Smith*. In *Carpenter*, however, the Court distinguished CSLI, noting that cell phones have become critical to everyday life such that warrantless, long-term monitoring of one's every move by government officials is a constitutional bridge too far. Likewise, given the indispensability of electricity in one's home, individuals cannot be required to assume the risk that, in acquiring it, government officials can access granular data about its differential use throughout the residence for prosecutorial use without a warrant. **B** is the best answer.

D.   The Closer

QUESTION 5. Philanderin' Phil.   Philip was found dead in his home wearing a shirt with lipstick on its collar. When detectives interviewed his fiancée, Lauren, at the police station, they noticed that she was wearing lipstick similar in color to that found on Philip's shirt collar. After she left, they seized the can of soda she had been drinking and sent it to the lab for testing.

Meanwhile, the following day, Officer Dan interviewed Lauren's grandmother, Granny, with whom Lauren lived. After Dan told Granny that her life would become very "difficult" if she did not cooperate, Granny disclosed that Lauren had told her in confidence that she (Lauren) had been phoning a woman repeatedly with whom Lauren discovered Philip had been having an affair.

Wishing to locate Philip's paramour, Dan obtained Lauren's phone records from the phone company, BigBell, without a warrant and noticed that one number had been dialed repeatedly. When BigBell reported that the phone number did not belong to one of its customers, Dan asked a BigBell representative to call the number to glean information to aid his investigation. The representative did so and disclosed that the number belonged to Suzy, who had received threatening phone calls from Lauren.

If introduced at her murder trial, which of the following most clearly violates Lauren's Fourth Amendment rights?

A.   The testing of the lipstick on Lauren's soda can.
B.   Granny's statements about Lauren's anger over Philip's infidelity.
C.   The phone records seized from Lauren's apartment.
D.   The testimony from BigBell's representative about her conversation with Suzy.

ANALYSIS. This problem reviews the case law on personal characteristics, private conversations, and public versus private records. Answer **A** posits that the forensic analysis of the lipstick on the soda can exceeds constitutional limits. For this argument to succeed, the forensic process must constitute a "severe . . . intrusion upon cherished personal security." It is hard to see how it does. Skin lodged underneath one's fingernails is not readily observable. If it were, police officers would not need to detain an individual involuntarily to obtain a physical sample, as they did in *Cupp*. Here, the sample was obtained without compromising Lauren's liberty at all. In addition, the material tested, lipstick, is "worn" on the face and, thus, is clearly visible to everyone who sees Lauren. Finally, while the lipstick was tested by police personnel, handwriting exemplars are also reviewed by experts specially trained to determine their similarity to other samples. Nonetheless, the U.S. Supreme Court declined to extend Fourth Amendment protection in this context. See *Mara*, *supra*. For the foregoing reasons, **A** is not the best answer.

The suppression of Granny's statements under the Fourth Amendment would presumably assert that Granny's divulgence of the content of a private conversation with Lauren violated the latter's expectation of privacy. The "false friend" cases, however, foreclose this line of argument. The fact that Dan pressured Granny into revealing Lauren's statements does not alter the analysis, since the effect on Lauren's privacy is the same with or without police coercion. **B** is wrong.

The remaining answers concern the information linked to Lauren's phone records. **C** focuses on their seizure from the telephone company. Under *Smith v. Maryland, supra*, there is no Fourth Amendment problem with this conduct. While Lauren may subjectively expect this information to be kept private, this expectation is not reasonable, since data concerning the phone numbers dialed is freely and voluntarily exposed to a third party in the ordinary course of business. **C** is wrong.

There is a difference, however, between a phone company disclosing the numbers dialed by a customer and its taking further action to gather information for the police involving a noncustomer. By exceeding the scope of information knowingly exposed to the phone company, its representative is effectively acting as an agent of the police conducting the criminal investigation. Because the representative's actions violated Lauren's reasonable expectation of privacy, the content of the representative's conversation with Suzy would be inadmissible under the Fourth Amendment at Lauren's trial.

D is the best answer.

Cornwell's picks

1. Caught in the crosshairs   **A**
2. A third ear   **C**
3. Teaming with trouble   **D**
4. Off the grid   **B**
5. Philanderin' Phil   **D**

6

Privacy in Your Person and Effects

A.   Bodily Privacy and Liberty

The Fourth Amendment prohibition on the unreasonable search and seizure of one's "person" precludes law enforcement officers from invading bodily privacy without cause. In later chapters, we will explore the extent to which certain events, such as arrest, render external bodily searches by police reasonable, in the absence of consent. Without this sort of justification, police officers may not invade an individual's body, or the clothing covering it, without a warrant.

Of course, an officer may violate the Fourth Amendment without ever coming into contact with an individual's body. Our right to bodily "liberty" precludes a seizure of one's person without reasoned grounds for doing so. Thus, in *Florida v. Royer*, 460 U.S. 491 (1983), federal agents exceeded constitutional limits by detaining a traveler on an airport concourse without sufficient cause while retaining her credentials and announcing that she was under criminal investigation.

QUESTION 1. **Of boots and billfolds.**   Gwen, Sylvia, and Corlette were standing in line at Barnes & Noble, waiting for Rita Pita to sign their copies of Pita's latest cookbook. While they waited, Officer Melvin approached Gwen and asked when she had arrived at the store. Gwen estimated that she had arrived thirty minutes earlier, which Sylvia and Corlette confirmed.

Melvin remarked that a customer had reported that his billfold had been stolen by someone inside the store forty-five minutes earlier. As a result, Melvin was searching all bags carried by the 95 to 100 persons who were in the store at that time. Although Gwen stated she was not present in the store at that time, Melvin asked to search her purse anyway. When Gwen refused to consent to the search of her purse, Melvin required her to exit the line and accompany him to his office.

Outraged, Corlette and Sylvia joined Gwen to offer moral support. After five minutes, Sylvia left, explaining that she needed to pick up her daughter from day care. Corlette stayed as Melvin questioned Gwen about her movements within the store. When he finished, Melvin told Gwen to remove the boots she was wearing. He then looked inside the boots and found the missing billfold inside the left boot. Melvin's conduct violated the Fourth Amendment rights of:

A. No one.
B. Gwen only.
C. Gwen and Corlette only.
D. Gwen, Corlette, and Sylvia.

ANALYSIS.   This problem explores the parameters of the general right to bodily privacy and liberty, as applied to the three ladies whose movements were influenced by Officer Melvin's investigation. We will start with Gwen, the target of the investigation.

Melvin clearly "seized" Gwen when he involuntarily removed her to his office. His subsequent search of her boot is likewise subject to Fourth Amendment constraints. Therefore, Melvin would need reasoned grounds to render these actions valid. The facts do not disclose any reason for suspecting that Gwen had stolen the billfold. Gwen stated that she had not yet arrived at the store when the theft occurred, and her friends corroborated her account. Lacking any basis for the detention and subsequent search, Melvin's actions toward Gwen were constitutionally indefensible.

Corlette and Sylvia accompanied Gwen into the office. Corlette remained until after the search of Gwen's purse, while Sylvia left earlier. If the removal of the ladies to the office was involuntary, the difference in time frame is irrelevant, since both would have been subjected to a restraint on bodily liberty. This is not the case, however. The facts indicate that they accompanied Gwen to offer "moral support," not because Melvin forced them to do so. Because their conduct was voluntary, it does not implicate the Fourth Amendment.

Because Melvin's conduct violated only the Fourth Amendment rights of Gwen, the correct answer is **B**.

B.   Higher-Level Invasions of Bodily Privacy

In certain circumstances, searches that invade the body itself may be permissible, provided the police can demonstrate a compelling need for the procedure. In *Schmerber v. California*, 384 U.S. 757 (1966), the defendant was arrested for driving under the influence of intoxicating liquor. His erratic driving caused an accident, and he was taken to the hospital. While he was receiving treatment for his injuries, a blood sample was taken to confirm his level of intoxication, at the direction of the police. The U.S. Supreme Court found that the officer's "seizure" of the defendant's blood did not violate the Fourth Amendment, noting the evanescent nature of blood-alcohol evidence and the lack of sufficient time "to seek out a magistrate and secure a warrant." In its totality-of-the-circumstances analysis, the majority also noted that the procedure presented virtually no risk, trauma, or pain and was performed in a clinical setting by medical personnel. Thus, on balance, and in light of the "special facts" presented, the warrantless blood test was reasonable.

While they did not overrule *Schmerber*, more recent cases have significantly undermined its significance. In *Missouri v. McNeely*, 133 S. Ct. 1552 (2013), the Court reasoned that, in light of the significant invasion of "bodily integrity" occasioned by a blood-alcohol test, where officers can "reasonably obtain" a warrant before drawing blood without "significantly undermining the efficacy of the search," they must do so. See also *Birchfield v. North Dakota*, 136 S. Ct. 2160 (2016) (Blood tests "pierce the skin and extract a part of the subject's body.") Breath tests, by contrast, do not implicate significant privacy concerns; therefore, they may be administered without a warrant incident to arrests for drunk driving. *Birchfield*.

McNeely and *Birchfield* are consistent with other cases where the Court has found that the government's need to invade the body to recover evidence does not outweigh a defendant's privacy interest. For example, in *Winston v. Lee*, 470 U.S. 753 (1985), the state sought an order to compel the surgical removal of a bullet from under the defendant's collarbone to prove that it came from a particular gun. Distinguishing *Schmerber*, the U.S. Supreme Court noted that the surgery requested involves an extensive intrusion on privacy and bodily integrity wherein the defendant loses all control over his body and is "drug[ged] . . . with narcotics and barbiturates into a state of unconsciousness." Moreover, the prosecution was not dependent on the forensic evidence, as in *Schmerber*, because there was abundant additional evidence linking the defendant to the crime.

Likewise, in *Safford Unified School District #1 v. Redding*, 129 S. Ct. 2633 (2009), the Court deemed the strip search of an eighth grader unreasonable, finding that the intrusiveness of the search was excessive in light of the proffered justification: the belief of school administrators that she was in possession of prescription-strength ibuprofen, a commonly used pain reliever marketed under brand names such as Advil and Motrin. While supportive of the principal's desire to provide a safe environment for his students, the "limited threat" posed by the drugs did not justify, according to the majority, the "exposure of intimate parts" of the teenager's body to school personnel.

QUESTION 2. Rockin' Robin.   Officer Frank was called to a bar to break up a fight reported by the owner between two patrons. As Frank approached the fighters, one of them, Robin, placed small objects into his mouth and fled the bar. Frank gave chase and apprehended Robin one block away. Frank asked Robin why he had fled. When Robin opened his mouth to respond, Frank saw a small, rock-like substance in his mouth that appeared to be crack cocaine. Frank ordered Robin to spit out the contents of his mouth.

Robin disobeyed the order and swallowed the contents, claiming they were candy. Frank then took Robin to a nearby hospital and had his stomach pumped, which revealed that the objects in question were, in fact, crack cocaine. If Robin argues that the pumping of his stomach violated the Fourth Amendment, which of the following is LEAST relevant in analyzing the merit of his claim?

A. Frank needed to determine how much crack he possessed to determine the severity of the drug offense with which to charge Robin.

B. Frank needed to protect Robin's physical well-being since Robin had swallowed drugs.

C. The pumping of Robin's stomach was performed by medical personnel.

D. Robin refused to spit out the contents of his mouth when ordered to do so by Frank.

E. Stomach-pumping is an invasive medical procedure.

ANALYSIS.   *Schmerber*, *McNeely*, *Lee*, *Redding*, and *Birchfield* instruct that, in determining the permissibility of highly intrusive searches to acquire incriminating evidence, courts should balance the nature and severity of the intrusion against the government's need for the evidence in question. It is against this backdrop that we must evaluate our five choices to determine which is least relevant to Robin's claim.

McNeely and *Birchfield* underscore the serious Fourth Amendment concerns attendant to invasions of bodily integrity, procedures that implicate "an individual's most personal and deep-rooted expectations of privacy."

Therefore, it is clearly relevant for Fourth Amendment purposes that stomach-pumping (like drawing blood) is an invasive medical procedure since it sheds light on the severity of the intrusion. Likewise, in *Schmerber*, the U.S. Supreme Court considered the fact that medical personnel performed the procedure to be important in assessing its reasonableness, since the clinical setting safeguards the defendant's health in an atmosphere less punctuated by police domination. Thus, **C**, like **E**, is relevant.

Distinguishing *Schmerber*, the U.S. Supreme Court in *Lee* noted that the surgery requested by the police was unnecessary since the police had other evidence to prove their case. Similarly, we must consider the extent to which Frank needed the "physical" crack cocaine evidence to prove a case against Robin. Because the possession of greater quantities of a drug merits higher-level charges, **A** is a relevant consideration. Remember, **A** does not state that the procedure is clearly necessary; rather, it imports that Frank's need to determine the quantity of crack is relevant in assessing the reasonableness of the procedure — in light of, and in addition to, his ability to acquire the information through other, less invasive means.

Answer **D** focuses on Robin's noncompliance with Frank's order to spit out the contents of his mouth. In assessing the reasonableness of this forced extraction, it is clearly relevant to consider this fact, since it goes to the very need for the procedure in the first place. More specifically, it supports Frank's argument that his conduct was reasonable, since he had attempted to acquire the evidence through far less invasive means with which Robin chose not to comply.

We are left, then, with answer **B**. In *Redding*, the majority emphasized the limited threat posed by the contraband in question, noting that school administrators had no evidence that large quantities of drugs were present in the school potentially threatening the well-being of the student body in general. Likewise, while Frank's concern for Robin's physical well-being might have some relevance if he had cause to believe Robin had swallowed a large amount of crack, the facts do not support this conclusion. Absent any reason to believe that Robin was in imminent danger, concern over his health is inapposite.

B is least relevant.[1]

C.   Personal Effects: Vehicles

Just as the text of the Fourth Amendment protects one's "person," so does it shield his or her "effects" from unlawful search and seizure. As we will see, the extent of this protection depends on a number of factors, including the location of the object, its relationship to the owner, and the use to which the "effect" is put. We will start with vehicles.

The U.S. Supreme Court has held that individuals have diminished privacy protection in their cars for several reasons. First, unlike residences, cars

---

1. This problem does not address the challenge that Robin could legitimately assert under the Due Process Clause of the Fourteenth Amendment. See, e.g., *Rochin v. California*, 342 U.S. 165 (1952).

rarely serve as "the repository for personal effects." Second, they are routinely subject to public scrutiny because they travel on roads where both the vehicles' contents and their passengers are plainly visible. Finally, due to the pervasive regulation of automobiles, operators expect greater intrusion on privacy by the state in the enforcement of periodic inspection and licensing requirements. See *New York v. Class*, 475 U.S. 106 (1986).

We will examine, in a later chapter, the necessity *vel non* of a warrant to physically invade and search the inside of an automobile for contraband. With respect to information gleaned from the exterior of a car, however, the Court has been willing to eschew the warrant requirement. For example, in *Cardwell v. Lewis*, 417 U.S. 583 (1974), the police took paint scrapings from the exterior of a car and examined the tire tread on the vehicle's operative wheel. While the officers had probable cause to believe that the vehicle was an instrumentality of crime, they lacked a warrant to search it. Writing for a plurality of the Court, Justice Blackmun deemed the warrant unnecessary, reasoning that any invasion of privacy under these circumstances was "abstract and theoretical."

Likewise, the justices have found no reasonable expectation of privacy in a vehicle identification number (VIN). Under federal law, the VIN must be located inside the passenger compartment in an area clearly visible to an individual with 20/20 vision. As such, the Court likened the VIN to the car's exterior, rather than to internal areas whose contents were not plainly visible to one standing outside the car, such as the trunk or glove compartment. Police officers conducting a traffic stop may, therefore, view and record the VIN without contravening the Fourth Amendment. In addition, if the officer's visual access to the VIN is obscured, the officer may remove any items necessary to permit the visual inspection. See *New York v. Class, supra*.

QUESTION 3. Secret stash.   To deter the use of automobile glove compartments to hide drugs, the Setonia legislature passed a law requiring all motorists to leave their glove compartments open when parking their cars in a public place to enable police officers to view the contents of the glove compartment from a position outside the vehicle. Police Officer Sarah is responsible for enforcing the law.

Sarah received a tip that Tim was stashing cocaine in his glove compartment, and she approached his car after he left it in a mall parking lot. Looking into the car, Sarah did not observe any drugs inside the open glove compartment, but she determined that Tim could have hidden some in the back, behind a first-aid kit located in the compartment. She entered the car and removed the first-aid kit. As she expected, she found a bag of cocaine behind the kit. If Tim claims that Sarah violated his Fourth Amendment rights, he will:

A. Succeed, because Sarah entered his car.
B. Succeed, because Sarah moved the first-aid kit.
C. Fail, because Setonia law required glove compartments in parked cars to be open.
D. Fail, because Tim's placement of the first-aid kit in the glove compartment concealed drugs.

ANALYSIS.   To successfully answer this problem, you need to think carefully about the reasoning of the U.S. Supreme Court in *New York v. Class*. In *Class*, the justices reasoned that federal law removed any privacy expectation in the VIN by requiring motorists to make it visible from outside the car. Likewise, in this problem, Setonia law removes any privacy expectation in the contents of glove compartments that officers can view when standing outside the vehicle.

In the problem, Sarah is able to view the contents of the glove box, but, believing that contraband is lurking in an area she cannot visually access from the outside, she enters the car and moves the contents of the glove compartment to allow a full inventory of its contents. At first blush, this may seem indistinguishable from *Class*, where the majority permitted law enforcement officers to move papers that impeded their ability to record the VIN. This case is different, though, because the Setonia law requires only that motorists enable police officers to view the contents of the glove compartment from outside the vehicle. Sarah was able to do this, noticing a first-aid kit and other items.

It is inevitable that some items will be located in a part of the compartment where visual access will be difficult, if not impossible, from outside the car. As such, officers will not be able to inspect these items. If the legislature intended to allow officers to have visual access to *all* contents, it should have written the law differently. As presently constituted, the statute removes the expectation of privacy only in those items within the glove compartment that may be viewed from the outside. Because the contraband in question does not fall within these parameters, its seizure was unlawful.

C and **D** are wrong. **C** merely restates the law which, as discussed above, is insufficient to justify Sarah's conduct. **D** suggests that Sarah's actions are nonetheless permissible since they led to the discovery of contraband. This is plainly wrong, as it imports that any police conduct, no matter how egregious, is permissible if officers find evidence of illegality in the end. It is the conduct that led to the discovery, not its fruits, that determines its constitutionality.

Both **A** and **B** are technically correct. Because Sarah only had the right to view the contents of the glove box from the outside, both her entry into the car and the subsequent moving of the first-aid kit were unlawful. **B** is better, however, because it is the movement of the kit that actually revealed the cocaine. The entry into the vehicle, while impermissible, was less closely linked to the unlawful search and seizure on which Tim's challenge is based.

B is the correct answer.

D.   Abandoned Effects

If individuals abandon their personal effects, they surrender any privacy interest therein, inasmuch as their actions manifest an intention to relinquish control over the objects in question such that others are likely to gain access to them. Therefore, if the owner of an automobile treats it in such a way that any expectation of privacy is unreasonable, the Constitution does not prohibit police officers from searching the vehicle for criminal fruits. Likewise, the U.S. Supreme Court found no Fourth Amendment violation where federal agents seized two items, a hollowed-out pencil and a block of wood, left by the defendant in a hotel room wastebasket after he had paid his bill and vacated the room. "There can be," the Court concluded, "nothing unlawful in the Government's appropriation of such abandoned property." *Abel v. United States*, 362 U.S. 217 (1960).

The fact that an individual has relinquished control over private property temporarily does not, however, prove abandonment. In *Smith v. Ohio*, 494 U.S. 541 (1990), when the defendant was approached by two police officers, he threw the bag he was carrying onto the roof of his car and subsequently endeavored to shield it from the officers. The officers searched it nonetheless, finding drug paraphernalia inside. The U.S Supreme Court rejected the officers' claim that, under these circumstances, the bag was abandoned property. "[A] citizen who attempts to protect his private property from inspection, after throwing it on a car to respond to a police officer's inquiry, clearly has not abandoned that property."

QUESTION 4. **Yo, where's my shotgun?**   After Judson sold his house to Kathleen, he realized that his new house would not be available for occupancy until one month after the closing date with Kathleen. Kathleen permitted Judson to stay in the house for one month after the closing for a rental fee of $1,500. Judson readily agreed and paid Kathleen the $1,500 up front. Three weeks after the closing, Judson found out that he could move into his new house. He packed up his belongings and moved them into the new house that day. He called Kathleen and told her that he had moved out and she was free to occupy the house at any time. Kathleen told him she would pick up the keys he had left with a neighbor later that evening and would move in the following day.

The next day, while patrolling the neighborhood, Howie, a local cop, saw Kathleen struggling to carry a chair into her new house. He helped her carry it into the garage. Once in the garage, Howie discovered a box, sealed with masking tape and labeled "property of Judson." "Who's Judson?" he asked. "Oh," Kathleen responded, "he's the guy I bought the place from. I guess he left it here." When Kathleen exited the garage, Howie opened the box, finding a sawed-off shotgun inside. Later that day, Howie arrested Judson for possession of an illegal firearm. If Judson claims that Howie's search of the box was unlawful, Judson will:

A. Prevail, because Judson was paying rent when Howie opened the box.
B. Prevail, because the box was sealed and clearly belonged to Judson.
C. Fail, because Judson had given the house keys to Kathleen's neighbor.
D. Fail, because Kathleen owned the house when Howie opened the box.

ANALYSIS. In answering this—or, indeed, any—question involving abandoned effects, the analysis will always focus on the extent to which the actions taken by the owner manifest an intention to relinquish control over the property in question. Here, Judson has placed the firearm in a sealed box in the garage of a house he is, at the time of the search, renting from Kathleen. Typically, these facts would be totally inconsistent with abandonment.

In this instance, however, the situation is complicated by the fact that Judson has moved out of the house into his new abode. Because he retains a right of access to the premises throughout the period for which he has paid rent, Judson could have held onto the original house until the end of the month. Had he done so, he could argue that he had not abandoned the box in question because he was planning to come back for it before the rental period expired.

Judson chose, instead, to surrender occupancy of the house by leaving the keys with a neighbor for Kathleen. At the time the box was opened, Kathleen had retrieved the keys and was moving in. Judson's actions conveyed an intention to leave the premises for good; thus, the box appeared to be left behind with no intention to reclaim it. It was, in short, abandoned property.

As discussed above, both **A** and **B** would be correct if Judson still occupied the house at the time of the search. His payment of rent would distinguish him from the hotel guest who had checked out in *Smith v. Ohio*, and his ownership of the box, coupled with the steps taken to secrete its contents, would certainly demonstrate a subjective and reasonable expectation of privacy. However, his relinquishment of the premises to Kathleen negates these arguments.

D is incorrect because the fact of Kathleen's ownership, standing alone, does not defeat Judson's claim of privacy in the box. Rental of property, coupled with occupancy, is clearly sufficient to promote a claim of privacy in the premises and its contents. Were this not the case, renters everywhere would have lesser privacy rights than do owners, a result plainly at odds with the spirit of the Fourth Amendment.

Judson explicitly surrendered the property to Kathleen, leaving the keys with a neighbor, and Kathleen explicitly told Judson she would collect them later that evening. Judson's abandonment of any claim and Kathleen's access to the property the next day defeat Judson's Fourth Amendment claim with respect to the box. It does not matter that his rental period had not yet expired at the time of the search. He has voluntarily relinquished control over the dwelling and, by extension, over its contents.

C is the correct answer.

E.   A Spotlight on Garbage

Of all abandoned effects, garbage has probably received the most attention from the courts. In response to variations in the reasoning of lower court cases, the U.S. Supreme Court considered individuals' privacy rights in garbage left at the curb for collection in *California v. Greenwood*, 486 U.S. 35 (1988).

The Laguna Beach Police Department believed that defendant Greenwood was involved in drug trafficking. To help gather sufficient evidence to obtain a search warrant for his residence, a police investigator asked the neighborhood's trash collector to pick up the plastic garbage bags the defendant had left at the curb for collection and then hand them over to the police department without mixing them with the refuse left by other customers. The trash collector agreed to help and delivered the bags to the police as requested. The bags contained incriminating evidence, which the police used to obtain a search warrant for Greenwood's residence.

The U.S Supreme Court found that the warrantless search of Greenwood's garbage did not violate his Fourth Amendment rights. The majority reasoned that garbage placed on a public street is "readily accessible to animals, children, scavengers, snoops and other members of the public." Moreover, customers typically place no restriction on the garbage collectors' use of the refuse they collect; as far as Greenwood knew, the trash collector could have sorted through the garbage himself or handed it over to a third party for inspection. Indeed, as the justices noted, the trash of public figures has been searched by tabloid newspapers.

Because Greenwood knowingly exposed his trash to the public by placing it on a public thoroughfare for collection, he could not reasonably expect privacy protection in its contents any more than he could expect privacy in the numbers he dials on his telephone. See *Smith v. Maryland, supra.* "[T]he police cannot reasonably be expected to avert their eyes from evidence of criminal activity that could have been observed by any member of the public." *California v. Greenwood.*

QUESTION 5. One man's trash. . . .   Officer Alan received an anonymous tip that the Bracketts were selling marijuana at their home on 14 Drury Lane. Alan surveyed the property, hoping to witness suspicious behavior that, together with the tip, would furnish probable cause for the issuance of a warrant. On the fourth day of surveillance, Alan saw Mr. Brackett place a black, plastic bag outside his house in the back yard, leaning against the porch. Two hours later, he saw a dog enter Brackett's back yard from the street. The dog pawed at the bag and then dragged it out of the back yard and onto a neighbor's property. Seeing the neighbor in her front yard, Alan asked her if he could search the bag that the dog had dragged onto her lawn. She consented to the search, which turned up marijuana paraphernalia among various items of household trash. Brackett's claim that the search violated his Fourth Amendment rights will:

A. Succeed, because he has a privacy interest in his back yard.
B. Succeed, because he did not knowingly expose the contents of the bag to public view.
C. Fail, because the dog dragged the bag onto the neighbor's yard.
D. Fail, because the bag contained trash that Brackett meant to discard.

ANALYSIS. To successfully navigate this problem, you must determine which of the four answers contains the *dispositive* principle of law, as applied to the facts. That is, while each statement is accurate, only one resolves the problem, as we shall see.

As answer **A** notes, Alan does have a privacy interest in his back yard through the concept of curtilage, discussed previously. Therefore, his placement of the bag within the curtilage creates privacy protection inasmuch as an officer would need to invade the curtilage to access the bag. That is not, however, what happened here. Alan never entered Brackett's back yard. The privacy infringement was accomplished by a dog running free through the neighborhood. Since Alan had no control over the dog's actions, its conduct does not implicate the Fourth Amendment. (By contrast, if this had been a police dog, acting on Alan's command to enter the yard, the Fourth Amendment would have been violated.)

Likewise, answer **D** is insufficient to resolve this problem. While the bag contained trash, it may nonetheless merit Fourth Amendment protection if its location creates a reasonable expectation of privacy in its contents. For example, as just discussed, if the bag is placed inside the home or outside within the curtilage, its invasion will violate the Fourth Amendment, without regard to its contents. Thus, our focus must be on the bag's location at the time of the search and how Alan gained authority to search it from that location.

Answer **B** seems very attractive at first blush, since it tracks the governing legal standard of *California v. Greenwood*. In *Greenwood*, the U.S. Supreme Court held that the defendant lacked privacy protection in his garbage since, by leaving it at the curb for collection, he had knowingly exposed its contents to "animals, children, scavengers, snoops, and other members of the public" who might choose to access it.

Mr. Brackett's conduct differed significantly, however, from that of defendant Greenwood. Brackett did not leave his garbage in a public place; on the contrary, he placed it in a *private* area behind his house where members of the public would not have routine access to it. In fact, in order to do so, an individual would need to trespass onto Brackett's property. In *Greenwood*, by contrast, ordinary citizens would come upon the trash while proceeding on a public thoroughfare.

Even though Brackett's placement of the bag did not promote common access to it, it was nonetheless removed to a different location by a stray dog. Its newfound resting place in a neighbor's yard gave the neighbor authority over the bag. Thus, her consent to Alan's search of the bag was valid.

The correct answer is **C**.

F.   Luggage and Other Moveable Containers

It is clear that individuals have a right to privacy in luggage and other moveable "containers," such as wallets and purses, in that they contain personal items placed there by their owners. *United States v. Chadwick*, 433 U.S. 1 (1977). Therefore, a police officer may not stop individuals on the street and demand to search their suitcases without a warrant authorizing the search. This same prohibition applies to common carriers, such as buses.

In *Bond v. United States*, 529 U.S. 334 (2000), border patrol agents squeezed the defendant's luggage—in this case an opaque duffle bag—while conducting a check of the immigration status of all passengers. The U.S. Supreme Court found that, while a bus passenger may expect his bag to be handled, he does not anticipate that other passengers or bus employees will "feel the bag in an exploratory manner," as the agent did in this instance. This "physical manipulation" violated the Fourth Amendment.

The Court has also limited the amount of time that law enforcement officers may "seize" luggage believed to contain contraband or other evidence of crime. In *United States v. Place*, 462 U.S. 696 (1983), the U.S. Supreme Court held that government agents violated the Fourth Amendment by holding an air passenger's luggage for 90 minutes without probable cause after its arrival at its airport destination. This lengthy seizure interfered, the justices reasoned, with both the defendant's "possessory interest in his luggage, as well as his liberty interest in proceeding with his itinerary."

Note, however, that *Place* does not address the authority of airport personnel to conduct a thorough search of luggage as a condition of boarding an aircraft without proof that its owner has engaged in any wrongdoing. Preboarding searches and seizures do not compromise the traveler's possessory or liberty interests as in *Place*. Moreover, this common, 21st-century practice is almost certainly justified by the need to ensure passenger safety in light of contemporary challenges and realities.

QUESTION 6. **A helping hand.**   Jonathan is traveling by bus from Newark to Florida to visit his buddy, Brian. The bus is scheduled to leave at 12:45 P.M. At 12:30 P.M., uniformed Newark police officer Jake enters the bus, announces himself, and indicates that he will be passing through the bus to make a cursory inspection for contraband since, as Jake notes, "Newark is a well-known source city for drugs."

As Jake begins his inspection, Jonathan bursts onto the bus. He hurriedly places his duffle bag in the luggage rack and sits down. In his haste, Jonathan fails to secure the bag, and it falls to the floor in front of Jake. "Here, let me help you with that," Jake offers. Jake then picks up the bag to reposition it in the overhead luggage rack.

As Jake is doing so, Jonathan jumps up. "No, no! That's okay. I'll do it," Jonathan urges. As Jake is handing the bag back to Jonathan, Jake feels what appears to be the butt of a shotgun. Based on his discovery, Jake tells Jonathan that carrying a firearm on a bus is a felony and he (Jake) will need to seize the firearm. Jonathan is later charged with possession of an illegal firearm. He claims that Jake's search of his duffle bag violated the Fourth Amendment. This claim will likely:

A. Succeed, because Jake handled Jonathan's bag against Jonathan's wishes.

B. Succeed, because Jake lacked authority to handle Jonathan's bag.

C. Succeed, because Jake's handling of Jonathan's bag exceeded Jake's authority.

D. Fail, because Newark is a source city for drugs.

E. Fail, because Jake was merely acting courteously.

ANALYSIS. This problem primarily tests your understanding of *Bond v. United States* and its limits. Jonathan enters the bus at the last minute and, in his haste, fails to secure his luggage such that it falls to the floor just as Officer Jake is making an inspection. Jake picks up the bag to be helpful, much as any passenger might. When Jonathan indicates that he does not want assistance, Jake begins to hand the bag back to him. In the process of doing so, Jake detects the illegal firearm.

Bond imports that law enforcement officers cannot physically manipulate luggage "in an exploratory manner" without proof that its owner is engaged in criminal wrongdoing. By the same token, *Bond* recognizes that travelers on a common carrier should expect that the luggage they carry will be handled by others who may need to reposition it to create room for their own belongings.

Jake does not exceed his authority under this standard. He manipulates the bag only to the extent necessary first to place it in overhead storage and then to hand it back to Jonathan. Jake engages in no gratuitous "exploration" of the bag's contents. His initial contact with the bag was also reasonable, since he was doing no more than any fellow traveler might do to be helpful.

Answers **A**, **B**, and **C** are, thus, incorrect. To accuse Jake of handling the bag "against Jonathan's wishes" is unfair and somewhat misleading. Jake's initial contact with the bag was not an act of defiance toward Jonathan; Jake was merely trying to be helpful. When Jonathan indicates that he does not want help placing it overhead, Jake complies with this request and begins to pass the bag to Jonathan. The manner in which Jake handles the duffle bag is also reasonable. As explained above, Jake did not manipulate the bag unlawfully. As he hands the bag to Jonathan, Jake *immediately* senses that it is a firearm, without any additional exploration. Therefore, he does not exceed his authority under *Bond*.

As between **D** and **E**, **E** is the better answer. The fact that Newark is a source city for drugs does not give Jake the right to search Jonathan's bag. Indeed, this was precisely the point of *Bond*. Conversely, the courteous assistance Jake provided to Jonathan is clearly contemplated by *Bond*, as Jake's actions did not exceed that in which any other passenger might engage.

E is the correct answer.

G.   The Closer

QUESTION 7. **Garbage in, garbage out.**   The City of Peeyookey has been subject to a one-month citywide strike by sanitation workers. Residents of the city have been increasingly creative in finding ways to dispose of their trash. Needing to clear away the mounting garbage in his garage, Brock decided to fill an old duffle bag with trash and leave it on the curb next to his car, which Brock had parked on the street in front of his house.

Police Officer A.J., who had long suspected Brock of dealing drugs, saw the bag and decided to seize it, hoping it would contain illegal drugs. A.J. opened the bag and found, amidst the garbage, a clear baggie that contained what appeared to be marijuana. Because the forensics lab was temporarily closed for renovation, A.J. kept the bag for five days before submitting it to the lab for testing. In the end, A.J.'s suspicions proved correct: The contents of the baggie were indeed marijuana. If Brock moves to suppress the marijuana, he will likely:

A. Fail, because anyone could have accessed the bag.
B. Fail, because the bag contained garbage.
C. Succeed, because Brock left the bag next to his car.
D. Succeed, because A.J. physically manipulated the bag.
E. Succeed, because A.J. kept the bag for five days before testing it.

ANALYSIS.   To arrive at the correct answer to this problem, it is important to keep the "big picture" in mind. We know that, in determining if an item qualifies as abandoned property, courts look at whether an individual's actions manifest an intention to relinquish control over it. Brock has filled a duffel bag with garbage and left it at the curb unattended. On its face, these actions indicate an intention to abandon the bag, since Brock could not effectively prevent others from gaining access to or removing it. Therefore, **A** is presumptively correct, unless additional facts or considerations negate it.

Answer **B** notes that the bag contains garbage. We know that the U.S. Supreme Court has held that garbage left at the curb for collection is not protected by the Fourth Amendment, but, in so finding, the Court's emphasis was not on the contents of the bag but rather on the fact that it was left in a place where its contents were freely accessible to all members of the public, as well as animals. Thus, **A** is the better answer.

Answers **C** through **E** attempt, in different ways, to create privacy protection in the duffle bag. Answer **C** focuses on the bag's location next to Brock's car. This is inapposite, since the car is parked in a public area, most likely in the vicinity of other vehicles. Moreover, at any rate, there is nothing in the facts that links the bag to Brock's car. **C** is wrong.

Answer **D** assails A.J.'s manipulation of the bag. In *Bond*, the U.S. Supreme Court disallowed the exploratory manipulation of a duffle bag, but the context of that case is quite different from that of this problem. In *Bond*, the bag was located on a bus where passengers retain a privacy interest in it. Here, the bag's location on the curb communicated no expectation of privacy at all. Because privacy protection was unavailable to the bag in the first instance, A.J.'s actions in opening it could not violate the Fourth Amendment. **D** is wrong.

Place's prohibition on lengthy seizures of luggage is misplaced here for similar reasons. Police officers cannot retain a piece of luggage for an extended period because privacy protection inheres in moveable luggage used to transport personal items. *United States v. Chadwick, supra*. Brock's luggage was not employed for this purpose, however, making the reasoning of *Place* inapplicable. **E** is wrong.

A is the correct answer.

✦ Cornwell's Picks

1.	Of boots and billfolds	B
2.	Rockin' Robin	B
3.	Secret stash	B
4.	Yo, where's my shotgun?	C
5.	One man's trash. . . .	C
6.	A helping hand	E
7.	Garbage in, garbage out	A

7

The Warrant Clause: General Principles

CHAPTER OVERVIEW
A. The Need for a Warrant
B. Evidentiary Considerations
C. A Neutral and Detached Magistrate
D. The Closer
✦ Cornwell's Picks

A.   The Need for a Warrant

While the text of the Fourth Amendment makes explicit reference to warrants, the Framers did not specify the circumstances in which a warrant is a necessary precondition to an arrest or to the search or seizure of private property. Consequently, our understanding of the need for a warrant derives principally from the case law specifying when one is *not* necessary.

Generally speaking, unless an exception applies (see Chapters 10 through 14, *infra*), police officers need a warrant to search protected areas such as an individual's home, body, and personal effects. Arrest warrants are necessary only if the arrest takes place outside a public place. While the line dividing public and private space can be difficult to draw, the Court has approved the warrantless arrest of a suspect standing on the threshold of the front door of her home, reasoning that she "was as exposed to public view, speech, hearing and touch as if she had been standing completely outside her house." *United States v. Santana*, 427 U.S. 38 (1976). Police officers can also arrest individuals without a warrant for very minor offenses, including those punishable by fines alone, without running afoul of the Fourth Amendment. *Atwater v. City of Lago Vista*, 532 U.S. 318 (2001).

QUESTION 1. **Whoa, Nellie!**   Police Officer Paul was patrolling Main Street when he saw a vehicle making an illegal left-hand turn at an intersection. Paul followed the car into a residential neighborhood and observed the driver, Nellie, park her car on the street and subsequently enter her residence. After ten minutes, Nellie left the house. As she was reentering her car, Paul approached and asked to see Nellie's driver's license. She complied.

Paul ran a computer check, which indicated that Nellie's driving record was clear. He nonetheless decided to place her under arrest for violating the "no left turn" law, which is punishable by a fine of up to $100. Paul handcuffed Nellie, placed her in the back seat of the squad car, and transported her to the police station for booking. Nellie's claim that her warrantless arrest was unconstitutional:

A. Has merit, because Nellie had just left her home.
B. Has merit, because violating the "no left turn" law is not a jailable offense.
C. Has merit, because Nellie was not acting belligerently toward Paul.
D. Has merit, because Paul did not arrest Nellie at or near the location where the offense took place.
E. Lacks merit.

ANALYSIS.   Answers **A** through **D** offer a variety of rationales for requiring a warrant. **A** suggests that Paul would need a warrant because Nellie had left her residence just prior to her arrest. While a warrant would have been necessary if Paul had arrested Nellie in her home, he waited until she was in a public place. The recency of her presence in a protected area is irrelevant. **A** is wrong.

Because violating the "no left turn" law cannot result in incarceration, it would be unusual for a police officer to make a custodial arrest based solely on this infraction. However, in this instance, Paul believes that such action is appropriate. The U.S. Supreme Court has held that this practice does not violate the Fourth Amendment, even without any additional proof that the suspect's demeanor made the arrest necessary. **B** and **C** are wrong.

Answer **D** is a red herring. While it seems plausible that an officer would make the arrest at or near the location where the violation takes place, this is not a constitutional requirement. Remember to evaluate an answer based *only* on the principle of law specified in the problem — here, the Fourth Amendment. Do not substitute your subjective sense of what seems logical or fair.

Nellie's claim lacks merit. **E** is the correct answer.

B. Evidentiary Considerations

It is important not to confuse evidence admissible at trial with that which may be considered by police to furnish probable cause to search or arrest. For example, while the rules of evidence preclude the use of hearsay at trial, the U.S. Supreme Court has permitted its use in formulating probable cause. Likewise, whereas prosecutors may not refer to a defendant's prior arrests and pending indictments in their case-in-chief, such evidence may form part of the probable cause inquiry without compromising Fourth Amendment protections.

The differing rules of admissibility reflect the distinctions in the proceedings and their purposes. The purpose of a trial is to establish the defendant's guilt or innocence; as such, the prosecution bears the heavy burden of proof beyond a reasonable doubt coupled with stringent rules designed to ensure the reliability of potentially damaging evidence introduced against the accused. Because a search or arrest is less ominous, the requisite proof is more lenient, as are the rules governing the admissibility of evidence. See *Brinegar v. United States*, 338 U.S. 160 (1949).

Not all evidence inadmissible at trial may be used, however, to furnish probable cause that is otherwise lacking. In *Spinelli v. United States*, 393 U.S. 410 (1968), police officers obtained a warrant to search the defendant's apartment for evidence of illegal gambling. The warrant application relied on information gleaned from telephone records, a confidential informant, and FBI surveillance. When the Court deemed these sources insufficient, all that remained was the government's statement that Spinelli was "known" by the FBI and others to be a gambler. This, the justices held, "may not be used to give additional weight to allegations that would otherwise be insufficient."

> **QUESTION 2. Dalmatian plantation.** Cruella owned the Shake-a-Paw Puppy Palace. Officer Leonard received an anonymous tip that some of Cruella's dogs had been stolen from Dalmatian breeders in the area. Leonard set up surveillance outside the shop for five weeks. He noticed that, after hours, Cruella would often meet with Teddy Nogood, an unsavory individual whom Leonard had arrested several times for low-level theft offenses. On several occasions, Leonard noticed Nogood entering Cruella's shop carrying a blanket in his arms large enough to conceal a Dalmatian puppy. He was convinced that the blankets contained puppies stolen from local breeders.
>
> To test his theory, Leonard enlisted the help of his partner, Officer Janet. Each day for a week, Janet would enter the store undercover and ask Cruella if she had any new Dalmatian puppies. Each day, Cruella said no, always appearing nervous and agitated. On one occasion, as Janet approached Cruella, she heard her tell a customer, "I simply love

Dalmatian puppies! I can't get enough of them." On the seventh day Janet asked about the Dalmatian puppies, Cruella barked, "For the last time, you stupid woman, no! I don't have any, and I don't expect any, as I have told you before." Leonard applies for a warrant to search Cruella's shop for evidence of stolen Dalmatian puppies.

Which of the following statements contained in the affidavit supporting the warrant application should the court refuse to consider in evaluating probable cause?

A. "On several occasions, Cruella was seen in the company of Teddy Nogood, an individual who has committed theft offenses in the past."

B. "Teddy Nogood, a known criminal, was seen on several occasions entering Cruella's store carrying a blanket large enough to conceal a Dalmatian puppy."

C. "When asked by an undercover officer if she had any Dalmatian puppies, Cruella appeared nervous and agitated."

D. "On one occasion, an undercover officer heard Cruella state that she loved Dalmatian puppies and could not get enough of them."

E. All four statements would be considered.

ANALYSIS. As in the previous problem, our focus is not to determine whether the evidence gathered by the police is sufficient to furnish probable cause; rather, in this instance, we are evaluating the admissibility of the evidentiary statements proffered by the police in their effort to obtain a search warrant. In doing so, we must keep in mind that courts, in finding probable cause, may consider evidence that prosecutors would not be allowed to use at trial; however, statements that merely suggest that the subject of the warrant has a bad reputation are not useful.

Statement **A** accurately reports that Cruella has been seen with Teddy Nogood who has committed theft offenses. If it is permissible to consider prior arrests of the subject of the warrant, *a fortiori* a court may take cognizance of the criminal convictions of her associates.

Likewise, Statement **B** correctly reports that Teddy was seen carrying a blanket large enough to conceal a Dalmatian puppy. That it refers to Teddy as a "known criminal" is not problematic. Teddy has, in fact, been convicted of criminal offenses. As such, the reference is not analogous to the FBI agent's characterization of Spinelli as a "known gambler" where the agent's belief was based purely on speculation and innuendo. Moreover, Spinelli was himself the subject of the warrant; Teddy is not, and the statement makes no allegation about Cruella's criminal past.

Statement **C** references Cruella's nervousness and agitation when Janet questions her about the puppies. Again, this does not impermissibly comment on Cruella's bad reputation. It simply recounts the officer's impression of her demeanor when asked a question relevant to the crime under investigation.

Statement **D** does much the same. It contains no speculation about past activity, nor does it cast aspersions on Cruella's reputation either directly or through innuendo. It is, moreover, relevant to the alleged criminal activity, which focuses on the alleged theft of Dalmatian puppies from breeders in the area.

Because all four statements are admissible to establish probable cause for the issuance of a search warrant for the Shake-a-Paw Puppy Palace, **E** is correct.

C.   A Neutral and Detached Magistrate

In *Johnson v. United States*, 333 U.S. 10 (1948), the Supreme Court held that the authority to issue warrants rests exclusively in "neutral and detached magistrates" who, unlike law enforcement officers and agents, are divorced from "the often competitive enterprise of ferreting out crime." Thus, a state attorney general cannot perform this function, since his or her investigative and prosecutorial responsibilities may compromise the ability to independently evaluate the evidence. *Coolidge v. New Hampshire*, 403 U.S. 443 (1971).

While magistrates are usually judicial officers with formal legal training and experience, the Court has never held that only lawyers or judges can grant warrants. The justices have required only that an issuing magistrate be able to determine whether probable cause exists for the arrest or search at issue. Accordingly, *Shadwick v. City of Tampa*, 407 U.S. 345 (1972), found that municipal court clerks were competent to issue arrest warrants for breaches of ordinances, even though the position required neither a law degree nor any legal training. One does not need a law degree, the Court opined, to assess the likelihood of guilt for "impaired driving, breach of peace, drunkenness, trespass, or the multiple other common offenses covered by a municipal code." The justices emphasized, at the same time, that the clerks had no authority over more complex factual inquiries, such as the issuance of search warrants or arrest warrants for violations of state law.

Shadwick also found no reason to question the neutrality of the clerks. Unlike the attorney general in *Coolidge*, the clerks were removed from police and prosecutors; they worked, instead, within the judicial branch under the supervision of municipal court judges. As such, the requisite "severance and disengagement from activities of law enforcement" was manifest.

> **QUESTION 3. Justice denied?**   When preparing a budget for the upcoming fiscal year, the Albertville Town Council learned that the town's finances were in far worse shape than the council members had thought. Needing to trim municipal expenses by 40 percent, they instituted a variety of cost-cutting measures, including the consolidation of certain

government positions. One such consolidation concerned the justice of the peace (JP), a publicly elected official whose qualifications include graduation from an accredited or provisionally accredited law school in the United States.

Effective the beginning of the JP's next term, the JP assumed the responsibilities of both the registrar of voters and the town clerk in charge of real estate assessments. To justify the imposition of these additional duties with no corresponding increase in salary, the council removed responsibility for issuing search warrants from the list of the JP's official "salaried" duties. Instead, through a separate agreement, the town agreed to pay the JP a flat rate of $10 for each search warrant he or she issued.

After these new procedures took effect, police searched Tammy's home pursuant to a warrant issued by the JP. Tammy was charged with possession of stolen property, based on items found during the search. She has filed a motion to suppress, claiming that the JP was neither sufficiently qualified nor "neutral and detached" under the Fourth Amendment. Will Tammy prevail?

A. Yes, because a JP is not required to have law-related work experience.

B. Yes, because the JP is an elected official.

C. Yes, because the JP receives no compensation for search warrant requests that he or she denies.

D. Yes, because the JP is also responsible for real estate assessments and voter registration.

E. No.

ANALYSIS. This problem offers four challenges to the qualifications or neutrality of the JP who issued the search warrant of Tammy's home. We can start by eliminating **A.** The U.S. Supreme Court has never held that law-related work experience is a constitutional requirement of magistrates. In fact, while they only had the authority to issue arrest warrants, the municipal clerks in *Shadwick* were not required to have any legal experience whatsoever. It is also irrelevant that the JP is an elected official. Outside the federal system, judges are elected by popular vote in many jurisdictions, and the U.S. Supreme Court has acknowledged this practice without objection.

As a cost-cutting initiative, the council has made the JP responsible for voter registration and real estate tax assessment. This expansion of duties is problematic if it compromises the JP's neutrality, but there is no indication that it does so here. Voter registration and property valuation are not law enforcement functions that align the JP with police or prosecutors, as the responsibilities of the state attorney general did in *Coolidge*.

The same is not true, however, of the structure of the JP's compensation. The council has agreed to pay the JP a flat rate for every search warrant he or she issues. Therefore, if the JP rejects a request by law enforcement for a search warrant, he or she receives no money. By remunerating the JP only when he or she acquiesces to requests by law enforcement, the council's compensation structure introduces inherent prosecutorial bias. Unsurprisingly, reviewing facts very similar to ours, the U.S. Supreme Court found the magistrates insufficiently "neutral and detached." See *Connally v. Georgia*, 429 U.S. 245 (1977).

The correct answer is **C**.

D. The Closer

QUESTION 4. **Shady lady.**   Lorraine went to her local police precinct to complain about the steady influx of different men in and out of the house of her neighbor, Carol. Lorraine also claimed that she overheard Carol talking on her cell phone outside telling someone that she "could probably service him at 4:00 P.M. the next day" but would have to look at her appointment book, which she keeps "with all other business items" in a locked safe in her house. "These men," Lorraine explained, "are coming and going at all hours, and some look like real shady characters. If you ask me, she's turning tricks in there." Officer Ronnie conducted surveillance and confirmed Lorraine's story. Ronnie also noticed that Carol dressed very provocatively, favoring micro-miniskirts and tight-fitting shirts.

Assistant District Attorney Purvi applied for a warrant to find and then search the safe, believing it to contain business records and other items linked to prostitution. The affidavit supporting the warrant application included the details of Ronnie's surveillance—that is, the influx of men and Carol's provocative attire. Purvi also included the information obtained from Lorraine, most notably the overheard phone conversation and her belief that many of the men who entered the house looked "shady."

The warrant application was assigned to Magistrate Allan. Before the governor appointed Allan to the bench, he had worked as a prosecutor for twelve years. He joined the prosecutor's office right out of law school, which he attended at night while working as a police officer. Allan told Purvi that he was pleased her office was "finally" taking the "scourge of prostitution" seriously, commenting that it has been "infecting our streets for far too long." "Going after these so-called 'madams,'" Allan added, "is the right approach in my book." He then issued a warrant to find and search the safe.

Executing the warrant the following day, Ronnie started in Carol's bedroom. He entered her walk-in closet and, looking down, saw the safe. He opened it. Underneath a ledger, he found a $100 bill with a note, signed by "Bill," stating "Charlene was all you said she would be. Well worth the money." Ronnie placed Carol under arrest for promoting prostitution. Carol's argument that her Fourth Amendment rights have been violated:

A. Has merit, since statements about Carol's attire should not have been included in the warrant application.
B. Has merit, if the magistrate considered Lorraine's statements about the men.
C. Has merit, since the magistrate who issued the warrant was not neutral and detached.
D. Has merit, since Ronnie lacked a warrant to arrest Carol.
E. Lacks merit.

ANALYSIS.   In this closer, we follow Officer Ronnie as he investigates Carol's behavior, obtains a warrant to search a safe in her home, and searches the safe, finding incriminating evidence that leads to Carol's arrest. We must look at each step of the process to see whether—and, if so, where—Ronnie violated Carol's Fourth Amendment rights.

A and **B** address the warrant application process and the evidence presented to, and/or considered by, the magistrate. **A** is a bit of a red herring. While the evidentiary value of Carol's attire is indeed minimal, its inclusion by Purvi in the application does not violate Carol's constitutional rights. Were the magistrate to give it great weight in finding probable cause, Carol's argument would be stronger, but there is no such indication in the facts. Likewise, it is permissible for the court to consider evidence inadmissible at trial, both verbal and physical, in determining probable cause. Thus, Lorraine's statement that the men looked "shady" is fair game, provided the magistrate "does not use it to give additional weight to allegations that would otherwise be insufficient." See *Spinelli, supra.* **A** and **B** are wrong.

In questioning Allan's neutrality, Carol would presumably focus on his extensive law enforcement background before taking the bench and his comments to Purvi in court approving the prosecution of madams to combat the "scourge of prostitution . . . infecting our streets." We can summarily dispose of the first objection, as it is common for judges to have worked in law enforcement before "donning the robes." A judge's demonstration of prosecutorial bias on the bench is of far greater concern. Allan's comments to Purvi, however, do not nearly rise to this level. The fact that the magistrate applauds the prosecution of certain types of crime does not import that he is acting as an agent of law enforcement. Unlike the state attorney general in *Coolidge, supra,*

Allan's issuance of a search warrant does not undermine the separation of powers since Allan is not simultaneously working within two branches of government; his responsibilities are squarely—and exclusively—those of a judicial officer. **C** is wrong.

While Ronnie would ordinarily need a warrant to arrest Carol in her home, he does not in this instance. The purpose of the arrest warrant is to protect the independent privacy interests arrestees have in their residence—an interest that is not diminished by the restraint on liberty occasioned by the arrest. Here, Ronnie is already in Carol's home lawfully by virtue of the search warrant; thus, he can place Carol under arrest when she enters the bedroom. Requiring Ronnie to leave the house to obtain a warrant to allow his reentry for the purpose of an arrest would be illogical and unresponsive to the purposes of the Fourth Amendment. **D** is wrong.

The correct answer is **E**.

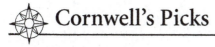

Cornwell's Picks

1. Whoa, Nellie!	E
2. Dalmatian plantation	E
3. Justice denied?	C
4. Shady lady	E

8

The Warrant Clause: Understanding Probable Cause

CHAPTER OVERVIEW

In those circumstances where a warrant is required, the Fourth Amendment provides that none shall issue "but upon probable cause." While this probable cause requirement is clear, the Framers did not define the term. As a result, law enforcement officers have looked to the courts for guidance as to the nature and quality of evidence necessary to furnish probable cause.

There are two applications of probable cause in the warrant context: arrests and searches. Probable cause to arrest requires a sufficient likelihood that a crime has occurred and that the arrestee has committed or is committing that offense. Probable cause to search mandates a sufficient likelihood that contraband or evidence of crime is presently in the place to be searched. Probable cause to search can go stale, since the likelihood that incriminating evidence is in a given location can diminish over time. By contrast, probable cause to arrest never erodes.

Notwithstanding this distinction, the quantum of proof necessary to establish probable cause is the same in the two contexts. Different standards would confuse police officers, the U.S. Supreme Court noted, as they generally "have only limited time and expertise to reflect on and balance the social and individual interests involved in the specific circumstances they confront." *Dunaway v. New York*, 442 U.S. 200 (1979).

A.   Probable Cause: General Principles

The U.S. Supreme Court has specified that the probable cause determination is a "practical, nontechnical conception." *Brinegar v. United States*, 338 U.S. 160 (1949) (see Chapter 7, *supra*). Based on the information available to them, officers must determine whether a person of "reasonable caution" would conclude that a crime has been committed or contraband is present at the place to be searched. *Beck v. Ohio*, 379 U.S. 89 (1964). The probable cause inquiry asks only if the evidence gathered by officers meets the applicable standard; an officer's subjective motivation in conducting a search or making an arrest is irrelevant. Thus, in *Whren v. United States*, 517 U.S. 806 (1996), the Court held that a pretextual traffic stop conducted by vice squad officers in a "high drug area" was constitutional, since the officers had probable cause to believe the driver had violated the motor vehicle code.

While this is an objective test, an individual officer may rely on his or her own experience in making a probable cause determination. For example, in *Johnson v. United States*, 333 U.S. 10 (1948), a police officer entered a room from which he detected the odor of burning opium. While the justices invalidated the entry on other grounds, they noted that probable cause may be found where "the affiant [is] qualified to know the odor, and it is one sufficiently distinctive to identify a forbidden substance."

In addition to on-the-job experience, a police officer may have specialized training that uniquely qualifies him or her to detect criminal misconduct. For example, Border Patrol agents receive specialized training in identifying illegal aliens and those who assist them in gaining entry into the United States. Based on their training, agents may suspect criminal activity based on conduct or circumstances that would seem innocent to other law enforcement officers. The U.S. Supreme Court allows lower courts to consider such training in evaluating probable cause. See, *e.g.*, *United States v. Brigoni-Ponce*, 422 U.S. 873 (1975).

QUESTION 1. **Trolling for "techno-mules."**   Jeanette was a police officer for the City of Los Angeles assigned to the airport. Because Los Angeles was known as an international entry point for the unlawful importation of computer chips from Asia, Jeanette's primary responsibility was the apprehension of computer chip "mules." Having been assigned to the airport for two years, Jeanette had noticed that many of the mules she had apprehended wore green or blue sweat pants and tops and carried a large, canvas carry-on bag. One afternoon, while patrolling in the international arrivals area, Jeanette saw Suzy, wearing an aquamarine sweat suit and carrying a large canvas tote. She approached Suzy and asked for permission to search her bag. When Suzy refused, Jeanette detained her for two hours while Officer Liz obtained a warrant. Suzy claims that her "seizure" by Jeanette was unlawful. Which of the following, if true, is LEAST relevant in evaluating Suzy's claim?

A. Jeanette was part of the Computer Chip Task Force, created to ferret out computer-chip smugglers.
B. Jeanette had apprehended six computer-chip smugglers at the airport who were not wearing blue sweats and were not carrying large canvas bags.
C. Twenty-five percent of female airport travelers wear blue sweat suits and carry large canvas bags.
D. Jeanette had previously apprehended five computer-chip smugglers dressed similarly to Suzy who were carrying large canvas bags.

ANALYSIS. This case requires us to determine which of the four considerations is least relevant in assessing probable cause. Note that it does not ask whether Jeanette had probable cause; indeed, it is questionable at best that she did. We need only focus on the importance of each of the factors in making that determination, however valid.

Answer **D** notes that Jeanette had made similar arrests before. This is clearly relevant, since *Johnson v. United States* teaches that an officer may rely on his or her experience in assessing probable cause. Likewise, it is also relevant if, as noted in Answer **A**, Jeanette is a member of a special task force designed to catch computer-chip smugglers, since we can reasonably assume that members of the task force receive specialized training tailored to their mission. As in *Brigoni-Ponce*, this specialized training would allow Jeanette to draw inferences about criminal behavior that officers without her specialized knowledge could not legitimately draw. Both **D** and **A** are, therefore, wrong.

The greater the number of travelers who present in a manner similar to Suzy, the weaker the justification for singling her out for investigation. To this end, **C** states that fully 25 percent of all female travelers share the characteristics used to target Suzy. Under these circumstances, it is difficult to see how a person of "reasonable caution" could identify Suzy alone as a computer-chip smuggler. Clearly, **C** provides information relevant to probable cause.

Answer **B** is, in a sense, the flip side of **D**. It provides that Jeanette had also apprehended six smugglers who were not wearing green or blue sweat suits and were not carrying large canvas bags. Standing alone, this does not compromise a probable cause finding with respect to Suzy. The facts state that many, not *all*, computer-chip smugglers had these characteristics. Thus, the fact that Suzy apprehended individuals who did not fit the "profile" is to be expected. It does not negate Jeanette's observations with regard to others.

B, therefore, is less relevant than the others in assessing probable cause and is the correct answer.

B.   The *Aguilar-Spinelli* Test

Determining whether probable cause exists is most challenging when police officers rely in whole or in part on hearsay from informants. To ensure a judicial officer's ability to fairly evaluate evidence from confidential sources, the U.S. Supreme Court created a two-part standard known as the *Aguilar-Spinelli* test, based on the two cases that inform its content: *Aguilar v. Texas*, 378 U.S. 108 (1964), and *Spinelli v. United States*, 393 U.S. 410 (1968).

Part one, the "basis of knowledge" prong, asks whether the information that underlies the probable cause conclusion is of sufficient character and quality that it is reasonable to rely on it. Part two, the "veracity" prong, explores whether the information giving rise to the probable cause determination is truthful so as to justify reliance on it. A deficiency in either prong defeats probable cause.

QUESTION 2. Hijinx on High Street.   Neighbors complained about the high volume of traffic in and out of Alison's house late at night. They reported that from midnight until 3:00 A.M. cars would pull up and someone would exit the vehicle, enter the house, and return to the car minutes later. The car would then drive off, only to be replaced minutes later by another. Police Officer David surveilled the residence for one week. He noticed nothing unusual on six of the seven nights, but on the seventh, a Saturday night, he did notice a higher volume of traffic in and out of the house late at night, with visitors staying for varying lengths of time. He also contacted "Ralph," an informant with many contacts in the drug-trafficking trade. Ralph agreed to make some calls and, after doing so, informed David that his sources confirmed that Alison was dealing drugs out of the residence.

Based on the foregoing information, David applied for a search warrant for Alison's home. His affidavit in support of the warrant application described what he had witnessed while surveilling the house and added that a police informant "spoke to individuals with personal knowledge of Alison's unlawful sale of drugs from her home." Relying on the affidavit, Judge Tammy issued a search warrant for Alison's residence at 18 High Street. Based on *Aguilar-Spinelli*, Tammy's issuance of the warrant was:

A. Improper, because she was given no information about the informant.
B. Improper, because she did not know how the informant's contacts acquired their information.

> **C.** Proper, because the informant's information was unnecessary to furnish probable cause.
> **D.** Proper, because the information provided in the affidavit was sufficient to grant the warrant.

ANALYSIS. In this problem, the warrant application is based on informant information and police surveillance. If the surveillance alone is sufficient to establish probable cause, we need not inquire into the value of the informant's contribution. We must ask, therefore, if the information David gleaned after a full week of surveillance indicated that it was likely that Alison was dealing drugs from her house.

Based on what David observed, it would be difficult to draw this conclusion. On six of the seven nights, he saw nothing unusual. On the remaining night, he did witness a greater volume of activity but, because it was Saturday night, this was not so unusual as to suggest illegal activity was taking place inside the residence. For example, Alison could have been entertaining friends or having a party. This information, standing alone, is insufficient to establish probable cause. **C** is wrong.

Having determined the necessity of the informant's testimony, we must now determine whether it satisfies the requirements of *Aguilar-Spinelli*. Under the two-prong test, the magistrate must be able to assess both the informant's veracity and his or her basis of knowledge. The affidavit specifies that the informant spoke with individuals with personal knowledge of Alison's drug dealing; this is adequate to establish his "basis of knowledge." **B** is wrong.

However, the magistrate received no information that would allow her to gauge the credibility of either the informant or the information provided. As such, the application fails to meet the "veracity" requirement. **A** is the correct answer.

C.   Removing the Strictures: *Illinois v. Gates*

Because *Aguilar-Spinelli* required proof of both an informant's basis of knowledge and his or her veracity, some complained that it inappropriately precluded probable cause determinations where, notwithstanding a deficiency in one prong or the other, police had sufficient evidence of wrongdoing to justify a search. In *Illinois v. Gates*, 462 U.S. 213 (1983), the U.S. Supreme Court agreed and abandoned the *Aguilar-Spinelli* framework.

In *Gates*, the police received an anonymous letter describing the drug-trafficking activities of a husband and wife. While they never learned the identity of the sender, the police verified many of the numerous, specific details provided in the letter and used this corroboration to obtain a warrant to search the suspects' residence. The justices deemed the warrant valid, even though it failed to meet the strict requirements of *Aguilar-Spinelli*. They reasoned that, viewed collectively, the information gathered by the police provided a "fair probability" that contraband would be found in the Gates home.

In this regard, the Court found that the police had corroborated enough of the tipster's information to allow the magistrate to make a "common-sense, practical" determination that probable cause existed. This finding takes account of and balances the reliability of the information obtained, as well as the informant's basis of knowledge and veracity. A serious weakness in one consideration may be offset by strength in the other.

Under *Gates*, probable cause is a "fluid concept" that is "not readily, or even usefully, reduced to a neat set of legal rules." Therefore, probable cause determinations should consider all relevant information; they should not be subject to an "inflexible set of evidentiary requirements." *Florida v. Harris*, 133 S. Ct. 1050 (2013) (invalidating the use of a strict evidentiary checklist to determine a drug-sniffing dog's reliability in establishing probable cause to search).

The *Gates* totality-of-the-circumstances test now defines the parameters of the Fourth Amendment probable cause requirement. However, a number of jurisdictions have rejected it and continue to follow *Aguilar-Spinelli*, deeming it necessary to fulfill state constitutional requirements.

QUESTION 3. Junk in the trunk.   A woman, who chose not to identify herself, called the police station to report that a balding, bearded Hispanic male with a dark complexion and wearing a dark blue suit was selling cocaine from a shopping bag kept in a car located in front of 15 Peaceful Lane. Responding to the call, Officer Larry drove to Peaceful Lane and noticed a man showing the contents of a grocery bag to another man. The man had a dark complexion, a receding hairline and a beard and was dressed in a dark green suit.

Larry observed the man toss the bag into the trunk of the car, close the trunk, and walk away. After he did so, Larry stopped the man and took the keys to his car. Searching the trunk, Larry found 100 packets of heroin inside the grocery bag. Under *Gates*, the man's best argument challenging probable cause to search the trunk is:

A. The tipster's identity was unknown.
B. The bag may have contained additional items that were not illegal narcotics.
C. The tipster did not indicate how she acquired the reported information.
D. Intimate details of the suspect's future behavior were neither predicted nor observed by the informant.
E. Larry did not sufficiently corroborate the tip before acting.

ANALYSIS.   While the replacement of *Aguilar-Spinelli* with *Gates* removed the rigidity of the probable cause evaluation, a tipster's information, combined with police corroboration, must indicate a "fair probability" that contraband will be found in the area searched. It is inapposite, therefore, that the bag may contain items other than narcotics, since it may still be probable that it contains contraband. **B** is wrong.

Police Officer Larry confirmed most of the details provided. While the color of the suit was incorrect, this small error would appear to be overcome by the accuracy of the remainder. **E**, therefore, is wrong.

A and **C** refer to the veracity and basis of knowledge prongs of *Aguilar-Spinelli*. Both considerations remain relevant under *Gates*. Weakness in one, however, may be overcome by strength in the other in combination with other factors — most importantly, police corroboration of important details provided by the anonymous tipster. Assuming sufficient corroboration, the anonymity of the informant and Larry's lack of knowledge as to how the tipster acquired her information does not preclude a finding of probable cause; indeed, both were lacking in the *Gates* case itself.

What is more problematic, however, is that the tipster neither claimed firsthand observation nor supplied sufficiently detailed information that personal knowledge of the facts could be logically inferred. Anyone on the street could have supplied the same details. Thus, the conclusion that the man was selling drugs was mere speculation. While predictive information is not required under *Gates*, its absence here undercuts significantly the reliability of the tip.

D is the correct answer.

D.   Probable Cause to Arrest

Probable cause to arrest requires a sufficient likelihood that a crime has occurred and the arrestee has committed or is committing that offense. Whether probable cause exists in a given situation depends upon the reasonable conclusion to be drawn from the facts known to the arresting officer at the time of the arrest. *Ornelas v. United States*, 517 U.S. 690 (1996). The evidence furnishing the grounds for arrest, once obtained, does not go stale. Thus, once acquired, the authority to arrest an individual does not diminish over time. See *United States v. Watson*, 423 U.S. 411 (1976).

If officers have probable cause to make an arrest for one offense but erroneously arrest an individual for a different offense for which probable cause was lacking, the arrest is valid. *Devenpeck v. Alford*, 543 U.S. 146 (2004). As the Supreme Court stated in *Whren v. United States*, 517 U.S. 806 (1996), "the fact that the officer does not have the state of mind which is hypothecated by the reasons which provide the legal justification for the officer's action does not invalidate the action taken as long as the circumstances, viewed objectively, justify that action." The officer's subjective intent does not undermine the validity of the arrest.

> **QUESTION 4. Yosemite Sam.**   While patrolling the public park one hot summer day, Officer Delia stopped to buy a bottle of water at a concession stand. The customer directly in front of her, Sam, also purchased water and handed the cashier a $100 bill as payment. The cashier was hesitant to accept the bill, commenting that area businesses had reported a rash of incidents in the last two weeks where customers had used counterfeit $100 bills to purchase goods. When Sam told the cashier that he had no other form of payment, Delia interceded and told the employee that she was experienced at identifying counterfeit bills. In fact, she was not. After carefully examining the currency, Delia concluded that the bill was a fake and she arrested Sam for felony counterfeiting.
>
> On the way to the station house, Sam told Delia that he was concerned about leaving his car in the park for a long period of time. He explained that he had left it unlocked with a loaded firearm in the glove compartment. Delia immediately called another officer who retrieved the firearm from the vehicle and brought it to the station house. A computer check revealed that Sam had failed to obtain a license to carry the firearm, which is a misdemeanor in this jurisdiction.
>
> Closer inspection by the crime lab revealed that the bill was not, in fact, counterfeit. If Sam challenges his arrest, is he likely to prevail?
>
> **A.** Yes, because Delia lacked probable cause for the arrest.
> **B.** Yes, because counterfeiting is a felony.
> **C.** No, because Sam had an unlicensed firearm in his car at the time of arrest.
> **D.** No, because an officer retrieved the firearm from the vehicle soon after the arrest.

ANALYSIS.   Delia arrested Sam for counterfeiting, an offense for which she did not have probable cause. At the time of his arrest, Sam was in possession of an unlicensed firearm, a misdemeanor for which she could have arrested him, but did not. (Remember: Officers have discretion to make arrests for any and all offenses under the Fourth Amendment. See Chapter 7, Part A, *supra*.) We must now determine if Delia's error renders the counterfeiting arrest invalid.

Devenpeck imports that the validity of an arrest rests on its objective reasonableness, rather than an officer's subjective intent. This objective inquiry relies, in turn, on the facts known to the officer at the time of arrest. Thus, in *Devenpeck*, the defendant's erroneous arrest for violating the state's privacy laws was found not to violate the Fourth Amendment since, at the time of arrest, officers had sufficient facts to arrest the defendant for the alternative offense of impersonating a police officer.

Our facts do not, however, mirror those of *Devenpeck*. While Sam had an unlicensed firearm in his car when he was arrested, Delia was not aware of its presence until later, when she was transporting Sam to the station house.

Therefore, viewed objectively, Delia lacked sufficient facts to arrest Sam for carrying an unlicensed firearm when she made the arrest for counterfeiting.

It is immaterial that the firearms offense is a misdemeanor and counterfeiting is a felony. Because officers have broad authority to make arrests, the firearm offense would have insulated Delia's error, if she knew of it at the time of the arrest. The fact that an officer promptly retrieved the firearm from Sam's car is similarly unavailing since it does not negate Delia's ignorance of the very existence of the unregistered firearm when she arrested Sam.

For the foregoing reasons, the correct answer is **A**.

E.   Arresting Multiple Parties

As mentioned in the introduction to this chapter, to arrest an individual police must have probable cause to believe that he or she has committed the offense in question. In *Maryland v. Pringle*, 540 U.S. 366 (2003), the defendant claimed that his arrest for felony possession of cocaine was improper under this standard where police found contraband in a car in which he was a passenger. Pringle's challenge focused on ownership of the contraband—five baggies of cocaine—that was equally attributable to the driver and the other passenger.

The U.S. Supreme Court agreed that ownership of the cocaine was unclear but held unanimously that Pringle's arrest was proper. The justices first noted that passengers in automobiles often "engage in a common enterprise with the driver and have a common interest in concealing the fruits or evidence of their wrongdoing." As such, an inference was especially appropriate in this case. All three occupants had access to the contraband, which police found in a backseat armrest. The additional discovery of $763 in the glove compartment suggested drug dealing, an activity that typically involves multiple parties. Finally, all three would be eager to conceal their participation in this felonious conspiracy. Ultimately, the Court found that probable cause to arrest Pringle (as well as the other occupants) existed, since police could reasonably infer that any or all of them had knowledge of, and exercised dominion and control over, the cocaine.

> **QUESTION 5. Dinner and dessert for two.** Police had been monitoring the Beefcake Escort Service for months. While the owner of the service claimed that its employees merely provided companionship to clients, undercover surveillance suggested that escorts provided sexual favors for a "surcharge" beyond the standard rate. One evening, Marianne, a female police officer posing as a client, arranged to meet an escort at the service's business office for a "date." She prearranged the fee, which included an additional $500 for sexual intercourse. At Marianne's request, the office

manager, Tina, arranged for Marianne to pick up a copy of her bill from a box on Tina's desk. When Marianne called and asked for the name of the escort, Tina told her she wasn't sure, but there would be three candidates present when she arrived who would have decided in advance among themselves which of them would take the assignment.

When Marianne arrived at the office, she picked up the bill, which included the standard fee of $250 plus a $500 "surcharge for additional services." There were three escorts present. Marianne identified herself as a police officer and asked which of the three had agreed to be her date for the evening. All three claimed they were not the one, each claiming it was one of the other two. Marianne then arrested all three for attempt to engage in prostitution, on the authority of *Maryland v. Pringle*. These arrests are:

A. Appropriate.
B. Inappropriate, because the alleged offense did not take place in a vehicle.
C. Inappropriate, because only one of the three men was going to accompany Marianne.
D. Inappropriate, because drug dealing and prostitution are not analogous activities.

ANALYSIS. This is a challenging problem that requires a close reading of *Pringle* to determine whether its facts are materially different from ours. In *Pringle*, the Court permitted the arrest of all three occupants of a vehicle based on a number of considerations. Most significantly, the Court emphasized the nature of the evidence, which suggested a "common enterprise" among all three men and the "reasonable inference" that all three men had knowledge of, and dominion and control over, the contraband.

The problem asks if the arrest is defensible under *Pringle*. Answer **B** is easily eliminated. The location of the unlawful activity was not dispositive in *Pringle*. The contraband's presence in a vehicle was important because it provided equal access to all three occupants; if another setting provided similar opportunity for all parties to engage in illegal activity, the Court's reasoning would apply with equal force.

Answer **C** is quite appealing at first blush. All three arrestees in *Pringle* could possess the cocaine if, hypothetically, the five baggies were divided among them. By contrast, only *one* of the three escorts would have accompanied Marianne. This distinction does not, however, remove Marianne's authority to arrest all three men. The *Pringle* Court noted, in this regard, that "any or all" of the men could have possessed the cocaine "solely or jointly." Thus, they did not require proof that more than one arrestee *actually* engaged in the unlawful activity immediately at issue, provided all three had sufficient knowledge and opportunity. Under this standard, the arrest of all three potential escorts is lawful.

Finally, as **D** states, drug dealing and prostitution are certainly not analogous. Their differences are relevant, however, only to the extent that they relate to the reasoning of *Pringle*. *Pringle* focuses on the "common enterprise" among the arrestees with respect to the activity in question. Here, the facts clearly indicate that the three escorts are engaged in a common enterprise with each other and with Tina, and all participants would want to conceal their participation in the illegal activity. Thus, the various differences between the two "businesses" are beside the point for our purposes. Their similarities are sufficient to justify the arrests.

Based on the foregoing, the correct answer is **A**.

F.   The Closer

QUESTION 6. All in the family.   Jill was found dead in her apartment by the cleaning lady. Jill had been stabbed to death with what police detectives concluded was a large serrated knife. Suspicion focused on her husband, Matt, who was the sole beneficiary of a $500,000 life insurance policy and claimed to be on a business trip when the body was found. Police later learned that Matt had been having an affair with Alison, whom he described to a co-worker as his "soul mate." Matt's mother, Liza, who lived with Jill and Matt, told police that she was not surprised about the affair, since "Jill was such a shrew." "My son," she commented, "deserved better but could not leave Jill since she had all the money. Now he will get what he should have had all along."

Sam, an experienced homicide detective, was in charge of the investigation. He believed that Matt, Alison, and Liza were all involved in the murder, but he did not have enough evidence to make an arrest. Then, two weeks after the murder, Sam received an anonymous letter from someone claiming to be a neighbor and close friend of both Jill and her husband. The letter stated that the writer had noticed "dried red dots" and hair on a bread knife in the couple's kitchen two days following the discovery of Jill's body.

Based on the foregoing information, Sam obtained a warrant to search Matt's residence for "blood and other tangible evidence related to the murder of Jill." Inside a kitchen drawer, he found a serrated bread knife with red dots that Sam recognized as blood. Strands of dark red hair, matching Jill's, adhered to the red dots. Sam seized the knife, which had been wiped clean of any fingerprints. When neither Matt, Liza, nor

Alison claimed any knowledge of the knife, Sam arrested all three and charged each with Jill's murder. Based on these facts, which of the following is FALSE?

A. The common enterprise theory supports Alison's arrest.

B. The issuance of the search warrant would be improper in an *Aguilar-Spinelli* jurisdiction.

C. The issuance of the warrant would be improper in a *Gates* jurisdiction.

D. Assuming the validity of the warrant, Sam had the probable cause necessary for seizure of the knife.

ANALYSIS.   This closer reviews the warrant clause's probable cause requirement. Here, Detective Sam is investigating a murder where suspicion falls on three suspects: the victim's husband, the husband's paramour, and the victim's mother-in-law. Sam eventually obtains a warrant to search the husband's residence for "blood and other tangible evidence" linking him to the crime. During this search, Sam finds what appears to be the murder weapon: a serrated kitchen knife with dried blood and hair attached to it.

The question asks which of the four statements is false. Let's start with **B** and **C**, which address the warrant's sufficiency. *Aguilar-Spinelli*'s two-prong test requires evidence supporting both the veracity of the informant and his or her basis of knowledge. These strictures are problematic here, since Sam's information about the bloody knife in Matt's house comes from an anonymous letter sent by someone alleging to be a close friend of both Matt and the victim. While this may satisfy the "basis of knowledge" requirement, Sam's lack of knowledge of the source of the information leaves him unable to satisfy the "veracity" prong of the test. Because both prongs are necessary, the warrant is insufficient under *Aguilar-Spinelli*. **B** is the wrong answer.

Gates is less rigid than *Aguilar-Spinelli* and allows magistrates to find probable cause based on a "totality of the circumstances." As in our problem, the probable cause finding in *Gates* relied in part on an anonymous letter; however, in *Gates*, the information was specific and detailed and was corroborated to a significant degree by the police before they applied for the warrant. Sam, by contrast, provides no corroboration, nor does he discover the identity of the informer. Without independent fact-finding to support its allegations, the letter's evidentiary value is substantially diminished. Because its information is critical in establishing probable cause, the warrant application fails under the *Gates* totality-of-the-circumstances test. **C** is the wrong answer.

If, on the other hand, the warrant were valid, would Sam's seizure of the knife be valid? Probable cause for the seizure is based on Sam's discovery of dried blood on a serrated knife to which hair, matching Jill's, is "glued." Sam's conclusion that the red dots are, in fact, blood merits deference, since he is an experienced homicide detective. This conclusion, coupled with the attached hair strands, is sufficient to support the seizure, especially since Jill's hair color (dark red) is less common than most. **D** is the wrong answer.

We are left, therefore, with **A**, which affirms Alison's arrest based on the "common enterprise" theory. There are a number of problems with this argument. First, homicide, unlike the drug-trafficking offense at issue in *Pringle*, is not by its very nature perpetrated by individuals acting in concert with others. Second, although Sam has a hunch that Matt, Liza, and Alison were acting in concert, he has no hard evidence to support his theory. Finally, even if he did, there is no reason to ascribe the possession or use of the weapon to Alison. Unlike Liza, Alison does not live with Matt. Thus, she lacks the "dominion and control" over the knife that is necessary for the common enterprise theory to apply.

In sum, because the common enterprise theory does not create a sufficient likelihood that Alison has killed Jill, **A** is the correct answer.

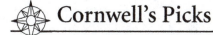 ## Cornwell's Picks

1.	Trolling for "techno-mules"	**B**
2.	Hijinx on High Street	**A**
3.	Junk in the trunk	**D**
4.	Yosemite Sam	**A**
5.	Dinner and dessert for two	**A**
6.	All in the family	**A**

9

The Warrant Clause: Understanding Particularity

CHAPTER OVERVIEW
A. General Principles
B. The Warrant Application and the Affidavit Supporting It
C. Reasonable Mistakes
D. The Closer
✦ Cornwell's Picks

A.   General Principles

The Fourth Amendment also states that warrants must "particularly describ[e] the place to be searched, and the persons or things to be seized." This particularity mandate was designed to prevent officers from using generally worded warrants to engage in broad-based fishing expeditions highly violative of personal privacy.

The U.S. Supreme Court explored the contours of this requirement in the 1976 case of *Andresen v. Maryland*, 427 U.S. 463 (1976), where a warrant authorized the search of an office for an exhaustive list of carefully described documents "together with other fruits, instrumentalities and evidence of crime at this [time] unknown." While this pendent clause sounds impermissibly broad, the Court did not find that it violated the particularity clause of the Fourth Amendment. Its seeming generality was saved constitutionally by the general context of the warrant, which made clear that the word "crime" referred to a specific offense — here, false pretenses with respect to a particular piece of property.

QUESTION 1. Dear diary. Officer Martha was investigating the brutal murder of Rhonda, a seventeen-year-old high school student from Amity Township. This was the third killing of a high school girl from Amity, all of whom had been immobilized with a stun gun, strangled to death with a rope and then dumped in the woods behind the town park. Suspicion for Rhonda's murder focused on her ex-boyfriend, Ryan, whom she claimed had been stalking her ever since their break-up and had once threatened to kill her if she did not agree to begin seeing him again. Ryan had never dated the other murder victims.

Martha was able to get a warrant to search Ryan's house. The first paragraph of the warrant authorized a search for "a stun gun, rope, and any tangible evidence related to the killing of Rhonda." Paragraph two provided as follows: "Police officers may also search for photographs, newspaper clippings, diaries and letters." When executing the warrant, Martha came upon a letter inside a diary in Ryan's bedroom that explained how he had killed all three girls. If Ryan challenges the warrant on particularity grounds, he will:

A. Succeed, because Officer Martha had no evidence linking Ryan to the other killings.
B. Succeed, because paragraph two of the warrant did not reference the killing of Rhonda.
C. Fail, because the warrant allowed Martha to search letters and diaries for evidence linked to Rhonda's murder.
D. Fail, because the *modus operandi* was the same for all three killings.

ANALYSIS. To answer this question correctly, you must remember that Ryan's claim is made on particularity grounds. This is important, because, based on the facts, the judge issuing the warrant may well have erred in permitting a search for the evidence specified in paragraph two in the absence of probable cause to believe that incriminating evidence would be found there. Thus, if Ryan had challenged the validity of the warrant on this ground, his claim might have been valid.

The particularity claim is on different footing, however. Based on *Andresen*, language that may appear to be overbroad on its face may nonetheless satisfy particularity requirements if it is logically linked to a crime specified elsewhere in the warrant. The first paragraph provides this link by explicitly referencing the killing of Rhonda in authorizing the search for tangible evidence. Thus, the warrant will not fail on particularity principles.

Answers **A** and **B** are, therefore, wrong—but for different reasons. **A** correctly notes that Martha had no evidence linking Ryan to the other killings, but this shortcoming goes to the issue of probable cause, not particularity. **B**, by contrast, sounds in particularity, but is an incorrect statement of law; as discussed above, paragraph two need not mention Rhonda's murder explicitly to satisfy particularity requirements.

Answers **C** and **D** present the same dichotomy. **D** focuses on the similar *modus operandi* for the three crimes. This consideration may influence the judge to authorize a broader search as provided in paragraph two, especially if there is evidence linking Ryan to the other murders. As with **A**, however, this concerns whether there is probable cause to justify the issuance of the warrant, not its sufficiency on particularity grounds.

By contrast, **C** invokes particularity principles. Remember, a particularity claim challenges the facial validity of the warrant, arguing that the language in question is overbroad and authorizes a "general rummaging" through the subject's belongings. *Andresen* reins in this potential overbreadth by interpreting otherwise expansive language through the lens of a previously referenced crime, in this case the killing of Rhonda.

C is the correct answer.

B.   The Warrant Application and the Affidavit Supporting It

When applying for a warrant, a prosecutor typically submits the application, together with an affidavit containing detailed information in support of the application. After reviewing all submitted materials, the magistrate issues the warrant, which specifically identifies the "place to be searched" and the "persons or things to be seized." The warrant may cross-reference other documents and may, in addition, incorporate these documents. Such incorporation must be explicit, however, and any documents so referenced should accompany the warrant to satisfy particularity requirements.

The warrant at issue in *Groh v. Ramirez*, 540 U.S. 551 (2004), illustrates how law enforcement officers can run afoul of these principles. In his application for a warrant to search the defendant's ranch for firearms and like materials, federal agent Groh submitted both an application and an affidavit describing in detail the basis for his belief that the listed items were concealed on the ranch. While the application was sufficiently particularized, the warrant issued by the magistrate was not. It failed to include any specific items and did not incorporate by reference the application or the affidavit. In the section entitled "person or property to be seized," it simply described the defendant's house. Under these circumstances, "there can be no written assurance that the Magistrate actually found probable cause to search for, and to seize, every item mentioned in the affidavit."

By the same token, a warrant may satisfy particularity demands without incorporating all relevant information contained in the supporting affidavit. In *United States v. Grubbs*, 547 U.S. 90 (2006), the affidavit specified that federal officers could not search the defendant's premises "unless and until" a certain parcel had been received and placed inside the residence. This condition was not included in the warrant, which otherwise included attachments describing the residence and the items to be seized. The U.S. Supreme Court held that the failure to include this "triggering condition" did not violate the particularity clause because the language of the Fourth Amendment explicitly requires the inclusion *only* of the place to be searched and the items to be seized — not "conditions precedent to the execution of the warrant."

QUESTION 2. **Hidden jewels.**   Prosecutor Mallory filed an application for a warrant to search Tim's residence for diamond rings and pieces of jewelry stolen from Kendall's jewelry store. Her application included an affidavit carefully describing the facts supporting the application, such as the month-long surveillance of Tim's movements and evidence gleaned from a wiretap on Tim's phone. The affidavit also specified that the search would not take place until Tim's alleged partner in crime, Dave, arrived at Tim's house from out of town the following Thursday.

The application also included two attachments. The first described in detail the physical layout of all three floors of Tim's home; the other contained a list of all the jewelry stolen from the store and the value of each missing piece. The magistrate issued the warrant, which did not explicitly reference either the affidavit or the attachments. It simply authorized a search of "the first floor of Tim's residence for diamond rings and other jewelry believed to be stolen from Kendall's jewelry store." If Tim challenges the warrant on particularity grounds, he will:

A. Prevail, because the warrant did not incorporate by reference evidence contained in the affidavit concerning the surveillance and the wiretap.
B. Prevail, because the warrant did not incorporate by reference the requirement that Dave arrive at the residence prior to its execution.
C. Prevail, because the warrant did not incorporate by reference the first attachment describing the physical layout of Tim's home.
D. Prevail, because the warrant did not incorporate by reference the second attachment describing in detail the items stolen from Kendall's store.
E. Lose.

ANALYSIS.   In answering this question, it is important to remember that the particularity clause requires that a warrant describe the "place to be searched" and the "persons or things to be seized." This information may be contained in affidavits and attachments, provided they are incorporated into the warrant by the issuing magistrate. No other information is constitutionally necessary.

A and **B** concern information provided in the unincorporated affidavit. The information relating to the surveillance and wiretap is relevant to whether or not there was sufficient probable cause to issue the warrant, not whether the warrant was sufficiently particularized. **B** contains the "triggering" provision, or condition precedent, to the execution of the warrant. As the Court clarified in *Grubbs*, inclusion of this information is not necessary in the warrant itself, since it relates neither to the place to be searched nor to the items to be seized. **A** and **B** are, therefore, wrong.

The first attachment gave a description of Tim's house that is far more detailed than that contained in the warrant itself. This difference is irrelevant, however, inasmuch as the language contained in the warrant itself satisfies constitutional requirements. Because the "first floor of Tim's residence" is an adequate statement of the place to be searched, **C** is wrong.

D is incorrect for similar reasons. While the warrant did not include the full list of items stolen from the store, its description was sufficient for particularity purposes. "Diamond rings and other jewelry believed to be stolen from Kendall's jewelry store" provides enough guidance to police officers to avoid the kind of fishing expedition of concern to the Framers. While inclusion of the exhaustive list of items contained in the attachment provides even greater specificity, this degree of precision is not constitutionally required.

Because Tim's motion will fail, **E** is the correct answer.

C.   Reasonable Mistakes

In determining whether a warrant satisfies the particularity requirement, courts consider the information police officers disclosed, or had a duty to disclose, to the issuing magistrate. If the officers later discover information indicating that the warrant was overbroad, it will not defeat particularity if the failure to acquire the information earlier was understandable and reasonable.

The U.S. Supreme Court's leading case addressing officers' "reasonable mistakes" in this context is *Maryland v. Garrison*, 480 U.S. 79 (1987). In *Garrison*, the police obtained a warrant to search "the premises known as 2036 Park Avenue, third floor apartment." Unbeknownst to both the officer who obtained the warrant and those who executed it, the third floor had two apartments. By the time officers conducting the search realized the error, they had entered the wrong apartment, where they found heroin, cash, and drug paraphernalia.

Turning first to the validity of the warrant, the Court found no constitutional error. The prosecutor had given the magistrate all information available at the time, and the warrant reflected that information. The subsequent discovery of facts indicating that the warrant was overbroad does not retroactively extinguish its validity.

Likewise, while the officers mistakenly entered the defendant's apartment when executing the warrant, their error was reasonable in light of what they knew at the time they acted. In addition, once they realized their mistake, they stopped the search. Under these circumstances, it cannot be said that the execution of the warrant was unreasonable.

QUESTION 3. Sorry—my bad.   Police Officer Jones had been monitoring an alleged heroin distribution ring for six months. He had reason to believe that drugs would be exchanged on Friday night at a poker game, but he did not yet know the game's location. Based on this information, the magistrate issued a warrant to search for "evidence relating to the sale and distribution of heroin at a location to be identified by Officer Jones prior to the execution of the warrant." On Wednesday, Officer Jones learned that the poker game was to take place on the second floor of a house at 66 Mockingbird Lane.

Two days later, Officer Jones executed the warrant. He opened the first door he saw at the top of the stairs on the second floor. The door turned out to be a storage closet rented by Melissa, a third party. Jones saw drug paraphernalia on the floor and seized it. He then saw a second door and opened it. Inside, he came upon a poker game and witnessed the exchange of drugs between two of the players. If Melissa challenges the search of the closet, she will likely:

A. Prevail, because Jones mistakenly opened the door to the closet.
B. Prevail, because the warrant was not sufficiently particularized.
C. Prevail, because Jones did not suspect Melissa of any wrongdoing.
D. Fail, because Jones reasonably believed that he was entering the location where the game was being played.

ANALYSIS.   This is a tricky problem that requires careful dissection of the facts and relevant law. On first impression, one might conclude that the search was unlawful because Melissa was the hapless victim of police error and there was no prior evidence implicating her in any criminal activity. This line of reasoning does not, however, square with Fourth Amendment case law. As discussed above, the lawfulness of the search centers not on its fairness to aggrieved third parties but rather on the reasonableness of the conduct of law enforcement personnel.

In this instance, based on the information available to him, Officer Jones had no reason to believe that the closet was not a door to the apartment. It was unmarked and unlocked, just like the door to the apartment, and the information he had acquired did not suggest anything to the contrary. If there had been a sign on the door saying "Storage Closet," Jones's conduct would be less defensible, but, based on what he knew, his mistake seems reasonable, and reasonable mistakes survive Fourth Amendment scrutiny. **A** and **C** are wrong.

D is an accurate statement of law. An officer's reasonable, though mistaken, belief that the warrant correctly identifies the premises to be searched precludes a subsequent challenge based on overbreadth. However, the fact that Officer Jones made a reasonable mistake when executing an anticipatory warrant does not necessarily mean that no constitutional infirmity is present. By allowing Officer Jones to determine the location of the search unilaterally, the warrant substitutes the authority of a neutral and detached magistrate for a "blank check" to be filled in by a police officer.

Anticipatory warrants typically pertain to contraband in transit, where police are aware in advance of an item's ultimate destination and/or the route to be followed in reaching that location. Because the contraband is not present at the location specified for the search when the prosecutor applies for the warrant, the magistrate must evaluate the likelihood that the specific item(s) will be at the designated location when the police execute the warrant. The delegation of discretion to the officer in this case was substantial, and not closely circumscribed, and there was no showing of an inability to relay the location to the magistrate by supplemental affidavit once Officer Jones learned it. As such, the warrant does not satisfy the Fourth Amendment's particularity requirement.

B is the correct answer.

D.   The Closer

> **QUESTION 4. Buckless, luckless Chuck.** Assistant District Attorney Vicki received reliable information from an informant that Eric planned to deposit the monetary proceeds from drug trafficking at a co-conspirator's residence at 18 Mountain Avenue at midnight that evening. The informant reported that a third party would move the money to an undisclosed location the following morning. She included this information in her affidavit requesting a warrant to search 18 Mountain Avenue upon the arrival of the criminal fruits that evening. The magistrate issued the warrant, which read, in its entirety, as follows: "In accordance with the information contained in the attached affidavit, I hereby authorize a search of the premises at 18 Mountain Avenue for any and all criminal fruits."
>
> Police Officer Alfred was assigned responsibility for executing the warrant. That evening, he staked out the residence, waiting for the arrival of the loot. At midnight, he saw Chuck enter the residence that Alfred believed was #18, carrying a duffle bag. Alfred knocked on the door, announcing that he had a search warrant. When Chuck opened the door, Alfred saw the duffle bag on the floor and told Chuck to open it. Chuck did so.

> Looking inside, Alfred found clothes and a large ziplock bag containing marijuana. Alfred later discovered that Chuck lived at 18A Mountain Avenue. The money had been delivered to 18B. The residence was a duplex, and the front doors of each unit, which were side by side, displayed their numbers. Alfred did not see the numbers from the road because of the darkness. Chuck is charged with felony possession of marijuana. If Chuck challenges the search, which of the following is his best argument?
>
> A. The warrant fails to adequately describe the location of the residence to be searched.
> B. The warrant authorizes too broad a search.
> C. The warrant does not specify the condition necessary to permit the officer to conduct the search.
> D. Alfred's erroneous belief that Chuck's residence was the correct location was unreasonable.

ANALYSIS.   This closer reviews the particularity cases from this chapter, as well as the Fourth Amendment allowance of police officers' "reasonable mistakes." Some of the rules are straightforward; others require more detailed analysis.

Grubbs held that the "triggering condition" in anticipatory search warrants need not be included in the warrant itself; it is sufficient if it is included within the supporting affidavit. Our problem complies with this requirement. The affidavit specifies that the money will be deposited at midnight that evening and then moved to another location the following morning. This is sufficient and **C**, therefore, is wrong.

On its face, the language of the warrant seems quite broad, authorizing a search for "any and all criminal fruits." As we learned in *Andresen*, however, the scope of a search can be limited by language elsewhere in the warrant that places the facially expansive language in context. In *Andresen*, for example, the phrase "together with other fruits and instrumentalities of crime at this time unknown" was held to satisfy particularity requirements through its implicit link to the specific crime referenced in the warrant. Likewise, prosecutors can successfully argue that the broad language in the warrant in this problem references criminal fruits linked to the drug-trafficking activity described elsewhere in the affidavit. **B** is wrong.

The location specified in the warrant incorrectly suggests that 18 Mountain Avenue is a single residence. In fact, it is a duplex, with one party residing at 18A and another at 18B. This error is reminiscent of *Maryland v. Garrison*, where the warrant failed to disclose that there were two separate apartments at the address provided. In that case, the Court found that the warrant satisfied particularity requirements on its face, since the police did not withhold information or otherwise engage in any subterfuge designed to violate the party's constitutional rights. The same is true here, making **A** incorrect.

Chuck's best strategy is to challenge the reasonableness of Alfred's erroneous belief that Chuck's residence was the one he was supposed to search. In finding the officers' mistake reasonable in *Garrison*, the Court noted that there was nothing that alerted them to the fact that there were two apartments before they conducted the search. Here, even if we credit Alfred's failure to see the number on the door from the street, he had twenty-five seconds to view it up close while waiting for Chuck to come to the door after he knocked.

Because **A**, **B**, and **C** will not work, **D** is Chuck's only option.

✴ Cornwell's Picks

1.	Dear diary	C
2.	Hidden jewels	E
3.	Sorry—my bad	B
4.	Buckless, luckless Chuck	D

10

Executing the Search Warrant

CHAPTER OVERVIEW

Once the judge or magistrate issues the warrant, law enforcement personnel conduct the search that it authorizes. To comply with the Fourth Amendment, the officers executing the warrant must satisfy two requirements: First, they must "knock and announce" their presence and purpose before forcibly entering the place to be searched and, second, they must search only those areas and items authorized by the language of the warrant. We begin by evaluating each requirement, in turn.

It is not uncommon for people to be present during the search, especially if the search is of a residence. Therefore, we will also discuss Supreme Court case law that has considered the extent to which officers can detain or search individuals present on the scene when executing the warrant.

A. The "Knock-and-Announce" Rule

At common law, police were required to knock and announce their presence and purpose before forcibly entering the place to be searched. In *Wilson v. Arkansas*, 514 U.S. 927 (1995), the Court declared that the knock-and-announce rule "forms a part of the reasonableness inquiry of the Fourth Amendment." The Court emphasized, at the same time, that lower courts should not apply the rule inflexibly; at times, the necessity of its application must give way to "contrary considerations."

The Court has clarified its position on the scope of the knock-and-announce rule in a series of post-*Wilson* cases. To justify a "no-knock" entry, the Court has required that police have a reasonable suspicion that knocking and announcing their presence would be dangerous or futile or would inhibit the criminal investigation — by, for example, allowing the destruction of evidence. *Richards v. Wisconsin*, 520 U.S. 385 (1997). Where reasonable suspicion exists, an unannounced entry is constitutional, even if destruction or damage to property was necessary in effecting the entry. *United States v. Ramirez*, 523 U.S. 65 (1998).

As to the time officers must wait after announcing their presence, the Court has accepted a wait of fifteen to twenty seconds in a small apartment where drugs were involved, accepting the government's contentions that the occupant had adequate time to get to the door and further delay would permit the disposal of the contraband. *United States v. Banks*, 540 U.S. 31 (2003). In so holding, the Court rejected the argument that twenty seconds was insufficient since the occupant was in the shower when the officers arrived. "The facts known to the police are what count in judging reasonable waiting time," the majority opined, and, in this instance, the officers were unaware of Bank's exact location.

QUESTION 1. **Too much TV.** After watching an episode of CSI, Doofus and Wingnut decided that they could earn lots of spending money by turning their house into a methamphetamine lab. Local police became suspicious when local pharmacies reported that the duo was going store to store attempting to buy as much Sudafed (an essential methamphetamine ingredient) as possible. After background checks revealed that both were full-time students at a local community college and neither had a criminal record, police decided to monitor the situation. The next week, when neighbors complained of a suspicious odor coming from Doofus and Wingnut's residence, Officer Ricky decided to take action and obtained a warrant to search it.

That evening, Ricky and his partner, Officer Alyssa, went to the apartment to execute the warrant. Ricky knocked and announced their presence and waited fifteen seconds. Hearing no response, the officers entered through the unlocked front door. As they did, Ricky accidentally damaged the ornamental vase worth $500 that was sitting next to the door. At that moment, Doofus and Wingnut ran downstairs, explaining that they hadn't heard Ricky's announcement since they were watching TV upstairs and had the volume turned up. If Doofus and Wingnut claim that the officers' forcible entry violated their Fourth Amendment rights, which of the following is most helpful to their position?

> **A.** Officer Ricky's entry destroyed a $500 vase.
> **B.** Doofus and Wingnut were full-time students with spotless criminal records.
> **C.** Doofus and Wingnut lived in a two-story residence.
> **D.** Doofus and Wingnut were upstairs when the officers arrived.

ANALYSIS.   Although the Supreme Court constitutionalized the knock-and-announce rule, its application is subject to numerous exceptions.

As a result establishing a constitutional violation based on non-compliance with the knock-and-announce rule is not easy. Nonetheless, the question asks you to identify Doofus and Wingnut's strongest argument in this regard. Ricky and Alyssa waited fifteen seconds before breaking into the residence. Doofus and Wingnut claim not to have heard Ricky's announcement, since they were upstairs watching TV at the time and had the volume turned up. In assessing the reasonableness of the waiting period, we must consider the facts known to the officers at the time. Because the officers did not know where Doofus and Wingnut were and what they were doing, the latters' presence upstairs watching television is irrelevant. **D** is wrong.

By contrast, the officers did know that Doofus and Wingnut were full-time students with no criminal history. This information would arguably inform the reasonableness of the officers' failure to knock and announce in the first instance. See, e.g., *State v. Anyan*, 104 P.3d 511 (Mont. 2004) (no-knock entry deemed unreasonable where occupants believed to be making methamphetamine in their home had no violent criminal record, no evidence suggesting they were armed, and no demonstrated risk of destruction of evidence in the time it would take to knock and announce). It seems far less relevant, however, to the amount of time officers must wait, once they announce their presence; the speed with which suspects reach the door or dispose of contraband does not depend on their criminal history or present occupation. **B** is wrong.

While Officer Ricky's entry inadvertently damaged a valuable vase, the destruction of property *per se* does not establish a Fourth Amendment violation. Claimants are more likely to succeed if they can show that an officer used excessive force to gain entry, but that is not the case here. **A** is wrong.

As they approach the house, Ricky and Alyssa could readily discern that it had two stories. In approving a fifteen-to-twenty-second wait in Banks, the Court emphasized that the residence was a small apartment, commenting that longer wait times would be necessary in larger structures. Thus, the size of Doofus and Wingnut's abode strongly suggests that more than fifteen seconds is necessary to allow them a reasonable opportunity to reach the door. See e.g., *Spradley v. State*, 933 So.2d 51 (Fla. Dist. Ct. App. 2006). Therefore, **C** best supports their claim.

B.   The Warrant's Terms and Limitations

The language of the warrant delineates the permissible scope of the search it authorizes. Thus, if the warrant allows officers to search only the "common areas" of a shared residence, officers would lack the authority to search a bedroom occupied by only one resident. Conversely, if the warrant authorizes a search of the entire premises, officers would have unrestricted access to all rooms.

A "premises" warrant does not necessarily give officers carte blanche, however, to invade all private spaces. Consider a warrant that authorizes a search of the subject's home for the pistol that police officers believe he used to commit a homicide. If the warrant contains no restriction on the rooms the officers may enter, they may search the entirety of the home. That does not mean, however, that they can search all items within these rooms, for some may not be large enough to house a pistol. For example, while a pistol may be hidden inside a shoebox in a bedroom closet, it could never fit inside a wallet or a bottle of aspirin. Thus, if officers searched these areas and discovered contraband there, the contraband would be inadmissible against the subject of the warrant.

> **QUESTION 2. Stocks, bonds, and blood.**   Police Officer Tadd was investigating the murder of Brent, a high-ranking manager of a prestigious brokerage house on Wall Street, who was found dead in his apartment in a pool of blood. The medical examiner believed that Brent was struck from behind with a heavy, blunt object. In the course of his investigation into the murder, Tadd discovered that Brent's most successful trader, Bobby, was conducting "phantom trades" to pad his profits and that Brent had become aware of the problem. At the time of his death, Brent was considering firing Bobby and notifying the federal authorities of Bobby's misconduct.
>
> After surveillance cameras disclosed that Bobby visited Brent at his home shortly before his death, Tadd obtained a warrant to search Bobby's residence for "bloody clothes and any evidence establishing the manner in which Brent was killed." When executing the warrant, Tadd opened a desk drawer in Bobby's living room and found a wad of documents, clipped together, with a cover memo from Brent to Bobby stating "We must talk about these trades as soon as possible." Tadd seized the documents. If Bobby moves to suppress the documents, arguing that their seizure was improper under the warrant, he will likely:
>
> A.   Prevail, since the seizure of the documents was improper.
> B.   Prevail, since Tadd had no right to search the desk drawer.
> C.   Fail, since the warrant permits Tadd to search the entire residence.
> D.   Fail, since the documents provide a motive for the murder.

ANALYSIS.   This problem tests your understanding of the proper scope of a warranted search. The language of the warrant sets the appropriate parameters. Here, the warrant allows Tadd to seize "bloody clothes and any evidence establishing the manner in which Bobby was killed." Therefore, Tadd is justified in searching anywhere within Bobby's residence where he might find garments and other incriminating evidence, such as the implement used to bludgeon Brent.

We do not know if the desk drawer is large enough to contain the large instrument used to bludgeon Brent, but, if it is large enough to hold the documents, it would be large enough to store bloody clothes as well. It does not matter that a desk drawer is not a common repository for clothes; we need only establish that it is large enough to accommodate them. Because Tadd's search of the drawer was lawful, **B** is wrong.

Answer **C** would admit the documentary evidence based on the breadth of the warrant. This consideration, standing alone, is insufficient to justify the search of the drawer. While the "premises warrant" allows entry into each and every room, it permits the opening of closed containers within the rooms only if they are large enough to contain the items sought. Thus, this answer says too little.

We are left, then, with **A** and **D**. While **A** deems the search improper, **D** would permit the search since the documents provide evidence of a possible motive for Bobby to have killed Brent. In choosing between the two options, it is important to focus on the precise language of the warrant. While proof of motive helps to explain a defendant's actions and may shed light on his state of mind when perpetrating the crime, it does not help in understanding the manner in which the victim was killed.

A, therefore, is the correct answer.

C.   Detaining and Searching Persons Who Are Present

Our final issue concerning the execution of search warrants is an officer's authority to detain and search persons who are present during the search. First, where a warrant authorizes a search of the premises, the mere fact that an individual is present does not justify, in and of itself, a search of his or her person. In *Ybarra v. Illinois*, 444 U.S. 85 (1979), when executing a warrant to search a tavern and its bartender for drugs, officers also conducted pat-down searches of the patrons, finding heroin on the defendant. Because there was no evidence that the tavern was frequented by persons illegally purchasing drugs, the Court invalidated the search. "[A] person's mere propinquity to others independently suspected of criminal activity," the majority reasoned, "does not, without more, give rise to probable cause to search that person."

Officers may, however, detain occupants of a residence while searching it. Detention prevents flight if incriminating evidence is found, facilitates an "orderly completion of the search," and minimizes the risk of harm to the officers by affording them "unquestioned command of the situation." *Michigan v. Summers*, 452 U.S. 692 (1981). The very issuance of a search warrant further justifies the detention of occupants since it establishes probable cause to believe that someone in the home is committing a crime. If such proof is sufficient to allow law enforcement to invade the residence itself, the detention of occupants during the search is also reasonable, given the connection between an occupant and his or her home.

The detention authority of *Michigan v. Summers* applies only to occupants found within or immediately outside the residence at the time of the search. Therefore, it was unlawful to detain recent occupants found one mile from the residence at the time officers were executing a search warrant of the premises. *Bailey v. United States*, 568 U.S. 186 (2013).

The Court has also permitted officers in the process of obtaining a search warrant to detain residents of the subject premises outside of the residence. In *Illinois v. McArthur*, 531 U.S. 326 (2001), the Court deemed a two-hour detention reasonable, emphasizing the following factors: First, the police had probable cause to believe that marijuana was present in the residence; second, if allowed to enter unaccompanied by an officer, the defendant would be able to destroy the drugs; and, third, the invasion of privacy was relatively minor since there was no warrantless search of either the defendant or the premises and the detention was for a limited time period.

QUESTION 3. Nosy neighbors. As Officers Andy and Kevon were patrolling Beechwood Avenue, Belinda flagged them down. Belinda told the officers that, two days earlier, she saw Drake, who lives at #85, selling drugs to someone in the living room of his house while his roommate, Anthony, looked on. The officers then interviewed Belinda's next-door neighbor, Kathy. Kathy said that she had witnessed three in-home drug sales by Drake and one by Anthony and had once heard a customer thank Drake for the "primo weed."

Based on this information, Andy and Kevon decided to apply for a warrant to search Drake's residence. As Andy left to secure the warrant, Drake arrived home accompanied by his roommate, Anthony, and Drake's friend, Chaz. Kevon told the three men that they could not enter the house "until further notice." Three hours later, Andy returned with a warrant that authorized a search of "the entire residence as well as Drake's person for drugs and drug paraphernalia."

After showing Drake and Anthony the warrant, Kevon allowed them, as well as Chaz, to enter the house. Kevon ordered all three to remain in the living room under his supervision while Andy searched the house. Stating that he wanted to leave, Chaz moved toward the front door. As he turned the doorknob, Kevon grabbed Chaz's arm and told him that he was not permitted to leave until Andy finished his search of the residence. As Kevon turned Chaz around, a baggie filled with cocaine fell out of Chaz's pocket. Kevon then conducted pat-down searches of Drake and Anthony, finding packets of marijuana in the pants pockets of both men.

If Drake, Anthony, and Chaz move to suppress the drugs seized by Kevon, who is most likely to prevail?

A. All three, because they were denied entry into the residence for an excessively long period of time.
B. Anthony and Chaz, because Kevon had no right to detain them while Andy searched the residence.
C. Chaz, because Kevon had no right to detain him while Andy searched the residence.
D. Anthony, because Kevon had no right to search his person.
E. Anthony and Drake, because Kevon had no right to search their persons.

ANALYSIS.   This question explores the parameters of officers' authority to detain and search individuals in the search warrant context. Officer Kevon denied entry to both residents (Drake and Anthony), as well as their guest (Chaz), for a period of three hours while Officer Andy obtained a search warrant. As in *McArthur*, there was probable cause to believe that there were drugs inside; thus, the risk of destruction of evidence if the men were allowed in seems reasonable. The duration of the exclusion was longer in our fact pattern, however, by one hour. The Supreme Court did not specify any maximum time period in *McArthur*, noting that the intrusion that resulted from the two-hour detention was "limited." While the additional hour may present a greater burden on the detainees' Fourth Amendment rights, it is unclear that it would render Kevon's actions unreasonable.

Once inside the home, Kevon detained all three men in the living room. He conducted pat-down searches of Drake and Anthony, finding drugs on each. The search of Drake is clearly lawful, since the warrant expressly authorizes it. Our warrant is similar, in this regard, to the one in *Ybarra*, which authorized a search of both the tavern and the bartender. The warrant does not include Anthony, much as the warrant in *Ybarra* did not include the tavern's patrons. However, in disallowing the searches of the patrons, *Ybarra* emphasized the absence of evidence linking the tavern to drug sales. In our fact pattern, by contrast, Belinda and Kathy witnessed drug sales taking place inside the residence. Moreover, while Drake conducted most of the transactions, Kathy identified Anthony as the seller on one occasion. These facts distinguish *Ybarra* and provide at least some justification for searching Anthony.

While he did not search Chaz's person, Kevon caused a baggie of cocaine to fall out of Chaz's pocket when he grabbed Chaz's arm to prevent his exit from the home. While conducting a search of a residence, *Summers* and *Bailey* allow officers to detain occupants found within or immediately outside the residence at the time of the search, based on the proof that the home is being used for criminal activity and the connection between the home and its occupants. *Neither case* addresses officers' authority to detain non-occupants, nor does their reasoning support such action. While the connection between a home and its occupants is self-evident, there is no obvious nexus between a residence and casual visitors.

Because Kevon's detention of Chaz lacks clear support in the case law, C is the best answer.

D.   The Closer

> **QUESTION 4. Phony Franklins.**   A local merchant notified Officer Luisa that a customer tried to pay for merchandise with a counterfeit $100 bill. The previous week, Luisa received a similar complaint from another area merchant. In both instances, the storeowners identified the suspect as Ben, a drifter who had lived in town on and off for years. The merchants also reported seeing Ben in the company of Alice, a former girlfriend and occasional police informant. Alice told Luisa that Ben was making counterfeit $100 bills in his apartment on Center Street.
>
> Based on the foregoing, the magistrate issued a warrant to search Ben's residence for "any machine used to manufacture counterfeit bills." Luisa and her partner, Ramón, arrived at Ben's apartment the following day to execute the warrant. Luisa knocked on the front door and identified herself as a police officer with a search warrant for the apartment. Within seconds, she and Ramón heard noise indicating a great deal of activity inside the apartment. In response, the officers forcibly entered the residence, causing a ceramic urn containing the ashes of Ben's father to crash to the floor in the process. The commotion, Luisa and Ramón discovered, had been caused by the four, six, and seven-year-old children of Ben's girlfriend, Amy. The children were staying with Ben that morning while Amy was at work.
>
> Ben told the children to wait in the kitchen during the search. Walking on the living room's hardwood floor, Ramón noticed a loose floorboard in the corner. When he walked on the board, it emitted a hollow sound, suggesting empty space underneath. Lifting the board, Ramón found a counterfeiting machine resting in a long, hollowed-out space. He seized it. Meanwhile, when searching Ben's bathroom, Luisa was surprised to find an empty candy wrapper sitting on a shelf in his medicine cabinet. When she picked up the wrapper, two pills fell out.

They were later identified as ecstasy, the possession of which is unlawful in this jurisdiction.

Midway through the search, Amy arrived at the apartment to take her children home. She was upset by the presence of Luisa and Ramón, who explained that they were executing a search warrant of the residence. Barking that there was no way she and her kids were "sticking around for this," Amy gathered her kids and moved quickly toward the door. As she did, she tripped over a toy and fell to the ground. The force of the fall caused her purse to fly open, and a small baggie of marijuana landed at Ramón's feet. He seized it. Did the execution of the search warrant by Luisa and Ramón violate the Fourth Amendment?

A. Yes, under the knock-and-announce rule.
B. Yes, by Ramón's lifting of the floorboard.
C. Yes, by Luisa's inspection of the candy wrapper.
D. Yes, by the involuntary exposure of Amy's baggie of marijuana.
E. No.

ANALYSIS. This question reviews each of the warrant execution issues addressed in this chapter. We begin with the knock-and-announce rule. Luisa and Ramón do not wait fifteen to twenty seconds before bursting into Ben's apartment, and the force of their entry shatters an urn containing his father's ashes. This harm to physical property and emotional well-being does not violate the Fourth Amendment, however, if the attendant circumstances justify their haste. They do.

After Luisa announces the officers' presence and purpose, the occupants offer no response. Instead, a frenzy of activity ensues, which may signal a frantic effort to hide or destroy contraband. That the noise was caused by Amy's visiting children is unavailing, since the officers were unaware of their presence. Based on what they knew, Luisa and Ramón's concerns were reasonable and justify their failure to wait longer before entering the apartment. **A** is wrong.

Ramón discovers the marijuana after Amy's purse explodes when she tumbles to the floor. Neither Ramón nor Luisa is responsible for Amy's fall; she trips over a toy left on the floor, presumably by one of her children. At that time, she is in the process of leaving the apartment and the officers are not attempting to detain her. Because Amy's own clumsiness exposes the contraband to public view, its discovery and seizure by Ramón do not violate the Fourth Amendment. **D** is wrong.

The "premises" warrant Luisa and Ramón are executing allows them to search for counterfeiting machinery. Because machinery may be hidden in a hollowed-out area beneath a loosened floorboard — indeed, it was — Ramón was justified in searching there. **B** is wrong. The candy wrapper, however, is a different matter. It is too small to house a counterfeiting machine; in fact, it is unclear if the medicine cabinet itself could do so. At any rate, even if we assume that Luisa's search of the medicine cabinet was appropriate, the warrant did not give her the right to inspect the candy wrapper, even if she regarded its presence as suspicious.

The correct answer is **C**.

✧ Cornwell's Picks

1. Too much TV	**C**
2. Stocks, bonds, and blood	**A**
3. Nosy neighbors	**C**
4. Phony Franklins	**C**

11

Exigent Circumstances

A. Hot Pursuit

The exigent circumstances exception is an umbrella with three distinct subparts, each with its own analytical mooring. The first allows police officers to make a warrantless entry into a home when they are in "hot pursuit" of an individual whom they have probable cause to search or arrest. If, upon doing so, an officer discovers contraband, she may seize it as an instrumentality of crime.

A police officer with the authority to enter a protected area without a warrant can search anywhere necessary to respond to the exigency. In so doing, the officer can ensure that the arrestee is the only person present and that there are no weapons present that may imperil his or her safety. See, e.g., *Warden, Maryland Penitentiary v. Hayden*, 387 U.S. 294 (1967). Police officers cannot, however, expand the search to areas or items outside the scope of the emergency that justified the warrantless intrusion.

> QUESTION 1. **Stop, thief!** Betty calls the police when she sees a man climbing through a ground-floor window in a house across the street. When Police Officer Alice arrives, she sees a man running out of the neighbor's house carrying a television set. When Alice yells, "Hey, hold up! I'm a police officer!," the man runs into the next-door neighbor's house.

Alice gives chase and enters the house, looking for the burglar. She opens a closet and does not find the burglar, but she does see a baggie labeled "marijuana." She seizes it and continues her search. In the master bedroom, Alice finds the burglar crouched in the corner. She arrests him. When he gets up, she sees a baggie labeled "heroin" on the floor behind where he was hiding. She seizes it. If the neighbor moves to suppress the marijuana and heroin, he will:

A. Prevail as to both, because Alice had no right to enter the home of a third party.

B. Prevail as to the marijuana, because Alice had no right to look inside the closet.

C. Prevail as to the heroin, because Alice had no right to enter the bedroom.

D. Prevail as to the marijuana and the heroin, because Alice had no right to enter the bedroom or look inside the closet.

E. Lose, as to both the marijuana and the heroin.

ANALYSIS. This problem explores the authority of police officers to invade protected areas when in "hot pursuit" of criminal suspects. **A** seems plausible at first blush. Fourth Amendment privacy rights are greatest in the home, and the infringement of those rights seems especially egregious here where they are directed at a third party against whom the police have no evidence whatsoever of wrongdoing. The pursuit of a fleeing criminal, however, excuses the warrantless entry into the home and its accompanying privacy infringements.

Answer **B** suggests that, even if the entry is defensible, the search of the closet is not. The key here is that the closet is a space large enough to conceal a burglar; since he might have been hiding there, its search is permissible and the marijuana found in plain view is admissible. By the same token, the burglar could have been hiding in the bedroom — indeed, he was! Thus, the entry into it to search for him is perfectly permissible, as is the seizure of the heroin baggie. **B** and **C** are, accordingly, incorrect and, therefore, so is **D**.

The correct answer is **E**. Remember: Officers can make a warrantless entry into a home to make an arrest *only* if they are in hot pursuit; otherwise an arrest warrant is necessary to enter the suspect's home and a *search* warrant is necessary to look for the suspect in the home of a third party.

B. Emergency Aid

The second category of "exigent circumstances" allows law enforcement officers to enter a home without a warrant to render emergency assistance to an injured occupant or to protect an occupant from imminent injury. Thus,

Brigham City v. Stuart, 547 U.S. 398 (2006), found officers' warrantless entry into a residence constitutional where, before entering, they witnessed an altercation inside involving five people, one of whom spit blood into a sink after being punched. These circumstances provided an objectively reasonable basis for believing that the injured adult might need help and that further violence may erupt. Because the U.S. Supreme Court deemed the officers' subjective motivation irrelevant, it did not matter if the officers entered primarily for the purpose of arresting the parties, as the lower court had found.

To invoke this "emergency aid" exception, officers do not need proof of a serious, life-threatening injury. In *Michigan v. Fisher*, 558 U.S. 45 (2009), an officer observed the defendant inside his residence with a cut on his hand and blood on a car and outside door. In addition, the defendant was screaming and throwing items about the house and refused an offer of medical attention. Under these circumstances, the officer's warrantless entry was justified, the Court reasoned, since he reasonably believed either that the defendant needed treatment for his injury or "was about to hurt, or had already hurt, someone else."

QUESTION 2. Party hardy. Scott and Linda Harrison were hosting a high school graduation party for their son, Philip. At midnight, as the party entered its fifth hour, their next-door neighbors became concerned when they heard a loud crash inside the Harrison's house. When no one answered the Harrison's phone, the neighbors called the police. Officer Joyce responded to the call. She had dated Scott in high school, and was devastated when he broke up with her. Though years later now, she still harbored deep resentment toward him.

When Joyce arrived, all seemed quiet at the Harrison's. When no one answered a knock at the door, Joyce looked through the window. She saw a shattered punch bowl on the floor and a small pool of blood alongside it. Scott was seated nearby, bleeding from his arm and staring blankly out the window. Wanting to confront him about his "mistreatment" of her years earlier, Joyce forced the door open. Once inside, she found two teens sitting on the stairs drinking beer. Joyce arrested Scott for providing alcohol to minors. If Scott challenges the warrantless entry, is he likely to prevail?

A. Yes, since Scott's injury did not appear to be serious.
B. Yes, since Joyce entered to confront Scott over their prior relationship.
C. No, since Scott appeared to be in need of medical attention.
D. No, since Joyce knocked before entering.
E. No, since Scott had committed a crime.

ANALYSIS. This problem asks whether the emergency-aid doctrine provides a sufficient exigency to justify Joyce's warrantless entry into the Harrison's home. **B** would invalidate the entry because Joyce's purpose was not to provide aid but, rather, to discuss her break-up with Scott years earlier. An officer's subjective intent is irrelevant, however, in assessing the constitutionality of a warrantless entry; therefore, **B** is wrong.

The fact that Joyce knocked at the door is a bit of a red herring, since it is inapposite to the warrantless nature of her entry. Scott's provision of alcohol to minors is likewise beside the point, since Joyce only became aware of this criminal activity once she was inside the residence. As such, it cannot justify a decision she made before acquiring this knowledge. **D** and **E** are wrong.

The need to address threats to individuals' physical well-being is at the heart of the emergency-aid doctrine. The injury, whether real or potential, may be to anyone inside the house and need not be serious or life-threatening. Before entering, Joyce noticed a cut on Scott's arm that had produced a small pool of blood and was still bleeding. Scott also appeared to be in a state of shock. These facts are unquestionably sufficient to justify Joyce's warrantless entry into the Harrison's home.

C is the correct answer.

C.   Evanescent Evidence

The third category of "exigent circumstances" permits a warrantless entry into a protected area to secure evidence that will be destroyed by delay. While cases are fact-specific, courts have deemed a number of circumstances relevant in finding exigency on this basis, including: whether efforts to obtain a search warrant would expose officers left at the scene to danger; the amount of time it would take to secure the warrant; the "ready destructibility" of the contraband and the reasonableness of the officer's belief that it will be destroyed in the event of delay; and the defendant's awareness of the presence of the police. See, e.g., *United States v. Rubin*, 474 F.2d 262 (3d Cir. 1973).

Officers may respond to exigencies created by their own conduct, provided they do not gain entry by means of an actual or threatened violation of the Fourth Amendment. Thus, if an officer's knocking at the door of a residence and announcing her presence causes occupants to attempt to destroy contraband, she may nonetheless enter the premises without a warrant to prevent the destruction of evidence. *Kentucky v. King*, 563 U.S. 452 (2011).

This concern for evanescent evidence has allowed police officers, without a warrant, to scrape a suspect's fingernails for evidence linking him to his wife's murder. *Cupp v. Murphy*, 412 U.S. 291 (1973). In determining whether the "ready destructibility" of evidence justifies dispensing with the warrant requirement, the Court considers the severity of the accompanying Fourth Amendment invasion. While the intrusion associated with fingernail scraping is "very limited," the interference with bodily integrity attendant to blood testing in drunk-driving investigations is far more extensive. Thus, the natural dissipation of alcohol in the bloodstream is not a per se exigency that justifies a warrantless blood test in this context absent special facts or circumstances that make it "impractical" to obtain a warrant. *Missouri v. McNeely*, 133 S. Ct. 1552 (2013). For example, in *Schmerber v. California*, 384 U.S. 757 (1966), a warrantless blood test of a drunk-driving suspect was reasonable since officers could not secure a warrant in a timely fashion due to the need to investigate the scene of the accident and to bring the accused to the hospital. See Chapter 6, part B.

The Court is also mindful of the gravity of the underlying offense when determining whether an exigency justifies overlooking the warrant requirement. Thus, in *Welsh v. Wisconsin*, 466 U.S. 740 (1984), the Court disallowed the warrantless entry into a man's home to arrest him for driving under the influence. The Court deemed this exigency insufficient to compromise the defendant's privacy interest in his home, since DUI was a non-jailable civil infraction under then-applicable state law.

QUESTION 3. Don't mess with Texas.   Mary Kate was manning the cash register at her family's convenience store at 1:00 A.M. in downtown Houston when a man entered the store, pointed a gun at her, and demanded that she empty the cash register. She remembered that her father kept a loaded pistol under the counter for protection. When the man looked away, she grabbed it and fired at his shoulder. As soon as he was hit, the robber ran out of the store. Mary Kate then called 911, reported the robbery, and described the robber to the police.

Two hours later, Anton turned up at the local hospital for treatment for a gunshot wound in the shoulder, which he claimed he had inflicted on himself accidentally. The police doubted his story and noted that he matched Mary Kate's description. They brought Mary Kate to the hospital. When she saw him, she exclaimed: "I think that's the man who tried to rob my family's store!" When Anton refused to allow the police to obtain a blood sample for comparison to blood left at the scene, the officer ordered a nurse to take the sample forcibly. If Anton challenges the officer's actions, he will:

A. Prevail, because Mary Kate was not sure of her identification.
B. Prevail, because a reliable blood sample could be obtained later.
C. Fail, because robbery is a felony.
D. Fail, because the procedure was performed in a hospital by medical personnel.
E. Fail, because the extraction of a blood sample from an unwilling suspect has been permitted by the U.S. Supreme Court.

ANALYSIS.   In this fact pattern, as in *McNeely* and *Schmerber* (also discussed in Chapter 6), blood is forcibly taken from a suspect for evidentiary purposes. In *Schmerber*, the procedure was necessary to determine if the defendant had been driving under the influence and special circumstances made it impractical to obtain a warrant. Here, the blood evidence will establish the suspect's presence at the scene of the crime.

In evaluating the permissibility of the procedure, we must be mindful of the considerations referenced by the court in *Rubin*. Unlike *Schmerber*, the blood evidence in this case is not "readily destructible." Whereas the body will "burn up" alcohol with the passage of time so as to hinder prosecution for DUI, delay has no impact on the ability of law enforcement personnel to match the suspect's blood to that found elsewhere. Neither will the delay place police officers in any danger, since the suspect is located in a medical facility.

Answer **C** is wrong. While *Welsh* provides that the gravity of the underlying offense is a relevant consideration in evaluating exigency, it does not suggest that the belief that an individual has committed a felony justifies highly invasive procedures in and of itself. Likewise, having a nurse draw the blood does not overcome the forcible nature of the extraction. In this context, by acting at their behest, the nurse becomes an agent of the police. **D** is wrong.

Answer **E** is an accurate statement of law, but it does not resolve the present inquiry. While *Schmerber* allowed the unconsented, warrantless taking of a blood sample from a drunk-driving suspect, *McNeely* clarified that special facts or circumstances are necessary to render such conduct reasonable. This fact-specific inquiry considers both the need for the procedure and the way in which it is accomplished. Here, it fails to pass constitutional muster.

While both **A** and **B** reach the proper conclusion, **A**'s reasoning falls short. The fact that Mary Kate was not sure of her identification suggests that the police need additional evidence to establish Anton's guilt. A match between his blood and that found at the scene is an example of the kind of evidence that would prove useful in this regard. The evidentiary value of the blood sample does not relate, however, to the necessity for a warrant to justify its extraction. As **B** indicates, relaxing the warrant requirement is unnecessary because no detriment will result from the delay in obtaining it. There is, in short, no exigency.

B is the correct answer.

D.   Automobiles: A Special Exigency

The U.S. Supreme Court first addressed the application of the warrant requirement to automobiles in the Prohibition-era case of *Carroll v. United States*, 267 U.S. 132 (1925). In upholding the warrantless search of a car believed to contain liquor, the Court emphasized that vehicles are readily movable, commenting that an automobile "can be quickly moved out of the locality or jurisdiction in which the warrant must be sought." Later cases continued to rely on the "ready mobility" of automobiles, as well as the limited privacy expectation individuals can expect in cars traveling on the open roadways due to pervasive government regulation. See *Pennsylvania v. Kilgore*, 518 U.S. 938 (1996); *California v. Carney*, 471 U.S. 386 (1985).

To obtain authority to search under the automobile exception, police officers need probable cause to believe that contraband will be found inside the vehicle. Probable cause gives officers the right to search the passenger cabin, the trunk, and *all* closed containers within them that might contain the contraband. *California v. Acevedo*, 500 U.S. 565 (1991). Ownership of the items placed in the vehicle is irrelevant; their presence in the car justifies the search without regard to any individual privacy interest that might otherwise attach.

Police may also order the occupants out of the vehicle while searching it. *Maryland v. Wilson*, 519 U.S. 408 (1997); *Pennsylvania v. Mimms*, 434 U.S. 106 (1977). However, they may not search the passengers' bodies or items worn by them without specific proof that they are in possession of contraband. Nor may officers enter the home or its curtilage to access a vehicle under the automobile exception; in light of the heightened privacy interests that attach to these areas, a warrant is necessary. *Collins v. Virginia*, 138 S. Ct. 1663 (2018).

QUESTION 4. A less-than-excellent adventure. Police Officer Adam's supervisor notifies him that a wrapped package containing a stolen Picasso painting is being transported in a black Nissan Altima with New York license plates containing the letters VYZ. Suddenly, Adam spots a car fitting this description traveling down the interstate. He pulls over the car and orders the driver, Bill, and his passenger, Ted, out of the vehicle.

Adam first searches the interior cabin of the car. Feeling under the passenger's seat, he finds a small zippered pouch labeled "Bill's CDs." He opens it and finds a marijuana cigarette inside. He seizes it. Proceeding to the trunk, Adam discovers a large suitcase with a tag identifying Ted as the owner. He opens it and finds the missing painting inside. He seizes it. The searches violate Fourth Amendment principles:

A. As to neither the CD case nor the suitcase.
B. As to the CD case only.
C. As to the suitcase only.
D. As to both the CD case and the suitcase, because the searches were impermissibly broad.
E. As to both the CD case and the suitcase, because Adam had no right to order Bill and Ted out of the car in the first place.

ANALYSIS. This question implicates three separate actions by Adam: the "seizure" of Bill and Ted when they are ordered to exit the vehicle; the search of the CD case under the passenger seat; and the search of the suitcase in the trunk. The seizure of Bill and Ted is clearly permissible. Police officers have plenary authority to order both drivers and passengers out of a vehicle when searching it. While their authority to order the occupants—particularly the passengers—to remain in the vicinity during the search is less clear, this situation is not presented by the facts. **E** is, therefore, wrong.

For the searches to be permissible under the automobile exception, they must be supported by probable cause. That is, the evidence must establish a fair probability that the stolen Picasso would be found in the car. There is ample evidence to support such a finding since the car matches the description provided by Adam's supervisor in all respects: color, make, and license-plate information.

Having satisfied the evidentiary standard, Adam is permitted to search the entire car, including the trunk. In searching items within the car, however, he is limited to those large enough to hide a painting. The suitcase in the trunk qualifies — indeed, the painting was located inside it! The small CD case under the passenger's seat is, however, a different story altogether. Because a painting could not fit inside it, Adam was not entitled to open it.

B is the correct answer.

E.   The Closer

QUESTION 5. **Pursuing Preston.**   Preston robbed Maria at gunpoint on Main Street. After securing Maria's purse, Preston sped off in his car. Having witnessed the crime from across the street, Officer Eric jumped into his car and gave chase. Five minutes later, Eric observed Preston pull into a driveway. Preston alighted from his car and ran into the house through a side door next to where he parked the vehicle at the top of the driveway. After calling for back-up, Eric entered the house. He started on the main level of the house, looking for Preston and the gun he used in robbing Maria. Unsuccessful, Eric ran upstairs, finding Preston hiding inside a bedroom closet. Eric arrested him, and confirmed that there was no else present in the house.

As Eric was driving away with Preston, Officer Tanya arrived. Eric radioed that he had taken Preston into custody but did not find inside the house the gun that Preston had used in robbing Maria. He told Tanya that the house was presently empty. Tanya subsequently searched the car and found the gun, which she seized.

Which of the following is most accurate?

A. Eric lawfully searched for the gun in the house, based on a theory of hot pursuit.

B. Eric lawfully searched for the gun in the house under the emergency-aid exception because it could be used to harm innocent third parties.

C. Eric lawfully searched for the gun in the house, because, if he did not do so, another occupant may later remove it.

D. Tanya lawfully searched the car for the gun, because Eric did not find it in the house.

ANALYSIS.   This closer explores the various "faces" of exigency, including its application to automobile searches.

We can start by eliminating **B**, which justified the search for the gun based on the potential of harm to third parties. In cases where courts have authorized warrantless searches based on the emergency-aid doctrine, there has been an extant, imminent threat to which they were responding. Here, the danger is too speculative. Eric has not identified any specific individual at risk, nor does he know the location of the weapon that could create the danger to this hypothetical person.

Likewise, the facts do not disclose the presence of a third party with access to the residence who could remove the gun before the police obtained a warrant or otherwise secured the premises. Without this information, there can be no exigency, based on the destruction of evidence. **C** is, therefore, wrong.

D would allow Tanya to search of the car because Eric did not find the gun in the house. Because Eric has already taken Preston into custody, and there was no one else in the house, exigent circumstances cannot justify a warrantless search for the weapon at this time. On the other hand, because Eric did not find the weapon in the house, Tanya would appear to have probable cause to believe that it is in the vehicle. However, the vehicle is parked inside the curtilage, and the recent case of *Collins v. Virginia* disallows an officer's entry into the curtilage to access a vehicle for a search under the automobile exception. Tanya's search is, therefore, unlawful.

Eric's best argument in support of a search for the gun is, therefore, the theory of hot pursuit. The facts of *Warden, Maryland Penitentiary v. Hayden, supra*, are instructive. In that case, police officers followed the defendant, who had committed an armed robbery, into a residence in "hot pursuit." Addressing the permissible scope of the officers' search inside the house, the Court held that they had authority to search for both the suspect and any weapons he may have used in the crime and carried into the house. Moreover, when Eric searched for the weapon, he did not yet know that the house was empty. Thus, Eric's "hot pursuit" of Preston fully justified his search for the gun used in the robbery.

A is the correct answer.

✦ Cornwell's Picks

1. Stop, thief!	E
2. Party hardy	C
3. Don't mess with Texas	B
4. A less-than-excellent adventure	B
5. Pursuing Preston	A

12

Searches Incident to Arrest and Inventory Searches

CHAPTER OVERVIEW
A. Searching the Person of the Arrestee
B. Searching an Arrestee's Car
C. Inventory Searches: The Jailhouse and the Impound Lot
D. DNA Collection Incident to Arrest
E. The Closer
✦ Cornwell's Picks

A. Searching the Person of the Arrestee

The U.S. Supreme Court has recognized repeatedly that custodial arrest is a highly significant event that both augments the police officer's authority to search and diminishes an arrestee's expectation of privacy. Accordingly, in *Chimel v. California,* 395 U.S. 752 (1969), the majority specified that, when arresting an individual, a police officer may search the arrestee's person and the area within his or her immediate control for weapons or evidence without a search warrant. The Court reasoned that a more extensive search would exceed the justification for this exception, which is grounded in concern for officer safety and the concealment or destruction of evidence. In addition, the search must not be remote in time or place from the arrest; it may, however, precede a "formal" arrest, provided the two events occur in close temporal and spatial proximity.[1] *Rawlings v. Kentucky,* 448 U.S. 98 (1980).

---

1. Lower courts have generally found searches of individuals and items immediately associated with their person to be "substantially contemporaneous" with their arrest even if the search is conducted some time after a lawful arrest and/or at a certain distance from the arrest's location. See, e.g., *United States v. Smith,* 549 F.3d 355 (6th Cir. 2008) (search at police station a few hours after the arrest); *Dunham v. District of Columbia,* 442 A.2d 121 (D.C. App. 1982) (search at police headquarters three hours after arrest); *United States v. Phillips,* 607 F.2d 808 (8th Cir. 1979) (search of defendant's wallet at station house "substantial period of time" after arrest).

In *United States v. Robinson,* 414 U.S. 218 (1973), the Court returned to *Chimel* when addressing the warrantless search of a man arrested for driving with a suspended license. The officer discovered capsules of heroin inside a crumpled cigarette packet stored in the arrestee's shirt pocket. The majority acknowledged the arresting officer's admission that the search was not motivated by any fear for his safety, nor did the target offense suggest the presence of any contraband. However, the Court deemed the search constitutional, reasoning that the validity of warrantless searches incident to arrest did not depend on the probability that weapons or evidence would be found on the suspect in a given case.

While *Robinson* authorizes searches incident to arrest of the body, clothing, and containers within an arrestee's immediate control, the Court has recently drawn the line at cell phones. In *Riley v. California,* 134 S. Ct. 2473 (2014), the justices unanimously disallowed searches of digital cell phone data incident to arrest, noting that this information implicates privacy interests "far beyond those implicated by the search of a cigarette pack, a wallet, or a purse." Because cell phone data presents no significant risk re officer safety or the destruction of evidence, the substantial infringement of arrestees' Fourth Amendment rights makes the routine seizure of such information incident to arrest unreasonable.

QUESTION 1. **Arresting developments.**   Having obtained an arrest warrant for Ben for securities fraud, Officer Don arrests the suspect at his place of work. At the time of the arrest, Ben is seated at his desk. Don asks him to stand, whereupon the officer searches Ben's person, finding a small packet of cocaine inside his wallet. When Don spots Ben's cell phone on the desktop, he examines it to make sure there is no dangerous instrument (like a razor blade) hidden between the phone and its case. Opening the bottom drawer of Ben's desk, Don finds a packet of marijuana. Believing there might be more drugs in the office, Don opens a filing cabinet on the other side of the room, inside of which he finds crack cocaine. Which of the following is most accurate with respect to the constitutionality of the three searches conducted by Don?

A. All of the searches are unconstitutional, because Ben was not likely to be armed or to be in possession of evidence that could be readily destroyed.
B. Only the search of the wallet is unconstitutional, because Don had no authority to open it.
C. Only the examination of the cell phone is unconstitutional, because Don had no authority to seize it.
D. Only the search of the desk drawer is unconstitutional, because it was closed.
E. Only the search of the filing cabinet is unconstitutional, because it was outside Ben's reach.

ANALYSIS. This problem illustrates the *Chimel/Robinson* "search incident to arrest" doctrine. The problem contains three separate searches incident to arrest. Take your time and analyze each separately. If you rush, you risk conflating them and choosing the wrong answer as a result.

Answer **A** posits that all of the searches are impermissible because they do not square with the justifications forwarded in *Chimel* for searches incident to arrest. While true, the Court in *Robinson* does not require that any given search reflect these justifications in a meaningful way. If the search of a cigarette packet in the shirt pocket of an individual arrested for driving with a suspended license satisfies the justificatory basis for searching incident to arrest, so do the searches here. Thus, answer **A** is incorrect.

While courts need not scrutinize a police officer's justification for searching incident to arrest, the searches conducted must not exceed the limits set out in *Chimel* and *Robinson*. **B** states that the search of the wallet is impermissible, because Don lacked the authority to open Ben's wallet. This argument will fail, since courts will liken the opening of the wallet to the opening of the cigarette packet in *Robinson*. While an individual may have a greater expectation of privacy in a wallet than in a cigarette packet, the fact of arrest sufficiently diminishes the privacy interest to validate the search, whatever the likelihood of actually finding a weapon or contraband therein.

Answer **C** is incorrect because it misconstrues the Court's recent decision in *Riley*. *Riley* disallows searches of the digital data stored in cell phones. It does not prevent officers from examining the physical aspects of a cell phone to ensure that it cannot be used as a dangerous weapon. In fact, the Court expressly affirms officers' authority to do exactly what Don did here.

Answer **D** is incorrect because *Chimel* permits the search of any area within an arrestee's immediate control. Because the drawer is not locked, Ben could have reached into it to procure a weapon during the arrest. *Chimel's* "immediate control" allows searches of areas within an arrestee's reach. Because the drawer satisfies this standard, it was permissible for Don to open it.

The analysis of **E** differs from that of **D** because, unlike the desk drawer, a filing cabinet located across the room is not within Ben's "immediate control." In fact, the *Chimel* majority expressly noted that the search-incident-to-arrest doctrine does not justify "searching through all the desk drawers or other closed or concealed areas" in the room in which the arrest is made. While *Chimel* is still good law, later cases disclose a willingness to grant officers greater authority to search areas within the room where the arrest is made. See, e.g., *Maryland v. Buie*, 494 U.S. 325 (1990). Still, it is the only search that arguably raises a constitutional flag.

E is the best answer. Remember: Do not conflate the existence of probable cause with the need for a warrant. Finding drugs in the drawer and on Ben's person undoubtedly furnishes probable cause to search further. To do so, police officers must obtain a properly issued search warrant, unless an exception to the warrant requirement applies. Therefore, in this problem, Don must obtain a warrant to search the filing cabinet, if *Chimel* is unavailing.

B.   Searching an Arrestee's Car

In Chapter 11, we addressed the automobile exception to the warrant requirement. It is important to remember, however, that not all automobile searches are governed by this provision. A police officer may choose from as many as five categorical exceptions to justify a warrantless search of an automobile. Because each exception has distinct justifications and limitations on the scope of the search, it is important to know the differences among them.

The U.S. Supreme Court first addressed the scope of a lawful automobile search incident to arrest in *New York v. Belton*, 453 U.S. 454 (1981). *Belton* announced a bright-line test governing all automobile searches incident to arrest without regard to the probability, in a given circumstance, of finding weapons or contraband in the vehicle. Accordingly, when a police officer custodially arrests the occupant of a vehicle, *Belton* permitted the officer to conduct a warrantless search of the entire passenger compartment of the vehicle, including any open or closed containers therein. The search must, however, be substantially contemporaneous with the arrest and could not extend beyond the passenger compartment. In addition, the arrestee must have been a "recent occupant" of the vehicle to provide a sufficient "temporal [and] spatial relationship" between the arrestee and the vehicle at the time of the search. See *Thornton v. United States*, 124 S. Ct. 2127 (2004).

In *Arizona v. Gant*, 129 S. Ct. 1710 (2009), the Court revisited the *Belton* doctrine, as applied to an individual arrested for driving on a suspended license who was handcuffed and locked inside the squad car before officers conducted the search of his vehicle. Overruling *Belton* and *Thornton* in part, *Gant* held that police may search a vehicle incident to arrest only if the arrestee is within reaching distance of the passenger compartment at the time of the search *or* it is reasonable to believe the vehicle contains evidence related to the offense for which the arrest was made. Thus, the search of Gant's car was unconstitutional: He was neither within reaching distance of the vehicle when it was searched nor could the police expect to find evidence related to driving on a suspended license inside it. Note that, if Gant had remained unsecured inside the vehicle at the time of the search, the search of the passenger cabin would have been lawful, since he would have been *within reaching distance of potential weapons and destructible evidence*.

QUESTION 2. Car trouble.   While patrolling the interstate, Officer Hawkeye noticed a car weaving in and out of its lane erratically. He pulled the car over. When the driver, Tippler, rolled down his window to ask Hawkeye why he had been stopped, Hawkeye immediately smelled alcohol on his breath. After Tippler failed the Breathalyzer test, Hawkeye arrested him for DUI.

> Hawkeye ordered Tippler out of the car and told him to sit on the hood while he searched the vehicle. Tippler stumbled out of the car. Hawkeye found an unlicensed firearm under the passenger seat, marijuana in the glove compartment, and cocaine in the trunk. He seized all three. Tippler moves to suppress all three items, claiming that the search violated his Fourth Amendment rights. He will prevail:
>
> **A.** On all three, since the arrest was for DUI.
> **B.** Only as to the firearm, since it was not in plain view.
> **C.** Only as to the marijuana, since it was in a closed container.
> **D.** Only as to the cocaine, since it was in the trunk.
> **E.** On nothing.

ANALYSIS. A is incorrect. While the DUI arrest based on a failed Breathalyzer test does not provide a reason to search the vehicle for criminal evidence, Hawkeye does not need to provide any such justification since, unlike Gant, Tippler is not secured at the time of the search. Because Tippler is unrestrained and is positioned in close proximity to the doors of the vehicle, he could access weapons inside the car that threaten Hawkeye's safety; thus, searching the vehicle is permissible under *Belton/Gant*.

Answer **B** is also incorrect. An officer may search under the passenger seat; therefore, the seizure of the firearm was proper, whether or not it was in plain view. **C** is wrong because the officer's authority to search extends to closed containers within the automobile's passenger compartment, including unlocked glove compartments.

The *Belton/Gant* rule for searching the vehicles of "unsecured" arrestees does not, however, allow officers to search the trunk of the car, since that part of the vehicle is clearly outside the arrestee's "immediate control." The facts in our problem underscore this point, since Tippler was positioned at the opposite end of the vehicle, sitting on the hood. Thus, in discovering and seizing the cocaine, Hawkeye exceeded the scope of his authority under *Belton* and *Gant*.

D is the correct answer.

C. Inventory Searches: The Jailhouse and the Impound Lot

Inventory searches take place primarily in two contexts: when personal effects are removed from an individual taken into police custody and when personal effects are removed from an impounded vehicle. These searches, regarded as part of the law enforcement "community caretaking" function, serve three law enforcement needs: protection of the owner's property, protection of the police against claims for lost or stolen property, and protection of the police from potential danger. *South Dakota v. Opperman*, 428 U.S. 364 (1976).

Fourth Amendment limitations on the scope of these searches focus on the applicable police department rules and regulations. If the regulations are reasonable and the police operate within them, any contraband seized is admissible against the owner without regard to prior suspicion of wrongdoing. In evaluating what is reasonable, deference to correctional officials is appropriate, in light of their expertise in devising policies "to detect and deter the presence of contraband in their facilities." *Florence v. Board of Chosen Freeholders*, 132 S. Ct. 1510 (2012). A search is not unreasonable, moreover, simply because a less intrusive procedure would have protected both the police and the owner's property. *Illinois v. Lafayette*, 462 U.S. 640 (1983).

In addition, regulations will not be considered unreasonable simply because they invest some discretion in police officers. In this regard, regulations need not require that either all or none of the closed containers be opened; it is reasonable, for example, to allow officers to open only those containers whose contents they are unable to determine from the outside. *Florida v. Wells*, 495 U.S. 1 (1990).

Inventory searches are invalid, however, if they are motivated by something other than the need to safeguard the owner's possessions or officer safety. *Colorado v. Bertine*, 479 U.S. 367 (1987). Ordinarily, an officer's subjective intent in carrying out a search is irrelevant under the Fourth Amendment, provided the officer's conduct has an objective justification. Inventory searches represent a rare exception to this rule due, in large part, to concerns that police might use the inventory procedure to gather criminal evidence where probable cause is otherwise lacking.

QUESTION 3. Protecting people and property in Podunk. The City of Podunk authorizes police officers to inventory all personal effects of individuals booked into jail, as well as the effects contained in the passenger cabin or trunk of any impounded vehicle. The relevant regulations specify that the officer conducting the search may seize "all contraband and any items of value. The officers also may, at their discretion, seize any items contained in closed containers."

Podunk Police Officer Marco arrested Anthony on Route 9 for possession of an illegal firearm. Marco took Anthony into custody and arranged for Anthony's car to be towed to the impound lot. Marco's partner, Bruno, waited for the tow truck and followed it to the lot. Once the car was deposited there, Bruno searched it thoroughly. Having learned at the police academy that "drugs and guns go together," Bruno seized an iPod, figuring that it might turn up trace amounts of cocaine or heroin. Bruno's suspicions proved correct; trace amounts of heroin were found on the iPod.

Meanwhile, as Marco was booking Anthony into the county jail, Marco removed a satchel Anthony was carrying. As Marco went to open it, Anthony asked him not to, stating that he (Anthony) would agree to waive any rights he might have against the police for lost property claims with respect to the satchel. Marco refused, noting that Podunk's booking procedures authorize the search of an arrested individual's personal effects. Inside the satchel, Marco found a bag of cocaine. If Anthony moves to suppress the heroin and the cocaine, he will prevail:

A. As to the heroin and the cocaine.
B. As to the heroin only.
C. As to the cocaine only.
D. As to neither the heroin nor the cocaine.

ANALYSIS. This problem presents two separate inventory searches. With respect to Officer Bruno's search of the impounded car, we must first determine if the governing regulations are reasonable. While they do allow police officers some discretion, discretion alone will not render them unconstitutional. Because permissive authority to seize items contained in closed containers does not seem unreasonable on its face, the regulations are likely to pass muster.

Next, we must ensure that Bruno did not exceed the lawful scope of inventory searches in Podunk. The regulations authorize the seizure of "any items of value," and iPods are certainly valuable. There is no mention, however, of any authority to test items seized by officers, and with good reason. Inventory searches are designed to safeguard private property, not to provide a ready substitute for searches for evidence of crime. Bruno's actions in this regard both exceeded the scope of his authority and constituted "bad faith." For both reasons, the heroin will be excluded.

As part of the booking process, Marco searches Anthony's satchel and finds cocaine inside. Anthony's willingness to waive any "lost property" claims against the police with respect to the contents of the satchel seems a clever way to avoid an inventory search, since it addresses directly the justificatory underpinning for these searches. The U.S. Supreme Court has been singularly unreceptive, however, to these sorts of efforts by criminal defendants. The Fourth Amendment requires only that the search be reasonable, and correctional officials enjoy judicial deference in the evaluation of search policies within their facilities. Moreover, a policy is not unreasonable simply because an alternative procedure would safeguard a defendant's privacy rights more completely. Because this search complies with reasonable departmental regulations, it is lawful. The cocaine will be admitted.

The correct answer is **B**.

D. DNA Collection Incident to Arrest

As described above, it is customary to inventory the belongings of individuals who are being held in police custody. Fingerprinting is also a routine part of the booking process to assist in arrestee identification. In its "DNA Collection Act," the State of Maryland also authorized law enforcement officers to collect DNA samples from all individuals arrested for committing, of attempting to commit, burglary or a crime of violence. In *Maryland v. King*, 133 S. Ct. 1958 (2013), the Supreme Court upheld the law, finding that it appropriately balanced "privacy-related and law enforcement-related concerns" so as to satisfy the reasonableness requirement of the Fourth Amendment.

With respect to privacy, the majority emphasized: the law's limitation to serious felonies; arrestees' diminished expectation of privacy; the minimal physical intrusion; and that the samples are only added after arraignment on formal charges and must be destroyed if a defendant is not convicted. Deeming the government's interest "substantial," the majority further noted the "unparalleled accuracy" of DNA testing and the benefits that DNA collection produces, such as aiding in individual assessments of dangerousness and allowing the innocent to go free.

In a blistering dissent, Justice Scalia described the law as having nothing to do with identification; it is, he opined, a thinly veiled and unconstitutional initiative designed to investigate and help solve past crimes. He fears, moreover, that the Court's reasoning will ultimately sanction DNA collection for non-serious crimes, including traffic offenses.

QUESTION 4. Summertime sadness. As Blake was strolling down Main Street one sunny day in July, a robbery took place at a convenience store two blocks from where he was walking. Officer Shareef pursued the robber and was about half a block behind him. Suddenly, the robber ran past Blake. When Shareef saw Blake, he mistook him for the robber, since Blake and the robber resembled each other. Shareef arrested Blake who was subsequently booked and fingerprinted. In addition, pursuant to state law, a DNA sample was taken by swabbing the inside of Blake's cheek. Based on *Maryland v. King*, which of the following would most likely make the entry of Blake's DNA profile into a national database unlawful?

A. Formal charges were never filed against Blake, because the prosecutor failed to establish probable cause for the arrest.
B. Blake pled not guilty and was acquitted at trial of the robbery.
C. No weapon or other dangerous instrument was found on Blake's person at the time of arrest.
D. Blake had no prior criminal record.

ANALYSIS.   This problem explores the scope of the Supreme Court's holding in *Maryland v. King*. Blake was mistakenly arrested for robbery. Because robbery is a serious felony, *King*'s reasoning applies to it. In fact, robbery was among the "crimes of violence" included in the Maryland statute.

Blake's lack of a criminal record and the police's failure to find any weapon or dangerous instrument on his person at the time of arrest might benefit Blake's defense to robbery charges, but they have no bearing on the state's authority to collect a DNA sample from him. That authority stems from the arrest itself. **C** and **D** are, therefore, wrong.

If Blake was acquitted of the robbery by a jury, the Maryland statute requires that the DNA sample be destroyed. That does not mean, however, that its entry into the database after the arraignment but before the acquittal was unlawful. Justice Scalia emphasizes this very fact in his dissent, criticizing the use of DNA evidence from individuals later proven to be innocent. **B** is wrong.

The prosecutor's failure to establish probable cause is another matter entirely. In upholding the Maryland law, the Court emphasized that no arrestee's DNA would be included in the database unless probable cause for the arrest had been established (or consent obtained). If Blake prevailed in a probable cause hearing, formal charges would not be supported and his DNA could not be entered into the database. **A** is the correct answer.

E.   The Closer

QUESTION 5. Wedding bell blues.   As soon as the grand jury issues an indictment for Shlomo's arrest on racketeering charges, Assistant U.S. Attorney Abigail radios Officer Lisa to arrest him. Lisa finds out that Shlomo has just left his home in New York to drive to Boston for a family wedding. As Shlomo enters the interstate, Lisa and her partner Ronnie pull him over and place him under arrest. Lisa orders Shlomo out of his car and, after declaring that he is under arrest, Lisa searches Shlomo's person, finding six packets of heroin inside his wallet each containing the same label: "for delivery in Boston."

Lisa places Shlomo in handcuffs in the back of the squad car, where Ronnie is sitting. Lisa then searches Shlomo's vehicle, finding two more packets of heroin under the front floor mat on the driver's side. Lisa then rejoins Ronnie in the squad car and they transport Shlomo to the county jail for booking. Shlomo's car is towed to the impound lot where Officer Mae conducts an inventory search of the vehicle. Three more packets of heroin are found in the inside of the rear passenger hubcap.

Departmental regulations allow inventory searches of "the interior cabin and all other visible areas of the vehicle." If Shlomo challenges the seizures of all the heroin packets, he will likely prevail:

A. As to those found in his wallet only.
B. As to those found inside the vehicle only.
C. As to those found in the hubcap only.
D. As to those found inside the vehicle and in the hubcap only.
E. As to all of them.

ANALYSIS. This closer reviews the three warrantless searches discussed in this chapter. **A** has Lisa searching Shlomo's wallet incident to arrest and finding heroin inside. It is immaterial that the crime for which Shlomo was arrested, racketeering, does not suggest the presence of readily destructible evidence. The defendant's offense in *Robinson*, driving on a suspended license, is similar in this respect and did not require the suppression of the evidence found in Robinson's wallet. In the custodial arrest context, the Court eschewed case-by-case scrutiny. Where, as here, the search takes place in an area within the reach of the arrestee, it is presumptively lawful.

In *Belton* and *Gant*, the Court extended to automobiles its preference for bright-line standards in the context of searches incident to arrest. Officers may search anywhere within the passenger cabin, so the floor mat is fair game. However, Shlomo is "secured" in the squad car when Lisa searches his vehicle, and she is not likely to find evidence of racketeering, the crime for which Shlomo was arrested, inside his car. Therefore, Lisa's actions are unconstitutional as a search incident to arrest under *Gant*.

However, Lisa's discovery inside Shlomo's wallet of six packets of heroin to be delivered in Boston provides probable cause to believe drugs may be located elsewhere in his car. Thus, under the automobile exception discussed in Chapter 11, she may search the entire vehicle without a warrant. (Remember: A fact pattern may implicate more than one warrant clause exception!) Therefore, the packets found under the floor mat are admissible.

We are left, then, with the search of the hubcap. Inventory searches are valid if they fall within the scope of reasonable departmental regulations. While the regulations appear reasonable on their face, Mae's search exceeds the scope of what they authorize. Hubcaps are not in the interior cabin of the car, nor are their contents otherwise visible to the naked eye.

For the foregoing reasons, **C** is the correct answer.

Cornwell's Picks

1. Arresting developments	**E**
2. Car trouble	**D**
3. Protecting people and property in Podunk	**B**
4. Summertime sadness	**A**
5. Wedding bell blues	**C**

13

Consent, Plain View, and Special Needs

I n some contexts, not only do police not need to obtain a warrant, an officer may need little proof of wrongdoing, if any, to justify a search. This is especially true where the government demonstrates "special needs," apart from law enforcement, that support a necessity to invade an individual's privacy. We will address this increasingly important doctrine at the end of the chapter. We begin by discussing two additional exceptions: consent and plain view.

A. Consent

If an individual gives police officers permission to search his or her person or effects, the necessity for a warrant vanishes. Moreover, an officer need not suspect an individual of any wrongdoing before asking for consent to search. Officers are free to ask any individual for consent to search, provided an individual is not unlawfully detained for the purpose of obtaining consent.

1. General Principles

For consent to be valid, it must be voluntary. The essence of voluntariness is freedom from duress or coercion on the part of law enforcement. An officer's failure to inform a detainee of his or her right to refuse consent will not frustrate the validity of the consent provided the "totality of the circumstances" suggests that consent to the search was freely given. *Schneckloth v. Bustamonte*, 412 U.S. 218 (1973).

With respect to a residence occupied by more than one person, consent to search may be given by anyone with common authority over the area searched. Thus, if a couple shares a bedroom, the consent of either party is sufficient; an officer need not obtain consent from both. *United States v. Matlock*, 415 U.S. 174 (1974).

If consent is obtained from an individual who lacks proper authority, the fruits of that search are nonetheless admissible if the officer conducting the search reasonably believed that the party providing consent had the authority to do so; in such circumstances, the "apparent authority" of the party providing consent validates the warrantless entry. *Illinois v. Rodriguez*, 497 U.S. 177 (1990).

QUESTION 1. What's cookin'?   Officer Allen was convinced that the house at 55 Speed Road contained a methamphetamine lab operated by Rusty. Allen knew that Rusty lived in the house with his wife and elderly mother. Because the mother rarely left the house, Allen had never seen her.

One day, while conducting surveillance, Allen saw Rusty leave. Five minutes later, Allen saw an elderly woman enter the unlocked house carrying a grocery bag. Allen approached the house and rang the doorbell. When the elderly woman answered, Allen identified himself as a police officer and politely asked for permission to search the premises for "evidence of wrongdoing." "Well," she replied nervously, "I suppose that would be alright." Allen then walked through the kitchen and discovered a small methamphetamine lab in an adjacent pantry.

As it turns out, the elderly woman was not Rusty's mother. She was a neighbor who had brought Rusty some fresh vegetables from her backyard garden. If Rusty challenges the search of his home, he will likely:

A. Succeed, because the neighbor lacked authority to consent to the search.
B. Succeed, if the neighbor did not know she could refuse Allen's request.
C. Succeed, because the neighbor appeared nervous.
D. Fail, since it was reasonable for Allen to think that the woman was Rusty's mother.
E. Fail, because Allen did not intimidate the neighbor.

ANALYSIS.   In evaluating the success *vel non* of Rusty's challenge to the consent provided by his neighbor, we can start by eliminating **B**. The U.S. Supreme Court has stated that an individual's lack of knowledge that she has the right to refuse consent is not dispositive; it is simply one among many factors to be considered in determining the validity of consent. Likewise, the fact that the neighbor appeared nervous is beside the point if her anxiety is not the product of duress or coercion by Allen. **C**, therefore, is wrong.

A, **D**, and **E**, on the other hand, all correctly state relevant principles of law. Consent is invalid if it is obtained coercively; thus, Allen's polite demeanor suggests that the neighbor granted him access voluntarily and thus permissibly (**E**). However, while she may have acted voluntarily, the neighbor lacked common authority over the premises; thus she could not validly consent to the search (**A**).

The neighbor's lack of "actual" authority to consent does not, however, invalidate the search if Allen's erroneous reliance on her "apparent" authority was reasonable. There are facts that support this conclusion: First, Allen knows that Rusty's mother lives in the house, but he has never seen her. He might reasonably assume, therefore, that an elderly woman entering the house without knocking is Rusty's mother. Second, the neighbor answers the door and grants Allen permission to search—conduct that would be considered unusual, to say the least, for non-residents. In light of these considerations, Allen was justified in relying on the grant of permission without further inquiry into the elderly woman's authority to consent.

D is the best answer.

2. Disagreeing Co-tenants

As discussed above, any individual with common authority over the area searched may provide consent. However, if co-tenants disagree regarding consent to search areas over which they share dominion and control, the objecting party prevails. *Georgia v. Randolph*, 547 U.S. 103 (2006). However, for the co-tenant's objection to govern, she or he must be present at the time of the search. Thus, in *Fernandez v. California*, 571 U.S. 292 (2014), the defendant's objection to the search of his home did not negate the consent of his live-in girlfriend since, at the time of the search, Fernandez had been arrested and removed from the home.

When a consent search occurs after an actual or potential objector is removed from the home, consent is undermined only if the removal was not objectively reasonable. Thus, since there was probable cause to arrest Fernandez for assaulting his girlfriend, his removal was proper and his girlfriend's subsequent consent to search the apartment was valid.

QUESTION 2. Less than ecstatic. Officer Harry of the Setonia police department has received an anonymous tip that Sandy is selling ecstasy out of her apartment. Sandy shares the apartment with a college classmate, Beth. Harry wants to search the apartment, but he is afraid Sandy won't consent to the search. Later that day, Harry discovers that Sandy has accumulated $550 worth of unpaid parking tickets. There is a Setonia statute that authorizes police to arrest anyone who has accumulated parking violations in excess of $500. While the police department has never enforced the law against anyone with less than $1,000 of unpaid fines, Harry decides to make an exception in Sandy's case. He goes to her apartment and, when Sandy answers the door, Harry places her under arrest for the $550 of unpaid citations. After taking her to the station house for booking, he returns to the apartment and obtains consent to search it from Beth. In a medicine cabinet in a shared bathroom, Harry finds a bottle labeled "Sandy's ecstasy." If Sandy claims that Beth's consent to search was invalid, she will:

A. Prevail, because no one else in Setonia had been arrested under these circumstances.
B. Prevail, because the arrest was motivated by Harry's desire to remove her from the apartment.
C. Fail, because Sandy violated the law for which she was arrested.
D. Fail, because Sandy had never told Beth or a police officer that she objected to the search.

ANALYSIS. This question applies the Supreme Court's decisions in *Randolph* and *Fernandez* re the validity of consent when co-tenants disagree. In our problem, Officer Harry obtains consent to search from Beth after arresting her roommate, Sandy, and thereby removing Sandy from the apartment. Harry expected Sandy to disagree, since she was selling ecstasy out of the apartment.

Answer **A** would invalidate the consent because the Setonia police department had never applied the statute under which Sandy was arrested to others in the same situation. The fact that others had not been arrested does not undermine Harry's authority to arrest Sandy on this occasion. Her conduct clearly violated the law, which justified Harry's decision to place her under arrest. **A** is wrong.

B is incorrect for similar reasons. Harry's motivation for arresting Sandy is irrelevant. As the *Fernandez* majority noted, an officer's subjective intent is very rarely relevant in the Fourth Amendment context, and it is not relevant here. All that matters is that the arrest is objectively reasonable, which it is, for the reasons discussed above.

D would dismiss Sandy's claim because she had never actually voiced her objection to the search before it took place. This is also irrelevant. Even if Sandy had previously told Beth or a police officer that she did not consent to a search of the apartment, this objection would not preclude Beth from overriding the objection if Sandy was not present at the time of the search.

C is the correct answer. Sandy's violation of the unpaid parking violation law provided an objectively reasonable basis for the arrest. Once Sandy was legitimately removed from the premises, Harry could validly obtain consent to search from Beth, which he did.

B.   Plain View

The plain view doctrine permits police officers to seize criminal evidence that they come upon in the course of a lawful investigation. For example, if an officer is lawfully searching for counterfeit currency in a banker's office and, in the course of the search, finds drug paraphernalia, he or she may seize the drug evidence as instrumentalities of crime.

While the officers need not discover the evidence inadvertently, they must have lawful access both to the place from which the item can be plainly seen and to the object itself. In addition, the incriminating nature of the object must be immediately apparent to the officer who discovers it. See generally *Horton v. California*, 496 U.S. 128 (1990). The police may not manipulate the item in any way to determine its criminal nature; even slight movement is impermissible for this purpose. See *Arizona v. Hicks*, 480 U.S. 321 (1987).

QUESTION 3. "Shear" revenge.   The police are investigating the death of Marjorie, whom the coroner determined was killed by a blow to the head with a sharp object. The investigation has focused on Marjorie's next-door neighbor, Sally, who had previously threatened Marjorie's life based on Sally's belief that Marjorie was having an affair with Sally's husband. The police have obtained a search warrant for Sally's house, authorizing them to search all interior rooms for any tangible evidence linking Sally to Marjorie's murder.

When Officer Sal executes the warrant, Sally and her husband are vacationing in the Bahamas. In searching the couple's bedroom, Sal discovers, in a dresser drawer, a diamond necklace similar to the one reported as missing from Marjorie's home at the time of the murder. When Sal moves the necklace to search the back of the drawer, its heart-shaped pendant turns over revealing an inscription with the name "Marjorie." Sal seizes the necklace.

Continuing on to the back of the house, Sal sees pruning shears outside on the patio beneath an awning. In the sunlight, Sal notices that the shears appear to have dried blood on them. He seizes them. As expected, the blood is Marjorie's, as is the diamond necklace. Sally has filed a motion to suppress both the pruning shears and the necklace. She will likely:

A. Fail as to both.
B. Prevail as to the pruning shears only.
C. Prevail as to the necklace only.
D. Prevail as to both.

ANALYSIS. The key to answering this question correctly is to remember the three requirements for plain view: lawful access to the place and to the item searched, and the item's criminal nature must be immediately apparent. The diamond necklace was found in a dresser drawer inside the couple's bedroom. Because the search warrant covered the entire interior of the house, Sal was justified in entering the bedroom. Once inside, he was authorized to search anywhere he might find tangible evidence linking Sally to the murder. Because a dresser drawer may contain relevant evidence, Sal was justified in searching it. When he did, he saw the necklace. He can seize it if, and only if, its criminal nature was immediately apparent. This is where the analysis gets tricky.

When Sal first opened the drawer, he suspected that the necklace might be Marjorie's, but it would be a stretch to conclude that it was "immediately apparent" that the item was stolen. There is no indication that Sally has a history of thievery. She may herself own a diamond necklace that she has placed in her dresser drawer for safekeeping. It is, therefore, only after Sal moves the necklace and discovers that it is engraved with Marjorie's name that his suspicions are confirmed sufficiently to justify the seizure of the necklace.

This physical manipulation of the necklace does not, however, remove the search from the purview of the plain view doctrine. While police officers may not move an item to determine if it is contraband, they may move it for other, legitimate reasons—for example, to gain access to areas or items that are blocked by the presence of the item in question. Thus, it was permissible for Sal to move the necklace to enable his search of the back of the drawer. Once the necklace was relocated for this purpose, the inscription became visible, thereby justifying its seizure as an instrumentality of crime.

The seizure of the pruning shears presents different challenges. When Sal spots them, he is lawfully standing inside the house, looking out onto the patio. From this vantage point, he sees what appears to be dried blood on the shears. The warrant, however, authorizes a search of the *inside* of the house only. Thus, Sal lacks the authority to search the patio. While sighting the bloodstained shears would clearly provide the probable cause necessary to obtain a second warrant, Sal seizes the shears before obtaining one. While exigency may obviate the need for a second warrant in certain circumstances, the present facts do not support the application of this exception. The occupants of the house are out of town and are thus unable to remove, or attempt to remove, the evidence. Also, because it is sunny and the shears are protected by an awning overhead, rain will not wash away the blood in the time it would take to obtain a warrant in person or by telephone.

Remember that evidence seized under the plain view doctrine need not relate to the crime that justifies the search. Therefore, the fact that Sal is searching for evidence relating to Marjorie's murder does not preclude his authority to seize the necklace, even though its theft may have had nothing to do with the murder. The converse is likewise true. The fact that the bloody shears provide evidence directly relevant to the crime under investigation does not relax in any way the application of the doctrine; all three requirements must be satisfied. In the case of the shears, they are not.

The correct answer is **B**.

C. The "Special Needs" Doctrine

The U.S. Supreme Court has recognized that the state may have "special needs" that eliminate the need for a warrant. In these circumstances, the search satisfies the Fourth Amendment if it is reasonable both at its inception and in its scope. The "special needs" doctrine was introduced in the 1985 case of *New Jersey v. TLO*, 469 U.S. 325, where the Court held that public school officials did not need a warrant to search a student's purse if they reasonably believed that she was violating school rules pertaining to smoking.

In later cases, the Court recognized special needs in a variety of contexts, including: sobriety checkpoints, *Michigan Dept. of State Police v. Sitz*, 496 U.S. 444 (1990); toxicological testing of railroad employees following impact accidents or incidents resulting in a fatality, *Skinner v. Railway Labor Executives' Ass'n*, 489 U.S. 602 (1989); drug testing of customs officials, *Treasury Employees v. Von Raab*, 489 U.S. 656 (1989); and public school children participating in extracurricular activities, *Board of Ed. of Indep. Sch. Dist. No. 92 v. Earls*, 536 U.S. 822 (2002). In evaluating the constitutionality of drug-testing policies, the Court balances a number of factors: the nature of the privacy interest, the "character" of the intrusion, the "nature and immediacy" of the government's concern, and "the efficacy of [the means used] for meeting it." *Vernonia School Dist. 47J v. Acton*, 515 U.S. 646 (1995). While the Court has required evidence of the need for the drug testing policy, it has not required "a demonstrated problem of drug abuse" in the target population. *Earls, supra*.

In finding special needs, the Court has required that the search be motivated by a concern for safety and/or security, rather than the desire to detect evidence of "ordinary wrongdoing." As such, the Court refused to apply the doctrine where state officials engaged in suspicionless searches of vehicles to interdict unlawful drugs. See *City of Indianapolis v. Edmond*, 531 U.S. 32 (2000). The Court also disallowed drug tests of pregnant women suspected of using cocaine; positive findings could result in arrest and prosecution. *Ferguson v. City of Charleston*, 532 U.S. 67 (2001). Finally, the Court rejected the suspicionless drug testing of candidates for elective office where the state's justification for the practice was purely symbolic—that is, to appear "tough on drugs." *Chandler v. Miller*, 520 U.S. 305 (1997).

QUESTION 4. Sadness at Happyville High. Rich and Megan, both seniors, are co-presidents of the Happyville High School's Future Bride and Groom Club of America. The Club competes against other schools in contests to see which couples know each other best. While unaware of any drug problem at the school, the principal orders random drug tests of all club members to ensure that its student representatives to other schools are "drug free." When producing a urine sample, students are accompanied in the bathroom by a same-sex monitor to ensure the integrity of the process. Students are permitted, however, to close the door of the stall while producing the samples.

After Rich's most recent sample tests positive for cocaine, he is kicked off the team, suspended for a week, and required to engage in drug counseling with the school's guidance counselor. Disappointed and dismayed, Rich decides to challenge the constitutionality of the policy. He will likely:

A. Prevail, because the school's justification for the policy is inadequate.
B. Prevail, because monitors accompanied him into the bathroom.
C. Prevail, because the school used the results of his test to punish him.
D. Prevail, because there is no history of drug use by members of the club.
E. Fail.

ANALYSIS. In evaluating the constitutionality of a drug-testing policy, the Court has required that the state's justification outweigh the privacy infringement of those subjected to it. In making this determination, the justices have examined the method in which samples are collected, the state's purported need for the policy, and the state's use of the information gleaned through testing.

In this instance, a monitor accompanies individuals into the bathroom while they produce the samples. This is a perfectly reasonable, and common, practice designed to ensure that those tested do not substitute another person's sample for their own. The privacy infringement is minimized, moreover, because the subjects can retreat behind the walls of a stall while producing the sample. For these reasons, **B** is wrong.

The policy's underlying purpose cannot be to collect evidence for use in a criminal prosecution. If this were permitted, non-law-enforcement personnel would be able to function as police officers without the necessity of warrants supported by probable cause. School officials may, however, severely discipline students who fail drug tests. Indeed, it would be odd if they did not! **C** is wrong.

In justifying their policy, school officials need not prove that there is a drug "problem" among members of the affected group. They must, however, demonstrate some need for the policy. Here, in the absence of any report of a drug "problem" at the school, the principal claims that it is necessary to ensure that its student representatives are drug free. This rationale would logically apply to any individual student or student groups that represent themselves as affiliated with Happyville High School. As such, this justification is essentially symbolic, much like the State of Georgia's mandatory drug testing of all candidates for statewide office. Because the policy is unrelated to any safety or security needs, it is unconstitutional.

A is the correct answer.

D.   The Closer

QUESTION 5. Sportin' and snortin'.   Amanda, the principal of a suburban public high school, was alarmed when a member of the swim team, Alex, admitted to using cocaine before a meet. Amanda became even more concerned when Alex reported that he knew of at least two other members of the team who routinely used illegal drugs. The following day, Amanda instituted a random drug-testing policy for all school athletic teams.

The first day the policy went into effect, Rachel and Sarah, who were on the racquetball team, were randomly chosen for testing. To emphasize the seriousness of the policy, Amanda herself monitored the tests. Sarah went first, producing a urine sample inside the bathroom stall. After she left, Rachel entered the stall and noticed Sarah's handbag on the floor. On her way out of the stall, Rachel picked it up to return it to Sarah. Amanda asked if she could search "her bag." Immediately upon opening the purse, Amanda spotted a marijuana cigarette nestled inside a tissue. She seized the cigarette. Rachel then told Amanda that the bag belonged to Sarah.

Rachel and Amanda left the bathroom and found Sarah waiting for Rachel at the end of the hallway. Sticking out of Sarah's rear pocket was a pipe, which Amanda recognized as being the sort used to smoke marijuana. Amanda seized it. Based on the foregoing, which of the following statements is most accurate?

A. The drug-testing policy is likely to be found unconstitutional, since there was no evidence of drug use on the racquetball team.
B. Rachel's consent to the search of the handbag will be found invalid, since the purse belonged to Sarah.
C. Even if Rachel's consent is invalid, Sarah will be unsuccessful in suppressing the marijuana cigarette, since it was discovered in plain view.
D. Sarah will be unsuccessful in suppressing the pipe, since it was discovered in plain view.

ANALYSIS. This closer reviews the three warrant clause exceptions covered in this chapter: consent, plain view, and special needs.

Amanda instituted the drug-testing policy for all athletes after learning of cocaine use among certain members of the swim team. Her decision to apply the policy to athletes who are neither personally nor collectively suspected of drug-related misconduct does not render the policy unconstitutional. Remember, the random drug-testing policy upheld in *Earls* applied to students who engaged in a wide range of extracurricular activities where, at most, there was no suspicion whatsoever of drug use among members. At least Amanda limited her policy to athletes. **A** is wrong.

Turning to the handbag, Rachel lacked *actual* authority to consent to its search, since it did not belong to her. Her consent is still valid, however, if Amanda reasonably believed that the bag was Rachel's. Because consent based on *apparent* authority is valid, **B** states an incorrect principle of law.

For the seizure of the cigarette to fall within the plain view doctrine, Amanda would need to immediately recognize it as contraband after lawfully accessing it. In this instance, Amanda does recognize the item as illegal but only after opening the purse. If Rachel's consent is invalid, Amanda would lack authority to enter the purse in the first place; thus, the plain view doctrine fails. **C** is wrong.

The correct response is **D**. Since the pipe was in plain view, and Amanda immediately recognized it as drug paraphernalia, its seizure is lawful.

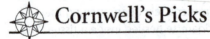 Cornwell's Picks

1. What's cookin'?	D
2. Less than ecstatic	C
3. "Shear" revenge	B
4. Sadness at Happyville High	A
5. Sportin' and snortin'	D

14

Lesser Intrusions on Liberty: *Terry* Stops

CHAPTER OVERVIEW
A. Investigating Suspicious Behavior
B. Informants' Tips and Reasonable Suspicion
C. The Use of Criminal Profiles in Establishing Reasonable Suspicion
D. Mistakes of Law and Reasonable Suspicion
E. Seizure of Persons
F. The "Brevity" Requirement
G. The Closer
✦ Cornwell's Picks

A. Investigating Suspicious Behavior

While the privacy infringement associated with a lengthy detention or an invasive search of one's person ordinarily requires a warrant supported by probable cause, lesser intrusions are not held to the same standard. In the seminal case of *Terry v. Ohio*, 392 U.S. 1 (1968), the U.S. Supreme Court first addressed this issue where police officers stopped and then patted the outer clothing of individuals believed to be engaging in suspicious activity. At the time they conducted this "stop-and-frisk," the police lacked probable cause to make an arrest. Nonetheless, in balancing the limited nature of the infringement of the defendants' privacy and liberty interests against the officers' interest in investigating potential criminal activity, the Court found the officers' conduct to be consistent with Fourth Amendment requirements.

While the Court's analysis focused on the lawfulness of the "frisk," subsequent decisions have credited *Terry* with authorizing the brief, investigative detention of individuals in the absence of probable cause, provided an officer "has a reasonable suspicion supported by articulable facts that criminal activity may be afoot." *United States v. Sokolow,* 490 U.S. 1 (1989). For example, in *United States v. Cortez*, 449 U.S. 411 (1981), the defendant argued that federal officers were not justified in stopping his vehicle near the Mexican border on the suspicion that he was smuggling aliens into the country. The Court disagreed. Using a "totality of the circumstances" test, the justices found that the panoply of factors considered by the border agents created a "particularized and objective basis for suspecting the particular person stopped of criminal activity."

QUESTION 1. Boob-tube baby.   Hyacinth told Police Officer Daisy that Hyacinth's neighbors, Rose and Violet, were planning to steal a portable television set from a warehouse on Main Street after closing hours that night. While walking her beat that night at 1:00 A.M., Daisy noticed two women fitting the descriptions of Rose and Violet walking down Main Street two blocks from the warehouse and pushing a baby carriage. When Daisy asked what they were doing out so late, they replied that they were taking the baby for a walk because he could not sleep. They said their names were Doris and Louise, but they had left their apartment without identification.

When Daisy asked to see the baby, they nervously said no, explaining that it might wake him and that they had to leave. Daisy said that they needed to answer a few more questions. At that moment, the blanket fell off the "baby" revealing a television. Daisy then placed the women under arrest. If Rose and Violet claim that the stop violated the Fourth Amendment, they will:

A. Succeed, because taking a baby for a walk is not unusual.
B. Succeed, because they did not attempt to flee from Daisy.
C. Fail, because it is likely that they were engaging in criminal activity.
D. Fail, because Daisy had reasoned grounds for detaining them.

ANALYSIS.   To navigate this problem successfully, it is important to keep two considerations in mind: First, reasonable suspicion is a totality-of-the-circumstances test; and, second, it requires less than probable cause. When Daisy stopped Rose and Violet, Daisy had received information specifically implicating them in a criminal plan. Rose and Violet's presence near the warehouse late at night was consistent with the tipster's information and was somewhat unusual on its face, since there was no commercial activity going on at that time. As such, it was reasonable for Daisy to stop the women to investigate her suspicions. Their seeming use of aliases, coupled with their nervousness, justified further inquiry and did not exceed the parameters of *Terry* since Daisy had, up until that time, detained the women quite briefly. In sum, Daisy's conduct did not violate the Fourth Amendment.

Because Daisy's conduct satisfied constitutional requirements, **A** and **B** are wrong. Taking a baby for a walk is not unusual in general, but doing so at

1:00 A.M., near a warehouse that a neighbor said you planned to burglarize, is far more suspicious than a daytime stroll through a residential neighborhood. In addition, while a suspect's flight from an officer attempting to question her raises suspicion, it is not necessary to justify a stop where other indicia are present.

In choosing between **C** and **D**, you must think carefully about which better captures the applicable standard of proof. As we discussed in Chapter 8, **C**'s preponderance-of-the-evidence language approximates the probable cause "fair probability" standard. By contrast, **D**'s reference to "reasoned grounds" is more akin to the reasonable suspicion standard applicable in the *Terry* context.

D is the correct answer.

B.   Informants' Tips and Reasonable Suspicion

Chapter 8 discussed the use of informants' tips in furnishing probable cause. Information from informants is equally useful in providing reasonable suspicion. Because the reasonable suspicion threshold is lower than that of probable cause, the Court has been especially mindful of the need to ensure the reliability of such information to prevent unwarranted interference with individuals' Fourth Amendment rights.

The Court has issued three major decisions delineating the evidentiary value of tips in the *Terry* stop context. In the first, *Alabama v. White*, 496 U.S. (1990), an anonymous tipster reported that a woman who was transporting cocaine would drive from a particular apartment building to a particular motel in a brown Plymouth station wagon with a broken right taillight. While deeming this a "close case," the majority held that the officers' corroboration of a number of these details made the tip reliable enough to create reasonable suspicion of criminal activity. By accurately predicting future behavior, the tipster demonstrated "a special familiarity with respondent's affairs," which in turn implied that the tipster had "access to reliable information about that individual's illegal activities."

In the second case, *Florida v. J.L.*, 529 U.S. 299 (2000), an anonymous informant reported that a young black male in a plaid shirt standing at a bus stop was carrying a gun. The tipster supplied no additional information about how he knew about the gun or the suspect's affairs, and the tip included no predictions of future behavior that could be corroborated to assess the informant's credibility. As such, this "bare bones" tip did not establish reasonable suspicion.

In the third case, *Navarette v. California*, 572 U.S. 393 (2014), an officer stopped a driver on suspicion of drunk driving after a 911 caller reported that a vehicle matching his had run her off the road. Deeming this a "close case" like *Alabama v. White*, the Court found that the tip contained sufficient indicia of reliability to justify the stop. The majority emphasized the tipster's purported "eyewitness knowledge" of dangerous driving; the contemporaneity of the incident and the tipster's report; and the disinclination of 911 callers to make false reports, due to the criminal nature of such conduct. Given the reliability of the tip, the stop was justified since the alleged "erratic behaviors" of the driver "are strongly correlated with drunk driving."

QUESTION 2. Going my way?   Campbell has disliked his law school classmate, Noreen, ever since she earned a better grade than he did in Criminal Law. To "get her back," he plants a small baggie of cocaine inside her wallet at the end of the school day when she is not looking. Immediately thereafter, Noreen leaves the law school and heads toward the parking lot. As she does, Campbell calls the local police station and anonymously reports that he just saw a drunk woman fitting Noreen's description get into her car in the law school parking lot. Campbell describes Noreen's car. A marked police car patrolling in the vicinity, driven by Officer Aaron, is alerted immediately and spots Noreen's car as it is leaving the parking lot. Aaron follows Noreen for five minutes along local roads and does not observe any erratic driving or traffic infractions. Nonetheless, he decides to pull her over. As he approaches the window, Noreen opens her wallet to retrieve her license. As she does, the baggie of cocaine becomes immediately visible to Aaron. He seizes it and arrests Noreen for possessing the drug. If Noreen claims that Aaron lacked reasonable suspicion to stop her vehicle, is she likely to succeed?

A. No, because Campbell claimed first-hand knowledge of her behavior.
B. No, because Aaron could have pulled her over as soon as she exited the parking lot.
C. Yes, because Campbell planted the cocaine in her wallet.
D. Yes, because she did not drive erratically when surveilled by Aaron.

ANALYSIS.   This question explores the extent to which police officers can rely on informants' tips to furnish reasonable suspicion. While our tipster does not identify himself to the police, we know that he is a law school classmate of the defendant who has set her up due to simmering, grade-based resentment. He falsely tells the police that she is driving drunk so they will pull her over and discover a baggie of cocaine that he has planted in her wallet. His plan succeeds.

Answer **C** would invalidate the search because Campbell planted the cocaine discovered by the officer. Sadly for Noreen, this is irrelevant in evaluating the legality of the stop, which is concerned solely with whether reasonable suspicion existed at the time Aaron pulled her car over. **B** is wrong for similar reasons. That Aaron could have pulled Noreen over when she exited the parking lot is beside the point; we must consider whether he retained that authority when he decided to do so five minutes later.

D would deem the stop unlawful because Aaron did not observe any erratic or unlawful behavior during the five minutes that he followed Noreen's car before pulling her over. While surprising, her ability to drive safely during this period does not, in and of itself, extinguish reasonable suspicion. In fact, faced with very similar facts in *Navarette*, the Court commented that one would expect that "the appearance of a marked police car would inspire more careful driving for a time." **D** is incorrect.

By contrast, Campbell's claim that he personally witnessed Noreen enter her car in a state of intoxication is exactly the kind of first-hand knowledge that enhanced the tipster's reliability in *Navarette*. In addition, like the 911 caller, Campbell's call to the police station appeared to be substantially contemporaneous with his witnessing the event. Finally, unlike the "erratic driving" tip in *Navarette*, the behavior reported by Campbell was directly linked to the public scourge of drunk driving. **A** is the correct answer.

C. The Use of Criminal Profiles in Establishing Reasonable Suspicion

The use of criminal profiles has been a particularly thorny issue for the U.S. Supreme Court. The justices first grappled with the issue in *United States v. Sokolow, supra,* where DEA agents stopped the defendant upon his arrival at Honolulu International Airport on suspicion of drug trafficking. The agents identified a number of factors that informed their suspicion and acknowledged that these factors also fit a "drug-courier profile" used by the DEA. The Court rejected Sokolow's argument that the existence of the profile had any bearing on the case. "The fact that the factors may be set forth in a 'profile,'" Chief Justice Rehnquist wrote, "does not somehow detract from their evidentiary significance as seen by a trained agent." See also *United States v. Arvizu,* 534 U.S. 266 (2002) (while defendants' conduct near a border crossing may appear innocent to an ordinary citizen, when viewed in its totality it may provide reasonable suspicion of alien smuggling to a trained INS officer).

The Court revisited profiles in *Illinois v. Wardlow,* 528 U.S. 119 (2000), where the issue was presented in a different way. In *Wardlow,* the Illinois Attorney General urged a bright-line rule that would allow the temporary detention of anyone who fled at the sight of a police officer. The Court refused to embrace such a rule but upheld the stop in question, noting that the unprovoked flight in this instance occurred in a high-crime area known for narcotics trafficking. The majority noted that officers must make "commonsense judgments and inferences about human behavior" in evaluating reasonable suspicion. The officer here did no more.

QUESTION 3. **The case of the suburban streetwalker.**   Citizens in a wealthy suburban town complained to the local police department that a young woman dressed in "inappropriate, provocative clothing" loitered most nights on a corner of Main Street near the entrance to the interstate. They further reported seeing her approaching cars, some of which she would enter before the car drove off, only to return later in the evening.

Police Officer Rick decided to set up surveillance over a two-night period. He did, in fact, observe a woman, approximately 20 to 25 years old, standing at the location indicated in the complaints, wearing a miniskirt and high boots. He also confirmed that she would sometimes approach cars stopped at the traffic light and would, on occasion, enter the cars, only to return approximately 30 minutes later. After concluding that her conduct satisfied four of the six factors in the police department's prostitution profile, Rick approached her for questioning. Upon seeing him, she ran down Main Street in the opposite direction. He caught up to her two blocks later and removed her to the police car for questioning. The suspect, Margarita, told Rick that she was an illegal immigrant who had fled from him because she feared deportation. Were Rick's actions justified?

A. Yes, because first-hand observation confirmed that Margarita's conduct at the street corner fit most factors in the profile, established by the police department, for prostitution.

B. Yes, because, viewed as whole, Margarita's conduct suggested criminal activity.

C. No, because Rick did not witness any illegal conduct and Margarita's conduct fit only some of the factors in the police profile.

D. No, because the unprovoked flight did not take place in a high-crime area.

E. No, because Margarita fled for reasons other than those Rick believed motivated her flight.

ANALYSIS.   This question couples the use of criminal profiles with the quantum of proof necessary to establish the reasonable suspicion necessary for an investigative stop. Here, Rick receives citizens' complaints about a woman's behavior. Before detaining a woman fitting the description in the complaints, Rick confirms, through first-hand observation, that her conduct suggests that she is a prostitute. He uses the police department's prostitution profile to inform his conclusions, noting that the woman's behavior fits a majority of the factors listed. When he approaches her, she flees, fearing deportation based on her status as an illegal immigrant.

In evaluating Rick's conduct, we should first place Margarita's flight in proper context for purposes of establishing the proof necessary for investigative detention. In *Wardlow*, the officer's suspicion was based on the suspect's presence in a high-crime area, coupled with flight. Here, Rick had decided to detain Margarita even before she fled, based on other factors. Because the flight preceded the detention, we may, of course, consider it, but, unlike the officer in *Wardlow*, Rick has more evidence to bolster his conclusion: Margarita's attire; her repeated loitering near the entrance to an interstate highway; her approaches to various vehicles stopped there; her entry into some of those vehicles; and her return to the same area a short time later.

Unsurprisingly, this suspicious behavior fits four of six factors in a prostitution profile created by the town's police department. While the U.S. Supreme Court has expressed concern about reflexive reliance on profiles, departments are free to use such profiles as a law enforcement tool, provided officers independently assess the extent to which the conduct of a given subject, viewed in its totality, informs their suspicions.

Considered as a whole, Margarita's conduct provides ample justification for detention, even without her flight as Rick approaches. Note that the facts do not tell us if Rick's questioning confirmed his suspicions, as this further information is irrelevant to the reasonableness of the initial stop. The permissibility of Margarita's detention turns entirely on the sufficiency of the evidence known to Rick at the time he acted, not on what he later learned that might have confirmed or dispelled his suspicions.

Based on the foregoing, **C** through **E** are necessarily wrong. Although Margarita's conduct fit only some of the factors in the profile, there is no bright-line standard as to how many, or what percentage, must be present in a given context. To provide this level of specificity would run counter, it seems, to the Court's general reluctance to focus too much attention on the use of profiling in law enforcement, which is one among many tools relied on by law enforcement in investigating behavior that is potentially criminal.

D and **E** focus on Margarita's flight. As discussed above, incidence of flight does not appear to be necessary to furnish reasonable suspicion. Inasmuch as it is, Margarita's presence in a low-crime area does not render flight irrelevant, nor does her *post hoc* explanation of why she fled, since those reasons were unknown to Rick at the time of the stop.

Both **A** and **B** are factually correct. However, **B** better identifies the relevant legal standard of reasonable suspicion based on a totality of the circumstances. **A** emphasizes the criminal profile, inappropriately suggesting that it, standing alone, may provide the requisite suspicion.

The correct answer is **B**.

D. Mistakes of Law and Reasonable Suspicion

In Chapters 9 and 13, addressing particularity and consent, respectively, we learned that reasonable mistakes of fact are compatible with Fourth Amendment principles. In *Heien v. North Carolina*, 574 U.S. 54 (2014), the

Court addressed an analogous question: whether reasonable suspicion can rest on an officer's mistake of law. In *Heien*, an officer conducted a traffic stop on the interstate after noticing that one of the brake lights on the suspect's vehicle failed to illuminate. In a subsequent consent search of the vehicle, the officer found cocaine inside a duffel bag and placed the defendant under arrest. The North Carolina Court of Appeals concluded that the officer had misinterpreted state law, which requires only one working brake light. The officer's error in turn rendered the stop "objectively unreasonable" under the Fourth Amendment in the court's view.

The U.S. Supreme Court disagreed. Mistakes of law, like mistakes of fact, do not automatically extinguish the reasonable suspicion necessary to justify traffic stops and other detentions authorized by the *Terry* doctrine. Cf. *Michigan v. DeFillippo*, 443 U.S. 31 (1979) (officers' reliance on ordinance later declared unconstitutional did not extinguish probable cause to arrest). The mistake must, however, be objectively reasonable. In this case, it was since the relevant statutory provisions relating to "stop lamps" were confusing at best, and contradictory at worst.

QUESTION 4. Texting trouble. The Setonia Motor Vehicle Code forbids drivers' use of cell phones to type or transmit a text message or an electronic-mail message while operating a motor vehicle. *All* other uses of cellphones by drivers are allowed, including: making and receiving phone calls; surfing the web; and reading driving directions and maps with GPS applications. In the course of passing a car driven by Maya on an interstate highway, Setonia Police Officer Amy saw Maya holding a cell phone in her right hand at stomach level with her head bent toward the phone. Amy concluded that Maya was texting and pulled her over. When questioned, Maya stated that she was not texting but merely reading a text sent by her sister. Amy replied that Setonia's texting-while-driving prohibition included reading texts. Before ticketing Maya for the infraction, Amy asked for permission to search the vehicle. Maya acceded to the request. The search turned up five pounds of heroin concealed in the spare tire in the car's trunk. Maya moved to suppress the heroin, arguing that Amy lacked reasonable suspicion to stop her vehicle. If the Setonia Supreme Court finds that reading texts is not prohibited by the Motor Vehicle Code, will Maya prevail?

A. Yes, because Amy could not have known whether Maya was texting based on what she observed.

B. Yes, because reading texts is not unlawful.

C. No, because when Amy observed her Maya could have been texting.

D. No, because Amy reasonably believed that the Motor Vehicle Code prohibited reading texts.

ANALYSIS. At a minimum, police officers need reasonable suspicion of unlawful conduct to justify pulling over a vehicle.[1] Officer Amy based reasonable suspicion on her belief that Maya was reading texts from her sister. However, reading texts is not prohibited under the applicable Motor Vehicle Code.

A vindicates Maya's Fourth Amendment claim based on Amy's lack of knowledge of the exact nature of Maya's conduct. The reasonable suspicion standard does not require that an officer be fully aware of a suspect's alleged unlawful behavior. It is only necessary that the officer have specific facts that suggest that an individual is violating the law. Because it misstates the applicable standard, **A** is wrong.

C would reject Maya's claim since, based on what Amy observed, Maya might have been typing or transmitting a text, which is unlawful. While this is true, Amy did not actually observe Maya engaging in unlawful activity. As such, what Amy saw was equally consistent with any number of lawful activities. Under similar facts, the U.S. Court of Appeals for the Seventh Circuit found reasonable suspicion to be lacking, noting that the "mere possibility" of unlawful use is insufficient to justify unlawful seizure and detention. See *United States v. Paniagua-Garcia*, 813 F.3d 1013 (7th Cir. 2016).

This leaves us with **B** and **D**. While merely reading texts is lawful, Maya will lose her motion if Amy's mistake of law was objectively reasonable. Here, it is not. The relevant provision is clearly limited to typing or transmitting texts, not reading them. Moreover, reading is expressly included in a number of other contexts. It would be illogical, for example, to allow reading for purposes of surfing the web but not texting. The clarity of the relevant provision also differentiates these facts from those of *Heien*, where the Court found that that the law's definition of what constituted a "stop lamp" (i.e., brake light) was inherently ambiguous. **B** is the correct answer.[2]

E.   Seizure of Persons

As the previous section illustrates, police officers may "seize" an individual under the Fourth Amendment by restraining his or her freedom of movement.

---

1. While the U.S. Supreme Court has never specified whether probable cause or reasonable suspicion is necessary to justify a traffic stop based on motor vehicle infractions, lower courts have favored the reasonable suspicion standard. See, e.g., *United States v. Stewart*, 551 F.3d 187 (9th Cir. 2009).

2. While admittedly illogical, the distinctions made in the fact pattern between reading texts and reading for other purposes while driving reflect those in effect in Indiana. See *Paniagua-Garcia*, 813 F.3d at 1013.

However, not all interactions with law enforcement qualify as seizures. In *United States v. Mendenhall*, 446 U.S. 544 (1980), the Court held that an individual is seized by a police officer only if a reasonable person would not feel "free to leave" in the given situation.

The facts of *Mendenhall* are instructive in this regard. Sylvia Mendenhall was approached by DEA agents on an airport concourse. The agents were not in uniform and displayed no weapons. They identified themselves, requested permission to see the defendant's ticket and identification, and posed questions relating to her travel plans. The Court deemed this encounter a non-seizure, concluding that Mendenhall had no "objective reason to believe that she was not free to end the conversation in the concourse and proceed on her way."

Eleven years later, the Court "clarified" the *Mendenhall* standard, noting that, where individuals claim they were seized by a show of police authority, it is not enough that they do not feel free to leave; the officer must, in addition, restrain their freedom of movement *or* the individuals must voluntarily submit to the officer's request. *California v. Hodari D.* 499 U.S. 621 (1991). Thus, where officers command a suspect to stop and she or he disregards the order, the suspect cannot claim unlawful seizure. Nor can a suspect claim seizure if police officers merely follow him or her in their car without ordering the suspect to stop, blocking his or her movement, displaying their weapons, or using the car's siren. *Michigan v. Chesternut*, 486 U.S. 567 (1988).

QUESTION 5. Fork it over.   Officer Ralph was patrolling a residential area beset by a number of nighttime burglaries. At 1:00 A.M., he saw Donny walking down an empty street alone, carrying a backpack. Ralph turned his car around and stopped fifty feet from Donny. As Ralph, carrying his nightstick, approached Donny, Donny ran. Ralph gave chase. Donny fell rounding the corner. When he hit the ground, the backpack opened, spilling silver flatware onto the pavement that later proved to have been stolen. Donny claims that Ralph seized him unlawfully. This claim:

A. Has merit, because Ralph did not have enough evidence to detain Donny.

B. Has merit, because Ralph was displaying his nightstick.

C. Lacks merit, because Ralph never ordered Donny to stop.

D. Lacks merit, because Donny was fleeing from Ralph when the backpack opened.

ANALYSIS. Whenever you confront a claim of unlawful seizure, you must start with the threshold issue: Was the defendant seized? If, and only if, you answer this question affirmatively should the analysis continue. We need not concern ourselves with the illegality of hypothetical, non-existent seizures.

When Officer Ralph turned his car around, stopped it in close proximity to Donny, and approached him with a weapon in hand, a reasonable person in Donny's shoes would most likely not feel free to leave. However, because this purported seizure is affected by a show of authority, Donny must also show that Ralph physically restrained him or that he submitted to Ralph's authority. Ralph never touched Donny; so, unless Donny submitted to Ralph's authority, there is no seizure.

When Ralph approached, Donny fled. The dislodging of the backpack from his person was the result of his stumble, not of any submission to Ralph's authority. On the contrary, Donny was actively attempting to evade Ralph at the time he fell. Plainly, Donny was not seized. Therefore, we need not consider his claim that the detention was invalid. **A** and **B** are wrong.

In choosing between **C** and **D**, it is important to analyze carefully the requirements for seizure. While a seizure does occur when an individual yields to an officer who orders him to stop, a verbal mandate is not necessary in all instances. For example, a seizure would have occurred if Donny submitted to a tacit show of authority demonstrated by the following course of conduct: Ralph's turning his car around upon seeing Donny; Ralph's alighting from the vehicle in close proximity to Donny; and Ralph's brandishing a nightstick and approaching Donny with the weapon in plain sight.

The correct answer is **D**.

F.   The "Brevity" Requirement

In allowing seizure in the absence of probable cause, *Terry* emphasized the limited nature of the infringement on liberty that it authorized. In a series of cases in the 1980s, the Court clarified the permissible temporal scope of a *Terry* stop. In *United States v. Sharpe*, 470 U.S. 675 (1985), the defendants claimed that the length of the stop, approximately twenty minutes, was indefensible under *Terry*, and thus evidence subsequently seized was inadmissible. The Court disagreed and refused to impose strict temporal limitations on *Terry* stops; the brevity inquiry focuses instead on whether police officers "reasonably" and "diligently" investigated their suspicions. In *Sharpe* they did, since any delay was caused by the evasive actions of the defendants.

Likewise, in *United States v. Montoya de Hernandez*, 473 U.S. 531 (1985), customs agents did not violate the Fourth Amendment by detaining a woman arriving from Bogotá, Colombia for sixteen hours where they had reasonable suspicion that she was an alimentary canal smuggler. As in *Sharpe*, the Court attributed the excessive length of the detention to the conduct of the defendant, not to the failure of law enforcement personnel to investigate their suspicions diligently. By contrast, in *United States v. Place*, 462 U.S. 696 (1983), the seizure of the defendant's luggage for ninety minutes at the airport while the police awaited the arrival of a canine unit was deemed unconstitutional, since the police could have averted the delay by, *inter alia*, arranging for the "sniff" while the defendant's flight was en route, since reasonable suspicion existed prior to departure.

QUESTION 6. Finding speed too slowly?   Homeland Savings & Loan was robbed by a masked man estimated to be twenty-five to thirty-five years old who was seen leaving the area in a dark green Toyota Camry. Ten minutes later, Police Officers Jamal and Sheila spotted a car fitting this description entering the interstate two miles from the bank. They pulled the car over.

The license of the driver, who was alone in the car, revealed that he was thirty-two years old and lived out of state. Asked to account for his whereabouts during the last hour, the driver replied that he had been shopping for a present for his girlfriend at Grant's, a department store downtown. While he did not buy anything, he remembered talking to a young female employee in the jewelry department about earrings. While Jamal stayed with the driver, Sheila took his license and went to Grant's to interview the store clerk.

In the meantime, Jamal summoned a canine unit. The dog arrived forty-five minutes later. As the canine unit arrived, Sheila returned and told Jamal that the clerk at Grant's confirmed the driver's presence at the store during the bank robbery. The officer who transported the dog immediately introduced the dog to the exterior of the vehicle. When the dog alerted to the trunk, Jamal searched it and found a "brick" of methamphetamine inside, which he seized.

The driver moves to suppress the drugs, claiming a violation of *Terry*'s brevity requirement. This argument will likely:

A. Succeed, because the dog was not immediately available to sniff the vehicle.

B. Succeed, because Jamal knew the driver had not robbed the bank before he initiated the search of the trunk.

C. Succeed, because Sheila's investigation took too long to complete.

D. Fail, because the U.S. Supreme Court has upheld *Terry* stops lasting far longer than this one.

E. Fail, because the driver's car matched the description of the getaway car.

ANALYSIS.   In answering this question, remember that the brevity requirement focuses on whether the police officers "reasonably" and "diligently" investigate potential criminal activity. Here, Officers Jamal and Sheila pull over a motorist whose car matches the description of one linked to a robbery that took place minutes earlier. Sheila leaves to confirm the driver's alibi that he was shopping for a gift for his girlfriend at a nearby department store. Meanwhile, Jamal calls for a canine unit that arrives just as Sheila returns to tell Jamal that the driver's alibi checks out. In the dog sniff of the outside of the vehicle that follows, the canine alerts to the trunk, which leads to Jamal's discovery of methamphetamine inside.

Answer **A** would invalidate the search based on the lack of immediate availability of the drug-sniffing canine. While the attendant delay of forty-five minutes is relatively lengthy, the U.S. Supreme Court has never held that drug-sniffing dogs must be *immediately* available to satisfy constitutional requirements. In determining whether the delay is acceptable, courts must consider the surrounding circumstances — most importantly, who bears primary responsibility for the delay, however long it may be. If the suspect's obstructionist behavior created the delay, an officer's failure to request the dog immediately will not count against him.

By the same token, U.S. Supreme Court precedent rejecting brevity challenges to far lengthier detentions (for example, sixteen hours in *Montoya de Hernandez*) does not mean that all stops of shorter duration satisfy the Fourth Amendment. What made the length of Montoya de Hernandez's detention reasonable was her refusal to agree to any intervention that would have permitted officers to investigate their suspicions more expeditiously. In our problem, by contrast, the driver cooperated fully with Officers Jamal and Sheila. Thus, it was the officers who prolonged the stop, not any misconduct on the part of the suspect. **D** is wrong.

B suggests an alternative theory: that the drugs must be suppressed because the sniff and search took place after the driver was cleared of suspicion for the robbery. First, this rationale does not fit comfortably into the analytical framework of brevity, which was the basis of the motion. Simply put, the conclusion of the robbery investigation does not mean that Jamal violated the brevity requirement by allowing a dog sniff that occurs moments later. Likewise, the fact that the driver's vehicle matched the description of the one seen leaving the scene of the robbery establishes the reasonable suspicion necessary to justify the stop, but it has nothing to do with the issue of brevity. **E** is wrong.

We are left, then, with **C**. Officers Sheila and Jamal will argue that the length of the stop was reasonable, since throughout the forty-five-minute period Sheila was diligently investigating the officers' suspicions that the driver was the masked robber. However, even if we assume that this is true, the fact that the driver bore no responsibility for the delay distinguishes our problem from the U.S. Supreme Court cases discussed above. Simply put, the Court has never held that *Terry* stops of such duration are permissible where responsibility for the delay rests entirely with the police. Accordingly, the best answer grants the driver's motion to suppress, based on the unreasonable length of Sheila's investigation.

The correct answer is **C**.

G.   The Closer

QUESTION 7. Nervous Nellie.   There have been a series of residential burglaries in Brenton, a middle-class suburban community. Officer Reggie was patrolling the targeted neighborhoods one evening at 9:00 P.M. when he saw Nellie walking briskly along a sidewalk. He followed her for two blocks and noticed that she continually looked behind her nervously as she walked. He also noticed that she was carrying a large shoulder bag and was wearing a raincoat, which struck him as odd since it had been a bright, sunny day and there was no rain in the forecast. Considered together, the bag, raincoat, and nervous demeanor made Reggie suspicious of Nellie. Her clothing and manner were, moreover, consistent with a burglar profile used by the Brenton Police Department, which included nervousness and the possession of items capable of concealing property.

Reggie stopped to question Nellie. As he approached, he asked if she would mind answering a few questions. "Sure, no problem," Nellie replied. First, upon Reggie's request, Nellie handed him her driver's license, which had an out-of-state address. Nellie then let Reggie look inside her shoulder bag, which turned up nothing out of the ordinary. Asked why she kept looking behind her, Nellie denied having done so. Asked what she did for a living, Nellie explained that she babysat the children of a family that lived in the neighborhood. She told Reggie that the family, Mr. and Mrs. Simon and their three daughters, lived around the corner at 45 Dunbar Street. Reggie knew Dunbar Street well and was certain that no house had the number 45. He then asked Nellie for the Simon's phone number, so he could call to verify her employment. She refused to provide it, commenting that she would get in trouble if she did, because the Simons are "private people" and "don't like being disturbed after dinner."

Nellie then asked to leave, claiming she had an appointment. Reggie told her she could leave as soon as he contacted the Simons and confirmed her employment. He called directory assistance, but they had no listing for a Simon on Dunbar Street. Reggie then called into the station house and asked a fellow officer to see if he could find the number and call the family to verify Nellie's employment. Growing tired, Nellie, sighing, walked to the side of the road to sit on the curb. As she sat down, a packet fell out of her coat, which Reggie immediately recognized as marijuana. He seized it. Five minutes later, Reggie's co-worker called back and reported that he had spoken to the Simons, who live at 47 Dunbar Street, and they confirmed that Nellie was their daughters' babysitter.

Will Nellie succeed in a motion to suppress the marijuana?

A. Yes, because her continued detention violated *Terry's* brevity
    requirement.
B. Yes, because the police department's use of a criminal profile in
    identifying suspicious persons was inappropriate.
C. Yes, because Nellie was, in fact, the Simons' babysitter.
D. No, because the dislodging of the packet was the product of a lawful
    detention.
E. No, because Nellie was not seized when the packet was dislodged.

ANALYSIS.   This closer explores the permissible scope of *Terry* stops. As is so often the case when analyzing fact patterns in criminal procedure, it is important to pay close attention to the sequence of events and to what the police officer knew, and did not know, at critical junctures.

In this problem, Officer Reggie, who is on the lookout for burglars, becomes suspicious of Nellie by virtue of her attire, her nervous demeanor, and her carrying of a large bag capable of concealing stolen items. While the foregoing facts provide reasonable suspicion that would allow Reggie to detain Nellie briefly for investigative purposes, their initial encounter does not, in all likelihood, constitute a seizure. Even if he was in uniform, Reggie simply asked Nellie if she was willing to answer questions, and she readily agreed to do so. Thus, as in *Mendenhall*, Nellie had no "objective reason" to believe that she was not free to leave.

While Reggie's search of Nellie's bag turns up nothing suspicious, she explains her presence in this neighborhood by referencing her employment as a babysitter for a family whose address she reports incorrectly. Nellie then declines Reggie's request for the family's phone number, which would allow him to confirm her employment. Reggie thereafter works diligently to find the number. He first calls directory assistance. When that proves unavailing, he enlists the support of a fellow officer back at the station house, who, minutes later, tracks down the number and speaks to the Simons, who verify Nellie's employment with them.

Reggie's actions do not violate *Terry's* brevity requirement, since he worked diligently to dispel his suspicions. Significantly, the delay that resulted from his difficulty in verifying Nellie's employment was her fault, not his, since she refused to provide the Simons' phone number, which forced Reggie to use alternative means of obtaining it. **A** is wrong.

Reggie's use of the criminal profile was also lawful. He did not rely on it reflexively, nor was the profile the only factor that created reasonable suspicion. The use of a profile in conjunction with specific articulable facts to form reasonable suspicion is constitutionally appropriate, and Reggie did no more here. **B** is wrong.

C is a red herring. The fact that Nellie did, in fact, work for the Simons (and presumably was not, therefore, the burglar) is irrelevant to the present analysis, which focuses on Reggie's conduct and the attendant circumstances at the time the marijuana packet fell out of Nellie's pocket. Short-term detention supported by reasonable suspicion is constitutional, whatever the final result. By the same token, detention in the absence of such suspicion is unlawful, even if the individual detained is later proven guilty of the targeted offense.

The marijuana packet fell out of Nellie's coat as she went to sit down at the curb. At this point, she had asked to leave and Reggie denied the request, requiring her to stay until he verified her employment. Because she submitted to his assertion of authority, Nellie was indeed seized at this time. **E,** therefore, is wrong.

D is the correct answer. While Nellie was seized when the marijuana became dislodged, her detention was lawful since specific, articulable facts provided the requisite reasonable suspicion. In addition, the length of the stop complied with *Terry*'s brevity requirement since, as explained above, any delay was caused not by Reggie but by Nellie's evasive actions.

Cornwell's Picks

1. Boob-tube baby	**D**
2. Going my way?	**A**
3. The case of the suburban streetwalker	**B**
4. Texting Trouble	**B**
5. Fork it over	**D**
6. Finding speed too slowly?	**C**
7. Nervous Nellie	**D**

15

Lesser Intrusions on Privacy: *Terry* Frisks and Protective Sweeps

CHAPTER OVERVIEW
A. Investigative "Frisks"
B. Automobile "Frisks"
C. Stops and Frisks on Mass Transit
D. "Protective Sweeps"
E. The Closer
✦ Cornwell's Picks

A. Investigative "Frisks"

In Chapter 14, we discussed a police officer's authority to detain an individual for a limited period to investigate the officer's belief that criminal activity "is afoot." An officer may also reasonably believe that the subject of his or her investigation is armed. In such circumstances, it is permissible for the officer to "frisk" the suspect to search for weapons or other items that threaten the officer's safety. Any such items, if discovered, may be seized by the officer.

A frisk is a pat-down of the suspect's body and outer clothing. Because the search is limited in scope, only reasonable suspicion is necessary; more invasive searches require the higher probable cause standard.

The sole justification for the frisk is officer safety. If, however, an officer discovers contraband while searching for weapons, he may seize it, provided its criminal nature is immediately apparent without tactile manipulation. Thus, in *Minnesota v. Dickerson*, 508 U.S. 366 (1993), the U.S. Supreme Court suppressed a vial of cocaine found during a *Terry* frisk since the officer identified it only after sliding his fingers up and down the object. When he did so, the officer knew that the item was not a weapon; thus, the only purpose of this further exploration was to confirm its identity as contraband. The "plain feel" doctrine—an analogue to the "plain view" doctrine discussed in Chapter 13—is unavailable in these circumstances.

QUESTION 1. Coochy-coo. Officer Jenny, working the night shift, was patrolling Main Street in the vicinity of Ted's, an electronics store that had been burglarized twice in the past week. On both occasions, the burglars stole laptop computers after gaining entry by shattering a heavy, plate-glass window near the store's rear entrance with a blast from a firearm. When Jenny drove through the downtown area at 2:00 A.M., there was very little activity, since all stores had closed hours earlier and there were no residential units within a mile in any direction. She was surprised to come upon a man and woman pushing a baby carriage in the otherwise desolate area. The carriage had a storage area below the basket in which a baby would be placed, and this section of the carriage was obscured by a dark cloth wrapped around it.

Jenny approached the couple on foot, asking what they were doing in this area at such a late hour. The couple did not want to engage in conversation, explaining that they needed to get home, since the baby was out well past his bedtime. Asked where they lived, the couple provided an address more than a mile away from their present location and nervously commented that they had wanted the baby to "get some fresh air."

As the couple began to move away from Jenny, she ordered them to halt. When she reached them, Jenny looked into the carriage and noticed a dark, sharp-edged object protruding from underneath the baby blanket. She also noticed what appeared to be a bulge beneath the male's sweater at his waist. Convinced that the two were responsible for the burglaries, Jenny frisked the male. Feeling a sharp object at his waist, she lifted up his sweater and found a screwdriver lodged in his waistband. Jenny removed it. Testing later revealed that it had been used to pry open locked areas inside the store. Jenny's conduct was:

A. Unconstitutional as to the stop, the frisk, and the seizure of the screwdriver.
B. Constitutional as to the stop only.
C. Constitutional as to the stop and the frisk only.
D. Constitutional as to the stop, the frisk, and the seizure of the screwdriver.

ANALYSIS. Officer Jenny encounters a couple with a baby carriage taking a walk in the middle of the night in a deserted commercial area. The couple is near a store that had been the target of two burglaries within the last week, where the wrongdoers gained access by shooting out a window and subsequently stealing laptop computers. Jenny's initial questioning does not dispel her suspicions, as the couple appears nervous and provides a home address at some distance from their present location. She orders them to halt. The decision is reasonable, since the foregoing facts provide reasonable suspicion that the couple is engaged in criminal wrongdoing.

Jenny next notices a hard-edged object protruding from beneath a baby blanket in the carriage. The carriage also has a storage area in its lower section, obscured by a cloth, in which stolen items could be secreted. Finally, Jenny notices a bulge at the male's waist, beneath his sweater. Collectively, these facts lead Jenny to frisk the male, as a result of which she finds a screwdriver in his waistband, which she seizes. Because Jenny has not arrested the couple, she must rely on a *Terry* frisk rationale to justify her actions. As such, Jenny must have reasonably believed that the subject was armed and dangerous.

The aforementioned facts provide a credible evidentiary basis for Jenny's belief that the couple perpetrated the burglaries. The object under the blanket could have been a laptop, and other laptops could have been placed clandestinely in the storage area. They also appear nervous. They purport to be taking their infant child for a walk, but this is suspicious, given the great distance from their home and the very late hour. The bulge could have been a weapon, and because Jenny knows that the burglars discharged a firearm to break the window glass, she could have reasonably believed that the male was carrying a gun.

The pat-down reveals a sharp object, which Jenny seizes. Consistent with Jenny's suspicions, the item turns out to be a screwdriver, which, while not commonly used for this purpose, is capable of inflicting bodily harm and thus is a potentially dangerous weapon. In this regard, it is important that Jenny felt a sharp object. Because frisks do not permit officers to manipulate objects tactilely, she cannot explore the object further. Faced with knowledge that the subject is carrying something sharp, Jenny must either remove it or hope it is not a knife or something similar that the subject could use against her. She decides to remove it, which is perfectly permissible in the interest of officer safety.

The correct answer is **D**.

B. Automobile "Frisks"

Vehicles have merited special consideration in the seizure context. This attention is the product of various factors, most notably the prevalence of traffic stops. If, in the course of a traffic stop, an officer has an "articulable and objectively reasonable belief" that the driver or a passenger is potentially dangerous, she or he may frisk that individual for safety reasons. *Arizona v. Johnson*, 555 U.S. 323 (2009). In addition, officers can "frisk" the car to make sure it does not contain any weapons that could be used to injure them. *Michigan v. Long*, 463 U.S. 1032 (1983). Concern for officer safety also allows police officers to order both the driver and any passengers out of the vehicle during the stop, without regard to individual suspicion. *Pennsylvania v. Mimms*, 434 U.S. 106 (1977); *Maryland v. Wilson*, 519 U.S. 408 (1997).

Because the justification for the search rests on officer safety, the frisk is limited to areas in the vehicle's passenger compartment within reach of an occupant and capable of hiding a weapon. While the desire to search for contraband does not justify a car frisk, it is lawful to seize contraband that is discovered in the course of a safety-motivated frisk, provided the criminal nature of the object discovered is immediately apparent to the officer.

Michigan v. Long, the Court's principal case addressing automobile frisks, is illustrative. Because Long was driving erratically, officers pulled over his car. Based on Long's demeanor, they concluded that he was "under the influence of something." After noticing a hunting knife on the floor, one of the officers frisked Long, finding no weapons. They then searched his car, finding marijuana inside an open pouch located under the armrest on the front seat. The marijuana was admissible, the Court held, since it was discovered in plain view during a search for weapons, motivated by concerns for officer safety, in an area where "a weapon may be placed or hidden."

QUESTION 2. Busted. Officer Evelyn was on traffic duty on the interstate when she noticed a car being driven with a broken taillight, a violation of the state's motor vehicle code. She pulled the car over and asked the driver for his license. When he looked at her, Evelyn noticed that his eyes were bloodshot. She ordered him out of the vehicle. Once he was outside, Evelyn asked him some routine questions and observed that he seemed nervous when responding. Believing that he might be hiding something in the vehicle, she searched the passenger cabin. Under the driver's seat, she felt what she immediately recognized as drug paraphernalia. She seized it and placed the driver under arrest.

If the driver moves to suppress the drug paraphernalia, he will likely:

A. Prevail, because Evelyn had no right to pull the car over.
B. Prevail, because Evelyn had no right to order the driver out of the car.
C. Prevail, because Evelyn had no right to search the car.
D. Prevail, because, while Evelyn had the right to search the car, she did not have the right to seize the drug paraphernalia.
E. Lose.

ANALYSIS. This problem begins with a fairly routine traffic stop. If an officer has reason to believe that someone is violating traffic laws or otherwise driving erratically, she or he has the right to pull the car over. Because Officer Evelyn notices the car has a broken taillight, she is fully justified in pulling the car over. **A** is therefore wrong. She then orders the driver out of the car, after noticing that his eyes were bloodshot. While it is unclear why she wanted him to exit the vehicle, courts will not second-guess an officer's preference in this regard. **B** is wrong.

Evelyn decides to search the car because the driver's nervousness leads her to believe that he may be hiding something in the vehicle. For this search to qualify as a *Terry* car "frisk," it must be motivated by concern for officer safety. The facts indicate, however, that Evelyn was looking for contraband, not weapons that might harm her. Likewise, the driver's demeanor was not belligerent or threatening, such that Evelyn would fear him.

If the car "frisk" theory is unavailing, the search is permissible only if it is supported by probable cause that the vehicle contains contraband. A broken taillight, bloodshot eyes, and nervousness do not suggest, collectively, that there is a "fair probability" that drugs or other illegal items are present. Thus, the search does not qualify under the automobile exception to the warrant requirement.

Note that, if the search were valid, Evelyn would have had the right to seize the drug paraphernalia because the items' incriminating nature was immediately apparent to her without physical manipulation. Thus, **D** is wrong on two accounts.

C is the correct answer.

C.   Stops and Frisks on Mass Transit

When a *Terry* stop involves a bus or other form of mass transit, rather than a privately owned vehicle, the seizure analysis is necessarily different. Whereas a motorist whose car is pulled over is clearly not "free to leave," police officers conducting a routine check of a bus for contraband in all likelihood have no authority to detain individual passengers; thus, any individual is free to leave when the officers enter the vehicle and before the search commences.

At the same time, if an officer does decide to question a passenger who remains, it makes little sense to evaluate seizure with reference to whether the passenger feels free to leave. Travelers stopped at an intermediate point in their journey would not readily choose to disembark, since doing so would leave them stranded in an unfamiliar place from which they would need to reformulate an itinerary to reach their final destination. Recognizing this distinction, the U.S. Supreme Court imposes a different seizure standard for public transport such as buses, asking whether the totality of the circumstances suggests that a reasonable innocent person in the detainee's position would feel free to disregard the officer's questions and go about his or her business.

In *United States v. Drayton*, 536 U.S. 194 (2002), three police officers entered a bus mid-route as part of a routine search for drugs and weapons. Officers first obtained permission to search the defendant's luggage and found nothing incriminating. Drayton thereafter consented to a search of his body, and police discovered he had drugs strapped to him. Drayton challenged the consent search, claiming that it was the product of an unlawful seizure. The Court disagreed, deeming the encounter a non-seizure since the "officers gave the passengers no reason to believe that they were required to answer the officers' questions." In so holding, the majority emphasized the officers' "polite, quiet voice" and unintimidating demeanor when approaching and questioning passengers.

QUESTION 3. Train trippin'. Mickey and Minnie booked tickets on the overnight train headed south from Charlotte, North Carolina. At a stop in Atlanta, federal drug enforcement agents boarded the train and announced that they would be conducting a random search for drugs. The agents were in uniform and were carrying weapons. Agent Duncan was assigned to Mickey and Minnie's car. He apologized for any inconvenience and explained to the passengers that this was a routine search and that they should soon be on their way.

Duncan stopped in front of Mickey when he noticed that Mickey was wearing gold jewelry and a track suit, apparel typical of drug dealers, in Duncan's experience. Duncan then asked Mickey: "Excuse me, sir, could you tell me where you are headed to and whether your trip is for business or pleasure?" Mickey explained that he and Minnie were on their way to Disney World. "Oh," Duncan continued, "you'll have a great time. Do you mind showing me some identification?" As Mickey was removing his wallet from his jacket pocket, a baggie containing LSD fell out. Duncan seized it and placed Mickey under arrest.

Mickey's claim that he was unlawfully seized:

A. Has merit, because he was obligated to answer Duncan's questions.
B. Has merit, because Mickey would not have wanted to exit the train in Atlanta.
C. Has merit, because Duncan was armed and in uniform.
D. Lacks merit, because Mickey could have chosen to exit the train.
E. Lacks merit, because Duncan's demeanor was cordial and nonthreatening.

ANALYSIS. When law enforcement agents conduct random searches of vehicles used in mass transit, individual travelers are seized for Fourth Amendment purposes only if their particular interaction with the officers suggests that they were not free to disregard any questions posed to them. Answers **B** and **D** concern Mickey's ability and desire to exit the train in Atlanta, an intermediate point in his journey. **B** is certainly accurate in that Mickey would not want to disembark there; this is beside the point, however, since the "free to leave" standard does not apply in the mass transit context. As such, **B** and **D** are wrong.

The fact that Duncan is armed and in uniform is of minimal relevance. *Drayton* specifically noted that wearing uniforms and displaying badges and firearms merits little weight in the seizure analysis since the public is widely accustomed to seeing officers attired in this manner. Only if Duncan were to brandish the weapon could the encounter be deemed sufficiently coercive to suggest seizure. **C** is wrong.

Answers **A** and **E** are better because they relate, specifically or impliedly, to the correct seizure standard. **A** posits that Mickey was seized because he was obligated to answer Duncan's questions. Realistically, most travelers would find it difficult to refuse to answer a federal agent's questions. This reality does not, however, resolve the seizure inquiry. If it did, all such questioning would constitute a seizure, and the U.S. Supreme Court has held that this is not the case.

In determining seizure in each instance, courts consider all relevant factors. Here, the agents were armed and in uniform, but they did not brandish their weapons at any time. They also indicated that the search was routine and should not take long. In addition, and perhaps most importantly, Duncan was polite and courteous at all times in interacting with Mickey. On balance, therefore, this encounter was a non-seizure.

E is the best answer.

D. "Protective Sweeps"

The authority to conduct a *Terry* frisk is predicated on concerns for officer safety. Previously discussed cases recognize that the danger an officer faces may emanate from a weapon carried on a suspect's person or stowed in his car. In *Maryland v. Buie*, 494 U.S. 325 (1990), the U.S. Supreme Court addressed, instead, the threat to an officer's physical safety posed by criminal cohorts lurking in other rooms during an in-home arrest.

Police officers arrested Jerome Edward Buie in his home on suspicion of armed robbery. At the time of the arrest, Buie was emerging from the basement. Concerned that dangerous individuals, including accomplices in the robbery, might be present in the residence, police entered the basement to safeguard their physical safety. While they did not locate any accomplices, they came upon criminal evidence in plain view, which they seized.

The court deemed the officers' "protective sweep" constitutional, reasoning that, during an in-home arrest, police may look for criminal confederates in any area immediately adjoining the place of arrest without reasonable suspicion, provided there is "a reasonable, articulable suspicion that the *house* is harboring a person posing a danger to those on the arrest scene." (Emphasis added.) To justify a sweep of more remote areas, officers must produce facts sufficient to allow a "reasonably prudent officer" to conclude that an individual who might threaten officer safety is present *in the area searched*.

QUESTION 4. One distressed diva. Police Officer Agnes had a warrant to arrest Bert, a stockbroker, for insider trading. They knew that Bert lived with his girlfriend, Martha, a local celebrity who hosted a weekly program on cable television's Home and Garden Network. The police had evidence implicating Martha in Bert's unlawful conduct, but they lacked sufficient proof for an arrest.

Agnes arrested Bert at 7:00 A.M. on his front porch as he was leaving his home for work. As he was being led away in handcuffs, he shouted to Martha, who was in an upstairs bedroom, that the police had arrested him and that she should call their lawyer and have him meet Bert at the station house. "Those bastards!" Martha shrieked. "Don't say anything to those vultures, Bert." Hearing Martha, Agnes's partner, Officer Nick, entered the home in search of her. He found her in the bedroom on the phone with the lawyer. Seeing Nick, Martha turned and threw a three-pound crystal vase at him, calling him a "f___ing jerk." The vase hit Nick on the side of the head, and the resulting wound required ten stitches. Nick arrested Martha for assaulting a police officer.

Martha's argument that Nick lacked authority to enter the bedroom likely:

A. Has merit, because Nick had no reason to fear Martha when he entered the residence.
B. Has merit, because Bert's arrest occurred outside the home.
C. Lacks merit, because Martha threw a vase at Bert.
D. Lacks merit, because Martha shrieked when she learned of Bert's arrest.

ANALYSIS. This protective sweep problem requires us to consider what is, and is not, within the analytical reach of *Buie*. Let's start with location. *Buie* concerned an arrest inside the home; Bert, by contrast, was arrested on his front porch. However, as we discussed in Chapter 2, the front porch may be considered part of the "curtilage" of the home and, as such, deserving of home-based constitutional protections. This seems especially true here, where a confederate positioned inside the home could easily access the front porch and threaten the safety of the officers.

Applying *Buie* to Bert's arrest gives Nick the right to search immediately adjoining areas for potential accomplices, provided he believes the house harbors someone who threatens officer safety. Here, Nick was specifically looking for Martha, whom he knew was present in an upstairs bedroom. Because this room did not adjoin the place of arrest, *Buie* further requires reasonable suspicion that Martha, specifically, posed a risk of harm to Nick and/or Agnes, since there is nothing to suggest the presence of other dangerous criminal confederates. This evaluation is made at the time of the officer's entry into the area searched.

When Nick entered the house, he knew that Bert was a stockbroker believed to have committed insider trading and, upon learning of his arrest, his girlfriend, Martha, shrieked and referred to the arresting officers as "bastards." These circumstances do not reasonably suggest that Martha, a local television celebrity, presented a risk to Nick or Agnes's physical well-being. Martha's reaction was a seemingly natural response to Bert's news, and the offense, a white-collar, "corporate" crime, does not connote violence.

In the end, Martha did aggress against Nick, throwing a three-pound object at him that caused an injury requiring medical attention. This unexpected occurrence does not change the fact, however, that at the time Nick entered the house he had no reason to fear for his physical safety. Thus, Nick's entry and search constitute an unlawful protective sweep.

The correct answer is **A**.

E.   The Closer

QUESTION 5. **Game over.**   Officers Carlos and Angie pulled a car over for running a stoplight in a residential neighborhood. When Carlos asked the driver, Martin, for his license, Martin became furious, telling Carlos to "get the f____ out of my face!" Carlos then ordered Martin and his passenger, Shelley, out of the car. As they exited the vehicle, Carlos noticed a bag of baseball bats on the floor in the backseat area, and Martin was wearing a baseball uniform with the word *Coach* printed on the back.

Shelley asked to leave, explaining that her house was a block away and "a team of hungry twelve-year-olds will be arriving any minute for a post-game pizza party." Carlos let her go. Carlos then asked Martin again to produce his license. Martin continued to rant, commenting that he was "about to lose [his] temper." Carlos proceeded to frisk him, while Angie searched the interior passenger compartment of the vehicle. Carlos felt a packet in Martin's front shirt pocket. After gently squeezing it, Carlos concluded, based on his experience, that it contained marijuana. He removed it and found it was indeed a packet of marijuana labeled "Shelley's stash." Meanwhile, Angie continued to search the car. She reached her hand under some papers inside the glove compartment, where she felt a six-inch, square plastic box. She removed it and, because it was clear, she immediately identified its contents as marijuana. She seized it.

After Martin provided Shelley's address, he was taken in handcuffs to the police station by a back-up officer who had arrived at the scene. Carlos and Angie proceeded to Shelley's house and rang the doorbell. When Shelley's mother came to the door, Angie explained what had happened and asked if they could enter to place Shelley under arrest. The

> mother agreed, stating that Shelley needed a "wake-up call." They found Shelley in the living room on the ground floor. While Carlos handcuffed Shelley, Angie conducted a protective sweep of the adjoining rooms, finding a packet of cocaine on the floor of a closet. She seized it.
>
> Martin and Shelley, respectively, challenged the frisks and protective sweep. On which are they likely to succeed? (Evaluate each one independently—that is, without regard to the constitutionality of the others.)
>
> **A.** The frisk of Martin only.
> **B.** The car "frisk" only.
> **C.** The protective sweep of Shelley's residence only.
> **D.** The frisk of Martin and the protective sweep.
> **E.** The frisk of Martin, the car "frisk," and the protective sweep.

ANALYSIS. Frisks and protective sweeps share a common justification: officer safety. Proceeding chronologically, we will start with Martin's frisk of Carlos. Martin was acting belligerently toward Carlos during the traffic stop, hurling expletives at him and admitting that he was struggling to control his temper. Because Carlos knew there were baseball bats in the vehicle, which Martin could use against Carlos, the frisk was justified. It does not matter that it is lawful to carry baseball bats; in *Michigan v. Long*, the suspect had a hunting knife in his car, which he was also permitted to carry. Both are items that are capable of inflicting serious bodily injury and, as such, they may be used to threaten the officer's physical safety.

During the frisk, Carlos discovers a packet, which he concludes is marijuana after gently squeezing it. This conduct exceeds the scope of a valid *Terry* frisk. At the time he squeezed the packet, Carlos knew it was not a weapon. Thus, he was endeavoring only to determine whether or not it was contraband. The absence of a nexus to officer safety renders the frisk unconstitutional.[1]

Angie's car "frisk" is justified by the same belligerent behavior that authorized the body frisk of Martin. She finds drugs in the glove compartment under a pile of papers. The glove compartment is a permissible search area, since it is located in the interior passenger cabin of the vehicle. Angie's removal of the six-inch plastic box is also permissible since it may contain a weapon. Instead, she discovers that the box contains marijuana. Because no further tactile manipulation was necessary to identify the contents of the box as contraband, the seizure was appropriate.

---

1. Lower courts have permitted officers to gently squeeze an object or explore its contours to confirm its identity as a *weapon*. See, e.g., *State v. Wright*, 1997 Wash. App. LEXIS 900 (Wash. Ct. App., June 6, 1997, Filed); *State v. Marvin*, 1996 Wash. App. LEXIS 352 (Wash. Ct. App., September 6, 1996, Filed). Here, however, Carlos did not believe the packet contained an item that posed any danger to him.

Finally, Angie conducts a protective sweep of Shelley's house and finds more drugs on the floor of a closet. Because the closet is located in an adjoining room, Angie may look for criminal confederates there, provided there is "a reasonable, articulable suspicion that the house is harboring a person posing a danger to those on the arrest scene." Here, Angie and Carlos have no reason to believe that anyone in the residence threatens their safety. Shelley is not a dangerous criminal; her arrest is for possession of a small amount of marijuana, consistent with personal use. Thus, there is no justification for a protective sweep.

In sum, the frisk of Martin was excessive in scope, and the protective sweep was not justified. The car "frisk," however, was permissible. The correct answer is **D**.

Cornwell's Picks

1.	Coochy-coo	**D**
2.	Busted	**C**
3.	Train trippin'	**E**
4.	One distressed diva	**A**
5.	Game over	**D**

16

The Exclusionary Rule: General Principles and Applications

CHAPTER OVERVIEW
A. Constitutionalizing the Rule
B. General Principles
C. "Standing"
   1. Standing Pre-*Katz*
   2. The Demise of Standing
   3. Invitees Revisited
D. Impeachment
E. The Closer
✦ Cornwell's Picks

The "exclusionary rule" provides that evidence obtained as a result of an unconstitutional search or seizure shall be excluded from the criminal prosecution of the party whose rights were violated. This remedy, declared by the U.S. Supreme Court in 1961 to be an "essential ingredient" of the Fourth Amendment, is not contained in the Amendment's actual language, however. It is useful to remember this when considering the limitations the U.S. Supreme Court has placed on the reach of the rule over the last fifty-plus years. Were exclusion an expressed Fourth Amendment guarantee, the scope of the protection it offers criminal defendants might well be different.

A. Constitutionalizing the Rule

The U.S. Supreme Court first mandated exclusion of evidence obtained in violation of the Fourth Amendment in *Boyd v. United States*, 116 U.S. 616 (1886), where the justices likened the introduction of the defendant's own unlawfully seized books and papers as "compelling him to be a witness against himself," which is prohibited under the Fifth Amendment. The Court waited nearly thirty years before revisiting the exclusionary rule in *Weeks v. United States*, 232 U.S. 383 (1914). In that case, the majority excluded evidence obtained by federal officials in violation of the Fourth Amendment but did not require exclusion of evidence gathered in a separate search by state officials. "[T]he Fourth Amendment is not directed," the Court noted, "to individual misconduct of such officials."

The U.S. Supreme Court reaffirmed *Weeks* in *Wolf v. Colorado*, 338 U.S. 25 (1949). In refusing to apply the exclusionary rule to evidence obtained by state officials in violation of the Fourth Amendment, the Court emphasized the absence of any language in the text of the Amendment providing for such a remedy and the express rejection of the rule by a majority of the states. Distinguishing *Wolf*, the Court subsequently affirmed the exclusion in state trial prosecutions of evidence unlawfully obtained by federal officials, ruling that to allow a federal officer to "use the fruits of his unlawful act in state or federal proceedings" would be to undermine the protection citizens deserve under the federal laws relating to search and seizure. *Rea v. United States*, 367 U.S. 643 (1956).

In the watershed case of *Mapp v. Ohio*, 367 U.S. 643 (1961), the U.S. Supreme Court overruled *Wolf*, holding that the exclusionary rule is an "essential ingredient" of the Fourth Amendment; thus, any evidence obtained in violation of it is inadmissible in a state court proceeding. A contrary decision would reduce the Fourth Amendment, the justices reasoned, to "a form of words." While the sweeping language of *Mapp* may appear to allow little exception to its mandate, the reality has been quite different. As we will see, the U.S. Supreme Court has significantly limited the reach of the rule in a host of cases decided after 1961.

United States v. Calandra, 414 U.S. 338 (1974), provides an early indication of the U.S. Supreme Court's willingness to be flexible in its application of the rule. There, the justices declared the rule "a judicially-created remedy designed to safeguard Fourth Amendment rights generally through its deterrent effect, rather than a personal constitutional right of the party aggrieved." Dissenting in that case, Justice Brennan worried that such language suggests a willingness, in later cases, "to reopen the door still further and abandon altogether the exclusionary rule."

QUESTION 1. Reefer mattress. As Mary and Todd sat watching television one evening, agents of a federal task force on drug interdiction stormed into their house without a warrant looking for drugs. After seizing a small quantity of crack cocaine, they left. Soon thereafter, state police officers broke a window on the ground floor in the back of the house and climbed into the couple's bedroom. They found marijuana

under the mattress. After the trial judge found that both searches violated
their Fourth Amendment rights, Mary and Todd moved to exclude all
drug evidence in a state court criminal proceeding commenced one year
prior to the U.S. Supreme Court's decision in *Mapp v. Ohio*. Which of the
following is TRUE?

A. All evidence must be excluded.
B. The decision as to whether to exclude any or all of the evidence
   is within the trial judge's discretion, since this is a state court
   proceeding.
C. The trial judge must exclude the crack, but not the marijuana.
D. The trial judge must exclude the marijuana, but not the crack.

ANALYSIS.   This is a fairly straightforward problem that tests your understanding of the U.S. Supreme Court's changing view of the exclusionary rule
in the years leading up to *Mapp v. Ohio*. As the explanation above indicates, the
Court expanded the reach of the rule incrementally in the years leading up to
1961. Because the proceeding described in our problem takes place in the year
prior to *Mapp*, *Wolf v. Colorado* provided the governing standard.

Like our problem, *Wolf* concerned the admissibility of unlawfully seized
evidence in a state court proceeding. In *Wolf*, however, the unconstitutional
conduct was perpetrated by state officials alone; here, as in *Rea*, we have federal misconduct as well. In *Rea*, the justices disallowed the use in a criminal
prosecution in state court of tainted evidence from federal officials, even
though *Wolf* declared the conduct of state officials to be beyond the reach of
the exclusionary rule. *Mapp* subsequently erased this distinction altogether.

Because our case is set in the *Wolf/Rea* era, the judge should not exclude
the marijuana evidence seized by the state police but should exclude the crack
cocaine obtained unlawfully by the federal agents.

The correct answer is, therefore, **C**.

B. General Principles

Generally speaking, the exclusionary rule prohibits prosecutors from intro-
ducing, in their case-in-chief, physical or testimonial evidence obtained in
violation of an individual's federal rights. As such, the rule does not apply to
violations of *state* law that do not implicate federal prohibitions. Therefore, in
Virginia v. Moore, 553 U.S. 164 (2008), exclusion of evidence found during a
search incident to arrest was unnecessary where the arrest, which was illegal
under state law, complied with Fourth Amendment requirements.

Likewise, because the exclusionary rule extends only to violations of federal *law*, it does not apply to federal agency rules when compliance with the

rule is not constitutionally or statutorily mandated. Thus, in *United States v. Caceres*, 440 U.S. 741 (1979), the Court allowed the use, in a criminal trial, of conversations obtained by the Internal Revenue Service through electronic surveillance that failed to comply with agency rules governing this sort of activity. In so holding, the Court emphasized that, because federal constitutional and statutory law did not require the IRS to adopt any particular procedural rules concerning electronic monitoring and recording of conversations, the agency's failure to abide by rules it voluntarily chose to implement did not implicate the Fourth Amendment's exclusionary rule.

The Supreme Court has also found the exclusionary rule inapplicable to grand jury proceedings and civil proceedings. Accordingly, the Court permitted the use in a federal civil proceeding of evidence unlawfully seized by a state criminal enforcement officer. Although the evidence in question was gathered under a search warrant that violated the Fourth Amendment, the majority reasoned that the societal costs of exclusion outweighed the likelihood that exclusion would deter future misconduct by state police personnel. *United States v. Janis*, 428 U.S. 433 (1976).

QUESTION 2. Hey, wiseguy. Conor is an agent with the Setonia Bureau of Investigation, a state agency similar to the FBI. For the past two months, Conor has been surveilling Kyle, whom Conor suspects is linked to organized crime in Setonia. One evening, after Kyle and his wife exit their residence, Conor breaks into their house, looking for incriminating evidence. In a dresser drawer in the couple's bedroom, Conor finds a note written by Kyle to a known mob boss detailing their joint criminal activities. Conor seizes the note and leaves the residence. Conor's conduct violates the rules governing searches of residences adopted by the Setonia Bureau of Investigation as well as the constitution of the State of Setonia. Conor's supervisor gives the note to federal prosecutors who indict Kyle for a host of federal offenses. Can the prosecution use the note in their case-in-chief at Kyle's federal criminal trial?

A. Yes, because Conor is not a federal officer.
B. Yes, because the Setonia Bureau of Investigation is an agency.
C. Yes, because Conor violated state law.
D. No.

ANALYSIS. This problem addresses the reach of the exclusionary rule, focusing on the relationship between federal law and state law/agency rules. Conor, who works for the State of Setonia, breaks into Kyle's house and seizes evidence. His conduct violates both the state constitution and the agency's internal rules. Because the evidence cannot be used against Kyle in a criminal proceeding in state court, the question asks whether the note can be used by prosecutors in a federal criminal trial.

A, B, and **C** posit that the evidence is admissible at Kyle's federal trial, relying alternatively on the fact that Conor works for a state agency and has violated its internal rules and state law. While these assertions channel *Moore, Caceres,* and *Janis,* they also differ from all three cases in critical respects. First, Conor's actions violated federal law. In the absence of some sort of exigency, searching someone's house without a warrant is impermissible under the Fourth Amendment, and the facts do not indicate any sort of emergency that would justify Conor's failure to obtain a warrant. In *Moore* and *Caceres,* by contrast, the misconduct at issue did not violate the Fourth Amendment.

In *Janis,* the evidence in question did, in fact, violate the Fourth Amendment; however, it was introduced against the defendant in a civil proceeding. Our facts indicate that the prosecution wants to use the note at Kyle's criminal trial. This it cannot do.

The correct answer is **D**.

C. "Standing"

Historically, to petition the court to exclude evidence, a defendant had to first establish that he or she had authority or "standing" to assert the claim. In the years prior to *Katz,* the standards used to evaluate standing relied on the property law principles widely used in the Fourth Amendment context. In the watershed case of *Rakas v. Illinois,* 439 U.S. 128 (1978), the U.S. Supreme Court abandoned standing as a distinct Fourth Amendment doctrine, choosing, instead, to fold the standing inquiry into the analysis of a defendant's substantive constitutional claim. "[W]e think the better analysis forthrightly focuses," the Court opined, "on the extent of a particular defendant's rights under the Fourth Amendment, rather than on any theoretically separate, but invariably intertwined, concept of standing."

1. Standing Pre-Katz

As noted above, in the years prior to *United States v. Katz,* courts looked exclusively to property law to frame Fourth Amendment principles. Accordingly, to gain standing to challenge a search or seizure, lower courts typically required defendants to allege either ownership or possession of the property seized or a possessory interest beyond that of an invitee or guest in the area searched. Accordingly, in *Jones v. United States,* 362 U.S. 257 (1960), the trial judge denied standing where the defendant did not claim ownership of the contraband in question and was merely a guest in the apartment where the search occurred.

The U.S. Supreme Court reversed, finding that the defendant had standing on two separate grounds. The first focused on the nature of the offense charged. The justices considered it problematic that a defendant, charged with a possessory offense, would need to claim ownership of the contraband in question to gain standing to challenge the search. If he lost, his admission of ownership would be used against him, resulting, almost certainly, in a conviction. To avoid this result, the Court conferred automatic standing on any defendant charged with a possessory offense.

The justices also took issue with the numerous lower court opinions that required ownership of, or a substantial possessory interest in, the premises searched to confer standing. They deemed it sufficient that the defendant was legitimately on the premises; because the defendant in *Jones* was present in the residence with the owner's permission, he satisfied this standard.

Under *Jones*, defendants charged with non-possessory crimes could not invoke the automatic standing rule. To obtain standing, they needed to establish ownership of the property seized or the place searched or their legitimate presence on the premises at the time of the search. Thus, the defendant in *Simmons v. United States*, 390 U.S. 377 (1968), faced a difficult choice. Charged with a non-possessory offense (armed robbery), he neither owned the premises in question nor was present when the search took place. To challenge the search, his only option was to claim ownership of the incriminating evidence seized. Reasoning that defendants should not be forced to surrender one constitutional right — the Fifth Amendment privilege against self-incrimination — to assert another, the U.S. Supreme Court disallowed the use at a subsequent trial on the issue of guilt of any testimony given in an evidentiary suppression hearing.

QUESTION 3. Officer Abigail: Slice Squad. Agnes worked weekends as a pizza delivery person for extra cash. One Saturday night, she was delivering pizza to Tadd at his apartment on Main Street. Tadd let her in and told her to wait in the living room while he retrieved his wallet from upstairs. While Tadd was upstairs, Officer Abigail entered the apartment, explaining that she smelled burnt marijuana as she was walking in the outside common-area corridor. She required Agnes to empty her purse, inside of which was a vial of cocaine. Abigail seized it. It turned out that the smell was actually emanating from the apartment next door. Agnes is charged with unlawful possession of narcotics and challenges the search. Which of the following should she argue to gain standing, based on the cases discussed above?

A. She was present in the apartment as an invitee when the search occurred.

B. She is charged with possession of narcotics.

C. Abigail found the cocaine in her purse.

D. She is charged with possession of narcotics and Abigail found the cocaine in her purse.

E. She was present in the apartment as an invitee when the search occurred, she is charged with possession of narcotics, and Abigail found the cocaine in her purse.

ANALYSIS.   In this problem, we are confronted with a warrantless search of Agnes's purse. As in *Jones*, Agnes is "legitimately on the premises" as an invitee at the time of the search. In *Jones*, however, the area searched was the apartment itself. Here, it is the defendant's personal effects that Abigail explores. In short, because the contraband was not found in a search of the apartment itself, Agnes's presence in the apartment is irrelevant for purpose of standing. Therefore, **A** and **E** are wrong.

It is important to consider the nature of the charge. Because Agnes is charged with a possessory offense, she will have automatic standing to challenge the search. In addition, she can acquire standing by showing ownership of, or a substantial possessory interest in, the area searched. Since the purse was hers, she clearly satisfies this standard.

Because Agnes can assert standing based either on the possessory nature of the offense or her ownership of the personal effect searched, the correct answer is **D**.

2. *The Demise of Standing*

Between 1978 and 1980, the U.S. Supreme Court decided a number of cases that eviscerated the standing doctrine created by *Jones*. In so doing, the Court rejected the very concept of standing, finding it more appropriate to consider "standing" questions as inquiries into the merits of defendants' substantive, Fourth Amendment claims. This shift conformed to the analytical repositioning of the Fourth Amendment in the years following *Katz*.

The first, and most significant, of the cases was *Rakas v. Illinois*. The defendant was a passenger in a vehicle in which police officers, during a roadside search, found contraband in the glove compartment and under the front passenger seat. Because the defendant neither owned the vehicle nor claimed ownership of the contraband, the trial court denied standing to challenge the search. The U.S. Supreme Court affirmed, but not because of a failure of standing due to the lack of ownership. Instead, they held that the defendant had no Fourth Amendment claim because he lacked a legitimate expectation of privacy in the areas searched. Mere presence as an invitee, without more, is insufficient to implicate Fourth Amendment interests. Compare *Byrd v. United States*, 138 S. Ct. 1518 (2018) (A driver in lawful possession and control of a rental vehicle has a reasonable expectation of privacy in the vehicle even if he is not listed on the rental agreement.)

The U.S. Supreme Court applied the reasoning of *Rakas* in a trio of cases decided in 1980. In *Rawlings v. Kentucky*, 448 U.S. 98 (1980), the Court denied relief under the Fourth Amendment to a man who stashed drugs in his girlfriend's purse as officers approached, finding that he had no reasonable expectation of privacy in it; the fact that he claimed ownership of the drugs was inapposite. Likewise, federal agents did not violate the Fourth Amendment rights of a bank customer by unlawfully searching a banker's briefcase that contained documents implicating the customer in criminal activity; as in *Rawlings*, the customer had no expectation of privacy in the area searched (here, the banker's briefcase). *United States v. Payner*, 447 U.S. 727 (1980). The fact that the agents acted intentionally, knowing that Payner lacked authority to challenge the search, did not alter the U.S. Supreme Court's analysis. Finally, *United States v. Salvucci*, 448 U.S. 83 (1980), formally abolished the automatic standing rule that *Simmons, supra,* had made unnecessary more than twenty years earlier by disallowing the introduction at trial of testimony proffered by defendants at prior suppression hearings to gain standing.

QUESTION 4. 30 grams has April. Officer June was convinced that April was running a drug distribution operation at State University. Through surveillance, she found out that April had four couriers who would transport the drugs to her customers for her. May was one of the couriers. One afternoon, June observed April handing suspicious-looking baggies to May, which May then placed in her (May's) backpack. After April left, June approached May, grabbed her backpack and began searching it. Though May protested, June did not desist, commenting "Don't worry, May, you're not the one I'm after." In an interior zippered compartment, June found four baggies containing marijuana, each with a label containing the name of the intended recipient and the words "from April." April is charged with drug trafficking and moves to suppress the evidence found in May's backpack. Does April's claim have merit?

A. Yes, because May has a privacy right in her backpack.
B. Yes, because June intentionally violated the Fourth Amendment.
C. Yes, because April was the target of the search.
D. No, because May was in possession of the baggies at the time of the search.
E. No, because April and May did not share the backpack.

ANALYSIS. Under *Rakas* and its progeny, the focus of our inquiry is privacy. Therefore, for April to state a valid claim, she must have a reasonable expectation of privacy in the area searched by June: May's backpack. Ownership of the items seized, which was sufficient to confer "standing" under *Jones*, is no longer dispositive.

A correctly notes that May has a privacy right in her backpack. Thus, June's actions implicate May's Fourth Amendment rights. It is April, however, who is the moving party here, and her privacy rights were not affected by a search of May's backpack.

B's assertion that June intentionally violated the constitutional norms is likewise correct. While we might find her conduct unsettling, it has no relevance to the merit of April's claim. In *Payner*, federal agents were advised to disregard Fourth Amendment principles in searching the banker's briefcase, knowing that the banker, who could challenge their actions, would not be criminally charged. While the U.S. Supreme Court stated that it did not condone the agents' conduct, it nonetheless denied the Fourth Amendment claim of the customer criminally implicated by the unlawfully seized evidence.

As the discussion of **B** suggests, being the target of police action does not create Fourth Amendment rights, in and of itself. In fact, the U.S. Supreme Court addressed this theory squarely in *Rakas* and rejected it. Thus, the fact that June was targeting April when she searched May's backpack is insufficient to support April's claim. **C** is wrong.

D would deny April's claim because May, not April, was in possession of the baggies at the time of the search. Like ownership, even a substantial possessory interest in the items seized is no longer sufficient to create Fourth Amendment rights. However, if April and May shared the backpack, April could reasonably claim a constitutional privacy interest in it that was violated by the search. Her claim would, in that circumstance, have merit.

The correct answer is **E**.

3. Invitees Revisited

In its more recent cases, the U.S. Supreme Court has clarified the Fourth Amendment rights of invitees. In *Minnesota v. Olson*, 495 U.S. 91 (1990), the justices held that overnight guests have a sufficient expectation of privacy to claim Fourth Amendment protection in the residence where they are staying. Thus, the defendant could claim constitutional injury from a warrantless entry into a friend's home in which he was temporarily residing.

Should *Olson* apply to someone merely present in the residence with the consent of the householder? *Minnesota v. Carter*, 525 U.S. 83 (1998), addressed that question in the context of two men using an apartment for approximately two-and-a-half hours to bag cocaine. The lessee, with whom they had no personal relationship, had consented to their presence and accepted a small quantity of narcotics as "payment." The U.S. Supreme Court declined to apply *Olson* in this context, pointing to three factors: the purely commercial nature of the transaction; the relatively short duration of the visit; and the lack of any previous connection between the defendants and the householder.

Finally, the U.S. Supreme Court returned to the Fourth Amendment rights of passengers during a roadside stop in *Wyoming v. Houghton*, 526 U.S. 295 (1999), and, more recently, in *Brendlin v. California*, 551 U.S. 249 (2007). Whereas *Rakas* held that passengers do not have a reasonable expectation of privacy in the car itself, *Houghton* addressed a passenger's privacy interest in personal effects carried into the car — in this case, a woman's purse. Finding that passengers' expectation of privacy in effects transported on "public thoroughfares" is "considerably diminished," the majority held that probable cause to search a vehicle includes passengers' belongings contained therein "that are capable of concealing the object of the search."

Whereas *Rakas* and *Houghton* addressed a passenger's Fourth Amendment rights in an automobile search, *Brendlin* considered the threshold issue of the stop itself. Ruling unanimously, the U.S. Supreme Court recognized the similar restraint on "privacy and personal security" experienced by drivers and passengers during a roadside stop. Accordingly, the justices extended the authority to challenge the lawfulness of the stop to both.

QUESTION 5. A rocky courtship. As Mary Jane was driving down Main Street late one morning, Police Officer Dwayne pulled her over because he thought she was pretty, and he wanted to meet her. She was one block from her house and was returning from the train station where she had picked up her former college roommate, Brandy. Brandy was going to spend the afternoon at Mary Jane's apartment so that the two of them could review the finances of a business they had started together at college providing SAT tutoring to high-school students. Brandy planned to return home that evening, but she had brought an overnight bag in case she decided to stay over.

After Dwayne pulled the car over, Brandy decided to walk to Mary Jane's apartment to start reviewing the bookkeeping ledgers Mary Jane had prepared for the business. She took her bag but left her purse in the car. After she had left, Dwayne returned to the car and, convinced that he had detected the odor of marijuana when Brandy walked past him, he grabbed Brandy's purse and searched it, over Mary Jane's objections. Inside, he found no marijuana, but he did discover a small quantity of methamphetamine. He then accompanied Mary Jane to her apartment to talk to Brandy. Once Mary Jane let them in, he saw Brandy's overnight bag and searched it, without Brandy's consent. He found cocaine inside.

Brandy's Fourth Amendment rights were violated:

A. By Dwayne's search of her purse.
B. By Dwayne's entry into Mary Jane's apartment.
C. By Dwayne's search of her suitcase.
D. By Dwayne's search of her purse and her suitcase.
E. By Dwayne's search of her purse and her suitcase and by his entry into Mary Jane's apartment.

ANALYSIS. This problem explores the extent of Brandy's Fourth Amendment rights as an invitee in Mary Jane's car and apartment. With respect to the car, *Brendlin* clarified that passengers' liberty interests are implicated by traffic stops, inasmuch as they, like the driver, are "seized" during the encounter. In our problem, however, Brandy was never truly seized, since she left the scene as soon as Dwayne pulled the car over. Had he ordered her to remain, *Brendlin* would apply. The mere inconvenience of having to walk the final block to Mary Jane's apartment does not implicate the Fourth Amendment.

Dwayne subsequently searches Brandy's purse, which she had left in the car after deciding to walk back to Mary Jane's house. *Houghton* instructs that passengers' privacy interests in effects left in someone else's car are greatly diminished in general; *a fortiori*, their interests in effects that have been left in the driver's exclusive control are even more attenuated. Therefore, Dwayne's interest in searching Brandy's purse, in light of his "plain smell" detection of marijuana as she walked past him, outweighs whatever privacy interest she had retained in its contents. The search is lawful.

Dwayne next searches Brandy's overnight bag inside Mary Jane's apartment without Brandy's consent. While Brandy's visit has a business purpose, her relationship to both Mary Jane and the apartment is different from that of the defendants and the householder in *Carter*. Unlike the defendants in *Carter*, Brandy and Mary Jane have a personal relationship and have known each other for a length of time. Also, Brandy would reasonably expect privacy in the bag and its contents, which are likely to contain personal items. The fact that she was not sure if she would stay does not negate this expectation of privacy.

Even though Brandy enjoys Fourth Amendment protection in Mary Jane's apartment, her rights do not extend to Dwayne's entry into the apartment, since Mary Jane afforded him access. The search of Brandy's bag is a different story, however. Only consent from Brandy would permit Dwayne to scrutinize its contents, and she did not grant him permission. Thus, the search of the bag violates Brandy's constitutional rights.

In summary, Dwayne's search of Brandy's purse did not implicate the Fourth Amendment since Brandy was not "seized" at the time of the search and the purse was, therefore, an effect of the car under Mary Jane's exclusive control in which Brandy consequently had a very diminished expectation of privacy. As a guest in Mary Jane's apartment, Brandy did have Fourth Amendment rights that were violated by the search of her overnight bag. Dwayne's entry did not violate the Fourth Amendment, because Mary Jane consented.

The correct answer is **C**.

D. Impeachment

Evidence obtained unlawfully by government agents is inadmissible in the prosecution's case-in-chief. *Mapp v. Ohio, supra*. Mindful of this prohibition, the assistant district attorney in *Harris v. New York*, 401 U.S. 222 (1971), sought its introduction only to impeach the credibility of the defendant on cross-examination. The U.S. Supreme Court held that the exclusionary rule did not apply in this context, since its application could be construed as promoting a defendant's "right to commit perjury."

The impeachment evidence need not contradict a particular statement made by the defendant. If a defendant's statements on cross-examination are "reasonably suggested" by the direct examination conducted by his attorney, these statements are subject to impeachment by evidence obtained unconstitutionally. *United States v. Havens*, 446 U.S. 620 (1980).

Unconstitutionally tainted evidence may not, however, be used to impeach the credibility of a defense witness. *James v. Illinois*, 493 U.S. 307 (1990). The U.S. Supreme Court worried that suspension of the exclusionary rule in this context risked chilling the willingness of defendants to put on their best defense through third-party testimony. Prosecutorial use of illegally obtained evidence in this way "would not just deter perjury; it would also deter defendants from calling witnesses in the first place, thereby keeping from the jury much probative exculpatory evidence."

QUESTION 6. Air traffic control. The Los Angeles drug interdiction task force had been monitoring Pierre's movements for a year, after noticing that he routinely traveled between Los Angeles and Bogotá, a well-known source city for street drugs in L.A. When Pierre arrived in Los Angeles after one of his many trips to Bogotá, customs agents at the Los Angeles International Airport searched his luggage thoroughly, finding nothing. Frustrated, DEA agent Marta stopped Pierre on his way out of the airport and unlawfully searched his person, finding a note card on which five names were written, including that of Jillian, with the heading "the best distributors in Los Angeles of imported, Columbian heroin." Two months later, federal agents obtained sufficient evidence against Pierre to charge him with drug trafficking. He took the stand in his own defense, and Jillian was called as a defense witness. Which of the following is most defensible?

A. Jillian testifies on direct examination that she has never sold heroin to anyone, and the prosecution on cross-examination introduces the information on the note card for impeachment.

B. Pierre testifies on direct examination that he has never brought drugs into the United States from Columbia, and the prosecutor introduces the note card on cross-examination.

C. Jillian testifies on direct examination that she has never met Pierre, and the prosecution introduces the information on the note card for impeachment on cross-examination.

D. Pierre testifies on direct examination that he has never known any drug dealers in the United States, and the prosecutor introduces the note card on cross-examination.

ANALYSIS. This problem examines the use of evidence obtained in violation of the Fourth Amendment for impeachment purposes only. **A** and **C** both involve a defense witness, Jillian, who gives testimony that is contradicted, either directly or impliedly, by the information on the note card. As such, introduction of this evidence would erode her credibility. The U.S. Supreme Court has decided, however, that the detriment of allowing potentially false testimony is outweighed by the chilling effect on a defendant's ability to mount a vigorous defense of allowing such evidence. Thus, unlawfully obtained evidence can *never* be used to impeach a witness's credibility even if, as in **A**, the tainted evidence directly contradicts a statement the witness makes on the stand. **A** and **C** are, therefore, indefensible.

B and **D** concern the ability of the prosecution to introduce constitutionally tainted evidence to impeach the credibility of the defendant. This practice is permissible as applied to anything within the scope of the defendant's direct testimony. Thus, tainted evidence may be used for impeachment if the prosecutor, in satisfaction of the rules of evidence, properly "lays a foundation" to create a bridge from the defendant's direct statement to the evidence.

As between the two, it will be easier for the prosecutor to introduce the note card in **D**. Because the card provides the names of heroin distributors, the prosecutor should be able to create a bridge between this evidence and Pierre's statement that he has never known any drug dealers in the United States. This task would be more difficult with respect to **B**, since the card does not indicate that Pierre himself has ever brought drugs into the country. That is, it is possible that he purchases drugs in Columbia and arranges for their shipment to the United States but does not personally handle the merchandise.

The correct answer is **D**.

E.   The Closer

QUESTION 7. Bill's pills.   Bill was driving down the interstate when Officer Diane pulled him over for driving with a broken taillight. She looked at his driver's license and let him go with a stern warning. After he pulled away, she ran his license and noticed that it had been suspended. Because driving with a suspended license is a serious infraction, Diane drove to Bill's house to issue a citation.

Through a ground-floor window, she saw Bill talking to a man, Christopher, inside the house. She rang the bell and announced that she was a police officer, but no one responded. After waiting two minutes, Diane climbed a ladder leaning against the house in an effort to enter through an open, second-story window. In so doing, Diane saw a plastic bag on a bedside table labeled "Bill's OxyContin—bought from Christopher for $200." She reached in and grabbed it. Christopher lives down the block from Bill. Bill admitted that he had been buying "black market" OxyContin from Christopher for two years. Christopher is subsequently charged with felony distribution of a controlled substance.

If we assume that Diane's actions were unconstitutional, which of the following statements is TRUE?

A. Christopher will succeed in suppressing the OxyContin under *Jones*, as well as under current case law.

> **B.** Christopher will succeed in suppressing the OxyContin under *Jones*, but not under current case law.
> **C.** Christopher will not succeed in suppressing the OxyContin under *Jones* or current case law.
> **D.** If Bill testifies on direct examination at Christopher's trial that he (Bill) had never received OxyContin from Christopher, the prosecutor can introduce the bag seized by Diane to impeach Bill's testimony.

ANALYSIS. We know that Diane's actions in seizing the bag of OxyContin violated the Fourth Amendment. To arrive at the correct answer, we must determine whose constitutional rights were violated and what this means under the exclusionary rule.

The OxyContin clearly belonged to Bill, who purchased it from his supplier, Christopher. Christopher did not live with Bill, nor was he staying with Bill; he lived down the block. As such, Christopher lacked any reasonable expectation of privacy in Bill's residence and, by extension, in the contents of the residence. Thus, under modern Fourth Amendment case law, Christopher would be unable to obtain suppression of the narcotics at his trial.

Under *Jones*, Christopher can gain "standing" to challenge the seizure in a variety of ways. Unfortunately for him, none is unavailing under the present facts. First, an individual can gain standing by demonstrating a possessory interest in the items seized. Here, the label on the bag indicates that the owner is Bill, not Christopher. Second, Christopher would have automatic standing if he was charged with a possessory offense. Here, however, the charge is for distribution, not possession.

Finally, individuals who are "legitimately on the premises" can gain standing to challenge a search of those premises. While the U.S. Supreme Court has interpreted this standard to include overnight guests, it has never indicated that invitees stopping by for a brief visit are included. Moreover, the Court has not extended Fourth Amendment protection to individuals who are present in a residence for purely commercial purposes. Thus, inasmuch as Christopher's visit is merely to deliver to Bill the narcotics Bill has purchased, his status as an invitee would be unavailing.

With respect to impeachment, prosecutors would be able to introduce the unlawfully seized evidence if Christopher took the stand in his own defense and, for example, denied any association with OxyContin. In this instance, however, it is Bill who takes the stand and gives false testimony. Because he is a witness, the prosecution will be unable to use the unlawfully seized bag of narcotics to impeach his credibility.

Thus, in summary, Christopher will be unsuccessful in obtaining the suppression of the OxyContin unlawfully seized by Diane under *Jones* or under current Fourth Amendment case law. In addition, the prosecution will be unable to introduce the bag of OxyContin to impeach the credibility of Bill, even if he makes a false statement directly contradicted by its presence in his home.

The correct answer is **C**.

✦ Cornwell's Picks

1. Reefer mattress	**C**	
2. Hey, wiseguy	**D**	
3. Officer Abigail: Slice Squad	**D**	
4. 30 grams has April	**E**	
5. A rocky courtship	**C**	
6. Air traffic control	**D**	
7. Bill's pills	**C**	

17

Challenging the Search Warrant

CHAPTER OVERVIEW
A. The "Substantial Basis" Test
B. The "Good Faith" Revolution
C. Categorical Exceptions to the "Good Faith" Doctrine
   1. Probable Cause, Particularity, and Bias
   2. Falsehoods and *Franks* Hearings
D. The Closer
◈ Cornwell's Picks

As we discussed in Chapters 8 and 9, to be valid, search warrants must be supported by probable cause and must particularly describe the area to be searched and the items to be seized. A defendant who believes that a warrant did not satisfy these requirements may challenge it in court. If successful, any evidence found during the search will be excluded from the prosecution's case-in-chief.

This chapter examines the standards courts use to evaluate a defendant's challenge of the validity of a search warrant. We will begin with "substantial basis," the standard announced by the U.S. Supreme Court in *Illinois v. Gates*, 462 U.S. 213 (1983). Next, we will turn to the "good faith" exception to evidentiary exclusion, which has limited criminal defendants to a significant extent from obtaining evidentiary exclusion. The final section of the chapter details the procedure by which defendants can obtain relief where the good-faith exception does not insulate a defective warrant.

A.   The "Substantial Basis" Test

As we learned in Chapter 8, *Illinois v. Gates* defines probable cause as a "common-sense, practical determination" as to whether there is a "fair probability" that contraband will be found in a given location. If, on appeal, a defendant challenges the magistrate's probable cause finding, the U.S. Supreme Court requires affirmance of the determination below, if there is a "substantial basis" for concluding that probable cause existed.

Applying this standard to the facts of *Gates*, the U.S. Supreme Court found a substantial basis for issuing the warrant. The magistrate based probable cause, in large part, on information contained in an anonymous letter, some of which was found to be inaccurate. The Court held that these inconsistencies did not extinguish probable cause since police officers confirmed "major portions of the letter's predictions." As such, there was necessarily "a substantial basis for concluding that probable cause . . . existed."

QUESTION 1. **Talc is cheap.**   Ricardo occupied the second floor of a two-family house. He shared an entrance with Albert, who lived on the ground floor. One day, their next-door neighbor, Alice, accidentally received a package addressed to Ricardo and opened it. It contained a pouch inside of which was a white powder that Alice believed to be cocaine. She notified the police, who set up surveillance of Ricardo's residence.

After the police noticed a lot of traffic in and out of the house over a one-week period, they filed for a warrant to search Ricardo's residence, explaining the cocaine and the high volume of traffic in and out of the house. They obtained the warrant, but the subsequent search turned up no cocaine. However, the police did find counterfeit hundred-dollar bills.

Later testing of the substance in the pouch revealed that it was talc, not cocaine, and the individuals traveling in and out of the house were high-school students whom Albert was tutoring. If Ricardo challenges the sufficiency of the warrant, he will likely:

A. Prevail, if there was not a fair probability that cocaine would be found in his apartment.
B. Prevail, because there is no connection between cocaine and counterfeiting.
C. Prevail, because the magistrate had insufficient credible evidence to issue the warrant.
D. Fail, because the police conducted surveillance of the house before obtaining the warrant.
E. Fail, because the information provided to the magistrate furnished probable cause.

ANALYSIS.   In answering this problem, it is important to remember the prevailing standard: If an appellate court concludes that the judge issuing the warrant had a substantial basis for finding probable cause, they must affirm. It is possible, therefore, that a reviewing court will uphold a warrant even if they do not believe that probable cause existed in the first instance; the evidence presented to the court can establish a *substantial basis for believing* that a fair probability exists even if a fair probability is, strictly speaking, lacking.

The magistrate based issuance of the warrant on the supposed cocaine in the package sent to Ricardo and on police observation of a high volume of traffic in and out of the house where he resided. Both sources of information proved ultimately unavailing. While a mistaken understanding of the evidentiary value of information does not necessarily preclude the finding of a substantial basis for issuing the warrant, the mistakes in this instance were too far-reaching and unreasonable to pass muster.

The surveillance of the house was a function of the assumed presence of cocaine in the pouch. As such, the failure of law enforcement officers and the magistrate to ensure that the substance was, in fact, cocaine is indefensible. This leaves the "suspicious" traffic patterns observed over a seven-day period. Because Ricardo shared the entrance with another tenant whom police did not investigate, this information, standing alone, fails to provide a substantial basis for issuing the warrant.

D and **E** are, therefore, incorrect. The fact that police conducted surveillance is useful in gathering sufficient evidence to obtain a search warrant, but it does not, in and of itself, provide adequate proof. If, moreover, the evidence presented to the magistrate failed to provide a substantial basis for issuing the warrant, *a fortiori* it would be insufficient to furnish probable cause.

Of the three answers that reach the correct result, we can first eliminate **B**. If there were sufficient evidence to justify the issuance of the warrant, the police would not need independent evidence to seize counterfeit bills discovered in plain view. As between **A** and **C**, the latter is clearly better, since **A** misstates the law. As discussed above, an appellate court need not find that probable cause existed to uphold a warrant based on the substantial-basis standard. Instead, Ricardo's challenge will succeed because the magistrate lacked sufficient credible evidence to issue the warrant.

The correct answer is **C**.

B. The "Good Faith" Revolution

In *United States v. Leon*, 468 U.S. 897 (1984), police officers executed a search warrant for residences and automobiles believed to be linked to drug trafficking. They found a multitude of drugs, which were subsequently suppressed by the trial judge, who concluded that the affidavit in support of the warrant application failed to establish probable cause. The prosecution appealed the decision, arguing that the exclusionary rule should not apply where the police acted "in reasonable, good faith reliance on a search warrant that is subsequently held to be defective." The U.S. Supreme Court agreed, reasoning that the "marginal or nonexistent benefits" of excluding reliable evidence were not justified where the police act in "objectively reasonable reliance" on a warrant issued by a magistrate.

This "good faith" exception to the exclusionary rule also applied where the police reasonably relied on a statute, later held unconstitutional. *Illinois v. Krull*, 480 U.S. 340 (1987). The deterrent function of the rule was inapplicable in such circumstances, the justices opined, since it was the legislators, not the police officers, who erred. Likewise, good faith insulated an arrest based on an invalid warrant where court personnel, not police employees, had failed to update the computer record. *Arizona v. Evans*, 514 U.S. 1 (1995).

Even if police personnel *are* responsible for an error that violates an individual's Fourth Amendment rights, exclusion is necessary only if the misconduct was "deliberate, reckless or grossly negligent." The exclusionary rule did not apply, therefore, where a recalled arrest warrant was erroneously reported as active due to simple, as opposed to gross, negligence on the part of clerks in the sheriff's office who were responsible for maintaining computer records. *Herring v. United States*, 555 U.S. 135 (2009).

QUESTION 2. Know when to fold 'em.   Detective Eddie has been gathering evidence for six months about an illegal gambling operation run by Annabelle Jones out of her house at 18 Cheaters Lane. He has been surveilling the residence both visually and electronically through a listening device. Having secured sufficient evidence for a search warrant, the district attorney made a formal application to the court, attaching an affidavit detailing the information collected by Eddie. The magistrate granted the warrant, authorizing a search of "the entirety of the residence of Annabelle Jones at 18 Cheaters Lane for evidence of illegal gambling."

Unfortunately, Annabelle Jones learned of the impending search through a "leak" in the department and moved out before officers were able to execute the warrant. Eddie knew she had relocated, but he did not inform any of the other officers in the department. Officer Rick executed the warrant two days later when Eddie was home sick with the flu. When Rick arrived at the residence, the new tenant, Marty Smith, answered the door. Rick showed him the warrant, and Marty told Rick that there must be some mistake, since he had never been involved in gambling, had never heard of Annabelle, and had just moved into the apartment by himself that week from out of state. Rick disregarded Marty's protests and proceeded to search the residence. In so doing, he found drug paraphernalia belonging to Marty and incriminating evidence pertaining to gambling inadvertently left by Annabelle.

If Marty moves to exclude the evidence against him, he will:

A. Prevail, because he claimed to reside alone in the apartment.
B. Prevail, if Annabelle challenges the search.
C. Fail, because Eddie was at home the day Rick searched the residence.
D. Fail, if Rick claims he did not believe Marty.

ANALYSIS. In this problem, the warrant issued by the court was sufficient at the time it was issued, but it was not sufficient at the time it was executed. When he arrived at the apartment, Rick was unaware that Annabelle had moved; thus, had Marty been absent at the time of the search, Rick's discovery and seizure of the contraband arguably would have been reasonable.

Prior to his execution of the warrant, however, Rick encountered Marty, who claimed that he, not Annabelle, currently occupied the residence. Rick chose to disregard Marty's protests and proceeded with the search. In light of the plausibility of Marty's assertions, it was objectively unreasonable of Rick not to inquire into Annabelle's continued association with the residence, particularly in light of the warrant's explicit reference to her ("the residence of Annabelle Jones"). Rick cannot, in short, claim in good faith that he did not believe Marty, without having undertaken further investigation. **D** is, therefore, wrong.

Answer **C** would suspend application of the exclusionary rule due to Eddie's absence from the station house the day of the search. This fact is irrelevant. While Eddie may have informed Rick of Annabelle's relocation prior to the search, there is no concrete evidence to support this. What we do know is that Rick had reason to suspect as much based on his conversation with Marty and failed to respond appropriately. **C** is wrong.

Answer **B** posits that Marty would prevail if Annabelle challenged the search. Annabelle may indeed attempt to do so, but she will not prevail. By abandoning the apartment, Annabelle lacks any reasonable expectation of privacy in it or its contents.

For the above reasons, Marty's claim to be the sole occupant of the apartment was credible, and Rick's decision to disregard it was unreasonable. Because Rick cannot claim that he executed the warrant in good faith, the exclusionary rule mandates the suppression of the drug paraphernalia.

The correct answer is **A**.

C. Categorical Exceptions to the "Good Faith" Doctrine

While the good-faith doctrine clearly creates a broad exception to the exclusionary rule, its reach is not boundless. *Leon* identifies four contexts in which the egregiousness of the warrant's insufficiency makes the doctrine unavailable because, in those circumstances, "the officer will have no reasonable grounds for believing that the warrant was properly issued."

1. Probable Cause, Particularity, and Bias

The first two contexts concern the core Fourth Amendment requirements of a valid warrant: probable cause and particularity. To overcome good faith, the deficits must be extreme. For example, the affidavit supporting the warrant must be "so lacking in indicia of probable cause as to render official belief in its existence entirely unreasonable." *Brown v. Illinois*, 422 U.S. 590, 610–611 (1975) (Powell, J., concurring in part). Likewise, if the warrant is "so facially deficient—*i.e.*, in failing to particularly describe the place to be searched or the items to be seized . . . officers cannot reasonably presume it to be valid." *Leon, supra.*

The third exception concerns the conduct of the magistrate or other judicial officer granting the warrant. If the court acts, for all intents and purposes, as a "rubber stamp" for the prosecution, this abandonment of judicial neutrality will negate an officer's ability to claim good faith. For example, in *Lo-Ji Sales, Inc. v. New York*, 442 U.S. 319 (1979), the town justice issued a warrant to search an adult bookstore and to seize material believed to be legally obscene. However, the justice subsequently proceeded to join the police on the search, acting as a leader of the party, ordering certain items to be seized, and leaving interpretation of various provisions of the warrant to the discretion of the police. Under these circumstances, the U.S. Supreme Court believed that the justice was acting less like a judicial officer and more like an "adjunct law enforcement officer." This absence of "neutrality and detachment" is antithetical to the notion of good faith.

QUESTION 3. Yes, Virginia, there is a search warrant. For two days each month, Virginia checked into a motel near the interstate. From there, she would travel to a nearby truck stop where she would sell marijuana to patrons of the truck-stop diner. Officer Lester learned of the monthly operation when he overheard a conversation between two truckers as he ate lunch at the diner. Lester confirmed their account with Sammy, an informer he knew from prior drug arrests. In addition, the manager of the nearest highway motel disclosed that a woman named Virginia Hamm had booked a room for the following Thursday night.

Lester applied to the local magistrate for a search warrant for the motel room. He supported his application with an affidavit stating that he "had received information from a confidential informant" whom he "knows personally and who has provided information in the past that has led to arrest and convictions." Referencing the affidavit, the magistrate issued a warrant to search Virginia's motel room for "marijuana and drug paraphernalia." She attached a note to the order, on her personal stationery, stating "Good luck." Upon searching the room an hour after Virginia checked in, Lester found six ounces of marijuana, a scale, and several small plastic bags. If Virginia moves to suppress this evidence, she will likely:

A. Prevail, due to the warrant's deficiencies in probable cause.
B. Prevail, due to the warrant's deficiencies in particularity.
C. Prevail, due to problems of judicial neutrality and autonomy.
D. Fail.

ANALYSIS.   This problem asks whether any of the categorical exceptions to the good-faith doctrine applies to the facts above. Remember that, in making this determination, "ordinary" deficits in probable cause and particularity will not overcome good faith; the shortcomings must be so significant that no reasonably well-trained police officer could rely on it. Likewise, if a judicial officer "wholly abandoned" neutrality in a manner similar to that of the town justice in *Lo-Ji Sales, supra,* there can be no objectively reasonable reliance by law enforcement personnel.

Particularity challenges are the easiest to dismiss. The warrant authorizes police officers to search for "marijuana and drug paraphernalia." While drug paraphernalia might describe a broad category of items, the phrase is not overly vague, particularly for police officers trained to recognize contraband of this nature. **B** is clearly wrong.

In issuing the warrant, the magistrate added a handwritten note stating "good luck." While clearly inappropriate, more than impropriety is necessary to negate good faith. The surrounding circumstances must suggest that the magistrate is functioning as a "rubber stamp" for the prosecution. There is evidence to the contrary, most importantly the magistrate's express reference to the affidavit in issuing the warrant. In addition, unlike the town justice in *Lo-Ji, supra,* the magistrate did not accompany police officers on the search, nor did she allow officers to interpret ambiguous search terms.

The content of the affidavit is of far more concern. Lester provided no information that would allow an independent determination of probable cause; rather, the affidavit essentially urged the court to trust Lester's personal belief that he had sufficient evidence to justify the search. Courts have rejected this sort of "bare bones" affidavit as insufficient to constitute good faith. See, e.g., *United States v. Barrington,* 806 F.2d 529 (5th Cir. 1986).

A is the correct answer.

2. *Falsehoods and* Franks *Hearings*

The final categorical good-faith exception focuses on misrepresentations used by the prosecution to obtain authority to search. In *Franks v. Delaware,* 438 U.S. 154 (1978), an affidavit used to secure a warrant to search the defendant's apartment for evidence linking him to a rape, kidnapping, and burglary contained certain misstatements by third parties. The defendant argued that the misrepresentations were made in bad faith and, thus, any evidence seized under the warrant should be suppressed under the exclusionary rule.

The U.S. Supreme Court agreed that an evidentiary hearing should be mandatory where a defendant has proof that an affidavit used to obtain a search warrant contained falsehoods material to the probable cause finding. To be sufficient, the misstatements must be made knowingly and intentionally, or with reckless disregard for the truth, meaning the affiant consciously disregarded a substantial risk that the information was false; misinformation included negligently or innocently is insufficient. Moreover, if probable cause exists with the misrepresentations set aside, no hearing is necessary.

If the court mandates a hearing, the defendant retains the burden of proof. She or he must demonstrate, by a preponderance of the evidence, that the challenged information is false and that it was included in the affidavit knowingly and intentionally or with reckless disregard for the truth.

QUESTION 4. The smell test. Agents of the Drug Enforcement Administration (DEA) were summoned by Federal Express agents when the shipping company received a package, addressed to Lonnie, that they believed might contain drugs, since it originated from a known source city for drug trafficking and was being sent to an area included on a "drug importation watch list" provided by the DEA to Federal Express. The DEA agents arrived with a narcotics dog. They "introduced" the dog to the package three times. The dog alerted to the presence of drugs on only one occasion; typically, when drugs are present, a narcotics dog would alert during two out of three introductions, at a minimum.

The agents provided all information to the U.S. Attorney's Office, which applied for a warrant to search the package. Jill, the assistant U.S. attorney who prepared the warrant application, mentioned the positive alert, but did not mention the two failed attempts, feeling that it was unnecessary to do so. Her supervisor disagreed and told her to include the results of all three attempts. She told him she would, and she planned to do so. She forgot, however, and the application was submitted to the court as originally drafted. The magistrate issued the warrant and, in the subsequent search of the package, the agents found a large quantity of cocaine.

To obtain suppression of the cocaine, Lonnie requests an evidentiary hearing under *Franks v. Delaware*. Should the request be honored?

A. Yes, because the dog sniff evidence was necessary to the finding of probable cause.
B. Yes, because Jill forgot to amend the warrant application.
C. No, because nothing contained in the warrant application was factually inaccurate.
D. No, because Jill intended to make the changes requested by her supervisor.

ANALYSIS. The right to have an evidentiary hearing under *Franks* depends on three requirements: The affidavit supporting the warrant application contains falsehoods; the falsehoods were included knowingly and intentionally, or with reckless disregard for the truth; and, if the misrepresentations were excluded, probable cause would not exist. Here, the dog sniff evidence is clearly necessary to proving probable cause. Without it, federal prosecutors would be left with the address information alone. Were this sufficient, government officials would have the right to open myriad packages based on no more than broad "profiling" information. This is not enough.

The falsehoods issue is more difficult. Unlike the situation in *Franks* itself, the misinformation concerns omissions, as opposed to statements that contain blatant, affirmative lies. There is no reason to believe, however, that excluded information cannot give rise to an evidentiary hearing under *Franks*, where the evidence in question both misleads the court and is necessary to the probable cause determination. The dog sniff omissions meet this standard. Because narcotics dogs typically alert at least two out of three times when introduced to a package containing drugs, the failure to include the two negative attempts deprived the court of material information that may well have influenced its decision to issue the warrant.

The tougher issue is Jill's *mens rea*, or state of mind, in failing to amend the warrant application. The facts suggest that her error was careless. As such, she acted negligently in failing to include the negative dog sniffs. To merit an evidentiary hearing, the misrepresentations would need to have been made at least recklessly. This consideration negates Lonnie's right to a *Franks* hearing.

Based on the above considerations, **A** and **B** are wrong. While the dog sniff evidence was necessary to the probable cause finding, Jill's careless failure to amend her affidavit to include all of it is not a sufficient basis for granting an evidentiary hearing.

C is also incorrect. While nothing contained in the warrant application was factually inaccurate, omissions can be the basis for a *Franks* hearing. It is, instead, Jill's good-faith intention to include the missing information that frustrates Lonnie's motion.

D is the correct answer.

D. The Closer

QUESTION 5. **The ring of Queens.** At midnight, Officer Sybil received a tip from a reliable informant that Gretchen would be driving from her residence in Manhattan to 18 High Street in Astoria, Queens, where her three drug trafficking co-conspirators would be waiting for her at what the informant termed the group's "unofficial meeting place." Gretchen would be carrying a gym bag containing three five-pound "bricks" of cocaine, one for each co-conspirator, to be divided by them later at a different location for distribution to "clients."

Eager to get a warrant to search the house before the drugs disappeared from it, Sybil sought an expedited search warrant. Bev, the assistant district attorney, agreed and telephoned the magistrate "on call" to make the request. After Bev provided the information supplied by Sybil, the magistrate ended the call abruptly, commenting, "Good enough. I hereby issue a warrant to search the premises at 18 High Street in the Borough of Queens, provided Gretchen arrives at this location, as indicated in the assistant district attorney's oral affidavit. Now, I am going back to bed." He hung up before Bev could clarify that the information she had conveyed was based on an informant's tip.

Unable to make it to Queens before Gretchen would have left, Sybil called her colleague, Officer Monique, who was closer to the residence. Gretchen read Monique the warrant as issued by the magistrate. Monique agreed to conduct the search, but she mistakenly went to 18 High Street in Jamaica, Queens, as opposed to Astoria, since the warrant failed to specify the appropriate section of the borough. At the mistaken residence, Monique found a baggie containing marijuana on a bedside table and seized it. Yolanda, the owner of the residence Monique mistakenly visited, is challenging the search. Which of the following is Yolanda's best argument?

A. The magistrate lacked a substantial basis for issuing the warrant.
B. The search was not in good faith, based on deficiencies in particularity.
C. The search was not in good faith, based on deficiencies in probable cause.
D. The magistrate's conduct demonstrated judicial bias.
E. By failing to specify that the information came from an informant, Bev recklessly misled the magistrate.

ANALYSIS. This closer considers the appellate review standard for warrants as well as the good-faith and *Franks* doctrines. You are asked to identify Yolanda's best argument in challenging the erroneous search of her apartment that turned up a baggie of marijuana on a bedside table.

Assistant District Attorney Bev requests, and the magistrate issues, an "anticipatory" search warrant—that is, one that takes effect only upon the occurrence of a "triggering" condition. (See Chapter 9, section B.) Because of the urgency of the situation and the late hour, the exchange between Bev and the magistrate takes place by telephone, which is perfectly appropriate. Bev recounts the information conveyed to Sybil by an informant, but she is unable to clarify its source, since the magistrate abruptly issues the warrant and ends the call.

A posits that the magistrate lacked a substantial basis for issuing the warrant. As discussed at the beginning of the chapter, the substantial-basis standard is not stringent and appears to require less than probable cause. The specific and detailed information provided by Bev more than met this standard. Although the magistrate may not have been aware that the information was provided by an informant, the addition of a triggering condition will require police corroboration of the tip before the warrant can take effect, thereby satisfying concerns about the reliability of the tipster or his information. **A** is not Yolanda's best argument.

To prove that the good-faith doctrine is unavailable due to the absence of probable cause, a defendant must show that the warrant is so egregiously lacking in probable cause that no reasonable officer would have relied on it. A substantial basis for issuing a warrant may, of course, exist in the absence of probable cause; that is, there can be a "substantial basis" for probable cause without *actual* probable cause. Nonetheless, it is difficult to imagine how a warrant can be *egregiously* lacking in probable cause where a substantial basis exists. **C**, therefore, is not persuasive.

While proof of judicial bias will likewise overcome good faith, there is nothing to suggest that the magistrate is acting as a "rubber stamp" for the prosecution. His conduct does not remotely approximate that of the justice of the peace in *Lo-Ji Sales, supra,* who accompanied the police on the search, acting, according to the U.S. Supreme Court, less like an impartial arbiter and more like an "adjunct law enforcement officer." While he could have been more thorough and thoughtful in considering the application, his conduct does not, on balance, suggest an abandonment of neutrality. **D** is not a good choice.

E invokes the "reckless falsehood" standard of *Franks v. Delaware.* Accordingly, Yolanda must prove that Bev consciously disregarded a substantial risk that she was misleading the magistrate by failing to specify that an informant was the source of the information relied on in seeking the warrant. Even if we assume that the magistrate did not know an informer supplied the information, it will be difficult for Yolanda to establish a *Franks* violation since, as discussed above, the triggering condition requires confirmation of much of the tipster's detail before the warrant can take effect.

In light of the difficulty prevailing on **E, B** is Yolanda's best argument. The warrant authorizes a search of the entire premises at 18 High Street in the "Borough of Queens." First, the address is insufficiently specific, such that the officer executing the warrant goes to an identical address in a different part of Queens. More importantly, the warrant authorizes a search of the entire premises, even though the tipster states that the only activity to take place at 18 High Street is Gretchen's delivery of three five-pound "bricks" of cocaine to co-conspirators. As such, the warrant authorizes an overbroad search and authorizes the kind of "fishing expedition" for criminal evidence that the Framers sought to avoid by including the particularity requirement.

The correct answer is **B**.

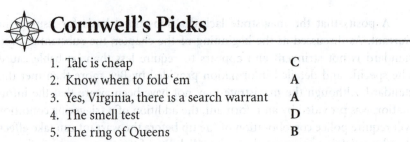

Cornwell's Picks

1. Talc is cheap   **C**
2. Know when to fold 'em   **A**
3. Yes, Virginia, there is a search warrant   **A**
4. The smell test   **D**
5. The ring of Queens   **B**

18

Beyond Good Faith: Additional Limits on Exclusion

CHAPTER OVERVIEW
A. Cost-Benefit Considerations
B. Independent Source
C. Inevitable Discovery
D. "Attenuation"
E. The Closer
✧ Cornwell's Picks

The exclusionary rule, profoundly weakened by the good-faith doctrine, has been further eroded by additional limitations announced by the U.S. Supreme Court. First, the Court has been generally unwilling to exclude evidence unless the deterrent benefits of doing so outweigh its social costs. The justices have also refused to apply the rule where there is a break in the causal link between the unconstitutional conduct and the criminal evidence that is subsequently discovered. Three doctrines achieve this break. The first two, "independent source" and "inevitable discovery," would waive exclusion on the premise that the unconstitutionally seized evidence would ultimately have been discovered through lawful means already being pursued at the time of the violation. The third, "attenuation," permits the introduction of evidence that would otherwise constitute "fruit of the poisonous tree," where intervening events have purged the taint of the original illegality.

A. Cost-Benefit Considerations

Police arrived at the home of Booker Hudson to execute a warrant authorizing a search for drugs and firearms. After announcing their presence, the officers waited three to five seconds before opening the unlocked front door and entering Hudson's residence. The subsequent search uncovered a loaded gun and large quantities of drugs. The prosecution conceded that the officers violated the knock-and-announce rule, discussed in Chapter 10. Based on this infringement of his Fourth Amendment rights, Hudson moved to suppress the criminal evidence found in executing the warrant.

The U.S. Supreme Court refused to apply the exclusionary rule noting, *inter alia*, that suppression of the evidence would entail "substantial social costs" in the absence of any meaningful deterrent benefit. *Hudson v. Michigan*, 547 U.S. 586 (2006). The costs of exclusion include, most notably, the risk of releasing dangerous criminals into society by providing a "get out of jail free card" to persons who have perpetrated serious felonies. The deterrence benefit, by contrast, is minimal at best since officers have little incentive to disregard knock-and-announce requirements, if and when they exist; as discussed earlier, reasonable suspicion of either the destruction of evidence or life-threatening resistance eliminates the need to knock and announce in the first instance.

QUESTION 1. County confusion.   Prosecutor Hafsa filed a petition for a search warrant for Anthony's residence for the weapon used to kill Anthony's wife, Stephanie. The warrant was signed by Judge Tatiana who sits on the criminal court of Laing County, where Anthony was believed to reside. In fact, Anthony lives in Torres County, which borders Laing County. While Anthony had previously lived in Laing County, the records relied upon by Hafsa had not been updated to reflect his change of address. Previous court orders had, however, listed Anthony's correct residence. Under state law, Tatiana has no authority to issue warrants outside of Laing County; thus, the warrant signed by her, while sufficiently particularized and supported by probable cause, is invalid.

In executing the warrant, officers did not find the murder weapon; however, they did find a firearm, whose possession by Anthony is illegal since he is a convicted felon. Anthony moves to suppress the weapon, based on Tatiana's jurisdictional ineligibility to issue the search warrant. Which of the following best supports admitting the evidence against Anthony?

A. The search warrant satisfied particularity and probable cause requirements.

B. Because Anthony is a convicted felon, it is important to enforce firearms restrictions against him.

C. Excluding the evidence would not deter future wrongdoing by law enforcement officers.

D. Anthony had previously resided in Laing County.

ANALYSIS.   In this problem, the police executed a facially valid warrant that was unenforceable under state law due to a jurisdictional defect. The invalidity of the warrant does not necessarily mean, however, that evidence gathered under it will be inadmissible. *Hudson* and later cases clarify that, for the exclusionary rule to apply, the deterrent benefit of exclusion must exceed its social costs.

That the warrant satisfies probable cause and particularity requirements is relevant to the admissibility inquiry, but it is insufficient *per se* to resolve the issue. If, for example, Hafsa had intentional flouted jurisdictional rules in applying for the warrant, exclusion might well be warranted to disincentive such conduct in the future. See, e.g., United States v. Master, 614 F.3d 236, 243 (6th Cir. 2010). **A**, therefore, is incorrect.

Likewise, the importance of keeping weapons out of the hands of criminals explains the prevalence across the country of laws criminalizing the possession of firearms by convicted felons. It does not justify, however, admitting such evidence where it is obtained in violation of federal constitutional requirements. Nor does the fact that jurisdictional requirements would have satisfied based on a previous address have any relevance in this context, especially where the correct address could have been discovered with greater diligence. **B** and **D** are wrong.

By contrast, excluding the evidence against Anthony would make probative, reliable evidence unavailable with arguably little deterrent effect on future misconduct by law enforcement. There is, for example, no evidence of improper motivation in seeking out a judge in Laing County, as opposed to Torres County. Under these circumstances, the social costs may outweigh the deterrent benefits of applying the exclusionary rule. **C** is the best answer.

B. Independent Source

The U.S. Supreme Court noted, in *Silverthorne Lumber Co. v. United States*, 251 U.S. (1920), that facts acquired unlawfully are not "sacred and inaccessible. If knowledge of them is gained from an independent source they may be proved like any others." This sentiment was developed more fully in subsequent years, finding its clearest expression in *Segura v. United States*, 468 U.S. 796 (1984).

In *Segura*, police officers unlawfully entered the defendants' apartment following an arrest. In so doing, they visually "seized" contraband that was subsequently "re-seized" physically through a validly issued search warrant. The U.S. Supreme Court allowed the introduction of the evidence at the defendants' trial, reasoning that there was an "independent source" for the seizure of the evidence. Significantly, none of the information used to secure the warrant was connected in any way to the initial, unlawful entry into the defendants' apartment; the information supporting the affidavit came from independent sources and was known to the agents prior to the illegal conduct. In short, "[n]o information obtained during the initial entry or occupation of the apartment was needed or used by the agents to secure the warrant."

QUESTION 2. Murder most foul. Sean was the primary suspect in the murder of his wife, Rita, which took place in their home. Officers Mack and Pete believed that Sean wanted her out of the way so that he could marry Rita's best friend, Jill, with whom he had been having an affair. Sean denied both the affair and any interest in Jill. To rebut Sean's claims, Mack and Pete were surveilling Sean's apartment to track his movements and, they hoped, to discover Sean and Jill together.

One night, the officers saw Jill arrive at the apartment. A little while later, Sean and Jill left together, with Sean carrying a large bottle of bleach. Pete left immediately to secure a search warrant. As he waited for Pete to return, Mack became increasingly concerned that Sean would return and destroy whatever evidence remained that might prove his guilt. While Sean and Pete were still gone, Mack entered the apartment, using the building manager's passkey. On the dining room table, he saw a book entitled *How to Murder Your Wife and Get Away with It*. Mack took a picture of the book and exited the apartment. Two hours later, Pete obtained a warrant to search the apartment for evidence related to Rita's murder. When executing the warrant, Pete seized the book.

Which of the following, if true, is IRRELEVANT in determining the admissibility of the book against Sean at trial?

A. Evidence pertaining to the book was necessary in finding probable cause for the search.
B. The warrant issued by the magistrate was found to be lacking in particularity.
C. Pete obtained the warrant after learning what Mack had done.
D. Before Mack entered the apartment, Jill returned, carrying a blowtorch.
E. Mack told the building manager that he was Sean's brother, visiting from out of town.

ANALYSIS. The independent source doctrine allows the introduction of evidence tainted by an unlawful search or seizure by virtue of an alternative lawful process that is independent of the previous unlawful conduct. Here, Mack's entry into the apartment violated Sean's Fourth Amendment rights. His free-floating concern about the destruction of evidence is far too speculative to constitute a valid exigency, particularly in light of Sean and Jill's absence from the residence at the time of entry.

As Mack is unlawfully entering the apartment, Pete endeavors to obtain a warrant. Because Pete is unaware of Mack's actions, Pete necessarily does not rely on any information discovered by Mack in obtaining authority for a search. Because the issuance of the warrant is, therefore, wholly independent of the illegality, the discovery and seizure of the book by Pete is lawful under the independent source doctrine.

Statements **A** through **E** provide additional information or change the facts in different ways, four of which would affect admissibility; we must identify the one that does not. **A** posits that evidence pertaining to the book was necessary to the probable cause determination. This is clearly relevant. If the probable cause necessary to issue the warrant depends on information pertaining to the book, the warrant will not provide an independent source for the seizure, since it would rely on the very illegality that it was meant to overcome. Likewise, if the warrant is found to be lacking in particularity, it would also fail to provide a *valid* independent justification for the seizure. As such, we would be left with two invalid seizures: Mack's and Pete's. **B** is, therefore, relevant.

D provides that Mack entered the apartment after seeing Jill reenter it carrying a blowtorch. Given her recent exit with Sean, it would be reasonable for Mack to conclude that the two are in the process of destroying evidence, first with bleach and now through burning. Based on these "exigent circumstances," Mack would be justified in entering the apartment without a warrant to secure the crime scene. **D** is relevant.

This leaves us with **C** and **E**. **C** states that Pete obtained the warrant after learning of Mack's unlawful conduct. This circumstance is potentially very important. For example, if Pete relied on any of the information conveyed by Mack in obtaining the warrant, the warrant would be invalid. Even if Pete does not do so, courts might be disinclined to deem the warrant an "independent source" if the application was tainted by an unlawful visual seizure of incriminating evidence.

E, on the other hand, is clearly irrelevant. Whether or not the manager knew that Mack was a police officer, Mack himself surely knew it! Thus, what the manager knew is potentially relevant only in assessing the extent to which his actions may subject him to liability in a civil suit brought by Sean or Jill. It has no relevance to the criminal proceeding against Sean.

E is the correct answer.

C.   Inevitable Discovery

Inevitable discovery is closely related to, but analytically distinct from, the independent source doctrine. The independent source doctrine allows the prosecutorial use of evidence tainted by an initial, unlawful search or seizure where such evidence is later seized through a lawful procedure wholly independent of the prior illegality. In the inevitable discovery context, by contrast, a police officer's unconstitutional conduct leads to the discovery of evidence that is not subsequently seized, or "re-seized," through lawful means. Prosecutorial use of such evidence rests on proof, by a preponderance of the evidence, that police officers would have inevitably discovered the evidence in question, based on the present state of their investigation into the relevant criminal activity.

The U.S. Supreme Court first recognized inevitable discovery as an exception to the exclusionary rule in *Nix v. Williams*, 467 U.S. 431 (1984). In *Nix*, a police officer violated a criminal defendant's Sixth Amendment right to counsel by interrogating him outside the presence of his attorney about the whereabouts of the dead body of an eleven-year-old girl Williams was charged with killing. As a result of the unlawful interrogation, Williams led the police to the girl's body. Because the discovery was inextricably linked to the Sixth Amendment violation in the absence of any independent source, the trial court excluded the evidence.

The U.S. Supreme Court reversed, reasoning that police officers would have inevitably discovered the body, based on the search currently underway. The Court pointed, in particular, to the "grid search" being used by local police to systematically inspect the wooded area where the body was believed to be located. At the time Williams led the officer to the body, the search party was only two and one-half miles from it and was closing in on its actual location.

As such, any bad faith on the part of the officer who conducted the interrogation was irrelevant, since the police would have found the body regardless.

QUESTION 3. Liar, liar. Responding to a tip, the United States Attorney's Office was investigating the securities trading activities of Lori, a rising star at Silverman Sachs. Through their investigation, federal officials discovered that Lori had falsely reported her trading activity to boost her profitability. In addition, her colleagues reported that they believed she was using cocaine, based on her erratic behavior and the fact that her nose was often running. (A perpetually runny nose is a symptom of frequent cocaine use.)

Based on the reporting misrepresentations and other trading irregularities linked to Lori, federal officers obtained a warrant to search her apartment for any documentary evidence that "proves, or tends to prove" securities fraud. While executing the warrant, officers found further evidence of fraudulent trading. They also seized several ounces of cocaine from a change purse located in Lori's jewelry box, an area they were not authorized to search. Dwight, the assistant U.S. attorney prosecuting Lori's case, argues that the cocaine is admissible nonetheless, based on inevitable discovery. Dwight's argument should:

A. Prevail, based on the information gleaned from Lori's colleagues.
B. Prevail, because the discovery of further evidence of securities fraud would have led officers to obtain authority for a broader search of Lori's apartment.
C. Fail, because securities fraud and cocaine are not closely linked.
D. Fail, because the evidence of cocaine use was too weak.

ANALYSIS. For the inevitable discovery doctrine to apply, Dwight would need to prove that it was more likely than not that federal officers would find the cocaine lawfully, based on the current state of their investigation into Lori's misconduct. At present, they have strong evidence that Lori has engaged in, and presumably is continuing to engage in, securities fraud. They also have learned that Lori's colleagues believe that she is using cocaine, due to her erratic behavior and frequently runny nose.

That officers have acquired further evidence in Lori's apartment linking her to securities fraud is likely to lead them to request additional search warrants—including, for example, a search of her office and, perhaps, a second, broader search of her apartment. The likelihood of this occurrence is irrelevant for our purposes, however, since any such warrant would logically extend only to *documents*, since evidence of securities fraud commonly takes this form. If the issuance of a warrant that includes a search for non-documentary evidence of the type that may be found in a pouch in a jewelry box is possible, it is certainly not inevitable, based on the facts provided. **B** is, therefore, wrong.

Answer **C** focuses, by contrast, on the lack of any necessary connection between the securities fraud and cocaine use in rejecting the inevitable discovery claim.

While the link between the two is tenuous at best, Dwight need not rely exclusively on the securities fraud evidence where, as here, there is independent evidence of drug use. That is, based on the information officers have lawfully acquired about Lori's drug use, Dwight can argue that the discovery of the cocaine in her apartment was inevitable without regard to the securities fraud issue. **C** is wrong.

Answer **A** makes this very argument, positing that the discovery of the cocaine was inevitable, in light of the information gleaned from Lori's colleagues. The problem with this argument is the strength of this evidence. Both Lori's erratic behavior and her runny nose, even if frequent, can be explained by myriad considerations other than cocaine abuse. (For example, knowledge that she was engaging in felonious misconduct would logically have an adverse effect on her physical and mental well-being!) Moreover, her co-workers' criticisms may be unreliable; jealous of her stellar productivity, their slings and arrows may be an effort to undermine and embarrass her.

In *Nix*, at the time of the unlawful discovery of the girl's body, the police were already engaged in a methodical search that would very soon have led them to it. Here, at the time of the unlawful search of Lori's jewelry box, we have only reports of illegal conduct from colleagues of questionable motivation. Her colleagues' comments are plainly insufficient to prove that the federal officers would have inevitably discovered the cocaine in Lori's apartment.

The correct answer is **D.**

D.   The "Attenuation" Doctrine

The doctrine of attenuation allows the introduction of evidence when the connection between unconstitutional police conduct and the evidence obtained is remote or has been interrupted such that "the interest protected by the constitutional guarantee that has been violated would not be served by suppression of the evidence obtained." *Utah v. Strieff*, 136 S. Ct. 2056 (2016). The application of the doctrine is necessarily case-sensitive and fact-specific. To this end, *Brown v. Illinois*, 422 U.S. 590 (1975), identified three factors which lower courts should weigh: the temporal proximity of the illegality to the acquisition of evidence; the existence of any intervening events and circumstances; and the purpose and flagrancy of official misconduct. See also *Strieff* (affirming the *Brown* factors).

The doctrine's seminal case, *Wong Sun v. United States*, 371 U.S. 471 (1963), provides an apt illustration of the principle. In *Wong Sun*, seven police officers invaded Toy's dry cleaning business in the late evening and, intending to intimidate Toy, proceeded to the back of the store where Toy resided with his family. They entered the bedroom and, while his terrified wife and children looked on, the officers arrested, handcuffed, and interrogated Toy. Finding that the arrest violated Toy's Fourth Amendment rights, the trial court disallowed the use of Toy's incriminating statements, as well as all information derived from them. Among the excluded "fruit of the poisonous tree" was the confession of Toy's confederate, Wong Sun. Toy had led police to Wong Sun through comments made during his interrogation. Later that same night, police arrested Wong Sun, who subsequently confessed to his involvement in drug trafficking.

The U.S. Supreme Court reversed, finding that Wong Sun's confession, as well as the heroin he provided, were admissible against him. Wong Sun had confessed at the station house two days after his arraignment and subsequent release on his own recognizance pending trial. The passage of time, coupled with his choice to provide incriminating testimonial and physical evidence voluntarily after consulting with counsel, "purged the taint" of the unlawful arrest and justified the introduction of the confession and heroin against him.

In *Strieff*, the temporal proximity was far greater. The defendant was arrested only minutes after an unlawful traffic stop, and a subsequent search incident to that arrest turned up methamphetamine and drug paraphernalia. The Court acknowledged that the time parameters favored the defendant but reasoned that the other *Brown* factors favored the defendant. First, the violation was not flagrant or purposeful, but merely negligent. Second, the arrest warrant was valid and existed prior to the stop. On balance, therefore, the Court felt that admission of the contraband was warranted.

QUESTION 4. Mary had a little scam. Mary was arrested in her home on Wednesday night when her neighbor, Madge, reported that Mary had stolen some jewelry. Officer Bill rang the doorbell and, when Mary refused to open the door, he pushed the door open and chased her into the rear of the house, where he grabbed her forcibly, threw her to the floor, and handcuffed her, in violation of her Fourth Amendment rights. Mary was held in the county jail and was arraigned two days later in state court. Unable to make bail, she was ordered back to jail, following the arraignment. Officer Rupert transported her back to jail in a police vehicle. In the car on her way back to jail, Mary told Rupert that Madge had too many jewels and that Mary deserved "at least one" for being such a good friend to Madge over the years. Mary now claims that her comments to Rupert should be suppressed, as a product of the unlawful arrest in her home. Mary's claim:

A. Has merit.
B. Lacks merit, because the confession occurred two days after the arrest.
C. Lacks merit, because Rupert was not the officer who unlawfully arrested Mary.
D. Lacks merit, because the confession occurred two days after the arrest and Rupert was not the officer who unlawfully arrested Mary.

ANALYSIS. Mary argues in this problem that her incriminating statement to Rupert should be suppressed as the "fruit'" of the previous, unlawful arrest in her home. Generally speaking, testimonial evidence linked to a Fourth Amendment violation is subject to exclusion, unless the "attenuation" doctrine applies.

Strieff and Brown instruct lower courts to balance three considerations to determine if attenuation has relevance in a given case. The flagrancy of the constitutional violation is one such factor. In this problem, Bill entered Mary's apartment against her will and physically abused her in effecting her arrest. As such, the misconduct is fairly egregious. The situation differs from *Wong Sun* in that Bill is acting alone and does not mistreat Mary in the presence of her children or other family members; however, the brutality and intimidating nature of his conduct is plainly evident and differs dramatically from the peaceful negligence of the officer's constitutional misconduct in *Strieff*.

A second consideration is the closeness in time of the constitutional violation and the confession. Here, as in *Wong Sun*, the events are separated by two days. The third factor looks to "intervening acts and circumstances." In *Wong Sun*, the defendant had been released from confinement prior to his confession and had consulted with counsel before acting. Moreover, he chose to come to the police station to confess. Mary's situation is quite different. Because she could not "make bail," she remained in police custody. In addition, the facts do not indicate that she discussed her confession with counsel, nor did she voluntarily place herself in the presence of law enforcement personnel at the time she spoke. This situation is also quite different from that of *Strieff* where the discovery of contraband was linked to a pre-existing, valid warrant.

For purposes of attenuation, the fact that Mary confessed to an officer other than the one who violated her Fourth Amendment rights is of questionable relevance. It is not a consideration emphasized by the U.S. Supreme Court in *Wong Sun* or other cases, nor does logic suggest that it should be. An individual who, like Mary, is a recent victim of police brutality is likely to be intimidated by any officer, particularly one with whom she is alone in police custody in a police vehicle on her way to jail.

Based on the foregoing, the only consideration that undermines Mary's claim is the two-day gap between her arrest and her confession. However, in light of the egregiousness of the constitutional infringement, Mary's failure to gain release from confinement during this period, and her involuntary presence in a police vehicle with only an officer present at the time she incriminates herself, the doctrine of attenuation will not apply.

The correct answer is **A**.

E.   The Closer

QUESTION 5. **While you were out.**   Martin was shocked when he arrived home one evening to find the door to his apartment open and Officer Brittany standing in his living room. Brittany was staring fixedly at a photograph depicting Martin directing what appeared to be a dogfight. Aware that dog-fighting is illegal is this jurisdiction, Brittany asked Martin where the photo was taken. Martin disregarded the question, instead asking Brittany what she was doing in his apartment. Brittany showed him a search warrant for the premises that, it turns out, was for the apartment on the floor below; Brittany had misread the address on the warrant. She apologized and left immediately.

Later that day, Brittany applied for a warrant to search Martin's apartment, based on the depiction in the photograph. The magistrate issued the warrant the next day. When Brittany returned to Martin's apartment to seize the photograph, Martin was out of town, but his wife, Martha, was present. Martha called Martin and explained that Brittany had seized the photograph and stated that Martin would be arrested upon his return. Martin arrived home the following day and went directly to the police station from the airport. Once there, he confessed his involvement in dogfighting to Brittany.

If Brittany's initial entry into Martin's apartment violated his Fourth Amendment rights, is either the seizure of the photograph or his confession nonetheless admissible?

A. Yes, the photograph is admissible under the independent source doctrine.
B. Yes, the photograph is admissible under the inevitable discovery doctrine.
C. Yes, the confession is admissible under the attenuation doctrine.
D. Yes, both are admissible.
E. No, neither is admissible.

ANALYSIS. This question asks whether any of the three doctrines discussed in this chapter can save Brittany's seizure of the photograph and/or Martin's confession from exclusion as the fruit of Brittany's unlawful initial entry into his apartment. For independent source to work, the physical seizure of the photograph must not rely on Brittany's prior unlawful entry in any way. For example, in *Segura, supra,* an unlawful entry that allowed police officers to view contraband played no part in other officers' efforts to secure a warrant to seize the same property; these officers had proceeded without knowledge of their colleagues' offending conduct. Here, Brittany relies entirely on the information she obtained from her initial entry to secure the warrant. This exercise of bad faith precludes the use of the independent source doctrine. **A** is wrong.

Conversely, the photograph is admissible if the prosecution can prove that, based on lawful activity currently underway, police officers would have inevitably discovered it. For example, in *Nix,* law enforcement officers were actively searching for the evidence in question and would have found it, even if the defendant had not led them to it "prematurely." In this problem, by contrast, the police investigation that gave rise to the discovery of the photograph concerned an entirely different party with no known connection to Martin and his involvement in dogfighting. There was, moreover, no additional information suggesting that Martin was engaged in any criminal wrongdoing. Discovery, in short, was far from inevitable. **B** is wrong.

The attenuation doctrine allows the admission of otherwise tainted information where its acquisition is the product of a suspect's free will, rather than prior, related, unlawful police conduct. Accordingly, in this problem, we must evaluate the strength of the connection between Martin's confession and Brittany's unlawful visual "seizure" of the photograph implicating him in dogfighting. To do so, we must apply the factors from *Strieff, supra,* and *Brown, supra.*

First, neither the nature nor the purpose of the officer's misconduct can be characterized as egregious. The constitutional infringement was careless, not willful, and Brittany left the apartment as soon as she realized her mistake. There was no physical mistreatment of Martin, nor any suggestion of psychological abuse. Second, two days elapsed between the unlawful entry and Martin's confession—the same time frame found sufficient for attenuation in *Wong Sun.*

Finally, in the period between the initial entry and the confession, Martin was free to do as he pleased and, in fact, traveled away from his home area by plane. He was at no time subjected to any official pressure and learned of his impending arrest from his wife, Martha. He also came to the station house voluntarily and chose to offer self-incriminating testimony. Based on the foregoing, prosecutors are likely to succeed in gaining admission of Martin's confession, based on the attenuation doctrine.

The correct answer is **C.**

✦ Cornwell's Picks

1.	County confusion	C
2.	Murder most foul	**E**
3.	Liar, liar	**D**
4.	Mary had a little scam	**A**
5.	While you were out	**C**

19

Entrapment and Due Process Defenses

CHAPTER OVERVIEW
A. Entrapment: The Majority Approach
B. Entrapment: The Minority Approach
C. The Due Process Clause
D. The Closer
✦ Cornwell's Picks

The defense of entrapment disallows criminal conviction where government officials implant in the mind of an otherwise innocent person the desire to commit the underlying offense and thereafter induce its commission. While often taught in criminal procedure courses, entrapment is conceptually akin to the affirmative defenses taught in substantive criminal law courses, such as necessity, duress, insanity, and self-defense. Like those defenses, entrapment does not derive from the federal Constitution. It was adopted by the U.S. Supreme Court in 1932 as a matter of federal law interpreting congressional policy. Since then, the defense has been recognized in all fifty states, through either legislation or judicial opinion. *Sorrells v. United States*, 287 U.S. 435 (1932).

The U.S. Supreme Court later found that covert government inducement of criminal activity may be so egregious that convicting nongovernmental participants would violate the Due Process Clauses of the Fifth and Fourteenth Amendments. For example, in *Raley v. Ohio*, 360 U.S. 423 (1959) and *Cox v. Louisiana*, 379 U.S. 559 (1965), the justices reversed convictions on due process grounds where government actors had encouraged the defendants to commit the crimes in question, representing that the acts promoted were lawful. Lower courts have recognized the viability of the due process defense in other circumstances as well where the government's involvement in manufacturing the crime was both indispensable and excessive.

A. Entrapment: The Majority Approach

As discussed above, entrapment occurs where the criminal design originates with the government, and its agents first implant in the mind of an innocent person the disposition to commit the crime and then induce it for purposes of prosecution. Thus, in *Sherman v. United States*, 356 U.S. 369 (1958), the U.S. Supreme Court overturned the defendant's conviction for selling illegal narcotics where a government agent, posing as a recovering addict, had solicited the defendant at a drug rehabilitation center, gained his sympathy and trust over time, and repeatedly asked him to sell the drugs over a three-month period before the defendant acquiesced. The foregoing constitutes, the Court reasoned, an impermissible course of conduct that "prays on the weakness of an innocent party and beguiles him into committing crimes which he otherwise would not have attempted." This characterization of the defendant as an innocent party imports that entrapment is unavailable to individuals whose prior conduct demonstrates a predisposition to commit the crime in question.[1]

Thus, in *United States v. Russell*, 411 U.S. 423 (1973), the Court rejected the defendant's entrapment defense to the crime of manufacturing methamphetamine, even though the government initiated contact with the defendant and provided a critical ingredient, because Russell was already engaged in this unlawful activity prior to the government's involvement. By contrast, in *Jacobson v. United States*, 503 U.S. 540 (1992), the Court found insufficient evidence of predisposition to violate the law where the defendant, who unlawfully purchased child pornography after more than two years of government inducement, had done so on only one prior occasion *when such conduct was legal*. If, however, Jacobson had agreed to engage in criminal activity with little inducement, his entrapment claim would have been unsuccessful, since an individual's "ready acquiescence" is sufficient in and of itself to demonstrate predisposition.

> **QUESTION 1. Blame Canada.** On January 1, 2006, it became a crime in the state of Setonia to buy watches manufactured in Canada. Two weeks earlier, as Nicole was browsing in a jewelry store on Main Street, she had seen Jeremy purchasing a watch with a maple leaf on the

---

1. Because Sherman had been convicted of two similar offenses in the past, the government had contended that he was predisposed. The Court rejected this argument, noting that the offenses in question were quite old (nine and five years, respectively) and therefore did not manifest "a readiness to sell narcotics," partic-ularly since he was trying to overcome his addiction when approached by undercover agents.

dial, commenting to the store owner that there is "nothing better than a Canadian-made timepiece." On January 5, Nicole contacted Police Officer Diane, head of the newly created Canadian Watch Task Force, and told her about Jeremy's purchase. Diane pursued Jeremy assiduously all year long, exhorting him to join a fictitious organization called Canadian Clock-a-Mania that offered a variety of Canadian timepieces at deep discounts. She also sent him catalogues and other printed materials offering a wide variety of well-priced Canadian merchandise. On at least six occasions, Jeremy declined to place an order. Finally, on November 12, 2006, Jeremy acquiesced and bought another Canadian watch. Diane thereafter arrested him. Jeremy's claim of entrapment will:

A. Succeed, because Canadian Clock-a-Mania is a fictitious organization.
B. Succeed, because Jeremy did not buy a Canadian watch soon after Diane began pursuing him in 2006.
C. Fail, because Jeremy was predisposed to purchase Canadian watches.
D. Fail, assuming the reliability of Nicole's information.
E. Fail, because Diane did not coerce him.

ANALYSIS. This is the type of question that rewards careful reading of the facts—a skill important not only for success on criminal procedure examinations, but on the bar exam as well. First, it is important to remember that the entrapment defense focuses analytically on the defendant's predisposition to commit the crime in question; if he is predisposed, the entrapment defense necessarily fails. As such, we can easily eliminate **A** and **E**.

Diane's attempt to solicit criminal conduct through the use of a fictitious organization is permissible and, like government coercion, it is irrelevant to the legal standard used to evaluate the defense. Answer **C** is appealing, inasmuch as it references the correct analytical framework—but don't choose too hastily. Remember that entrapment fails only when the defendant's past conduct demonstrates his propensity to engage in related *illegal* activity. Under the facts above, Diane had no evidence that Jeremy had ever broken the law when purchasing Canadian watches. As in *Jacobson*, the one purchase of which law enforcement was aware took place two weeks before the purchase of Canadian watches became illegal. Accordingly, **C** and **D** are wrong.

Had Jeremy purchased his second Canadian watch much earlier in 2006, shortly after Diane began her pursuit of him, his "ready acquiescence" would have demonstrated a predisposition to engage in relevant criminal conduct that would have eliminated his ability to claim the defense. Instead, he succumbed only after many months of concerted, aggressive intervention by law enforcement.

Answer **B** is correct.

B.   Entrapment: The Minority Approach

A minority of states follows the "objective" test of entrapment first articulated by Justice Frankfurter in his concurrence in *Sherman v. United States*. This test focuses on the methods used by law enforcement officials to elicit criminal conduct rather than on the defendant's predisposition. Accordingly, entrapment occurs where the overzealous actions of government officials are likely to induce criminal activity by those not otherwise ready and willing to engage in it. "The power of government is abused," Justice Frankfurter opined, "when [it is] employed to promote rather than detect crime and to bring about the downfall of those who, left to themselves, might well have obeyed the law."

QUESTION 2. **Birds of a feather.**   The U.S. Fish and Wildlife Service (FWS) has become increasingly concerned about the illegal killing of eagles on Indian reservations in South Dakota. The FWS attributes the problem to the willingness of consumers to pay "top dollar" for Indian handcrafts made from eagle feathers or carcasses. An area craftsman tells FWS Agent Jean that Carla, a cashier who works the "graveyard shift" at the local 711, is among the offenders. Carla is a single mother of four who receives public assistance to help make ends meet. Her criminal record is clean, except for a conviction two years earlier for possession of a small quantity of cocaine.

Jean waits one night until the store is empty and approaches Carla, asking if she is aware of anyone willing to make some money "on the side" by providing eagle feathers and carcasses. "I can pay," Jean adds, "up to $2,000 for each bird." Carla tells Jean that she can't help her, and Jean leaves. Jean returns each of the next two weeks, each time doubling the offer. On both occasions, Carla does not express interest in her offer. After the last visit, the FWS sends Carla an "official" letter stating that, effective immediately, her monthly public assistance will be reduced by 33 percent. Desperate, Carla contacts Jean the following day to tell her that she has decided to accept her offer and can produce "what [Jean] wants" by the end of the week. As Carla hands the dead bird over three days later, Jean places her under arrest for the unlawful killing and sale of protected wildlife. Carla claims entrapment. Under the minority approach, she is likely to:

A. Prevail, because Jean and the FWS impermissibly induced Carla's actions.
B. Prevail, because Carla had never committed a related criminal offense.
C. Fail, because Carla acquiesced within one month of initial contact by the FWS.
D. Fail, because Carla had a criminal record before Jean first approached her.

ANALYSIS. Because this question applies the minority test for entrapment, our focus is on whether the conduct of law enforcement officials is so egregious as to risk involving otherwise innocent people in criminal activity. This analytical benchmark is critical in identifying the right answer in that two of the four choices do not track this standard at all. Answer **B**, for example, credits the defense because Carla has never committed a similar crime. While this might suggest that she was not "predisposed" to commit this offense, predisposition is not a paramount concern in the objective test.

Likewise, while *Jacobson* required evidence of an individual's predisposition to engage in the illegal conduct in question, the U.S. Supreme Court was interpreting the majority approach in that case. **D** is, therefore, wrong. Our principal inquiry is not whether Carla's past indicates a propensity to engage in unlawful activity; we are asking, instead, whether the conduct of Jean or her employer was excessive in relation to its objective.

To that end, in deciding between the remaining two choices, we must evaluate the propriety of the government's conduct toward Carla. **C** would reject entrapment, since Carla "took the bait" within one month of her initial contact with Jean. This emphasis on time frame fails, however, to take account of the egregious nature of the government's conduct during this period. Most significantly, when increasing the amount of the offer proved ineffective, the FWS led Carla to believe that her public assistance would be reduced immediately by one-third. This false creation of panic and desperation over a single parent's ability to provide for her family's basic needs is beyond the pale.

A is the correct answer.

C. The Due Process Clause

In addition to the defense of entrapment, government involvement in criminal activity charged against the defendant may also be sufficiently outrageous to implicate the Due Process Clause of the Fifth and or Fourteenth Amendments to the federal Constitution. To violate principles of fundamental fairness, the U.S. Supreme Court had specified that the government's participation must violate "some protected right of the defendant." *Hampton v. United States*, 425 U.S. 484 (1976). Unfortunately, the justices have not clarified the precise meaning of the standard. In the few cases that have addressed this defense, the Court's splintered reasoning has undermined the clarity of its message.

A majority of justices has held that supplying contraband that is the *corpus delicti* of the crime is not a violation *per se* of due process. Beyond this, our understanding of the scope of the defense derives principally from *dicta* contained in various majority, concurring and dissenting opinions. Collectively, these opinions indicate that there are very few instances where government conduct would be sufficiently outrageous to violate due process. The justices have suggested, however, that a due process defense might be viable where the government's inducement includes the threat or actual use of violence against innocent parties, compromises First Amendment or other constitutional freedoms, or involves the provision of contraband indispensable to the criminal activity that is totally unavailable from other sources.

QUESTION 3. The hard sell.   Frustrated by law enforcement's inability to convict Rocco of racketeering charges, Officer Tom decided to pursue more modest goals. Knowing that Rocco was a drug user, Tom approached Rocco's best friend, Eric, for help in setting up Rocco. When Eric refused, Tom used physical "persuasion," knocking him to the ground and explaining that he could expect more of the same if he "did not wise up."

Fearful, Eric agreed to help Tom. The next evening, Eric met Rocco at Rocco's apartment. Eric begged Rocco to buy some cocaine, claiming that he needed it "real bad." When Rocco said he could not access any cocaine until the following week, Eric told him that he knew a dealer who could bring some over right away. Rocco resisted, stating that he would never buy from someone he didn't know. Eric became hysterical, screaming that he owed this dealer a lot of money. To buy some time, Eric had promised to find the dealer a new client that night. If Eric failed, the dealer said he would "relocate the nose" on Eric's mother's face. Reluctantly, Rocco acquiesced. He bought cocaine from Eric's dealer who was, in reality, an undercover cop.

Rocco's argument that the conduct of law enforcement violated due process should focus on which of the following?

A.   The use of Rocco's best friend as an undercover police agent.
B.   Tom physically harmed Eric to gain his cooperation.
C.   The potential harm to Eric's mother if he (Rocco) did not buy the cocaine.
D.   The fact that the police provided the contraband used to prosecute Rocco.

ANALYSIS.   As discussed above, due process claims based on outrageous government conduct are extremely difficult to prove and have been, as a result, largely unsuccessful. Note, however, that this problem asks you to identify the *best* argument, which may or may not be one that is likely to succeed. With this in mind, let's start with the arguments that seem weakest from the standpoint of due process.

Tom's use of Eric, Rocco's best friend, as an undercover informant is not outrageous. Whereas at least one court has found that a violation of due process occurred where the government initiates or exploits a sexual relationship to foster criminal activity, exploiting a friendship has not been considered to be of the same magnitude. See, e.g., *United States v. Hart*, 963 F.2d 1278 (9th Cir. 1992). Answer **A** is wrong.

Answer **D** is likewise incorrect. While the dissenters in *Russell* suggested that due process could be implicated where government officials supplied the contraband used to convict the defendant, their concern was for those situations where that contraband would have been totally unobtainable from other sources. Because Rocco represented that he could obtain cocaine from any number of dealers, this rationale is inapposite here.

The remaining two answers are more appealing in that both involve threatened or actual physical violence. At first blush, you may be inclined to favor **B**, since Eric is Rocco's best friend and he was coerced into assisting the police through physical brutality. While this may seem more egregious than the threat against Eric's mother, **B** has one serious shortcoming: The conduct in question had no direct impact on Rocco. The U.S. Supreme Court has emphasized that due process claims must compromise the personal constitutional rights of the *defendant*; in this instance, it was Eric's rights that were violated, not Rocco's, since Rocco was unaware of the violence perpetrated by Tom against Eric. By contrast, when Eric told Rocco about the threat against his (Eric's) mother, Rocco changed his mind and purchased the drugs. As such, the conduct is much more closely linked to his personal right to be free from outrageous government conduct.

C is the best answer.

D.   The Closer

QUESTION 4. **Seize the "A."**   Setonia's criminal code makes it unlawful to cheat on law school exams at any of the state law schools. Endeavoring to reduce cheating at Seton Hall, the dean decided to "plant" a file in the student lounge with the label "Answers to this semester's crim pro exams—confidential—do not open or remove." At the dean's request, state troopers set up and monitored a video camera to record student activity.

One hour after it was planted, Joe walked by. He looked at the file, hesitated and moved on. Curious, he returned five minutes later. He opened the file, leafed through and found the exam for his criminal procedure section. As he was removing it from the file, Trooper Mike rushed in and placed Joe under arrest for cheating. Joe has never before been arrested for any criminal offense, nor has he been the subject of any disciplinary proceeding in high school or college where cheating was alleged.

He moves to exclude the videotape evidence, claiming entrapment and a violation of his due process rights. His defense is plausible as to:

A. Entrapment under the majority approach.
B. Entrapment under the minority approach.
C. The Due Process Clause.
D. Entrapment, under both the majority and the minority approaches.
E. Entrapment, under both the majority and the minority approaches, and the Due Process Clause.

ANALYSIS. In this closer, Joe is a law student who commits the crime of cheating under Setonia law. We must determine the extent to which the actions of law enforcement, and/or Joe's response to those actions, support his claims of entrapment and a violation of due process.

Under the majority approach to entrapment, defendants who are predisposed to engage in the criminal activity in question cannot claim entrapment. Here, Joe has no criminal record, nor is there any record of prior disciplinary action taken against him by an academic institution for cheating. However, even if an individual has an unblemished past, his "ready acquiescence" to criminal activity will establish the predisposition necessary to preclude entrapment. Thus, because Joe attempted to remove the answers to the exam with no further encouragement by the state police or the dean, his entrapment claim fails under the majority approach.

Both the minority test for entrapment and due process claims focus on government misconduct rather than on the defendant's predisposition to engage in criminal activity. The evaluative framework for the minority approach regarding entrapment asks, essentially, whether the police conduct in question would lead an otherwise law-abiding individual to commit the target offense(s). Thus, in *State v. Powell*, 726 P.2d 266 (Haw. 1986), the Hawaii Supreme Court held that the conduct of the Honolulu Police Department constituted entrapment as a matter of law where the defendant stole the wallet of an officer pretending to be a drunken man lying on the ground in a high-crime area with the wallet sticking out of his back pocket. Deeming the "drunk decoy" operation police-manufactured crime, the Court reasoned that it "created a substantial risk that [theft] would be committed by persons other than those who [were] ready to commit it." Likewise, Joe can argue that, by tantalizing anxious law students with answers to a final exam, the police and dean manufactured the cheating offense and created a serious risk that innocent individuals would be ensnared in the criminal net.

While similar in certain respects to the minority approach to entrapment, the due process defense requires that the government misconduct be so outrageous as to violate principles of fundamental fairness. Accordingly, Joe would contend that it is outrageous and fundamentally unfair, given the competitive environment of law school, to offer students a highly useful and otherwise unavailable benefit that would give them a significant grading advantage over their classmates.

It is difficult to believe that this argument would prevail. As discussed earlier, this defense is very rarely successful and is reserved for government misconduct of the most egregious sort. Since law students, like lawyers, are held to lofty standards of professional and ethical conduct, it is tough to argue that it "shocks the conscience" to expect Joe not to do something that is not only highly unethical but also criminal.

In conclusion, of the three proffered defenses, only entrapment under the minority approach is at all plausible. The correct answer is **B**.

✦ Cornwell's Picks

1.	Blame Canada	**B**
2.	Birds of a feather	**A**
3.	The hard sell	**C**
4.	Seize the "A"	**B**

20

Due Process of Law and Confessions

CHAPTER OVERVIEW
A. Threats, Violence, and Physical Abuse
B. Beyond Physical Abuse
C. Promises and Mental Impairment
D. The Closer
✣ Cornwell's Picks

A.   Threats, Violence, and Physical Abuse

At common law, coerced confessions were excluded as untrustworthy. It was not until 1936 that the U.S. Supreme Court recognized that the federal Constitution imposes independent requirements for the admissibility of incriminating statements made before trial in state prosecutions. In that first case, *Brown v. Mississippi*, 297 U.S. 278 (1936), the Court held that the state violated the defendant's due process rights by admitting confessions obtained by whipping. Later cases addressed egregious police misconduct involving actual or threatened violence; the deprivation of food, sleep, or water; or intolerable conditions of detention. See, e.g., *Ashcraft v. Tennessee*, 322 U.S. 143 (1944). In these cases, the U.S. Supreme Court held that the Due Process Clause is violated with "no need to measure [the conduct's] effects on the will of the individual victim." *Stein v. New York*, 346 U.S. 156 (1953).

More recent cases, however, have regarded coercion as the focus of the due process analysis, even where the threat of physical force against the suspect was present. For example, in *Payne v. Arkansas*, 356 U.S. 560 (1958), the U.S. Supreme Court found that the defendant's confession violated due process because it was "not an expression of free choice" where the chief of police stated to the defendant that, if the defendant did not confess, the chief would let in an angry mob of thirty to forty people that "wanted to get [him]." Likewise, in *Arizona v. Fulminante*, 499 U.S. 279 (1991), the U.S. Supreme Court disallowed

225

a confession demanded from a government informant as "payment" for protection from other inmates who had threatened the defendant-confessor with bodily harm. Under these circumstances, the Court noted, "Fulminante's will was overborne in such a way as to render his confession the product of coercion."

QUESTION 1. A toxic relationship. Raymond's wife, Trixie, called the police, hysterical, claiming that she had found her husband dead on the living-room floor. Due to the uncertain cause of death, an autopsy was performed through which it was determined that Raymond had died from cyanide poisoning. Suspicious of Trixie, the police discovered that she had run a computer search two weeks earlier looking for web-based sources of cyanide. Trixie denied running the search, claiming that someone else must have used her log-in name and password. The police did not believe her. Frustrated at her unwillingness to confess, Officer Sanjay sent Trixie a letter, unsigned, on police department stationery stating "Confess to the murder, if you want your daughter to see her sixteenth birthday." Two days later, Trixie confessed. Charged with her husband's murder, she now seeks suppression of the confession on due process grounds.

Which of the following, if true, is LEAST relevant in evaluating her claim?

A. Sanjay did not sign the letter.
B. Trixie's daughter will turn sixteen three days after Trixie receives the letter.
C. Trixie waited two days to confess.
D. Trixie thought the letter was a joke.
E. Trixie had prepared a written confession before she received the letter.

ANALYSIS. For Trixie to prevail, she must prove that her confession was not the product of free will. Accordingly, we must choose the factual statement that, if true, is least likely to influence Trixie's decision to confess.

The age of Trixie's daughter is clearly relevant in that the letter states that the daughter will not "see her sixteenth birthday." If the daughter is currently three days shy of her sixteenth birthday, Trixie will feel pressured to act quickly to spare her life. **B** is incorrect.

By contrast, if Trixie thought the letter was a joke, her due process claim would necessarily fail, since the letter would have had no coercive effect on her at all. Likewise, Trixie's preparation of a written confession suggests that she had seriously considered confessing prior to receiving the letter; as such, it would be relevant in evaluating her claim. **D** and **E** are wrong.

The time period that transpired before Trixie confessed is relevant from the perspective of both the prosecution and the defense. The prosecutor can argue that, if Trixie took the threat to her daughter's life seriously, she would have responded immediately, so as not to take any chances that the threat would be carried out. The defense can argue, conversely, that Trixie's decision to confess before her daughter's birthday shows the impact the letter had on her. Either way, the time frame is relevant. **C** is wrong.

Sanjay's failure to sign the letter is not as significant as the foregoing. While his signature would have identified the specific source of the threat, the fact that the letter was written on police department letterhead and issued a specific threat against a family member is enough to render it credible in Trixie's mind. Trixie's lack of knowledge of the writer's identity is relatively insignificant in evaluating the letter's coercive effect.

A is the correct answer.

B.   Beyond Physical Abuse

The U.S. Supreme Court has acknowledged that a confession may be violative of due process in the absence of physical abuse. Police tactics may render the confession involuntary through psychological coercion created through official pressure, fatigue, and trickery. For example, in *Spano v. New York,* 360 U.S. 315 (1959), the defendant confessed after an eight-hour interrogation in the absence of counsel that included repeated entreaties from a friend, an officer in the police department, who falsely indicated that, if Spano did not confess, the officer would lose his job, which would be "disastrous" for the officer's three children and pregnant wife.

In applying the due process standard, courts use a "totality of the circumstances" test to determine if deception, trickery, and other tactics overbore the suspect's will. In *Frazier v. Cupp,* 394 U.S. 731 (1969), for example, the U.S. Supreme Court deemed the defendant's confession voluntary, even though it followed directly on the heels of the police interrogator's false statement that the defendant's accomplice had already confessed. This misrepresentation, "while relevant," was deemed insufficient to render an otherwise voluntary confession inadmissible. Conversely, in *Leyra v. Denno,* 347 U.S. 556 (1954), the U.S. Supreme Court found a confession involuntary where it was obtained through the efforts of a psychiatrist trained in hypnosis whom the defendant thought was a general practitioner brought in to treat a sinus ailment. Where, as here, a defendant is reduced "to almost trance-like submission by use of the arts of a highly skilled psychiatrist," the Due Process Clause is violated.

QUESTION 2. Divine justice.   Ellen's parents reported her missing, stating that they were afraid her long-term boyfriend, Sal, with whom they were close, had harmed her because Ellen was seen with him an hour before her disappearance. Sal had been increasingly paranoid for weeks, believing erroneously that Ellen had been cheating on him.

Officer Ann met Sal at his office at 3:00 P.M. and took him to the police station for questioning. Sal waived his *Miranda* rights. He seemed very nervous, but disavowed any knowledge of Ellen's disappearance. "We found her dead body," Ann lied, "and someone saw your car in the vicinity." While still very nervous, Sal insisted repeatedly that he had nothing to do with the death.

After twenty-four hours of nonstop questioning, Ann changed tactics. Knowing that Sal was a devout Catholic who attended mass every day, Ann told him that she was calling in a "special" officer whom Sal would "really enjoy talking to." Ann then summoned Marta, a police officer who is also a nun. "Come on, Sal," Ann urged. "Ellen's parents are sick about this. They can't stop crying. I know how much you love them, Sal. Give them peace of mind. Let's pray for them, you and Sister Marta and me, together." They held hands and prayed for God to comfort Ellen's parents. At the end of the prayer, Marta turned to Sal and said, "Enough, Sal. It's time to tell me what you did." At this point, Sal confessed to the murder.

Sal moves to suppress his confession as violating his due process rights. Which of the following is his best argument?

A. Playing on his relationship with Ellen's parents was unfairly prejudicial.
B. Lying to him about the death of the victim was fundamentally unfair.
C. Appealing to his religious nature was impermissible.
D. Depriving him of rest during twenty-four hours of questioning overbore his will.

ANALYSIS.   To answer this problem correctly, you must remember that the U.S. Supreme Court's due process analysis in the confessions context uses a "totality of the circumstances" test. Thus, in most instances, no one factor is clearly dispositive in proving a violation, even though you might personally consider the tactic to be highly suspect or offensive.

Answer **A** posits that Ann's exploitation of Sal's close relationship with the victim's parents was prejudicial. This might be so, but that fact alone does not render his confession involuntary, which is the standard that Sal must meet. Likewise, while Ann lied to Sal about the recovery of Ellen's body, the U.S. Supreme Court has held that this sort of trickery violates due process only if the surrounding circumstances suggest that the lie coerced the defendant to confess. In this instance, one cannot conclude that the lie produced the confession; on the contrary, Sal did not confess until countless hours later. Nor did Sal have a strong emotional reaction to the news of the recovery of the body. He was very nervous both before and after hearing that statement. **B** is wrong.

Answer **C** suggests that using Officer Marta to appeal to Sal's religious nature violates due process principles. This argument is problematic. First, in contrast to *Leyra v. Denno*, the defendant is not misled as to the identity of the interrogator. While Ann refers to Marta as "Sister," Marta is, in a fact, a nun and Ann also identifies Marta as a police officer. Second, while his confession follows the prayer, there is no indication that Marta's conduct has overborne Sal's will. Awakening an individual's conscience or moral values does not extinguish free will.

We are left, therefore, with **D**. While lengthy questioning is not always enough, in and of itself, to render a confession involuntary, it is certainly a relevant consideration. Moreover, it is the only answer that does not appear, on its face, to be incorrect.

D is, therefore, the best answer.

C.   Promises and Mental Impairment

Promises made to defendants during an interrogation have presented another thorny area for the U.S. Supreme Court. In *Bram v. United States*, 168 U.S. 532 (1897), the Court held that a confession "obtained by any direct or implied promises, however slight" would be involuntary. More recent cases have clarified that, for promises to violate due process, they must have overborne a suspect's will, in light of the totality of circumstances present. See, e.g., *Arizona v. Fulminante, supra*.

Accordingly, courts have found oblique promises of leniency — for example, assuring a suspect that the district attorney will be informed of his cooperation and/or that the prosecutor will consider a lower sentencing recommendation if he confesses — to be insufficiently coercive to trigger due process concerns. More specific guarantees of favorable treatment in exchange for a confession — such as promises of non-prosecution, lessened charges, or medical treatment — are far more likely to result in exclusion.

Whatever the individual circumstances, the focus of the due process inquiry is *always* government coercion. In *Colorado v. Connelly*, 479 U.S. 157 (1986), the defendant walked up to a police officer on the street and confessed to a murder he had committed several months earlier. The following day, he became visibly disoriented and indicated, for the first time, that "voices" had told him to confess. The state's psychiatrist later concluded that the defendant was a chronic schizophrenic who was psychotic at the time he confessed.

The U.S. Supreme Court deemed his confession voluntary, holding that the police officer to whom Connelly confessed engaged in no coercive conduct; in the absence of "police overreaching," there can be no due process claim. The majority was unwilling, in their words, to recognize a new constitutional right to confess "only when totally rational and properly motivated." Nor was the confession's unreliability an alternative ground for invalidation since the rules of evidence, not the Due Process Clause, govern the admissibility of "presumptively false evidence."

QUESTION 3. **Mother knows best.**   Police responded to the sounds of gunfire at the Sunnyvale Savings & Loan. When they arrived, they found the security guard dead and three men in their twenties running out of the bank. They apprehended the men, all of whom had guns, two blocks away. At the station house, Officer Marilyn questioned one of the three, Buddy. Buddy's address was a halfway house for developmentally disabled adults. When she handed Buddy a card with his *Miranda* rights, Marilyn could tell he could not read it. She calmly and patiently explained his rights to him, after which Buddy said he would talk to her. During the next two hours of interrogation, Buddy consistently refused to tell Marilyn who had killed the guard.

At that moment, Buddy's mother arrived, and Marilyn brought her into the interrogation room. "Look, Buddy," Marilyn commented, "I know you want to come clean and clear your conscience. You did a bad thing, Buddy, and you know it. I'll tell the district attorney," Marilyn added, "that you belong in a hospital, not a prison. I promise you that." "Buddy, do you hear the lady?" his mother asked. "You'll go to a hospital, not a jail. It's time to tell her what happened." At that point, Buddy started crying uncontrollably. Five minutes later, he confessed to killing the security guard.

If Buddy moves to suppress his confession under the Due Process Clause, he will:

A. Prevail, because his mother pressured him to confess.
B. Prevail, because Marilyn told Buddy he could go to a hospital instead of to prison.
C. Prevail, because Buddy's confession is not reliable, since he is developmentally disabled.
D. Fail.

ANALYSIS.   This problem requires close scrutiny of the interaction between Buddy and Marilyn, as well as consideration of the significance, if any, of the contributions of Buddy's mother. When Marilyn begins the interrogation, she knows that Buddy has significant cognitive limitations, since he is unable to read the *Miranda* card. She interrogates him nonetheless and ultimately obtains a confession. Under *Connelly*, our due process analysis must focus on whether Marilyn coerced Buddy to confess, not on the logic or rationality of Buddy's conduct.

The facts in the problem offer significant parallels to those in *Connelly*. In both cases, the police officer does not interact with the suspect in a hostile or intimidating manner. The tone of voice used by both officers is polite and controlled, and they are careful to read the suspects their rights. The difference, of course, is in the nature of the disability; Connelly is severely mentally ill, whereas Buddy's impairment relates to his intellectual capacity.

This difference does not affect the due process analysis, however. Our focus is on whether the facts uncover coercion by Marilyn, not whether Buddy's cognitive challenges make his confession less reliable. Reliability, the U.S. Supreme Court noted in *Connelly*, is the province of the rules of evidence, not the Due Process Clause. **C** is incorrect.

Frustrated at her inability to extract a confession from Buddy, Marilyn attempts to move him off the mark by raising the possibility that he could serve his sentence in a hospital rather than a prison. While this tactic would raise a constitutional flag if it falsely communicated a guarantee of relocation outside the jail setting, Marilyn is careful not to do this. She promises only that she will tell the district attorney that Buddy *belongs* in a hospital. The prosecutor is free to disagree with this assessment and to place Buddy in a penal facility.

Moreover, it is not at all clear that Marilyn's statement produces Buddy's confession. As soon as the words are out of Marilyn's mouth, Buddy's mother jumps in and tells Buddy to confess, telling him he will "go to a hospital, not a jail." It is after the mother's intervention, rather than Marilyn's, that Buddy confesses. It is not Marilyn's fault that Buddy's mother misconstrues the import of Marilyn's comment. Thus, Marilyn's conduct is not coercive either in substance or in effect. **B** is wrong.

Answer **A** is factually correct. Buddy's mother did pressure him to confess. She is not, however, a government agent. Nor is she acting at the behest of the state. Had the police department sent her in there to obtain a confession from her son, the mother's conduct would implicate constitutional norms. As a private actor, it does not. **A** is incorrect.

Based on the foregoing, the correct answer is **D**. The facts do not disclose that Buddy's confession was obtained in violation of the Due Process Clause of the Fourteenth Amendment.

D. The Closer

QUESTION 4. Good cop, bad cop. The police arrested Martin based on evidence that he was involved in a conspiracy to aid terrorists planning to bomb a federal building. Officer Alice left him in an interrogation room, commenting that she would be back to talk to him after she got some coffee. As soon as she left, Martin heard screams from the room next-door, followed by a male voice, stating, "I'll burn you again, if you don't talk." Crying, a different voice responded: "Okay, Officer, anything to stop the pain."

At that moment, Alice returned. After Martin refused to answer her questions, she told him that terror suspects who did not cooperate were kept in solitary confinement indefinitely. Although she did not in fact have any authority over inmate cell assignments, Alice told Martin that, if he talked to her, she would "get him a better deal." When Martin still refused to cooperate, Alice left and Marcus entered. As soon as he spoke, Martin recognized the voice as that of the tormenter in the room next-door. Marcus was smoking a cigarette, which, upon entry, he forcefully put out in front of Martin while maintaining eye contact. Smiling wryly, Marcus told Martin that he (Marcus) was brought in because other suspects had found him "very persuasive." Marcus then asked Martin to name his co-conspirators. Martin remained silent.

Five minutes later, Alice returned with a police dog she claimed to be training. The dog was aggressive and growled repeatedly at Martin, who was visibly on edge. She told Martin he would not be transported back to jail for three hours and that she and the dog would stay with him until then. Alice knew that Martin was very afraid of dogs and added: "Of course, if you answer my questions, I can probably get you out of here much sooner." Martin still refused to answer her questions.

Fifteen minutes later, Marcus returned. He pressed his face against Martin's, commenting "I think you had best start cooperating right now." As the dog lunged toward him, Martin relented. "Okay," he whimpered, "I'll talk to the lady officer but, first, I want you and that mutt out of here." He pointed at Marcus and the police dog, his hand shaking. "Afterwards I want to go back to my cell." He proceeded to answer Alice's questions, implicating himself and others in the conspiracy. When he finished, Officer Perry entered to take Martin back to jail. As soon as Perry spoke, Martin recognized his voice as that of the "victim" whom Marcus was abusing in the room next-door.

At trial, Martin moves to suppress his statements to Alice, claiming the officers had violated his due process rights. In evaluating this claim, which of the following considerations is LEAST relevant?

A. Alice's promise to have Martin moved out of solitary confinement.
B. Marcus's conduct suggesting that he would burn Martin if he did not answer Alice's questions.
C. Alice's introduction of the police dog into the interrogation room.
D. Alice's statement that Martin could probably leave sooner if he answered her questions.

ANALYSIS. This chapter explores the scope of the due process defense to the admissibility of confessions. While initially the Due Process Clause applied only to egregious physical abuse by law enforcement, the U.S. Supreme Court has subsequently vindicated broader availability where the abuse is more psychological than physical in nature. Whatever the context, the analytical framework is the same, requiring proof that police misconduct rendered the confession involuntary by overbearing the defendant's will.

In our problem, a trio of officers—Alice, Marcus, and Perry—worked together to obtain incriminating information from Martin by weakening his resistance. Martin has moved to exclude his statements on due process grounds, and the question asks you to identify which of four evidentiary considerations is *least* relevant. Remember that we are using a "totality of the circumstances" test; therefore, two or more factors can work together to overbear a defendant's will. Our job is to identify which of the four choices appears *least* influential in this context.

Each of the four answers corresponds to a different tactic used by the trio to overcome Martin's resistance. Alice instigated three of the four. First, she promised to move Martin out of solitary confinement if he cooperated. She then brought an aggressive police dog into the interrogation room, knowing that Martin was very afraid of dogs. Finally, with the dog by her side, she told Martin that she could probably end the interrogation early if he answered her questions.

The ruse engineered by Marcus and Perry was more complicated. It began with Marcus pretending to burn a shrieking Perry, who was posing as a suspect being interrogated within earshot of Martin in the room next-door. The script then continued as Marcus took over from Alice in the interrogation room. Marcus adopted a very intimidating tone and posture when interacting with Martin, intimating through his actions that Martin could be his next victim if he remained recalcitrant.

Considered together, all four tactics have the potential to render Martin's confession involuntary by impliedly threatening physical harm, making a false promise of favorable treatment, or preying on a known psychological weakness. To determine which of the four tactics is least important in this regard, we need to consider the extent to which each influenced Martin's ultimate decision to confess.

Immediately before Martin agreed to cooperate, the police dog lunged at him, and Marcus, using a hostile tone with face-to-face physical contact, issued what Martin could have believed was a veiled threat of violence if he did not cooperate. Significantly, Martin became visibly shaken and demanded that both Marcus and the dog leave the room as a *quid pro quo* to his answering Alice's questions. By contrast, Martin showed no emotion when Alice promised to have him moved out of solitary confinement. In addition, he indicated that he wanted to return to his cell as soon as possible after the interrogation, with no mention of, or request for, reassignment.

The correct answer is **A**. Because Alice's promise to have Martin moved out of solitary confinement proved far less influential than the other tactics in overcoming his will, it is the least important factor in the due process analysis.

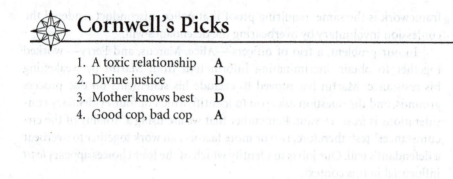

Cornwell's Picks

1. A toxic relationship   **A**
2. Divine justice   **D**
3. Mother knows best   **D**
4. Good cop, bad cop   **A**

21

Miranda: Remedying Police Coercion

CHAPTER OVERVIEW
A. Core *Miranda* Rights
B. The "Custody" Requirement
   1. A Two-Step Inquiry
   2. Age and Location
C. The "Interrogation" Requirement
D. The "Testimonial" Limitation
E. The Closer
✦ Cornwell's Picks

Until 1966, if a criminal defendant in a state court proceeding wished to challenge the admissibility, on federal constitutional grounds, of an incriminating statement made before the filing of formal charges, he was limited to the Due Process Clause of the Fourteenth Amendment and its "voluntariness" standard. (See Chapter 20.) *Miranda v. Arizona* introduced an additional challenge under the Self-Incrimination Clause of the Fifth Amendment and, in so doing, revolutionized constitutional criminal procedure. In a sweeping five-to-four decision, the U.S. Supreme Court repudiated police practices that worked to undermine a suspect's free will and made necessary the imposition of "adequate protective devices . . . to dispel the compulsion inherent in custodial surroundings."

It is important to remember that *Miranda* is designed to remedy police misconduct in the context of custodial interrogation *only*. As we will see, both "custody" and "interrogation" have specific definitions for *Miranda* purposes. Accordingly, when questioning takes place in a non-coercive setting, such as when suspects talk to an undercover informant whom they mistakenly believe to be a friend who will keep their confidence, the protections of the Fifth Amendment do not apply. See, e.g., *Illinois v. Perkins*, 492 U.S. 292 (1990) (*Miranda* inapplicable to jail cell interrogation of defendant by undercover agent posing as fellow inmate).

A.   Core *Miranda* Rights

Most of us are familiar with the rights enumerated in *Miranda* by virtue of their frequent recitation to suspects on television drama series featuring lawyers and police officers. These rights include, most significantly, the right to remain silent and the right to counsel. The right to counsel affords the right both to consult with an attorney and to have that attorney present during questioning. To ensure equal justice for all, regardless of wealth, suspects must also be told that, if they cannot afford an attorney, one will be appointed to represent them at no cost. Finally, suspects must be informed of the consequences of choosing to forgo silence and/or the benefits of counsel; before they waive *Miranda* rights and speak to the police, they must be instructed that anything they say "can and will be used against [them] in court."

While it is common practice for police departments to include these rights on a "*Miranda* card," which an officer reads to a suspect, the U.S. Supreme Court does not require such mechanistic precision. In *California v. Prysock*, 453 U.S. 355 (1981), the Supreme Court clarified that the terminology used is sufficient if it "reasonably conveys" the core rights detailed above. Thus, *Florida v. Powell*, 130 S.Ct. 1195 (2010), held that officers' satisfied this standard in telling a suspect he had the right to counsel before answering their questions and "at any time you want during this interview." The suspect claimed that the officers' words suggested that he was afforded a one-time opportunity to consult with an attorney, not the right to have the attorney present at all times during the interrogation. Acknowledging that this was not the "clearest possible" communication of the *Miranda* right to counsel, the majority concluded that the words nonetheless "were sufficiently comprehensive and comprehensible when given a commonsense reading."

While jurisdictions typically provide counsel to indigent defendants before trial, *Miranda* does not require them to do so. Thus, in *Duckworth v. Eagen*, 492 U.S. 195 (1989), the justices upheld Indiana's policy of telling suspects facing custodial interrogation that, while they had the right to a lawyer, they could not have one presently but one would be appointed "if and when [they] go to court." *Miranda* did not, the Court reasoned, require jurisdictions to pay for lawyers prior to trial; it simply disallowed pretrial custodial interrogation in the absence of an attorney when a suspect asked for one to be present.

> **QUESTION 1. Chip off the old cell block.**   Martin is the CEO of a Fortune 500 company that manufactures widgets. After a two-year federal investigation, Martin is indicted for multiple counts of money laundering and racketeering. The grand jury also indicts Martin's son, Junior, for similar offenses. Junior is currently a law student. Throughout the investigation, federal investigators and attorneys at the U.S. Attorney's Office handling the case had been in contact with Martin's lawyer.

> Following the issuance of the indictment, both Martin and Junior are arrested and brought to the U.S. Attorney's Office to meet with Rochelle, the lead attorney on the case. Not accustomed to providing *Miranda* rights, Rochelle fails to provide the full set of warnings. If so, which of the following omissions is least likely to result in the exclusion of a confession obtained thereafter?
>
> **A.** Rochelle does not tell Martin that he has the right to remain silent.
> **B.** Rochelle does not tell Junior that he has the right to counsel.
> **C.** Rochelle does not tell Martin that, if he cannot afford one, an attorney will be appointed to represent him at no cost to him.
> **D.** Rochelle does not tell Martin that anything he says can and will be used against him at trial.

ANALYSIS. In *Miranda*, the U.S. Supreme Court identified four "core" warnings: the right to remain silent, the right to counsel, the right of indigent arrestees to have an attorney appointed for them, and the acknowledgment that any incriminating statement made by arrestees during interrogation can be used against them at trial. Of our four possible answers, each contains a failure to communicate one of these core warnings. Thus, strictly speaking, *Miranda* rights were not "reasonably conveyed" to the defendants.

While this is true, courts have excused oversights of this magnitude where the circumstances clearly indicate that the suspect was aware of the omitted right. Since the essence of *Miranda* is making suspects facing custodial interrogation aware of available constitutional protections, lower courts are loath to elevate form over substance where such awareness is present and police conduct communicates respect for those rights and the intention to honor them. It is in this context, then, that we must evaluate our choices.

Junior's status as a law student does not allow police officers to dispense with *Miranda* warnings. In the majority opinion, the justices rejected a case-by-case inquiry into what a given suspect knew, noting that inevitably the process relied on speculation. This admonition has led lower courts to require lawyers to receive *Miranda* warnings; *a fortiori*, a law student merits at least as much. **B** is wrong.

A, **C**, and **D** ascribe an omission regarding each of the remaining three core warnings to Martin. The failure to apprize Martin of his right to remain silent and of the consequences of an incriminating assertion is clearly inexcusable. The same is not true, however, of the right to appointed counsel for indigent defendants. While courts are reluctant to speculate as to a given suspect's wealth, they have been far more willing to overlook the warning on appointed counsel when the police or prosecutor knows that the suspect has retained private counsel. Because the U.S. Attorney's Office has been dealing with Martin's attorney throughout the two-year investigation, the failure of the lead prosecutor to advise him of his right, if indigent, to appointed counsel is a far less serious oversight than the others.

C is the correct answer.

B. The "Custody" Requirement

To understand the U.S. Supreme Court's definition of custody under *Miranda*, it is important to remember that *Miranda*'s prophylactic rules were designed "to dispel the compulsion inherent in custodial surroundings." Accordingly, *Miranda* custody is "a term of art that specifies circumstances that are generally thought to present a serious danger of coercion." *Howes v. Fields*, 565 U.S. 499 (2012). One may, therefore, be in custody "in a technical sense" but not for purposes of *Miranda*. For example, defendant-inmate Fields was not in custody under *Miranda* during an interrogation in the conference room of the prison where he was housed since "isolation from the [dangerous] general prison population . . . does not suggest on its own the atmosphere of coercion that concerned the Court in *Miranda*."

1. A Two-Step Inquiry

Determining whether custody exists is a two-step process. Step one, sometimes called the "freedom-of-movement test," requires the court to ascertain whether a "reasonable person would have felt he or she was not at liberty to terminate the interrogation and leave." *Thompson v. Keohane*, 516 U.S. 99 (1995). If an individual's freedom of movement was curtailed in this way, we next ask "whether the relevant environment presents the same inherently coercive pressures as the type of station house questioning at issue in *Miranda*." *Howes v. Fields, supra.*

Custody requires satisfaction of both parts of the inquiry. Thus, in *Berkemer v. McCarthy*, 468 U.S. 420 (1984), the Court deemed routine traffic stops noncustodial for *Miranda* purposes. While they clearly constrain the motorist's freedom of movement, traffic stops are typically brief and, unlike interrogation at the police station, roadside interrogation takes place in public view and is generally less "police-dominated."

QUESTION 2. Love gone bad. Jill, a twenty-seven-year-old teacher, was reported missing by her parents. Her live-in boyfriend, Randy, came into the police station voluntarily to help the search effort. Officer Mireille thanked Randy for coming in and asked when he had last seen Jill. He answered "five days ago," which conflicted with information from Jill's best friend, Megan, who said she had seen the two together two days earlier. Suspicious of Randy, Mireille told him that it would be "in his best interest" to stay when he rose to leave. Surprised, Randy indicated that he would stay but asked if he could use the restroom before continuing. "Sure," Mireille replied, "right around the corner to the left."

When Randy returned, Officer Mike had joined Mireille, and the two questioned Randy for ninety minutes about his relationship with Jill, sensing that he was holding back valuable information. Randy remained cooperative, but his answers did not provide any information suggesting a motive to kill Jill. Frustrated, Mireille reached across the table, grabbed Randy's hand, looked into his eyes and said, calmly but forcefully, "C'mon, Randy, we need to find her. Where is she? You need to tell us." Suddenly tearful, Randy then admitted that he had killed Jill during a heated argument and had dumped her body in the ocean.

Was Randy's interrogation custodial?

A. Yes, when Mike entered the room.
B. Yes, when Mireille grabbed his hand.
C. No, because Randy could have terminated the encounter at any time.
D. No, because Randy did not come to the station house at the direction of the police.

ANALYSIS. To be in custody for *Miranda* purposes, two requirements must be met: First, viewing the totality of circumstances objectively, a reasonable person would have felt he or she was not at liberty to terminate the interrogation and leave; and, second, the environment presents inherently coercive pressures that mirror those associated with station-house questioning.

When the interrogation began, it was clearly noncustodial. Randy came to the station house voluntarily, offering to help in finding his missing girlfriend. Officer Mireille's demeanor changed, however, when she concluded that Randy was lying to her about his contact with Jill. Her comment that it would be in Randy's "best interest" to stay when he rose to leave reflects this atmospheric shift. Still, Randy was not ordered to remain and was granted leave to use the restroom upon his request. Had he simply left the station at this point, or communicated his intention to do so, there is nothing to suggest that the interrogation would have continued.

Officer Mike's entry into the room may have made the atmosphere appear more "police-dominated," but the facts do not suggest that his conduct was threatening or coercive. On the contrary, Randy's relaxed demeanor throughout the ninety-minute interrogation with both Mike and Mireille suggests the opposite. The fact that Mireille grabbed Randy's hand does not change this. Her actions did not forcibly restrain him and are equally likely to be seen as an affiliative, friendly act. Thus, Randy's subsequent confession does not appear to be the product of official coercion but, rather, of his own feelings of guilt or remorse.

As between **C** and **D**, **C** is the better answer. The fact that Randy came to the station house of his own accord establishes only that the interrogation was noncustodial at the outset. It is the fact that he was free to terminate the encounter at any time that made the duration of the exchange noncustodial.

C is the correct answer.

2. Age and Location

The custody determination is objective and is based on a totality of the circumstances. *Stansbury v. California*, 511 U.S. 318 (1994). It is consistent with the objective nature of the custody inquiry to take account of a child's age, if age is relevant *and* either the officer was aware of the child's age at the time of questioning or the child's age would have been objectively apparent to a reasonable officer. *J.D.B. v. North Carolina*, 564 U.S. 261 (2011). Age is less likely to be a "determinative, or even significant" consideration the closer the child is to the age of majority. *Id.; Yarborough v. Alvarado*, 541 U.S. 652 (2004) (17½-year-old suspect's age irrelevant in custody evaluation). A suspect's prior history with law enforcement is *never* relevant to the custody inquiry, whatever his or her age at the time of the interrogation. *Yarborough.*

While interrogation that occurs at the police station is more likely to be custodial than questioning that occurs in less "formal" settings, location is not dispositive in determining custody. Accordingly, in *Orozco v. Texas*, 394 U.S. 324 (1969), the U.S. Supreme Court found custody where federal agents entered the suspect's bedroom at 4:00 A.M. and questioned him about a shooting. Under these circumstances, the "potentiality for compulsion" mirrored that of the station house. By the same token, the Court has found interrogation at the station house and at a probation office to be noncustodial where, for example, the suspect came on his own accord, was familiar with the location, was in the presence of family members, and believed he could end questioning and leave at any time. See, e.g., *Yarborough; Minnesota v. Murphy*, 465 U.S. 420 (1984); *Oregon v. Mathiason*, 429 U.S. 492 (1977).

QUESTION 3. Bummer, dude. A police informant told Officer Tonya that Marius had information about a string of burglaries of commercial establishments on Main Street. The informant added that Tonya could find Marius in the town park at 4:00 P.M., when he and his friends met to play ultimate frisbee. After the informant left, Tonya and her partner, Luther, learned that Marius was a fifteen-year-old high-school sophomore with no criminal record.

That afternoon at 4:30 P.M., Tonya and Luther went to the park and, as expected, found Marius playing frisbee with his friends. They called him out of the game and told him they believed he had information about the burglaries. They then asked if he was willing to speak to them "in private." Marius agreed to do so, and the officers led him to an isolated part of the park about a quarter-mile away. Tonya and Luther found an empty bench and sat down, inviting Marius to sit between them. After he sat down, Marius asked if he was "in trouble" and Tonya answered: "Well, you might want to tell us what you know." "You know," Luther added, "I bet you'll feel better if you come clean with us. You're involved in this, aren't you?" "Yeah, man," Marius said regretfully. "I don't know what I was thinking."

Marius moves to suppress his confession, claiming that Tonya and Luther's failure to administer *Miranda* warnings violated his Fifth Amendment rights. The prosecutor argues that *Miranda* warnings were unnecessary because the officers' questioning was not custodial. Is Marius likely to prevail?

A. Yes, because the questioning took place in a coercive environment.

B. Yes, because the questioning took place in an environment that would be perceived as coercive by an individual Marius's age.

C. Yes, because the questioning took place in an environment that would be perceived as coercive by an individual Marius's age with no criminal record.

D. No.

ANALYSIS. This problem continues our evaluation of *Miranda* custody with a focus on age and location. Turning first to age, *J.D.B.* held that age should be considered in evaluating custody where the officer was aware of a suspect's minority, or a reasonable officer would have been, and where it was relevant. Tonya and Luther knew Marius's age when they questioned him. With respect to relevancy, *J.D.B.* noted that a minor's age is not always "determinative, or even significant," and that teenagers close to the age of majority are likely to perceive interrogation much like "a typical 18-year-old."

Because he is only fifteen, Marius is not close to the age of majority, in contrast to 17½-year-old Michael Alvarado. Thus, his age should be factored into the custody analysis. Inasmuch as Marius's "clean" record suggests a lack of experience with law enforcement and the criminal process, *Yarborough* deemed this consideration irrelevant to the custody inquiry. In sum, then, we must determine whether the atmosphere was sufficiently coercive that a reasonable fifteen-year-old would not have felt free to end the interrogation and leave.

The fact the questioning took place outside in public space away from the "inherently coercive pressures" of the station house suggests an absence of custody. A number of factors, however, push in the opposite direction. First, while Tonya and Luther encountered Marius in the presence of friends, they questioned him in a location one-quarter mile away where neither his friends nor anyone else was present. Second, there were two officers and only one suspect, a juvenile, and they positioned themselves on either side of him, creating an uncomfortable feeling of being "surrounded" by cops. Third, Tonya enhanced this discomfort by remarking, when Marius asked if he was in trouble: "Well, you might want to tell me what you know." These circumstances, viewed in their totality and in light of minors' greater susceptibility to influence and outside pressures than adults (*J.D.B.*), are sufficiently coercive that a reasonable fifteen-year-old in Marius's position would not have believed he could terminate the interrogation and leave.

The correct answer is **B**.

C.   The "Interrogation" Requirement

If a suspect incriminates himself in a custodial setting without having first received (and waived) his *Miranda* rights, his confession is inadmissible, provided the incriminating statements were the product of police interrogation. The word "interrogation" clearly includes the typical question-and-answer format, but what about more subtle forms of eliciting information from a suspect? In *Rhode Island v. Innis*, 446 U.S. 291 (1980), police officers arrested a man believed to have committed a robbery several hours earlier with a sawed-off shotgun that was not found at the crime scene. With the suspect in the back seat of the police car, the two officers discussed how the crime had taken place in the vicinity of a school for handicapped children and that it would be terrible if a handicapped girl came upon the discarded weapon and accidentally killed herself with it. Upon hearing the officers' conversation, the suspect, who was not part of the dialogue, told them that he would show them where the gun was located "to get [it] out of the way because of the kids in the area in the school."

In determining whether the officers' conduct constituted interrogation for *Miranda* purposes, the U.S. Supreme Court recognized that statements need not be phrased in the form of a question to qualify. Words or actions are the "functional equivalent" of interrogation if the officers "should have known" that they are "reasonably likely to elicit an incriminating response." In evaluating "reasonable likelihood," the focus is on the perceptions of the suspect, not the intent of the police. Accordingly, any knowledge an officer has about a suspect's "unusual susceptibility . . . to a particular form of persuasion" is relevant in assessing what the officer "should have known."

Applying this standard to the facts in *Innis*, the Court held that the officers did not interrogate the suspect. In reaching this conclusion, the majority noted that the officers had no special information suggesting that Innis was "peculiarly susceptible to an appeal to his conscience concerning the safety of handicapped children." The officers' comments, moreover, were not particularly "evocative." In sum, their words and actions amounted to no more than "subtle compulsion," which, standing alone, does not constitute interrogation for *Miranda* purposes.

QUESTION 4. **Say goodnight, Gracie.**   Dwayne, aged ten, was killed by a hit-and-run driver while he was crossing Delancy Street on foot. Betsy witnessed the accident from a distance and reported that the driver ran a red light and struck Dwayne, who was proceeding lawfully. Betsy had noted the vehicle's license plate number, which Officer Andrea traced to Gracie, aged eighty.

The following day, Andrea went to Gracie's home and found her sitting on her porch with her twelve-year-old grandson, Billy. After Andrea whispered to Gracie that her car was linked to a homicide, Gracie told Billy to go inside to watch television. After Billy left, Andrea asked Gracie if she had been driving her car in the vicinity of Delancy Street the day before. Gracie replied that she "did not want to talk about that right now." Andrea then placed Gracie under arrest and administered *Miranda* rights. She then added, "Gracie, you don't need to talk to me, but I will need to take you down to the station house for booking."

As Gracie went to get her coat, Andrea pulled out a crime scene photo of the victim lying in the road after the accident. When Gracie returned, Andrea handed her the photograph and remarked, "In case you were wondering, this is the boy who was killed yesterday. Let's go now." As Andrea turned to leave, Gracie began to cry and commented, "He's even younger than my Billy. What have I done? Please forgive me!"

If Gracie claims that she was unlawfully interrogated, she will likely:

A. Prevail, because Andrea knew Gracie was elderly.
B. Prevail, because Gracie's statements were elicited by the photo.
C. Fail, because Andrea had turned to leave when Gracie spoke.
D. Fail, because Andrea was not preying upon a known susceptibility.
E. Fail, because Andrea did not pressure Gracie to confess.

ANALYSIS.   In determining whether Andrea interrogated Gracie, the *Innis* standard asks whether Andrea should have known that her conduct was reasonably likely to elicit an incriminating response. In evaluating reasonable likelihood, the focus of the *Innis* inquiry is on the perceptions of the suspect, not the intent of the police officer. *Innis* further instructs that a police officer's manipulation of a suspect's known susceptibility is relevant to what the suspect should have known.

Answer **C** seems largely irrelevant. The fact that Andrea turned to leave after showing Gracie the photo has a tenuous relationship to the likelihood that Gracie will incriminate herself. It is the showing of the photo, not Andrea's movement around the porch, that is most relevant in establishing whether interrogation took place. As such, **C** is not the correct answer.

Likewise, the fact that Andrea did not overtly pressure Gracie to confess does not mean that there was no interrogation. The essence of interrogation is words or actions that are likely to lead a suspect to provide incriminating information. Coercion is not a necessary part of this conduct; for example, an officer can custodially interrogate a suspect while adopting a seemingly friendly, sympathetic tone. **E** is not the best answer.

Answer **A** would characterize Andrea's conduct as interrogation because of Gracie's age. This incorrectly suggests that the interrogation standard is different when applied to elderly suspects. While age may be a relevant factor in determining whether an officer's conduct constitutes interrogation in a given case, it is not a "silver bullet" that, standing alone, converts all police questioning into interrogation. Because it states too much, **A** is not the correct answer.

This leaves us with **B** and **D**. **D** deems Andrea's conduct non-interrogation because she was unaware of any particular susceptibility that Gracie may have had to children who were killed. *Innis* instructs that an officer's reliance on a suspect's known susceptibility to a particular police tactic mediates in favor of finding interrogation. Andrea, however, did not know Gracie personally and, thus, would have been unaware of what, if any, vulnerabilities Gracie may have had.

That said, conduct may constitute interrogation even if an officer does not take advantage of a suspect's known susceptibilities. In *Innis*, where the officers had no special information about the suspect's vulnerabilities, the majority labeled the conversation between the two officers about handicapped children non-interrogation after noting that it was not especially "evocative." Andrea's conduct in showing Gracie a photo of the lifeless victim is far more visceral, particularly since Gracie has a grandson who is roughly the same age, and Andrea knows this. This distinction from *Innis* is significant and supports the conclusion that Andrea's conduct is, in fact, interrogation.

B is the best answer.

D.   The "Testimonial" Limitation

Miranda requires suppression of incriminating statements made by a suspect during a custodial interrogation where the requisite warnings were not given. Because the Fifth Amendment self-incrimination guarantee on which *Miranda* is based is a testimonial privilege, *Miranda* will not require suppression of any responses that are not testimonial in nature.

In *Pennsylvania v. Muñiz*, 496 U.S. 582 (1990), the defendant, who was arrested for driving while intoxicated, was asked a series of questions — including his name, age, and address — without first receiving *Miranda* rights. He argued that the presentation of his videotaped responses to the jury violated *Miranda* by virtue of the incriminating effect of his demeanor, as well as his difficulty answering certain questions. Turning first to his demeanor, the U.S. Supreme Court deemed "slurring of speech and other evidence of lack of muscular coordination" a nontestimonial display of the defendant's physical state and, as such, beyond the reach of *Miranda*. See, also, *Schmerber v. California*, 384 U.S. 757 (1966) (forcible extraction of blood held nontestimonial as applied to arrestee for drunk driving). The justices also concluded that responses to questions that are a routine part of the booking process—such as name, age, and address—are essentially nontestimonial.

The majority distinguished, however, one question from the rest: the date of Muniz's sixth birthday. The Court reasoned that the coercive environment compelled him to answer, and any response he would give was incriminating since his inebriation made him unable to answer correctly. Because this response was testimonial and the question was not part of the routine booking process, the absence of *Miranda* warnings mandated its exclusion.

QUESTION 5. Truth be told. The police arrested Leroy for bank robbery after a witness picked him out of a photographic array. To give Leroy a chance to prove his innocence, qualified police personnel administered a polygraph (*i.e.*, lie detector) test. During the test, Leroy was asked a series of questions, some relating to the crime in question and others not. Wires attached to his skin measured his physiological response to each question. These responses were then used to determine whether he appeared to be lying or telling the truth when answering questions about the robbery. Because the results of polygraph tests are inadmissible at trial, they are used principally as an investigative tool to help law enforcement personnel decide whether to proceed against a given suspect. Are Leroy's answers to questions in the polygraph test sufficiently testimonial to violate *Miranda* if Leroy had never received the requisite warnings prior to the administration of the polygraph?

A. Yes, because Leroy was forced to take the test.
B. Yes, because the questions posed are not a routine part of the booking process.
C. No, because the results of the test are inadmissible at trial.
D. No, because the test measures only Leroy's physical state at a given moment.

ANALYSIS. This problem requires careful consideration of the parameters of the testimonial requirement in *Miranda*. To determine the correct answer, we must evaluate whether the polygraph test is more similar to the display of physical characteristics required as part of the booking process or, instead, to the "sixth birthday" question deemed testimonial in *Muniz*.

Like the field sobriety tests at issue in *Muñiz*, polygraph tests reveal a suspect's physical state. Polygraphs are different, however, in that the information they provide is not static; rather, they measure differences in a suspect's physiological response to a number of questions covering a range of topics, only some of which address criminal activity. The responses, viewed collectively, are then interpreted by an expert who concludes, based on the totality of information, whether the suspect is lying or telling the truth. Thus, while the polygraph machine measures a suspect's physical state "at a given moment," these individual snapshots are used in combination to draw broad conclusions about the suspect's veracity. **D**, therefore, is not the best answer.

Likewise, the inadmissibility of polygraph results at trial does not mean that the administration of the test does not violate *Miranda*. To so hold conflates improperly the constitutional violation with the use of evidence obtained as a result. Moreover, the evidence gleaned from polygraph tests is instrumental in making important investigative decisions, including the ultimate decision as to whether to prosecute the suspect or set him free. **C** is not the correct answer.

Because the administration of the polygraph implicated Leroy's *Miranda* rights, we must choose between **A** and **B**. **A** focuses on the forcible nature of the test. Being required to submit to a test or procedure does not necessarily implicate *Miranda*. For example, in *Schmerber*, the defendant's *Miranda* rights were not implicated where he was forced to submit to a blood test to determine if he had been driving drunk, since the test required only a display of his physical characteristics.

The better answer is **B**. The U.S. Supreme Court has affirmatively exempted routine booking questions from the reach of *Miranda*. Since polygraph examinations are not a routine part of the booking process, they would fall outside this exception.

B is the best answer.

E. The Closer

QUESTION 6. **Maurice's magical lotion.** The police knew that Maurice was defrauding women by selling skin products that falsely claimed to reverse the aging process. They could not prosecute him, however, because Maurice charmed the women into refusing to cooperate with detectives. To overcome this obstacle, the detectives devised a clever plan. They asked Maurice to come to the station house to pay for a surfeit of parking tickets he had accumulated. Once there, they told him that he would need to wait in an interrogation room while they "processed the paperwork."

Another man, Ted, was present in the same room. When the police officers left, Ted told Maurice that he had been arrested for "some trumped up fraud charge" and was waiting for his lawyer. "Those idiots thought I'd speak to them," Ted commented. "No way. I know about my right to remain silent and to a lawyer and that anything I say can come back at me in court, so I'm not saying nothing. They'll never get me to admit to what I done." Suddenly Maurice, who had seemed disinterested in Ted's ramblings, changed course. "Hey, Ted, my friend, I run a business that you might want in on." "Sure," Ted replied eagerly. "What do you do?" "Well," Maurice stated in a hushed voice, "I sell these face and body creams for a hefty sum to wealthy, middle-aged housewives and claim they stop them from getting old. Truth is, they don't do anything." At that point, Ted told Maurice he was an undercover police officer, and Ted placed Maurice under arrest.

If Maurice claims that Ted violated his *Miranda* rights, Maurice will:

A. Fail, because Maurice was not custodially interrogated.
B. Fail, because Ted's responses were insufficiently testimonial.
C. Prevail, because Ted failed to communicate Maurice's *Miranda* rights effectively.
D. Prevail, because Maurice was questioned in an interrogation room at the station house.

ANALYSIS.   This closer revisits the core requirements of the *Miranda* doctrine. Throughout the questioning, the suspect is unaware that the person he is talking to is a police officer. He thinks that Ted is a fellow suspect. Maurice "takes the bait" and becomes interested in Ted as a potential business partner upon learning of Ted's alleged involvement in fraud. Ted then succeeds in getting Maurice to admit to selling bogus anti-aging products.

We can start by eliminating **B**. Maurice's answers were most definitely testimonial since they are neither part of the routine booking process nor a display of Maurice's physical characteristics. **D** also misses the mark. As discussed earlier, the location where questioning takes place is not dispositive in determining *Miranda* custody. While a police-dominated atmosphere is not uncommon inside the station house, a casual and friendly encounter between a police officer and a suspect will typically be considered noncustodial, wherever it takes place.

This leads us to **A**. Because Maurice thought Ted was a fellow detainee, the atmosphere in the interrogation room was devoid of the "inherently coercive pressures" that informed the U.S. Supreme Court's decision in *Miranda*. While the police are undoubtedly using trickery to obtain incriminating information from Maurice, the Court declined to apply *Miranda* under similar facts in *Illinois v. Perkins, supra*, where an inmate secretly working for the police secured incriminating information from a fellow inmate whom he had questioned.

C correctly posits that Ted did not "reasonably convey" Maurice's *Miranda* rights. Ted did not state that, if Maurice could not afford an attorney, one could be appointed for him. More fundamentally, it is unclear that Maurice was even listening to Ted when he recited the remaining *Miranda* warnings, since he did not think Ted was a police officer! Still, this oversight is irrelevant since, as explained above, the absence of an atmosphere infused with police domination and coercion made *Miranda* inapplicable.

The correct answer is **A**.

✦ Cornwell's Picks

1.	Chip off the old cell block	C
2.	Love gone bad	C
3.	Bummer, dude	B
4.	Say goodnight, Gracie	B
5.	Truth be told	B
6.	Maurice's magical lotion	A

22

Waiving *Miranda* Rights

CHAPTER OVERVIEW
A. "Voluntary, Knowing, and Intelligent" Waivers
B. Implied Waivers
C. Limited Waivers
D. The Closer
◈ Cornwell's Picks

Before the police can begin a custodial interrogation, suspects must waive their *Miranda* rights. While criminal defense attorneys generally advise clients not to talk to police detectives, most do — as many as 84 percent, according to one study. Paul G. Cassell & Bret S. Hayman, *Police Interrogation in the 1990s: An Empirical Study of the Effects of* Miranda, 43 UCLA L. REV. 839 (1996). In this chapter, we will examine the requirements and the scope of an effective waiver.

A. "Voluntary, Knowing, and Intelligent" Waivers

For a waiver to be valid, it must be knowing, intelligent, and voluntary. As in the Fourteenth Amendment due process context (see Chapter 20), the Supreme Court has interpreted the voluntariness requirement to mean freedom from government coercion. Pressure that derives from other sources does not meet this standard; thus, when a psychotic defendant waived *Miranda* rights and confessed to a murder because God told him to, the waiver was not involuntary. *Colorado v. Connelly*, 479 U.S. 157 (1986).

Waivers are "knowing and intelligent" if defendants understand their rights and the consequences of abandoning them. Applying this standard in a controversial 5-4 decision, the Court found a waiver to be valid where the suspect was not informed that his lawyer had called in and wanted to be present during any interrogation. While this information may have influenced the suspect's decision, the majority deemed it irrelevant, since the suspect understood both his core *Miranda* rights and that the confession he subsequently gave could be used against him. *Moran v. Burbine*, 475 U.S. 412 (1986).

Likewise, police need not inform suspects of the subject matter of the planned interrogations before they waive their rights. In *Colorado v. Spring*, 479 U.S. 564 (1987), a defendant waived his rights and was questioned about criminal activity unrelated to the crime for which he was arrested. In the eyes of the Court, the fact that he did not expect to be questioned about this matter did not affect the validity of the waiver. "The Constitution," the majority opined, "does not require that a criminal suspect know and understand every possible consequence of a waiver of the Fifth Amendment privilege."

QUESTION 1. An offer he can't refuse.   Officer Caroline arrested Gene for the burglary of Jessica's Jewelbox, an upscale store specializing in precious stones. Caroline read Gene his *Miranda* rights, which he acknowledged he could recite himself since he was an avid fan of *Law & Order*. When they arrived at the station house, Caroline handed Gene over to another officer, T.J., who had just gotten off the phone with Gene's lawyer, Becky. Becky told T.J. that, if Gene wanted to talk to her, he could call her on her cell, adding that Gene knew the number.

T.J. took Gene into the interrogation room and asked him if he was willing to talk. Gene replied that he wasn't sure and was "thinking about" calling his lawyer, Becky. "Well," T.J. continued, "I don't have all day. If you want me to help you with the district attorney, you have to talk to me now — just the two of us. Once I walk out of this room, the offer expires. They'll be sending in my partner instead — a real ballbuster. It's up to you." T.J. then stood up and moved toward the door. "Okay, okay," Gene urged. "I'll talk." T.J. first asked Gene if he had ever met Jessica. When Gene denied knowing her, T.J. then asked why letters addressed to her husband were found in his belongings when he was booked into jail. Flustered by the question, Gene nervously stammered, "I didn't mean to take them." Gene was later charged with misappropriation of U.S. mail, in addition to the burglary charge.

Which is Gene's best argument that his *Miranda* waiver was insufficient, thus excluding his statement about taking Jessica's husband's mail?

A. Caroline, not T.J., established that Gene understood his rights.
B. Gene's decision to speak to T.J. was involuntary.
C. T.J. should have told Gene that he could reach Becky on her cell.
D. T.J.'s question about Jessica's husband's mail was inappropriate, since it did not relate to the burglary.

ANALYSIS. This problem requires us to evaluate the sufficiency of Gene's *Miranda* waiver to identify his best argument to invalidate it. While the prosecution must establish that the decision to waive was knowing and intelligent, it is irrelevant which officer meets the state's burden. Thus, it is sufficient that Caroline, and not T.J., established that Gene understood his rights. **A** is wrong.

Likewise, T.J.'s failure to tell Gene that his attorney had called does not invalidate his waiver. Becky told T.J. that, if Gene wanted to speak with her, she was available on her cell phone and that Gene knew the number. Thus, T.J.'s conduct did not in any way compromise the waiver by affirmatively impeding a suspect's stated desire to speak with counsel. Where no such request is made, there is no violation. As Justice O'Connor opined in *Moran v. Burbine*, a suspect does not have the right to "a flow of information to calibrate his self-interest." **C** is wrong.

The validity of a *Miranda* waiver is not dependent, moreover, on a suspect's knowledge of the subject matter of the interrogation. Here, Gene expects to be asked about the burglary and is surprised to be interrogated about his unlawful taking of mail from the burglary victim's husband. While he may have been flustered by the question, his emotional response does not make his waiver unintelligent, nor does it constitute police coercion. **D** is wrong.

This leaves us with **B**. While T.J.'s comments clearly influenced Gene's decision to waive, it is not certain that all courts would find his conduct impermissibly coercive. Still, it is Gene's best shot. Considered together, T.J.'s remarks pressure Gene to waive immediately to secure any potential leniency and to avoid interrogation by an officer known for his harsh treatment of suspects during interrogation. This police intimidation suggests involuntariness.

B is the best answer.

B.   Implied Waivers

While police often request that suspects waive their *Miranda* rights in writing, waivers need not be "express." A suspect may, instead, waive his rights implicitly through actions and words indicative of a desire to speak with police interrogators. *North Carolina v. Butler*, 441 U.S. 369 (1979). Interrogators may secure the waiver *after* the interrogation begins, provided the suspect has an opportunity to invoke the right to silence or counsel before answering questions.

Thus, *Berghuis v. Thompkins*, 560 U.S. 370 (2010), found that a suspect had waived his right to remain silent by answering a detective's question almost three hours into an interrogation in which he had previously remained mute. The defendant received his *Miranda* rights, understood them, and had the opportunity to assert his right to silence or counsel before answering. Under these circumstances, the Court reasoned, he waived the right to remain silent by making an "uncoerced" statement to the police.

The government bears the burden of establishing waiver by a preponderance of the evidence. *Colorado v. Connelly*, 479 U.S. 157 (1986). The waiver evaluation is based on a totality of the circumstances. *Fare v. Michael C.*, 442 U.S. 707 (1979). To this end, courts must consider "the particular facts and circumstances surrounding that case, including the background, experience, and conduct of the accused." *North Carolina v. Butler.*

QUESTION 2. Minor difficulty. Officer Mara arrested seventeen-year-old Darius for the shooting death of Christopher, a rival gang member who had gunned down a member of Darius's gang the day before. Mara read Darius his *Miranda* rights, pausing after each of four core warnings to ask if Darius understood what she was saying or had any questions. He asked Mara no questions and said he understood the rights because he had heard them "the other time" he was arrested.

In the squad car on the way to the police station, Mara asked Darius if he wanted to talk about the killing. He did not respond. She then told him how she understood why he would want to do it, since Christopher was "scum" for killing Darius's "brother." While Darius did not answer, Mara noticed that her comment peaked his interest. Feeling that she was making progress, Mara decided to extend the car ride by taking a longer route to the station house. While she drove, Mara continued to talk to Darius about his gang and its rivalry with Christopher's. Darius said nothing until, one hour into the journey, Mara asked what his mother would think about what he had done. At that point, Darius teared up and commented: "My mom always told me to stay away from the gang. She'll be so angry that I did this."

Darius moves to suppress his statements to Mara, claiming that he never waived his *Miranda* rights. Is this argument valid?

A. Yes, because Mara manipulated Darius.
B. Yes, because Darius was a minor.
C. No, because Darius's conduct demonstrated his desire to answer Mara clearly and convincingly.
D. No, because Darius chose to answer Mara's question.

ANALYSIS. Darius will not succeed in suppressing his statements if the facts demonstrate that he impliedly waived his *Miranda* rights. To do so, he must understand the rights and have the opportunity to invoke them before answering any questions. In making this determination, courts use a totality-of-the-circumstances approach that considers the accused's background, experience, and any other facts or circumstances relevant to the waiver inquiry.

Answer **B** would invalidate the waiver because Darius is a minor. While age is a relevant factor, it is not dispositive. The validity of a waiver executed by a juvenile must be assessed on a case-by-case basis, in light of the attendant circumstances. Because Darius is seventeen, he is relatively close to the age of majority. He also indicates that, due to his prior experience with law enforcement, he is familiar with the warnings. Finally, Mara makes a point of pausing after each core warning to ask if Darius understands or has any questions. He confirms his understanding, and there is nothing to suggest any intellectual or cognitive deficit that would undermine his assertion. In sum, then, Darius's age does not invalidate the waiver. **B** is wrong.

Police coercion will invalidate any waiver, whether express or implied. Answer **A** posits, to this end, that Darius's incriminating statements were the product of his impermissible manipulation by Mara. Mara did extend the trip to the police station artificially by taking a longer route. She also communicated empathy by calling the victim "scum" and appealed to Darius's emotions by referencing his mother. While these facts suggest that Mara manipulated the situation to her benefit, they do not rise to the level of unlawful coercion; viewed collectively, Mara's tactics did not impermissibly force Darius to respond. **A** is wrong.

Therefore, Darius understood his rights and had an opportunity to invoke them during the ride. Instead of doing so, he answered Mara's question in the absence of police coercion. Under *Berghuis v. Thompkins*, this conduct constitutes a valid, implied *Miranda* waiver that the government will be able to prove by a preponderance of the evidence. Because it misstates the applicable evidentiary burden, **C** is wrong.

D is the correct answer.

C.   Limited Waivers

In waiving his rights, either expressly or impliedly, a suspect need not waive all protections afforded by *Miranda*. For example, in *Connecticut v. Barrett*, 479 U.S. 523 (1987), the defendant confessed to the crime orally after repeatedly expressing his willingness to talk to the police while, at the same time, refusing to make a written confession outside the presence of counsel. The Court recognized that this distinction may be illogical but held that it did not invalidate the defendant's waiver of his right to speak with the police without counsel where his conduct otherwise suggested an understanding of his rights and the consequences of abandoning them. Cf. *Wyrick v. Fields*, 459 U.S. 42 (1982) (defendant's limited waiver of *Miranda* rights for purpose of taking polygraph extended to questions based on the results of the polygraph).

Suspects who execute limited waivers of the right to remain silent typically do so in one of two ways. They may refuse to discuss certain specified topics. See, e.g., *Michigan v. Mosley*, 423 U.S. 96 (1975) (suspect would not discuss the robberies for which he had been arrested); *United States v. Lopez-Diaz*, 630 F.2d 661 (9th Cir. 1980) (defendant would not discuss the drugs found in his van). Conversely, suspects may indicate a willingness to discuss *only* certain specific subjects. See, e.g., *United States v. Soliz*, 129 F.3d 499 (9th Cir. 1997) (defendant agreed only to answer questions about his citizenship).

QUESTION 3. Cargo embargo. Officer Mary sees Jonathan loading a package believed to contain unlawfully imported Cuban cigars into his car. Mary pulls the car over and searches the package finding, as expected, smuggled cigars. She also opens a suitcase positioned next to the package and finds a pouch hidden between two shirts labeled "Primo Cuban weed." Mary places Jonathan under arrest for conspiracy to smuggle Cuban cigars into the United States. Mary had arrested Jonathan twice before, so the two know each other. "Well, Jonathan, you know what happens now," Mary states. "Sure," Jonathan replies. "It's *Miranda* time. Let me hear it."

Mary recites Jonathan's *Miranda* rights in the squad car on the way to the station house. "Any comments or questions?" Mary asks. "Not at all," Jonathan responds. Mary then asks Jonathan if he wants to talk. He shrugs his shoulders and does not otherwise respond to the question. "Well," Mary remarks a few minutes later, "if I were you, I'd sure want to cooperate." "Why?" Jonathan queries. "Face the facts," she continues. "You were caught with both cigars and drugs in your car. Cigar smuggling is bad enough, but drug dealing? That adds up to a heap of jail time, but I can't help you if I don't know what you were up to." "Look," Jonathan replies, "me and my best friend got hooked into the cigar business, okay?" "How about the marijuana?" Mary presses. "I'm not saying a word about the drugs," Jonathan barks back. "Fine," Mary responds, "but tell me: Did you travel with your friend to Cuba to get the cigars?" Jonathan acknowledges that he did. "And did you buy them together?" Jonathan admits that they did. "And did you buy the marijuana or did he?" "I did," Jonathan comments, refusing thereafter to answer any more questions.

If Jonathan moves to suppress the incriminating statements he made to Mary, he will likely:

A. Succeed as to all of them.
B. Succeed as to all but the first statement.
C. Succeed only as to the last statement.
D. Fail as to all of them.

ANALYSIS. This problem requires us to evaluate whether Jonathan has waived his *Miranda* rights and, if so, the scope of his waiver. In establishing that Jonathan's waiver was knowing and intelligent, the prosecution may rely on Jonathan's prior experience with the criminal justice system and his lack of interest in asking Mary any follow-up questions about his rights when she invites him to do so. These facts, considered together, are sufficient to establish that Jonathan understands his rights and the consequences of abandoning them.

Jonathan is initially ambivalent about speaking to Mary but, when she answers his invitation to explain why cooperating with her would be in his best interest, he decides to submit to questioning. While Mary's comments are fairly characterized as custodial interrogation, her conduct in obtaining Jonathan's cooperation cannot be labeled coercive since she did not, in any way, force Jonathan to talk. As such, Jonathan's initial statement is admissible.

When asked about the marijuana, however, Jonathan clearly expresses his unwillingness to engage with Mary on this issue. Mary nonetheless asks him whether he bought the drugs. It is irrelevant that Jonathan voluntarily answered the question or that the questions immediately preceding it were proper subjects of interrogation. Jonathan had executed a limited waiver of his *Miranda* rights by deeming a specific subject matter, drugs, out of bounds. Mary's last question violated that assertion and, accordingly, Jonathan's response will be inadmissible.

The correct answer is **C**.

D.   The Closer

QUESTION 4. **Mon dieu!**   Myron flagged down a police car driven by Officer Henrietta in front of a gas station on Main Street. As Henrietta approached Myron, he blurted that he had shot his sister and felt "real bad" about it. Henrietta told Myron that she would like to talk to him further about this but would need, first, to tell him what his rights were so he could decide what he wanted to do. She then read Myron his *Miranda* rights, pausing after each one to ask if he understood what she was saying. In each instance, he said that he did. When Henrietta finished the *Miranda* rights, she asked Myron if he wanted to talk to her about his sister. Myron turned suddenly silent, remarking that he wasn't sure he was "ready to do that." Henrietta then placed him under arrest, placed him in the squad car, and took him to the station house.

They arrived twenty minutes later and, as they were exiting the car, Myron said he would not speak a word but, if Henrietta asked a question, he would write the answer in French, in which he was fluent. "If

God says it's okay, I will translate my written answers into English for you later, but only if he lets me." In response to questioning from Henrietta, Myron then described in writing in French how he had killed his sister the day before. Myron was angry that his confession was later translated into English by a police department interpreter and was used at trial to convict him. If Myron challenges the validity of his *Miranda* waiver, he will likely:

A. Prevail, because his waiver was involuntary.
B. Prevail, because his waiver was illogical.
C. Prevail, because he did not understand that the government would translate his words into English.
D. Fail.

ANALYSIS. In this closer, Myron confesses in a highly unusual manner to killing his sister. Specifically, he chooses not to speak to Officer Henrietta but is willing to write his answers to her questions in a foreign language (French), which he will later translate for police purposes, if God ordains it. However, a police department interpreter translates his statements into English and prosecutors use the confession to convict Myron of his sister's murder.

A addresses the voluntary nature of Myron's waiver. As in other contexts, voluntariness is satisfied if the suspect's decision to waive is not the product of police coercion. Here, there is no evidence whatsoever that Henrietta pressured Myron to waive. As in *Connelly, supra,* any coercion Myron experienced came from a spiritual source, not a governmental one. Because the waiver was voluntary, **A** is wrong.

In assessing the knowing and intelligent nature of Myron's waiver, it is important to differentiate that inquiry from consideration of the wisdom of his conduct. Inasmuch as Myron has assumed that a confession written in French will disadvantage him only if *he* personally translates it, pursuant to a directive from God, he has made a poor decision. Still, this misperception does not mean that he does not understand his *Miranda* rights and the consequences of abandoning them. To this end, after stating each and every *Miranda* right, Henrietta asked if Myron understood what she was saying. He indicated affirmatively that he did. He is, therefore, much like the defendant in *Connecticut v. Barrett, supra,* who was willing to issue an oral, but not a written, confession without counsel. Like Barrett, Myron has made an improvident, even illogical, decision; this misfortune does not, however, render his limited waiver insufficiently knowing and intelligent for *Miranda* purposes. **B** and **C** are, therefore, wrong.

The correct answer is **D**.

Cornwell's Picks

1. An offer he can't refuse   **B**
2. Minor difficulty   **D**
3. Cargo embargo   **C**
4. Mon dieu!   **D**

23

The Rights to Silence and Counsel Under *Miranda*

CHAPTER OVERVIEW
A. Invoking and Respecting the Right to Silence
B. "Lawyering Up"
C. Determining Whether a Suspect Has Invoked the Right to Counsel
D. The Scope of the Right to Counsel
E. The Closer
✧ Cornwell's Picks

The previous chapter addressed waiver, the first of three options available to a suspect facing custodial interrogation. In this chapter, we discuss the remaining two: invocation of the right to silence and the right to counsel. As we will see, an assertion of the right to counsel constrains future police contact with a suspect to a far greater degree than invoking silence. Respecting a suspect's desire for the assistance of counsel when confronting the coercive environment of custodial interrogation is at the very heart of the *Miranda* doctrine; as such, the U.S. Supreme Court has been consistently protective of this right while embracing, at the same time, far greater flexibility with respect to other issues in the confessions context.

A. Invoking and Respecting the Right to Silence

In *Berghuis v. Thompkins*, 560 U.S 370 (2010), officers brought the defendant to the station house for questioning about a fatal shooting outside an area mall. The defendant remained largely non-responsive for two hours and forty-five minutes but did not affirmatively state either that he wanted to remain silent or that he would not talk to the police. He then made an inculpatory statement in

259

response to an officer's question. Moving to suppress the statement, the defendant claimed, *inter alia*, that he had implicitly invoked the right to remain silent through his refusal to answer myriad questions about the crime over a nearly three-hour period. The Supreme Court disagreed, holding that suspects must invoke the right to remain silent unambiguously.

Once a suspect unambiguously invokes silence, officers must "scrupulously honor" the assertion. In *Michigan v. Mosley*, 423 U.S. 96 (1975), the defendant declined to speak to the police about the robberies for which he had been arrested. Two hours later, a different detective sought to question Mosley about an unrelated murder. After receiving his *Miranda* rights anew, Mosley elected to speak to the officer and made incriminating statements. The Court deemed these statements admissible, finding that the suspect's waiver was valid since the officer had "scrupulously honored" his desire to remain silent. In making this finding, the majority referenced the passage of a significant amount of time since his initial assertion, the detective's repetition of the suspect's *Miranda* rights, and the different subject matter of the second interrogation. The Court did not indicate that any single factor is dispositive or indispensable, holding simply that Mosley's right to cut off questioning was "fully respected" in this case.

QUESTION 1. Mercurial Milli. Officer Erinn arrested Milli for stealing merchandise from Malley's department store, where Milli had obtained temporary employment as a salesperson during the busy Christmas season. Erinn ushered Milli into an interrogation room and gave her *Miranda* rights. In response, Milli stated that she "didn't want to talk right now." Two hours later, Erinn's partner, Officer Susan, entered the room and politely asked Milli if she had changed her mind. "Um, no, not yet," Milli replied. "Maybe later." "How much longer will you need?" Susan continued, sighing. "Forget it, Officer," Milli offered as Susan turned to leave. "That's okay. I'll talk now." Milli then executed a written *Miranda* waiver and confessed, in response to a question from Susan, to stealing top-quality garland from the trim-a-tree department.

Milli's confession is likely to be ruled:

A. Admissible, because Milli expressly waived her *Miranda* rights.
B. Admissible, because Susan's demeanor was polite and courteous.
C. Inadmissible, because Susan pressured Milli to talk to her.
D. Inadmissible, because Susan questioned Milli about the same crime for which she had asserted the right to silence.
E. Inadmissible, because Milli unambiguously invoked her desire to remain silent.

ANALYSIS. This problem explores the constitutional standards for invoking, and then respecting, the right to remain silent. Suspects need to invoke the right unambiguously and Milli clearly did so when she told Erinn she "did not want to talk right now." Erinn and Susan now must "scrupulously honor" this invocation. *Michigan v. Mosely* presented a number of considerations that informed the majority's conclusion that the police had respected the suspect's invocation: the passage of time, a change in subject matter, and repetition of *Miranda* warnings. At the same time, the Court noted that no single factor, either alone or in combination, was dispositive in the analysis.

Here, there was no change in subject matter, nor did Susan repeat Milli's *Miranda* rights. Susan also showed disappointment with Milli's indecision, sighing audibly when Milli asked for more time. By the same token, Susan clearly communicated her willingness to give Milli more time to make her decision and had turned to leave when Milli relented. While Susan made clear that she was going to continue to honor Milli's desire to maintain silence, Milli changed her mind, effectively drawing Susan back into the room and subsequently executing an express waiver that would permit the interrogation to commence.

While Susan's sigh may have influenced, in some respect, Milli's decision to speak to her, it is difficult to conclude that it constituted impermissible pressure. Remember: After sighing in Milli's presence, Susan turned to leave. Thus, Milli could not have reasonably believed that Susan would make her talk or otherwise coerce her. **C** is wrong.

While our facts do not include all of the factors present in *Mosley*, the Court did not require that all be present, nor did it indicate that any single factor had a dispositive effect in the analysis. To this end, lower courts have found, on numerous occasions, that police have scrupulously honored a suspect's invocation where one or more of the *Mosely* factors is absent. See, e.g., *Gore v. Sec'y for Dept. of Corr.*, 492 F.3d 1273, 1299 (11th Cir. 2007) (questioning about same offense); *Weeks v. Angelone*, 176 F.3d 249, 268-269 (4th Cir. 1999) (questioning about same subject matter and no new *Miranda* warnings); *United States v. Hsu*, 852 F.2d 407, 411 (9th Cir. 1988) (questioning about same subject matter thirty minutes after invocation). Thus, the fact that Susan questioned Milli about the same offense is not sufficient, in and of itself, to violate Milli's Fifth Amendment rights, especially in light of Susan's affirmative indication that she would continue to leave Milli alone to ponder her decision. **D** is wrong.

In light of the foregoing, **E** is also wrong. Milli did effectively invoke the right to remain silent by doing so unambiguously. However, this does not preclude the admissibility of her subsequent confession since Erinn and Susan "scrupulously honored" the assertion and secured a *Miranda* waiver.

We are left, then, with **A** and **B**. Both correctly affirm the admissibility of the statement at Milli's trial, but **A** better represents the legal basis for such admissibility. Susan's polite and courteous manner, standing alone, does not resolve the admissibility question. For example, an officer can be both polite and coercive at the same time, negating any notion of scrupulously honoring a suspect's invocation of silence. While Susan did not act coercively, her pleasant demeanor does not necessarily convey respect for Milli's constitutional rights.

A, therefore, is the best answer. Milli decided to expressly waive her *Miranda* rights after Susan had turned to leave, clearly communicating to Milli her intention to give Milli additional time to decide what she wanted to do. As such, Milli's waiver is valid and supports the introduction at trial of Milli's incriminating statement obtained during custodial interrogation.

B.   "Lawyering Up"

In *Edwards v. Arizona*, 451 U.S. 477 (1981), the defendant-arrestee expressed interest in negotiating a deal with the police but wanted to talk to a lawyer before doing so. At that point, he was transported to the county jail where he was detained overnight. The following day, when police detectives arrived at the jail, Edwards was informed, over his objection, that he had to talk to them. Upon being advised again of his *Miranda* rights, he chose to waive them and proceeded—in response to police questioning—to implicate himself in criminal activity.

The U.S. Supreme Court held that, whenever an accused asserts the right to have counsel present during custodial interrogation, all interrogation must cease until counsel has been made available, unless the suspect himself initiates further communication with the police. Accordingly, the majority deemed Edwards's confession inadmissible, since the police, not Edwards himself, initiated questioning at the jail the morning after he requested counsel. Compare *Oregon v. Bradshaw*, 462 U.S. 1039 (1983) (by asking "what is going to happen to me now?" defendant initiated further communication with police under *Edwards*) (plurality opinion).

To implicate the *Edwards* doctrine, the Fifth Amendment requires invocation of a suspect's *Miranda* right to *counsel*. Thus, *Edwards* would not apply where a juvenile asked to talk to his probation officer, as in *Fare v. Michael C.*, 442 U.S. 707 (1979). Such requests should be considered, however, in evaluating the voluntariness of a suspect's subsequent *Miranda* waiver.

QUESTION 2. Otherwise engaged. Bill was arrested for soliciting a prostitute. After receiving his *Miranda* rights, Bill signed a waiver card. Detective Mary told him she would be willing to recommend probation if Bill admitted his guilt. Bill then asked to speak to his fiancée, Marita, commenting that he did not want to admit to anything without first talking to "the woman to whom I gave my heart but have tragically wronged today." Mary suspended the interrogation while Bill telephoned Marita. After he hung up, Bill turned to Mary and stated somewhat sadly that he had cleared his conscience and felt much better now. "I was lucky to get in touch with her," Bill continued. "She had just gotten back from lunch with her fellow lawyers at the firm." "So," Mary replied, "do you want to get back to it, then?" Bill then agreed to resume the interrogation, during which he confessed, in response to a question from Mary, to soliciting the prostitute.

Did Mary violate Bill's rights under *Edwards* at any time during the interrogation?

A. Yes, because Mary failed to obtain a *Miranda* waiver before resuming the questioning.
B. Yes, because Mary asked Bill to resume the interrogation, knowing Marita was a lawyer.
C. No, because Bill was asking to speak to a loved one, not to a lawyer.
D. No, because Bill initiated the conversation with Mary after he spoke to Marita.

ANALYSIS. This is the first of four problems in this chapter addressing the assertion of the Fifth Amendment right to counsel. Requesting counsel fundamentally alters the dynamic between the police interrogator and the suspect by severely limiting an officer's ability to gather information. As such, a suspect's decision to "lawyer up" is a disappointing moment, to say the least, for a police officer.

In this fact pattern, Bill asks to speak to his fiancée, Marita, who happens to be a lawyer. His purpose in speaking to Marita is not, however, to obtain legal advice; rather, he wants to "confess his sins" to her before admitting them to the police detective. Initially, Mary does not know that Marita is an attorney. Mary finds out, however, before she begins the interrogation. For his part, Bill, who has previously executed a *Miranda* waiver, is willing to submit to questioning by Mary once he has spoken to Marita. During the interrogation that follows, Bill admits to soliciting a prostitute.

Under *Edwards*, once a suspect asserts the right to counsel, all interrogation must cease unless he himself initiates it. Here, we have a threshold question of whether Bill did, in fact, ask for an attorney. The rationale of the *Edwards* rule is that a suspect who asks for a lawyer is communicating his desire to have the protection of counsel whenever he faces custodial interrogation; thus, his invocation must be respected. Here, however, that is not what Bill was communicating. He was not asking to speak to a lawyer; he was asking to speak to his fiancée, who happens to be a lawyer, for personal reasons. His reference to her profession was anecdotal and in no way suggested that he wanted her present with him to safeguard his rights. Thus, because he did not invoke his right to *counsel*, there was no constitutional infirmity in Mary's resumption of the interrogation. **B** is wrong.

A can also be discarded. Bill had already expressly waived his *Miranda* rights only minutes earlier. While there was a short break in the sequence of events, this disruption was hardly significant enough to negate the effectiveness of Bill's waiver. It is difficult, by the same token, to interpret Bill's remarks as an invitation to Mary to resume the interrogation. He was merely reporting that he had spoken to Marita and, having done so, he felt much better emotionally. It was Mary who initiated the interrogation after the phone call when she asked Bill if he was ready to "get back to it." **D** is wrong.

The correct answer is **C**. In asking to speak to Marita, Bill was seeking an emotional release, not the protections of a lawyer. Because he did not assert the right to counsel, Mary did not violate Bill's rights under *Edwards*.

C.   Determining Whether a Suspect Has Invoked the Right to Counsel

In *Davis v. United States*, 512 U.S. 452 (1994), after waiving his *Miranda* rights, the defendant reconsidered his decision ninety minutes into the interrogation, commenting "Maybe I should talk to a lawyer." Before proceeding, agents asked Davis if he was in fact requesting a lawyer. Davis answered that he did not want a lawyer. The interrogation then resumed for an additional hour during which time Davis gave incriminating responses to the agents' questions. The Supreme Court deemed those statements admissible, holding that a request for counsel made after a suspect has waived his *Miranda* rights must be clear and unambiguous. Moreover, if a suspect makes an ambiguous assertion, as Davis did, the police are under no obligation to clarify the ambiguity; they may simply continue the interrogation.

While *Davis* concerned a post-waiver request for counsel, subsequent case law indicates that *all* requests for counsel under *Miranda* must be unambiguous. For example, in *Berghuis v. Thompkins*, *supra*, the Court reasoned that, because invocation of the *Miranda* right to counsel must be unambiguous, there is "no principled reason" for adopting a different standard in the context of the right to remain silent. Citing "the logic of *Berghuis*" the Court recently opined that "[a] suspect who stands mute has not done enough to put police on notice that he is relying on his Fifth Amendment privilege." *Salinas v. Texas*, 133 S. Ct. 2174 (2013) (plurality opinion) (applying the "express invocation requirement" to noncustodial police interview conducted without *Miranda* warnings).

Once a suspect unambiguously asks for an attorney, all interrogation outside the presence of counsel must cease. *Edwards*, *supra*. If an officer continues and the suspect thereafter shows a willingness to respond, any incriminating statements made in response to the officer's questions will be inadmissible; "*post-request* responses to further interrogation may not be used to cast retrospective doubt on the clarity of the initial request itself." *Smith v. Illinois*, 469 U.S. 91 (1984).

QUESTION 3. Passing the buck.   Officer John arrested Clara for distributing counterfeit currency after a number of phony $20 bills were traced to her. John gave Clara her *Miranda* rights, which she clearly understood, and asked her what she wanted to do. "Hmmm," Clara mused, "what indeed? I'd like to talk to you, but I am going to wait until I have a lawyer. That's what my boyfriend would want me to do." "So," John retorted, "do you let your boyfriend make important decisions for you?" "No," Clara responded defensively, "of course not." "Good," John said, "because I'd hate to think you're not capable of making important decisions on your own. If you talk to me, maybe we can clear everything up here and now. What do you say?" Unnerved yet charmed by John's remarks, Clara agreed to talk to him after all. John then asked Clara how she got mixed up in counterfeiting. "With the debt that I have," Clara chuckled, "I should've been pedaling fifties, not twenties."

If Clara moves to suppress her last statement, she will likely:

A. Prevail, because John's remarks about her boyfriend were impermissible.
B. Prevail, because she asked for a lawyer.
C. Fail, because she never clearly requested a lawyer.
D. Fail, because she decided to talk to John.

ANALYSIS.   This problem asks whether Clara asserted her *Miranda* right to counsel. While *Davis* requires an unambiguous invocation, *Smith* disallows any intervention by law enforcement to negate a request for counsel that was clearly stated. Here, Clara tells John that she wants "to wait until she has a lawyer." This is a clear, unambiguous request for counsel. The motivation for the invocation—here, her boyfriend—is irrelevant. **C** is wrong.

While Clara decides that she will talk to John after all, *Smith* does not permit subsequent responses to "cast retrospective doubt on the clarity of the initial request itself." Thus, Clara's change of heart cannot nullify her prior unambiguous request. **D** is wrong.

John's remark about Clara's boyfriend clearly offended her and may have influenced Clara to change her mind about wanting a lawyer. It is her request for counsel, however, that is directly responsible for the suppression of her confession as a matter of law. It does not matter whether John's comments about the boyfriend do or do not constitute further, unlawful interrogation.

B, therefore, is the best answer.

D. The Scope of the Right to Counsel

Following his arrest for burglary, Ronald Roberson asserted his right to counsel under *Miranda*. Three days later, while still in police custody, he was questioned by a different officer about a separate, unrelated burglary. Before initiating the interrogation, the officer read Roberson his *Miranda* rights, which Roberson waived. Roberson subsequently made incriminating statements about the second burglary, in response to the officer's questions.

The U.S. Supreme Court found these statements inadmissible under *Edwards*. The majority reasoned that, when a suspect asks for an attorney, he is communicating his desire to have that attorney present whenever he is custodially interrogated, without regard to subject matter. Because the invocation of counsel is not offense-specific, the detectives were precluded from questioning Roberson about *any* offense. Rereading Roberson his *Miranda* rights was unavailing, moreover, since the waiver that followed was necessarily invalid due to "the presumption of coercion that is created by prolonged police custody." *Arizona v. Roberson*, 486 U.S. 675 (1988).

Likewise, the assertion of counsel is not satisfied by affording the opportunity to consult with counsel. In *Minnick v. Mississippi*, 498 U.S. 146 (1990), the suspect spoke to his attorney on two or three occasions after invoking his right to counsel. Two days later, law enforcement officers summoned Minnick to the interrogation room and, after providing his *Miranda* rights again and obtaining a waiver, Minnick incriminated himself during the questioning. The U.S. Supreme Court suppressed the statements finding that the police had violated *Edwards* by permitting interrogation outside the presence of counsel. As in *Roberson*, the waiver obtained after reminding the suspect of his *Miranda* rights was unavailing.

Finally, the protections afforded by *Edwards* continue as long as the suspect remains in custody and for the first fourteen days following his release. Fourteen days is sufficient, the majority explained in *Maryland v. Shatzer*, 130 U.S. 1213 (2010), to discourage abuse of a "break-in-custody rule." It also gives a suspect the opportunity "to get reacclimated to his normal life, to consult with friends and counsel, and to shake off any residual coercive effects of his prior custody." Police are free to seek a *Miranda* waiver at the expiration of this period.

QUESTION 4. Pilfered pumps. Rachel was arrested when she tried to use a stolen credit card to purchase designer shoes at an upscale Park Avenue boutique. Officer Seth read Rachel her *Miranda* rights on the way to the station house, and she said she wanted to speak to her lawyer. Seth permitted her to call her personal attorney, Brent, on her cell phone and to arrange for Brent to meet them at the station house.

Which of the following custodial interrogations is lawful?

A. Prior to Brent's arrival, Officer Theresa questions Rachel about an unrelated murder, after obtaining a *Miranda* waiver.

B. Prior to Brent's arrival, Seth persuades a public defender who is meeting another client to sit in the room while Theresa questions Rachel about an unrelated murder.

C. Brent meets Rachel at the station house, and they confer. As Brent leaves, Theresa asks Rachel if her talk with Brent was productive. Rachel acknowledges that it was and adds that Brent said it would be okay for Theresa to question her outside his presence. Theresa then questions Rachel about an unrelated murder, after obtaining a *Miranda* waiver.

D. Brent meets Rachel at the station house, and they confer. After he leaves, Rachel is taken to a holding cell where she is kept overnight. The following day, she makes bail and is released. One week later, Seth waits for Rachel to exit her apartment. When she does, he asks to speak with her. Seth readministers *Miranda* rights and Rachel signs a waiver form. Seth then questions Rachel about an unrelated murder.

E. None of the above.

ANALYSIS. This problem presents a fairly straightforward set of facts. Rachel is arrested, *Mirandized*, and invokes her right to counsel before being delivered to the station house. As we discussed earlier, the police are extremely limited in their ability to interrogate a suspect who has asked for a lawyer. Thus, we must determine if any of the four scenarios provides an exception to the general prohibition on post-invocation, uncounseled custodial interrogation.

First, it is important to remember that the Fifth Amendment is *not* offense-specific. Therefore, the fact that the interrogation relates to an unrelated offense is unavailing. When suspects invoke their *Miranda* right to counsel, *all* custodial interrogation must cease without regard to subject matter. Thus, there is no constitutional difference between questioning Rachel about her use of a stolen credit card or about the murder; both are presumptively prohibited.

We can start by eliminating **A.** As discussed above, the subject matter of the questioning is irrelevant. The fact that Theresa obtained a *Miranda* waiver is likewise inapposite. The core principles that *Edwards* and its progeny embrace is the insufficiency of a *Miranda* waiver after a request for counsel. Theresa's interrogation is unlawful.

B appears, at first blush, to satisfy *Edwards* inasmuch as an attorney is present in the interrogation room while Theresa is questioning Rachel. However, the facts do not state that the public defender is actually acting as Rachel's counsel. This attorney is not representing Rachel and agrees "to sit in the room" as a favor to Officer Seth. *Miranda* and *Edwards* clearly contemplate the presence of a lawyer who is actively engaged in protecting the client's rights. Because the facts provide no such assurances, **B** is not the best choice.

C is also problematic. Under *Edwards*, once a suspect invokes the right to counsel, no further questioning is permitted unless the *suspect* initiates it. A suspect's opportunity to consult with counsel does not change this rule. *Minnick*. Here, Rachel reports that her attorney would allow uncounseled interrogation; however, Rachel does not affirmatively state that she wants to speak with Theresa. In addition, it is Theresa, not Rachel, who initiates contact after Rachel has spoken to her attorney. Viewed in their totality, these circumstances do not constitute initiation.

Edwards discredits *Miranda* waivers obtained after a request for counsel to combat the coercion that flows from police custody. Under *Shatzer*, the request for counsel remains in force while a suspect remains in custody and for the first fourteen days following release. In **D**, Seth obtains a waiver from Rachel outside her apartment one week after her release from the holding cell. Because he did not wait until the fifteenth day, the waiver is invalid and the accompanying interrogation is unlawful.

Because all four interrogations are unlawful, the correct answer is **E**.

E.   The Closer

QUESTION 5. **Barry's fiery temper.**   Barry was arrested at his home when forensic evidence linked him to the arson of his neighbor's house. After the arresting officer, Tammy, read Barry his *Miranda* rights, he told Tammy he "neede[ed] a minute to compose himself." Tammy told Barry to sit on the sofa in the living room. She sat beside him, doing paperwork.

After fifteen minutes, Tammy began questioning Barry about his relationship with the neighbor and his recent purchase of incendiary devices. Tammy then changed course, asking Barry if it was true that his teenage daughter tried to kill herself after the neighbor's son, Mitch, broke up with her. At that point, Barry balked. "Hold on, Officer, leave my daughter out of this. If you're gonna head down that road, I might need a lawyer to help me out." "So," Tammy queried, "you don't want to answer my question? Looks like Mitch put her through the ringer." "That bastard!" Barry barked. "I wish he was in that house when it burned."

Tammy then took a ten-minute break, during which Barry called his lawyer. When questioning resumed, Tammy asked Barry if he knew anything about the vandalism of Mitch's car the day before the fire. Barry smiled, remarking, "Glad I saved that old baseball bat." Barry is charged with arson and vandalism and moves to exclude his statements about Mitch and the baseball bat. He will likely succeed:

A. As to the statement about Mitch only.
B. As to the statement about the baseball bat only.
C. As to both statements.
D. As to neither statement.

ANALYSIS.   This closer reviews assertions of the right to silence and counsel and the effect an invocation has on a police officer's authority to conduct an interrogation thereafter. After receiving *Miranda* rights, Barry tells Tammy he "needs a minute to compose himself." She waits fifteen minutes before initiating the interrogation. Invocation of the right to silence must be unambiguous. If Barry's comment qualifies as an invocation under this standard, which is unclear, it appears that Tammy "scrupulously honored" the request since he asked for "a minute" and she waited fifteen. Thus, there is no violation of the *Miranda* right to silence.

By answering Tammy's questions, Barry impliedly waives his *Miranda* right to counsel; however, he reconsiders his decision when Tammy begins to question him about his daughter's attempted suicide on the heels of her failed relationship with his neighbor's son, Mitch. Barry eventually incriminates himself both for the arson of his neighbor's home and for the vandalism of the car owned by the neighbor's son, Mitch.

Under *Davis*, Barry's ruminations about counsel must amount to a clear and unambiguous request for a lawyer. Barry's statement that he "might need a lawyer" does not meet this standard. *Davis* also refused to require police officers to clarify an ambiguous request for counsel. It is irrelevant, therefore, that Tammy disregards Barry's comment about possibly needing a lawyer and continues, instead, to question him about his daughter's conduct.

Tammy thereafter takes a break and, ten minutes later, resumes the interrogation. Her questioning now focuses on a new topic: the vandalism of Mitch's car. Barry's *de facto* admission that he took a baseball bat to the vehicle is fully admissible. Barry has still failed to clearly ask for counsel, and the fact that he spoke to his lawyer during the break does nothing to change this reality. If Barry had requested counsel, *Minnick* provides that his consultation with his lawyer would not undermine the need for counsel to be present when questioning resumed; however, *Minnick* has no relevance where, as here, there is no valid assertion in the first place!

For the foregoing reasons, both statements are admissible. The correct answer is **D**.

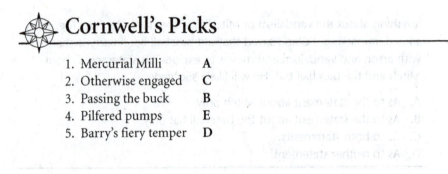

Cornwell's Picks

1. Mercurial Milli   **A**
2. Otherwise engaged   **C**
3. Passing the buck   **B**
4. Pilfered pumps   **E**
5. Barry's fiery temper   **D**

24

Limiting the *Miranda* Doctrine

CHAPTER OVERVIEW
A. Curing Constitutional Defects: Attenuation in the *Miranda* Context
   1. Purging the Taint from, and Through, *Miranda*
   2. *Elstad* Revisited
B. Beyond the Reach of *Miranda*: Public Safety and Physical Fruits
C. The Closer
   ✦ Cornwell's Picks

W hile *Edwards* and its progeny have strongly affirmed the *Miranda* right to counsel, the U.S. Supreme Court has recognized significant limitations on the doctrine in a variety of other contexts. The number and force of these exceptions, addressed in this chapter, led the Court to consider, in 2000, whether *Miranda* was a constitutionally based decision or, by contrast, a set of prophylactic protections that may be overcome by a countervailing statutory standard of admissibility. By a vote of six to three, the Court held that *Miranda* "announced a constitutional rule that Congress may not supersede legislatively." *Dickerson v. United States*, 530 U.S. 428 (2000). Still, as we explore the various limitations on the reach of *Miranda*, you should consider the extent to which these decisions are consistent with the core principles emphasized by the Court in 1966.

A. Curing Constitutional Defects: Attenuation in the *Miranda* Context

In Chapter 18 we discussed the "attenuation" doctrine, which provides that, under certain circumstances, evidence linked to prior unconstitutional conduct may be admissible against the defendant. To prevail, the prosecution must demonstrate that the subsequent evidence, whether tangible or testimonial, was the product of the defendant's free will. The cases we discussed all involved Fourth Amendment violations that resulted from an unlawful arrest, search, or seizure. We now consider how attenuation principles play out when the violation sounds instead in the Fifth Amendment *Miranda* doctrine.

1. Purging the Taint from, and Through, Miranda

In *Oregon v. Elstad*, 470 U.S. 298 (1985), police officers went to the home of an eighteen-year-old burglary suspect, Elstad, intending to place him under arrest. Before giving the suspect his *Miranda* rights, one of the officers questioned him about the crime, in response to which Elstad admitted his involvement. Approximately one hour later, after the officers transported Elstad to the station house, the suspect was read his *Miranda* rights. He elected to speak with the officers and issued a full, written confession.

Elstad subsequently moved to suppress the station-house confession as a "fruit" of the earlier *Miranda* violation. The U.S. Supreme Court denied the motion, holding that "a suspect who has once responded to unwarned yet uncoercive questioning is not thereby disabled from waiving his rights and confessing after he has been given the requisite *Miranda* warnings." In so holding, the majority rejected as "speculative and attenuated" the defendant's contention that the presumptive compulsion of the first interrogation compromises the constitutional validity of the second since the "cat is out of the bag."

The Court did note, however, that the administration of *Miranda* warnings would be insufficient to purge the taint of a previous admission obtained through "inherently coercive police tactics or methods offensive to due process." In such circumstances, the involuntariness of the initial confession would so severely compromise a suspect's free will as to render him unable to invoke the protections subsequently provided to him under *Miranda*.

QUESTION 1. Of mice and men.   Ronald works for the Taylors as a farmhand. In exchange for helping care for the animals and crops, the Taylors pay Ronald a weekly salary and provide lodging in a one-room cottage next to the barn. Ronald is nineteen years old and severely learning disabled. He dropped out of high school at sixteen and has limited reading ability and life skills. One evening, Isaac, the Taylor's nephew and a paroled felon who lives with his aunt and uncle, invites Ronald to go to a local tavern with him. On the way there, Isaac sees a hitchhiker and tells Ronald that they should rob him. Isaac then stops near the hitchhiker and, while Isaac holds a gun to his head, Ronald removes the hitchhiker's wallet from his back pocket. Ronald hands the wallet to Isaac who proceeds to kill the hitchhiker and dump his body by the roadside. Isaac tells Ronald, who is terrified, that he will kill him if he (Ronald) tells anyone about the incident.

The police investigation soon focuses on Isaac. Knowing that he spends time with Ronald, Officer Budd comes to Ronald's cottage at

2:00 A.M. one night, wakes him up, and asks him to get into the police car so they can talk. Budd is silent until they arrive at the place where the body was found. Budd tells Ronald that a "man was found dead here" and they think Isaac killed him. Budd stresses how serious the crime is, adding that, if Ronald knows anything about it, he had better speak up now because it will only be worse for him later. As tears well up in his eyes, Ronald admits that he was with Isaac when Isaac killed the man. Budd then explains Ronald's *Miranda* rights to him carefully, making sure he understands them. When they arrive at the police station twenty minutes later, Budd repeats the warnings. Ronald states that he does not want a lawyer and will "tell his story" to the police. He then gives a full, oral confession.

Is this second confession admissible under *Elstad*?

A. Yes, because it took place in a different location from the first and was obtained after Budd repeated the *Miranda* warnings.
B. Yes, because Budd did not force Ronald to admit his presence at the crime scene.
C. No, because it was closely connected in time to the first.
D. No, because the environment in which the first admission was elicited was inherently coercive.

ANALYSIS. *Elstad* allows the introduction of incriminating statements from an individual "who has once responded to unwarned yet uncoercive questioning," provided police officers obtain a valid *Miranda* waiver prior to the second confession. Because Ronald waived his *Miranda* rights before incriminating himself at the station house, this confession is admissible, provided his earlier admission in the police car to having been present when Isaac killed the hitchhiker is not the product of police coercion.

In addressing this question, it is important to identify the type of police compulsion that will invalidate subsequent admissions. The fact that *Miranda* warnings were necessary initially indicates that the atmosphere in which the suspect made his first confession was sufficiently "police-dominated" to render any incriminating statement "presumptively compelled." The *Elstad* majority holds, however, that custodial interrogation is insufficient, in and of itself, to invalidate subsequent confessions, reasoning that the psychological effect of having "let the cat out of the bag" is too indeterminate to presume ongoing coercive taint. Excluding subsequent statements requires, in addition, that police elicited the initial statement through *actual* compulsion — for example, "physical violence or other deliberate means calculated to break the suspect's will."

This fact pattern is based on *Shelton v. State of Arkansas*, 699 S.W.2d 728 (Ark. 1985). The Arkansas Supreme Court suppressed the second confession, finding that the first was made in an inherently coercive setting that impaired the defendant's freedom of choice and action. Like Ronald, Shelton was a teenager with impaired cognitive abilities who was taken out of his residence in the middle of the night, driven to the crime scene, and asked for information about the crime while sitting at the scene in a police car. In both fact patterns, the subsequent confession followed the first closely in time and was likewise obtained in the wee hours of the morning in a custodial setting. As such, the administration of *Miranda* warnings is insufficient to restore the suspect's free will so as to permit the introduction at trial of the station-house confession.

A incorrectly asserts that the administration of *Miranda* warnings and the change of location before securing the second confession is enough to purge the taint of the initial violation. While factually correct, **B** states an incorrect principle of law: A confession may be deemed involuntary even if it is not obtained by force. The police can compromise a suspect's free will by placing him in an atmosphere that is inherently coercive, as Budd did to Ronald. Finally, while **C** correctly indicates that the temporal proximity of the two confessions is relevant in assessing admissibility, its significance depends analytically on the inherent compulsion that infected Ronald's roadside admission.

D is, therefore, the best answer.

2. Elstad *Revisited*

Patrice Seibert intentionally burned down her mobile home and, in so doing, killed Donald Rector, a mentally ill teenager who had been living with Seibert and her children. Five days later, police arrested Seibert at 3:00 A.M. in the hospital where she was staying with one of her children who was being treated for burns sustained in the fire. Officers transported Seibert to the station house where Officer Hanrahan questioned her for thirty to forty minutes until she incriminated herself. After a twenty-minute break, Seibert received *Miranda* warnings for the first time. Hanrahan thereafter obtained a written waiver and resumed the interrogation. Confronted with her pre-warning statements, Seibert again confessed her involvement in the arson and murder.

Officer Hanrahan later acknowledged that he had intentionally withheld *Miranda* warnings in the first instance. He explained that he was following an interrogation technique learned at the police academy in which an officer questions a suspect first, then provides warnings, and then, after obtaining a waiver, "repeat[s] the question 'until I get the answer that she's already provided once.'" The state argued that Seibert's post-waiver statements are admissible under *Elstad* since the provision of *Miranda* warnings cured any constitutional defect associated with her previous incriminating admissions.

The U.S. Supreme Court disagreed, holding that *Elstad* does not support the admissibility of the second confession. *Missouri v. Seibert*, 542 U.S. 600 (2004). A four-justice plurality reasoned that the "question first, warn later" technique did not adequately convey to Seibert the message that she retained a choice about whether to continue answering the officer's questions. "When *Miranda* warnings are inserted in the midst of continued and coordinated interrogation," the plurality opined, "they are likely to mislead and 'depriv[e] a defendant of knowledge essential to his ability to understand the nature of his rights and the consequences of abandoning them.'"

Providing the fifth vote in favor of suppression, Justice Kennedy did not join the plurality opinion. Concurring in the judgment, he believed that the principles of *Elstad* did not govern under these facts only because the officers intentionally endeavored to undermine *Miranda* in a situation where the confessions were substantively related and the police had made no effort to purge the initial taint before securing the second confession. The result may have been different, he opined, if, for example, there had been "a substantial break in time and circumstances between the statements" or if Officer Hanrahan had provided "an additional warning that explain[ed] the inadmissibility of the prewarning custodial statement."

QUESTION 2. **Clean green.**   The grand jury issued an indictment on Friday morning at 10:00 A.M. charging Benny with multiple counts of racketeering and money laundering. The U.S. Attorney's Office obtained an arrest warrant one hour later. Agent Ted and his supervisor, Agent Ramón, waited until 2:00 A.M. that night to make the arrest, figuring they might get more information from Benny if he was groggy. Ramón and Ted further agreed that Ramón would ask Benny about his criminal activity as soon as Ted placed him under arrest.

As expected, Benny was awakened out of a sound sleep when the agents rang the doorbell and announced their presence. The moment Benny opened the door, Ted told him he was under arrest and had to come to the station house with them. "What are you talking about?" Benny asked, yawning. "You heard him," Ramón retorted. "Get your coat." As Benny opened the coat closet adjacent to the front door, Ramón continued, "So, Benny, how long did you think you could launder that drug money without us noticing?" "Five years and counting," Benny chuckled, as he put on his jacket.

Benny rode to the station house with Ted, who administered *Miranda* warnings on the way. Ted told Benny that he would do what he could to help him out if Benny cooperated. When they arrived at the station house ten minutes later, Ted gave Benny his *Miranda* rights again, and Benny executed a written waiver. In response to Ted's questions, Benny admitted his involvement in money laundering and other criminal activities linked to organized crime. Which of the following is Benny's best argument regarding the inadmissibility of the station-house confession?

A. The station-house confession directly followed the unwarned admission.
B. The initial questioning took place when Benny was awakened from a sound sleep.
C. The agents agreed in advance to question Benny upon arrest without *Miranda* warnings.
D. The agents purposely waited until 2:00 A.M. to arrest Benny.

ANALYSIS.   This thought-provoking problem requires careful consideration of the fine points of *Missouri v. Seibert*. While significant in signaling a reluctance to expand *Elstad*, *Seibert*'s analytical clarity is complicated by the justices' 4-1-4 split. As a result, the more limited reach of Justice Kennedy's concurrence in the judgment necessarily holds sway, since he would join the four dissenters to form a majority for any "excess" urged by the plurality.

Most importantly, unlike the plurality, Justice Kennedy believed that the constitutional infirmity in the police practice at issue in *Seibert* was its intentionality in the absence of effective countervailing redress. If, by contrast, officers violated a suspect's *Miranda* rights negligently, he presumably would continue to apply *Elstad*. Because the federal agents in our problem intentionally endeavored to undermine Benny's *Miranda* rights, *Seibert* applies both under the plurality *and* under Justice Kennedy's framework.

Based on the foregoing, we can eliminate **A** and **B**, since neither references the intentional nature of the agents' acts. Both **C** and **D** do. In deciding which is the better answer, keep in mind the principal issue(s) that *Seibert* addressed. The justices' primary concern with respect to the "question first, warn later" interrogation technique was its tendency to undermine a suspect's belief in the vitality and meaning of his *Miranda* rights. As such, the agents' decision to question Benny before providing these rights tracks *Seibert*'s analytical framework closely. By contrast, the decision to arrest Benny in the middle of the night lacks a direct link to *Miranda*. For example, if the agents, upon awakening Benny at 2:00 A.M., immediately administered *Miranda* warnings, *Seibert* would not appear to apply.

The correct answer is **C**.

B.   Beyond the Reach of *Miranda*: Public Safety and Physical Fruits

In *New York v. Quarles*, 467 U.S. 649 (1984), police entered a supermarket into which a man had fled after perpetrating a rape while armed. Upon locating and frisking the suspect, an officer discovered an empty gun holster and, after handcuffing the suspect, the officer asked him where the gun was. The suspect responded that it was "over there" and gestured in the direction of some empty cartons. The officer then retrieved the loaded weapon from inside an empty carton, placed the suspect under arrest, and administered *Miranda* rights.

The U.S. Supreme Court conceded that the officer's question as to the location of the gun constituted custodial interrogation prior to the administration of *Miranda* rights, but the majority deemed the response admissible nonetheless. In so holding, the Court recognized a "narrow" exception to *Miranda*, where an officer's question is "reasonably prompted by a concern for public safety." This exception does not depend on the officer's motivation. Thus, the fact that this officer did not fear for his safety when he posed the question is irrelevant where the facts otherwise disclose a legitimate risk to public safety. Only where there is "actual" coercion by the questioning officer does the Constitution mandate exclusion.

The Court's willingness to recognize limits on the reach of *Miranda* in *Quarles* was underscored dramatically in *United States v. Patane*, 542 U.S. 630 (2004). During an unlawful custodial interrogation in which Patane failed to receive *Miranda* warnings, he told officers where to find a firearm that, as a convicted felon, Patane was forbidden to carry. While it excluded his incriminating statement, the majority admitted the gun found as a result. Because *Miranda* sounds in the self-incrimination clause of the Fifth Amendment, the justices reasoned that it does not apply to "the nontestimonial fruit of a voluntary statement." A statement is involuntary, according to the majority, only if it is "actually" coerced. Thus, because the defendant's statement as to the location of the gun was voluntary, the "fruit" of the statement—the gun itself—was outside the reach of *Miranda* and, therefore, admissible.

QUESTION 3. Mercury rising. Police officers gathered information indicating that Martin, a student with a history of antisocial behavior and mental illness, had purchased items over the previous two weeks consistent with making an explosive device. Martin had also told a fellow student that something "really big" was going to happen the next day. After a search of Martin's apartment and car failed to turn up any of the bomb-making items he had purchased, Officer Lucy brought him in for questioning.

After denying that he purchased the bomb-making materials, Martin told Lucy that he did not want to answer any questions. Lucy then told him that he was going to be "jammed up here" for a while. She stayed with him in the interrogation room, asking every fifteen minutes if he was ready to talk. Forty-five minutes later, Martin agreed to talk and admitted, in response to questioning, that he had hidden a partially constructed bomb in his parents' basement. Lucy seized it there later that day, and the district attorney charged Martin with attempted arson.

> If Martin files a motion to suppress based on the Fifth Amendment
> *Miranda* doctrine, he will succeed:
>
> **A.** As to the statement and the bomb.
> **B.** As to the statement only.
> **C.** As to the bomb only.
> **D.** As to neither the statement nor the bomb.

ANALYSIS. In answering this question, we can start by addressing the admissibility of the partially constructed bomb. As *Quarles* and *Patane* make clear, the admissibility of incriminating statements about the bomb and the bomb itself may, or may not, align. If, for example, the statement is admissible as an exception to *Miranda*, the defendant cannot object to the introduction of the bomb discovered through the statement. If, by contrast, the statement is excluded, the bomb is admissible nonetheless in the absence of actual coercion since, under *Patane*, it would be a "physical fruit" that does not implicate the self-incrimination clause of the Fifth Amendment from which the U.S. Supreme Court derived the *Miranda* doctrine.

To exclude the statement, the court would need to find that it was the product of custodial interrogation *and* that the "public safety" exception does not excuse Lucy's failure to administer *Miranda* warnings. There is little doubt that Lucy's questioning of Martin was custodial. She detained him for more than forty-five minutes at the station house after telling him he would be "jammed up" there for a while. She also remained in the room with him, repeatedly asking if he was ready to talk. In sum, Martin faced the kind of inherently coercive custodial environment that *Miranda* was designed to redress. See *Howes v. Fields, supra.*

Lucy's conduct is motivated, however, by the desire to protect the public, since Martin had stated that "something big" was going to happen the next day and the police knew he had purchased bomb-making materials. In light of this "public safety" nexus, his response to her question about the bomb's location is admissible, unless it was elicited through *actual* coercion. It was not. While Lucy's conduct clearly violated Martin's assertion of the right to silence under *Miranda,* see *Berghuis* and *Mosley, supra,* she did not engage in the kind of physical or psychological abuse that is the hallmark of this higher standard. Thus, Martin's statement is admissible.

The foregoing also supports the admissibility of the bomb itself. In *Patane,* the U.S. Supreme Court held that physical fruits derived from *Miranda* violations are inadmissible only if the *Miranda* violation is coupled with actual coercion. Therefore, because Martin's confession as not actually coerced, the bomb comes in.

The correct answer is **D.**

C.   The Closer

QUESTION 4. Parental involvement.   State University President Thad contacted the police when he received a letter from Rita stating that she had a bomb and, unless he admitted her son, she would detonate it in the student union. While Officer Ted searched Rita's apartment for the explosive, Officer Rick went to her place of work to arrest her. As Rick arrived, Ted called to report that the bomb had not been found in the apartment.

Rick placed Rita under arrest, immediately asking her where she had hidden the bomb. When she refused to answer, Rick pushed Rita against the wall and, pinning her shoulders, told her that if she didn't tell him the location of the bomb immediately, she had "better prepare for pain." Rita then told him where she had hidden it. While Rick sped off to the location, his partner, Officer Abigail, transported Rita to the police station.

Once they arrived at the station house, Abigail read Rita her *Miranda* rights, after getting her a soda. Abigail then asked Rita if she would be willing to speak with her. Rita said that she would, and she signed a *Miranda* waiver form. In response to Abigail's questions, Rita confessed that she had constructed the bomb and planned to use it to secure her son's admission to State University. Rick found the bomb at the location provided by Rita, and the bomb squad successfully deactivated it.

Rita moves to exclude her statement to Rick about the bomb's location, her station-house confession, and the bomb. She is likely to succeed as to:

A. The statement as to the location of the bomb, the station-house confession, and the bomb.
B. The statement as to the location of the bomb and the station-house confession.
C. The statement as to the location of the bomb only.
D. The station-house confession only.
E. Nothing.

ANALYSIS.   This chapter addresses the admissibility of evidence, both physical and testimonial, following a *Miranda* waiver where a suspect has previously made incriminating statements that are inadmissible under *Miranda*. Here, Rick gets Rita to tell him where she hid the bomb by pinning her to the wall and threatening to inflict pain on her. While he speeds off to retrieve the bomb, Abigail obtains a fuller confession at the station house. Rita moves to exclude her incriminating statements to both Rick and Abigail, as well as the (deactivated) bomb itself.

Because Rick is motivated by the desire to protect public safety, *Quarles* excuses the *Miranda* violation, provided he does not resort to actual coercion to elicit the information. Unfortunately, he does just that, threatening and physically manhandling Rita to learn the location of the bomb. As such, Rita's statement is clearly inadmissible under *Miranda*, as well as the Due Process Clause of the Fourteenth Amendment. (See Chapter 20.)

Under *Elstad* and *Seibert*, obtaining a *Miranda* waiver before subsequent questioning can purge the taint of the preceding *Miranda* violation so as to allow the later statements to be admitted into evidence. Unfortunately for Abigail, the *Miranda* waiver is ineffective in purging the taint of "actual" compulsion where, for example, the initial confession was the product of threats of physical violence. Thus, because Rick threw Rita against the wall, her station-house confession is inadmissible, even though she executes a written *Miranda* waiver.

Likewise, under *Patane*, physical fruits that are ordinarily admissible in the context of a *Miranda* violation are inadmissible if actual coercion is present. While the prosecution may argue that Abigail did not coerce Rita, Rita disclosed the bomb's location to Rick, not to Abigail. Therefore, Abigail's professional demeanor is irrelevant.

The correct answer is **A**.

✧ Cornwell's Picks

1. Of mice and men	D
2. Clean green	C
3. Mercury rising	D
4. Parental involvement	A

25

Confessions, Counsel, and the Sixth Amendment

CHAPTER OVERVIEW
A. Indigent Defendants' Right to Counsel Under the Sixth Amendment
B. The *Massiah* Doctrine: Limiting Pretrial Interrogation Without Counsel
C. Defining Interrogation and Waiver Under the Sixth Amendment
D. Jail "Plants" and the Sixth Amendment
E. Custodial Interrogation in the Sixth Amendment Context
F. The Closer
✧ Cornwell's Picks

The Sixth Amendment provides the third constitutional vehicle for challenging the admission of a confession at trial. Unlike the Fifth Amendment *Miranda* doctrine and the Due Process Clause of the Fourteenth Amendment, the Sixth Amendment provides an *express* guarantee of counsel "[i]n all criminal prosecutions."

The application of the Sixth Amendment to pretrial police conduct was first recognized by a majority of the U.S. Supreme Court in the watershed case of *Massiah v. United States*, 377 U.S. 201 (1964), which we will discuss in Section B. *Miranda*, handed down two years later, overshadowed *Massiah* and became, in the years that followed, the nearly exclusive vehicle used by lower courts to exclude pretrial confessions. *Brewer v. Williams*, 430 U.S. 387 (1977), discussed in Section C, affirmed the broad availability of the Sixth Amendment in the pretrial context and, in so doing, reinforced its constitutional vitality in regulating police conduct.

This chapter is divided into five sections. Section A identifies when indigent defendants are entitled to the assistance of counsel under the Sixth Amendment. Sections B through E address the scope and meaning of the Sixth Amendment's guarantee of counsel in various contexts. Section B defines when the Sixth Amendment attaches and the offenses to which it applies in a given case. Section C specifies the meaning of "interrogation" under the Sixth Amendment. Section D addresses Sixth Amendment limits on the use of confessions elicited from defendants detained in jail pending trial. Finally, having already discussed custodial interrogation in the Fifth Amendment *Miranda* context, Section E evaluates the rules and standards that apply to custodial interrogations under the Sixth Amendment.

A.   Indigent Defendants' Right to Counsel Under the Sixth Amendment

Prior to 1963, states were required to provide counsel at trial for an indigent defendant in a felony case only if "special circumstances" existed, such as a possible death sentence, unusually complicated facts or legal issues, or some sort of impairment on the part of the defendant. See, e.g., *Betts v. Brady*, 316 U.S. 455 (1942); *Powell v. Alabama*, 287 U.S. 45 (1932). *Gideon v. Wainwright*, 372 U.S. 335 (1963), eliminated the "special circumstances" rule and made appointed counsel available in state cases to all indigent felony defendants.

Gideon did not address the right to counsel of indigent defendants in misdemeanor cases. Nine years later, *Argersinger v. Hamlin*, 407 U.S. 25 (1972), applied *Gideon* to a misdemeanant sentenced to jail time. The U.S. Supreme Court later specified that the right to counsel does not extend to misdemeanants who do not receive jail time as part of their sentence. Thus, the refusal to provide counsel to the defendant in *Scott v. Illinois*, 440 U.S. 367 (1979), did not violate the Sixth Amendment's "actual imprisonment" standard, since he was only required to pay a $50 fine following his conviction for shoplifting.

A valid uncounseled conviction may, however, be used as an enhancement for a subsequent offense where jail time is ordered by the U.S. Supreme Court. Thus, in *Nichols v. United States*, 511 U.S. 738 (1994), it was permissible for the sentencing court to use the defendant's uncounseled prior conviction for DUI to increase the jail time imposed for a subsequent felony to which he pled guilty with the assistance of counsel.

QUESTION 1. Joint custody.   Louise, who is indigent, borrowed a friend's car to go to the grocery store. On her way to the store, she was pulled over for speeding. The officer ordered her out of her car and, as she stepped out, a marijuana cigarette fell out of her purse. The officer arrested her for misdemeanor possession, an offense punishable by a fine of up to $200 and/or jail time of up to three months. Although Louise requested counsel, appointed counsel was not available for misdemeanor offenses. Louise, therefore, represented herself and pled guilty. The judge ordered her to pay the full $200, but she received no jail time.

The following year, Louise was one of five people arrested in her apartment building as part of a sting operation to identify individuals who were selling drugs in public housing. She was charged with a single felony count of drug distribution. Her lawyer persuaded her to plead guilty, in light of the strength of the evidence against her. At the sentencing hearing, the judge cited a state law that allowed him to exceed the maximum authorized sentence in drug distribution cases where the defendant's criminal record contains one or more convictions in "drug or drug-related" cases. Based on this provision, the judge sentenced Louise to four years in jail plus $10 for every person to whom she had sold drugs. The statutorily specified penalty for this offense is two to four years of incarceration.

Louise's claim that the judge violated her Sixth Amendment rights:

A. Has merit, because of the penalty prescribed for the misdemeanor.
B. Has merit, because of the penalty imposed for the misdemeanor.
C. Lacks merit, because she had counsel for the felony.
D. Lacks merit, because the enhancement consisted of a fine only.

ANALYSIS. Choosing the correct answer to this fact pattern requires a careful application of the rules detailed above. Louise is subject to a sentencing enhancement for her second offense based on her prior, uncounseled conviction for the first. *Nichols* approves this practice, reasoning that the enhancement provision "do[es] not change the penalty imposed for the earlier conviction," provided the denial of counsel for the first offense was appropriate.

Louise's first offense was for misdemeanor possession. For this offense, under the "actual imprisonment" standard of *Argersinger/Scott*, she was not entitled to appointed counsel as an indigent defendant unless she was sentenced to jail time. Remember: It is not the *potential* for jail time that is relevant; a defendant has to actually receive a sentence of incarceration to trigger the counsel requirement. Thus, because the penalty imposed by the judge consisted of a monetary fine only, the denial of Louise's request for counsel was constitutional. Accordingly, **A** and **B** are wrong.

D is a bit of a red herring. The fact that the enhancement imposed by the judge was in the form of a fine, as opposed to a longer term of imprisonment, is irrelevant. The previous conviction either permits enhancement or it does not; it does not permit some forms of enhancement but not others.

Gideon requires appointed counsel for all felony offenses. Because the drug distribution offense was a felony, Louise had the right to appointed counsel, which she received. As such, the sentence imposed by the judge was constitutional.

The correct answer is **C**.

B. The *Massiah* Doctrine: Limiting Pretrial Interrogation Without Counsel

Winston Massiah was indicted for federal drug offenses and, after posting bail, was released pending trial. His co-defendant, Colson, invited Massiah to discuss the case in Colson's car. Massiah accepted the invitation, unaware that Colson was cooperating with the prosecution and had agreed to the placement of a radio transmitter in the vehicle that allowed a federal agent to listen to the conversation. The federal agent's testimony at Massiah's trial as to the substance of the overheard conversation was held to have violated the Sixth Amendment, since the covert interrogation took place in the absence of counsel. *Massiah v. United States*, 377 U.S. 201 (1964).

Massiah was revolutionary in its use of the Sixth Amendment to regulate pretrial police conduct. The U.S. Supreme Court later clarified that the Sixth Amendment attaches "at or after the time that adversarial judicial proceedings have been initiated" against the defendant. *Kirby v. Illinois*, 406 U.S. 682 (1972). Once that moment arrives, uncounseled interrogation is forbidden, in the absence of a waiver.

Unlike the Fifth Amendment, the Sixth Amendment is "offense specific." As such, the Sixth Amendment right to counsel applies *only* to those offenses with which a defendant has been formally charged. If, therefore, an indicted defendant makes incriminating statements during covert interrogation by an undercover police officer, only those statements concerning the offense for which he has been indicted are inadmissible. *Maine v. Moulton*, 474 U.S. 159 (1985).

Interrogation about uncharged crimes is permissible under the Sixth Amendment even if those crimes are "very closely factually related to" and "interwoven with" the offense charged. In *Texas v. Cobb*, 532 U.S. 162 (2001), the defendant had been indicted for the burglary of a home whose residents had gone missing. While he initially denied any knowledge of their whereabouts, he later confessed to their murder during an interrogation at which his counsel was not present. The confession, which secured a conviction on two counts of capital murder, was deemed admissible, since burglary and murder are not the "same offense." To be considered the same offense under the Sixth Amendment, all of the statutory elements of one offense must be included in the other; because both the burglary and the murder statutes contain elements not found in those of the other, they do not qualify. *Cobb* (citing *Blockburger v. United States*, 284 U.S. 299 (1932)).

QUESTION 2. The spy who bugged me. Having obtained a warrant to arrest Brad for stealing Lindsay's diamond ring, Detective Billy Bob took Brad into custody at his home. Later that day, Brad was arraigned on one count of second-degree felony theft. His attorney was present with him in court. After posting bail, Brad was released on his own recognizance pending trial.

> Afraid that the evidence against Brad was thin, Billy Bob persuaded Brad's girlfriend, Angelina, to ask him questions about the crime while wearing a recording device that allowed Billy Bob to hear the conversation from his squad car parked outside the residence. When Angelina asked Brad why he stole Lindsay's ring, Brad stated that he had wanted to "shake her up." Angelina then asked Brad if he had been carrying his weapon when he took the ring, commenting that that "would really put a scare into ol' Linds." Brad chuckled. "Yeah, it sure seemed to. Glad I brought it."
>
> Unaware of the presence of a weapon, Billy Bob raised the issue with Lindsay, who then remembered seeing the gun and "being transfixed by it for a while." Based on this new information, the district attorney indicted Brad for robbery. Robbery is defined as "theft perpetrated while carrying a weapon." (Theft does not require proof that the defendant was armed.) At Brad's robbery trial, Billy Bob recounts the conversation between Brad and Angelina. This testimony is likely to be:
>
> **A.** Admissible, because Brad initiated the conversation about the crime.
> **B.** Admissible, because theft and robbery are different offenses.
> **C.** Inadmissible, because the conversation took place after Brad was arrested.
> **D.** Inadmissible, because Brad had been indicted for theft before the conversation took place.

ANALYSIS. This problem explores the Sixth Amendment limits on post-indictment police interrogation. Like *Massiah* and *Moulton*, the interrogation in our fact pattern is covert, in that Brad does not realize that a police officer is listening to his conversation with Angelina. As such, it is permissible only as to topics other than the theft offense with which he has been charged.

Angelina asks Brad about weapons. Theft does not require proof that a defendant is armed; robbery does. This may lead you to conclude that they are not the same offense under the Sixth Amendment, like burglary and murder in *Cobb*. But there is a difference here. Because burglary and murder each contain an element not included in the other, proof of one will never automatically prove the other. Robbery, however, is simply theft with an additional element: The defendant was armed when the theft took place. Therefore, when the prosecution proves robbery, it automatically proves theft. Because theft is a "lesser-included" offense of robbery, the two would be considered the "same offense" for purposes of the *Blockburger* test, cited by the U.S. Supreme Court in *Cobb*.

Based on the foregoing, **B** is wrong. **A** is also incorrect. It is irrelevant that Brad initiated the conversation with Angelina since, in doing so, he did not realize that he would be speaking to a police informant. In fact, in *Moulton*, the defendant also initiated contact with the informant, and this circumstance had no impact on the Court's Sixth Amendment analysis.

C is wrong because the Sixth Amendment does not attach at the time of arrest. The initiation of adversarial *judicial* proceedings is necessary to trigger its protections. This occurs most commonly when the prosecutor files a charging document, sometimes referred to as "criminal information," with the court. The issuance of a grand jury indictment can also trigger Sixth Amendment protections if its issuance precedes the filing of formal charges. An arrest warrant is insufficient for this purpose.

Because Brad had already been indicted for theft, his Sixth Amendment rights had attached to that offense. Thus, because robbery and theft would be considered the same offense under the reasoning of *Cobb/Blockburger*, questions about either would be improper.

The correct answer is **D**.

C. Defining Interrogation and Waiver Under the Sixth Amendment

In Chapter 21, we discussed the meaning of interrogation in the Fifth Amendment *Miranda* context. The Sixth Amendment standard is different, mainly in its focus on officer intent. The U.S. Supreme Court clarified this distinction in the famous case of *Brewer v. Williams*, 430 U.S. 387 (1977). Williams was arrested and arraigned for the killing of an eleven-year-old girl. He asserted his right to counsel at the arraignment. While transporting Williams to the appropriate jurisdiction after the arraignment, the police detective elicited a confession from the defendant by delivering what attorneys dubbed the "Christian burial speech." In it, the detective appealed to Williams's strong religious beliefs by, among other things, referring to him as "Reverend" and stating that, if the little girl's body was not found soon, the falling snow would impede its recovery and prevent her parents from giving the child a "proper Christian burial." The majority held that the detective's conduct constituted interrogation, since he had "deliberately and designedly set out to elicit [incriminating] information."

Interrogation may exist in the absence of direct questioning. In *Fellers v. United States*, 540 U.S. 519 (2004), the Court unanimously held that federal agents had "deliberately elicited" incriminating information from the defendant when, upon entering the defendant's home, they announced that: They had come to discuss his involvement in methamphetamine distribution; Fellers had been indicted for conspiracy with four other people to distribute methamphetamine; and they had a warrant for his arrest.

Once Sixth Amendment rights have attached, interrogation in the absence of counsel is permissible only if the defendant's conduct manifests an "intentional relinquishment or abandonment" of his right to have his attorney present. *Johnson v. Zerbst*, 304 U.S. 458 (1938). The U.S. Supreme Court has likened this standard to that used in the *Miranda* context, requiring that the waiver be knowing, intelligent, and voluntary. *Patterson v. Illinois*, 487 U.S. 285 (1988). In short, the accused must "know what he is doing" such that "his choice is made with eyes wide open." *Adams v. ex rel. McCann*, 317 U.S. 269 (1942). Applying this standard in *Brewer*, the Court concluded that Williams had not waived, since he repeatedly referenced his attorney during the car ride and stated that he would tell the police "the whole story" after meeting with counsel.

QUESTION 3. Correction facility. Denise and Marta were indicted for conspiracy to sell narcotics. Both were released on bail, pending trial. After Marta's attorney told her that Denise had decided to plead guilty, Marta called Denise and left her a message asking to meet. Denise immediately called the district attorney, who asked her if she would wear a wire at the meeting "to back up" her testimony at Marta's trial. Denise agreed, and she called Marta back to arrange a time and place to get together.

Marta preferred to meet at a "neutral" location, explaining that she was concerned about surveillance. Marta also told Denise that she had been afraid that Denise would "set her up," but she had decided in the end to trust in their friendship. "C'mon, Marta," Denise retorted, pretending to be insulted, "how could you think that about me?" Denise then showed Marta the confession she planned to read in court when the judge took her plea and asked Marta what she thought of it. "It's okay," Marta answered nervously. "Would you change anything?" Denise asked. "Yeah," Marta replied, "you say our first sale was in November. That's wrong. It was December."

If Denise recounts this conversation at Marta's trial, would this violate Marta's Sixth Amendment rights?

A. Yes, because Denise wanted Marta to incriminate herself.
B. Yes, because Denise led Marta to believe that they were speaking in confidence.
C. No, because Marta was not being interrogated by Denise.
D. No, because Marta waived her right to counsel.

ANALYSIS. This fact pattern is loosely based on *United States v. Johnson*, 954 F.2d 1015 (5th Cir. 1992). Denise's testimony would violate Marta's Sixth Amendment rights if Denise's conduct constituted interrogation in the absence of a valid waiver of the right to counsel. The interrogation inquiry asks whether Denise "deliberately and designedly" elicited the incriminating information obtained from Marta. This focus on intent distinguishes the interrogation standards of the Fifth and Sixth Amendments; while the intent of a law enforcement official, or his agent, is not irrelevant in the Fifth Amendment context,[1] the analytical focus there is on the perceptions of the suspect.

The difference can be important. For example, the prosecution can argue that it was not reasonably likely that Denise's conduct would lead Marta to incriminate herself in light of Marta's awareness of the plea bargain and her concern about a set-up. Denise cannot deny, however, that her purpose was to elicit incriminating information from Marta. The district attorney's comment about using the information acquired to back up Denise's trial testimony indicates as much.

Because Denise's conduct constitutes interrogation, it violates the Sixth Amendment, unless Marta waived her right to counsel. The waiver need not be "express," provided her conduct demonstrates an "intentional relinquishment or abandonment." Since the U.S. Supreme Court has interpreted this standard to be similar to that used in the Fifth Amendment *Miranda* context, we must ask whether the accused "was made sufficiently aware of his right to have counsel present during the questioning, and of the possible consequences of a decision to forgo the aid of counsel." *Patterson.*

As the Fifth Circuit noted in *Johnson,* it is difficult to conclude that Marta has intentionally waived her right to counsel when she does not even know that she is being questioned by someone who is acting as a government agent. If she knew that Denise was recording their conversation for prosecutorial use, Marta would almost certainly not have wanted to speak to Denise without her attorney present.

Having established that Marta's Sixth Amendment rights were violated, we have eliminated **C** and **D**. We can also eliminate **B**. The fact that Denise leads Marta to believe that the two are speaking confidentially creates a Sixth Amendment violation *only* if the conversation that they subsequently have deliberately elicits incriminating information.

Accordingly, **A** is the best answer. Denise wanted Marta to confess to satisfy the district attorney with whom she was cooperating.

D. Jail "Plants" and the Sixth Amendment

The U.S. Supreme Court has separately examined the extent to which police informants working undercover inside jails and prisons can encourage defendants to speak about charged offenses without "deliberately eliciting" incriminating information. In *Henry v. United States,* 447 U.S. 264 (1980), government agents instructed an inmate at the city jail to "be alert to any statements made" but not to "initiate any conversation with or question Henry about the bank

---

1. In the context of interrogation under *Miranda*, intent "may well have a bearing on whether the police should have known that their words or actions were reasonably likely to elicit an incriminating response." *Innis, supra.*

robbery" for which Henry had been indicted. The informant had "some con-versations with the defendant," during which Henry admitted his involvement in the crime. The Court excluded the confession, holding that the govern-ment had deliberately elicited it "by intentionally creating a situation likely to induce Henry to make incriminating statements without the assistance of counsel." The Court identified three factors that informed its decision: that the informant was being paid by the government; that the defendant believed the informant to be a fellow inmate; and that the defendant was in custody and under indictment at the time of the incriminating conversation.

Mindful of *Henry*, prosecutors in *Kuhlmann v. Wilson*, 477 U.S. 436 (1986), instructed an informant not to question his cellmate but simply to "keep his ears open" for incriminating information. The defendant subsequently told the informant the story he had already provided to the police about the crime. In response, the informant said the story "didn't sound too good." The defen-dant began to change his story over the next few days; however, he told the informant the whole story only after meeting with his brother, who told the defendant that his family was upset because they believed he was guilty.

The U.S. Supreme Court distinguished this factual scenario from that of *Henry*, holding that the informant in *Kuhlmann* acted more like a "listen-ing post." The lone exception—his remark that the defendant's story did not sound good—was insufficient, the majority concluded, to constitute inter-rogation, particularly since the brother's visit was the immediate catalyst for the confession.

QUESTION 4. Secrets and spies. Eric, a prominent businessman and former state assemblyman, was arrested and arraigned for the murder of his girlfriend. The jail warden placed him in a cell with Patrick, a govern-ment informant who had been promised leniency if he cooperated with the authorities and produced testimonial evidence that could be used against Eric at trial. The district attorney told Patrick to listen but not to instigate conversations about the murder.

Eric was agitated when he entered the cell and readily talked about the charges against him. When asked what he was "in for," Patrick lied and said he had been charged with murdering a store employee during a robbery that got out of hand. During "free time" later that afternoon, a number of inmates were gathered around the television watching the news. Eric and Patrick joined them just as the station was reporting Eric's arrest for his girlfriend's murder. Eric wept as the girlfriend's parents were interviewed. "We loved him like a son," the mother sobbed. "We hope some day to understand why he did this."

Later that day, as they were getting ready for "lights out," Eric teared up as he told Patrick what great people his girlfriend's parents were. "I felt bad for them," Patrick replied as he climbed onto the

top bunk. "I guess things just don't make sense to them right now."
Distressed, Eric proceeded to tell Patrick how he warned his girlfriend
not to break up with him "but she wouldn't listen. I just did what any
guy would do, you know?" Eric added. "I gave her one last chance
before I cut her."

Eric's claim that Patrick violated his Sixth Amendment rights is likely
to:

A. Prevail, because Eric thought Patrick was a fellow inmate.
B. Prevail, because Patrick lied about being charged with murder.
C. Fail, because Patrick was not being paid for his efforts.
D. Fail, because Patrick never questioned Eric about the murder.

ANALYSIS. Arriving at the correct answer to this problem requires careful consideration of its similarities to, and differences from, both *Henry* and
Kuhlmann. *Henry* identifies three factors that influenced the U.S. Supreme
Court's finding that the informant's conduct constituted interrogation, among
which was the defendant's belief that the informant was a fellow inmate. In
Kuhlmann, however, the defendant had a similar understanding that was considered insufficient to characterize the informant's conduct as interrogation. **A**
does not, therefore, seem the best answer.

B references Patrick's dishonesty in stating that he had been charged with
murder. While the informant in *Henry* did not lie about his charges, dishonesty
seems a strange basis on which to find interrogation, since the larger context of
the interaction between the informant and the defendant is false. That is, the
informant is falsely holding himself out as no more than a fellow inmate and
is fostering a relationship with the defendant to obtain incriminating evidence
for prosecutorial use at trial. If this arrangement is insufficient, in and of itself,
to constitute the "intentional creation of a situation in which the defendant is
likely to incriminate himself," the addition of a lie about charges seems unlikely
to change the result—particularly where the alleged circumstances surrounding the false charge are different from those of the defendant's offense.

C rejects a finding of interrogation based on the fact that, unlike the informant in *Henry*, the informant in this problem is not being paid by the prosecution. While this is one of the factors relied upon by the U.S. Supreme Court
in *Henry*, the reference is not so much to money *per se* as it is to the favorable
treatment available to the informant if he is able to provide the government
with useful information. In this problem, the district attorney has promised
leniency in exchange for incriminating testimonial evidence. Like a monetary
reward, this "carrot" provides an incentive for the informant to secure a confession. **C** is, therefore, wrong.

While Patrick was not, strictly speaking, a "listening post," like the informant in *Kuhlmann*, he makes only one remark relevant to the interrogation

inquiry. The comment here—that the victim's parents don't understand why she was killed—is not enough to satisfy *Henry*. First, it is not posed as a question that directly invites a description of the killing. Second, and more importantly, it is simply a reiteration of what Eric heard and saw in the news broadcast hours earlier. Seeing the parents interviewed had a strong emotional effect on Eric at the time, and he was still thinking about them at the end of the evening when he mentioned to Patrick what wonderful people they were. Patrick's reflective response was just that and no more. Because Patrick's conduct does not constitute interrogation, Eric's Sixth Amendment rights were not violated.

The best answer is **D**.

E.   Custodial Interrogation in the Sixth Amendment Context

In Chapter 21, we identified the legal standards that govern custodial interrogations under the Fifth Amendment *Miranda* doctrine. We now return to this topic, this time in the context of the Sixth Amendment.

The Sixth Amendment protects criminal defendants at all "critical stages" of the prosecution, which includes interrogations that take place after formal charging. See, e.g., *Massiah, supra*. Therefore, when a formally charged defendant is custodially questioned by law enforcement, he is protected by both *Miranda and* the Sixth Amendment.

Informing suspects of their *Miranda* rights is generally sufficient to inform them of their Sixth Amendment right to counsel as well; likewise, a *Miranda* waiver generally qualifies as a valid waiver of the corresponding Sixth Amendment right to counsel. *Patterson, supra*. However, because the Sixth Amendment's protection of the attorney-client relationship exceeds that provided by the Fifth Amendment through *Miranda*—see, e.g., *Maine v. Moulton, supra*—there will be cases where a waiver that would be valid under *Miranda* will not suffice for Sixth Amendment purposes. For example, police officers who fail to inform suspects during questioning that a lawyer is trying to reach them do not compromise the validity of the suspects' *Miranda* waivers; however, Sixth Amendment waivers would not exist in such circumstances. *Patterson*.

Moreover, the appointment of counsel at a Sixth Amendment hearing, such as an initial arraignment at which suspects hear the charges filed against them and a judge sets bail, does not invalidate a subsequent Sixth Amendment waiver for purposes of custodial interrogation. *Montejo v. Louisiana*, 556 U.S. 778 (2009). Accordingly, incriminating statements made by the defendant during the interrogation are admissible, provided the prosecution demonstrates that the defendant waived his right to counsel knowingly, intelligently, and voluntarily.

QUESTION 5. Peddle to the metal.   Julio was arrested on January 1 for conspiracy to import stolen cars into the United States from Mexico. He was arraigned later that afternoon, following the filing of formal charges against him by the U.S. Attorney's Office. At the hearing, he requested counsel, claiming he was indigent. The assistant U.S. attorney (AUSA) objected to the appointment of counsel, claiming that Julio was not indigent. The magistrate stated that she would look into the matter and asked the AUSA for proof that Julio had sufficient means to pay for counsel. Julio was remanded to custody.

On January 5, Detective Jane, newly assigned to the case, brought Julio to an interrogation room at the jail. Before beginning the questioning, Jane read Julio his *Miranda* rights and obtained a written waiver that stated, "I, Julio, understand that I have the right to have an attorney with me and voluntarily agree to speak to the police without that attorney present." In response to Jane's questions, Julio implicates himself in the conspiracy.

On January 6, Julio receives a letter from the court, dated January 4, that states "Effective January 5, an attorney from the Office of Federal Defender will represent you, Julio, on the conspiracy charge filed January 1 by the U.S. Attorney's Office." Based on this letter, Julio's attorney moves to suppress the statements made to Jane as violative of his Sixth Amendment rights. The motion will likely:

A. Succeed, because Julio requested counsel on January 1.
B. Succeed, because Julio was represented by counsel when Jane interrogated him.
C. Fail, if Jane was unaware of Julio's request for counsel.
D. Fail, because Julio did not know counsel had been appointed when Jane interrogated him.
E. Fail, because Julio waived his Sixth Amendment right to counsel.

ANALYSIS.   This problem presents a somewhat complicated and convoluted procedural history. Most of the detail, however, is completely irrelevant to the ultimate question of the admissibility of Julio's incriminating statements. To avoid getting bogged down in extraneous detail, it is important to focus on the big picture and the relatively straightforward rule that governs in these circumstances: Defendants can validly waive their Sixth Amendment right to counsel at a custodial interrogation even if they have requested counsel at a previous Sixth Amendment hearing.

Accordingly, you can eliminate **A** and **B**, since they are at odds with the U.S. Supreme Court's recent decision in *Montejo v. Louisiana*. Neither Julio's request for counsel at his initial arraignment nor the Court's subsequent appointment of counsel for him prior to the interrogation extinguishes the authority of the prosecution to interrogate him without his attorney present, provided Julio validly waives his Sixth (and Fifth) Amendment rights.

C and **D** address Julio and Jane's lack of awareness of the court's appointment of counsel at the time the interrogation took place. As with **A** and **B**, the admissibility of Julio's confession does not turn on what either party knew about the court's response to Julio's request for counsel based on indigence on January 1. As long as Julio's agreement to speak to Jane on January 5 constitutes a knowing, intelligent, and voluntary waiver of his right to counsel, constitutional requirements are satisfied, without regard to what either party knew or did not know about the status of Julio's prior request at that time.

As discussed above, providing *Miranda* rights is generally sufficient to apprise defendants of their Sixth Amendment right to counsel. Therefore, in reading Julio his *Miranda* rights, Jane has satisfied the Sixth Amendment requirements in this regard. Julio subsequently executes a written waiver that acknowledges his right to counsel and affirmatively states that he has decided voluntarily to speak to Jane without an attorney present.

Because Julio executed a valid waiver of his Sixth Amendment right to counsel, his statements to Jane are admissible. **E** is the correct answer.

F.   The Closer

> **QUESTION 6. Canadian fakin'.**   Joyce and Andy, both American citizens, were indicted for conspiracy to import phony Rolex watches from Canada. Joyce posted bail and was released pending trial, but Andy could not raise the necessary collateral and was remanded to custody. One week later, Detective Thomas, working undercover, approached Joyce in a supermarket and struck up a conversation about the rising cost of groceries. Joyce was charmed by him and accepted an offer to meet for coffee the next day.
>
> At that meeting, Thomas asked Joyce seemingly innocent questions about herself, such as where she lived and what she did for a living. He told her he was from Canada and asked if she had ever been there. When Joyce said that she had, he asked if she had ever been to Montreal, his home town. She said that she had visited many times and loved it. Asked where she stayed, Joyce named a hotel on Saint-Antoine Street. The prosecution had grainy surveillance video from that hotel of a man and woman resembling Joyce and Andy handing phony Rolex watches to an informant the week before. Asked if she had stayed there recently, Joyce admitted to staying there the previous week "with a friend."
>
> A second undercover officer, Barry, posing as an inmate sharing a cell with Andy, used a similar "script." Barry stated that he used to travel a lot

"on business" and particularly loved Montreal. After Andy commented that he also liked Montreal, Barry lamented that he had never managed to find a hotel he liked and wondered if Andy "had any recommendations." Andy then mentioned his stay, the week before his indictment, at the same hotel referenced by Joyce.

At Joyce's trial, Thomas testified about his conversation with Joyce. At Andy's trial, Barry did not testify; instead, information about the substance of the conversation between Barry and Andy was provided by Trey, a prison security guard who had listened in while conducting a strip search of an inmate in an adjacent cell. Joyce and Andy claim that allowing Thomas and Trey's testimony violated their Sixth Amendment rights. This argument has merit:

A. As to both Joyce and Andy.
B. As to Joyce, but not Andy.
C. As to Andy, but not Joyce.
D. As to neither Joyce nor Andy.

ANALYSIS. This Sixth Amendment review problem involves two interrogations, effectively identical, conducted by officers acting undercover. One takes place in a coffee shop with the officer posing as a potential suitor to defendant Joyce, the other in a jail cell where the officer pretends to be an inmate sharing the cell with defendant Andy. Both Joyce and Andy have been indicted; thus, because formal charges have been lodged, Sixth Amendment protections apply to both.

The two conversations between the officers and the defendants are substantively similar. We will start, then, by determining whether the conduct in question constitutes interrogation. There is no question that the information obtained from Joyce and Andy was "deliberately elicited." The officers intentionally sought out the defendants and fostered relationships with them in the hope they would unwittingly offer incriminating information. This is unlawful, provided Thomas and Barry were questioning Joyce and Andy about the crime with which they were charged: conspiracy to import Rolex watches.

Joyce and Andy's admission that they were present at the hotel in Montreal meets this standard. It provides persuasive evidence that the individuals seen trading phony Rolexes on the videotape were, in fact, the defendants. Proof of this fact would be highly useful to the prosecution in proving conspiracy, much like the defendant's identification of the location of the victim's dead body was in *Brewer v. Williams*.

Applying *Henry*, Barry's placement in Andy's cell "intentionally creat[ed] a situation likely to induce Henry to make incriminating statements without the assistance of counsel." Barry's conduct was akin to that of the detective in *Henry* who had "some conversations" with the defendant-cellmate. The undercover officer in *Kuhlmann*, by contrast, acted more like a "listening post," offering only one comment that encouraged an incriminating response, which was not, in the end, the primary catalyst for the confession subsequently offered.

Unlike *Henry*, however, the undercover officer is not the one testifying at trial. Instead, a security guard who overheard the conversation takes the stand. Because the guard is acting as a "listening post," the conclusion that *Kuhlmann* permits the introduction of his testimony seems tempting, at first blush; *Kuhlmann* does not apply, however, to the fundamentally different factual scenario presented here.

"Listening posts" are allowed to testify because the incriminating information they convey is not the product of unlawful interrogation. The confession detailed by the informant in *Kuhlmann*, for example, was not "deliberately elicited" by him or by any other state actor; it was the product primarily of the defendant's feelings of remorse after meeting with his brother. Here, by contrast, the confession in question was indeed deliberately elicited by an individual working for the prosecution. The fact that the trial testimony is provided by a different state official, one who merely listened to the unlawful exchange, does not insulate or sanitize the unconstitutionality of the government's conduct. Were this the case, the government could subvert Sixth Amendment requirements by adding an extra person to merely witness, but not actively engage in, violations of constitutional rights.

Likewise, the fact that Andy confessed within earshot of third parties does not constitute a valid waiver of the Sixth Amendment right to counsel. Do not conflate the Sixth Amendment waiver with the laws applicable to lawyer/client privilege under state and federal rules of evidence. Andy could not intentionally relinquish his right to counsel because he did not know he was speaking to an officer. That Trey only eavesdropped on Andy's conversation with Barry does nothing to change that fundamental reality.

Based on the foregoing, the court should have excluded the testimony of both Thomas and Trey. By failing to do so, it violated Joyce and Andy's Sixth Amendment right to counsel. The correct answer is **A**.

✦ Cornwell's Picks

1. Joint custody	**C**	
2. The spy who bugged me	**D**	
3. Correction facility	**A**	
4. Secrets and spies	**D**	
5. Peddle to the metal	**E**	
6. Canadian fakin'	**A**	

26

Identifications

CHAPTER OVERVIEW
A. Identifications and the Right to Counsel
B. Due Process and Identifications
C. Remedial Considerations
D. The Closer
✦ Cornwell's Picks

The identification of a defendant at trial by an eyewitness to the crime is among the most powerful weapons in a prosecutor's arsenal. Because identification creates a powerful association in the mind of the jury between the defendant and the crime, the U.S. Supreme Court has endeavored to ensure that it is admissible only where a witness's recollection derives from the crime scene. If a tainted pretrial identification procedure compromises the reliability of an in-court identification, the Due Process Clause of the Fourteenth Amendment mandates its exclusion. Similarly, the evidentiary importance of witness identification triggers Sixth Amendment protection to guard against police misconduct in administering line-ups and show-ups taking place after formal charges have been filed.

This chapter explores the constitutional parameters of challenges to methods of witness identification under the Sixth Amendment and the Fourteenth Amendment Due Process Clause. Law enforcement agencies use three identification procedures: a line-up, where the accused is one among several persons shown to the witness; a "show-up," in which the accused alone is shown to the witness; and a photographic array, in which a witness views a number of photographs, including that of the accused. Section A discusses the constitutional right to counsel in the identifications context, addressing both Fifth and Sixth Amendment implications. Section B focuses on the Due Process Clause of the Fourteenth Amendment, highlighting the role of witness reliability under the prevailing standard. Finally, Section C addresses remedies, identifying when and how constitutional infirmity in pretrial identifications precludes their introduction at trial, as well as a witness's in-court identification.

A. Identifications and the Right to Counsel

In *United States v. Wade*, 388 U.S. 218 (1967), police officers required the defendant, who had been indicted for bank robbery, to take part in a line-up where each participant was forced to wear tape on his face, as the robber had done, and to utter the words used by him in perpetrating the crime. Wade argued that this procedure violated his Fifth Amendment privilege against self-incrimination as well as the Sixth Amendment, since it occurred outside the presence of counsel.

The U.S. Supreme Court rejected the Fifth Amendment claim. Because the prosecution was using the defendant's appearance and words at the line-up purely for purposes of identification, the defendant's conduct was insufficiently "testimonial" to implicate the privilege against self-incrimination.[1] Displays of one's physical characteristics, whether voluntary or forced, generally lack constitutional significance.

The Sixth Amendment claim, however, proved meritorious. The Sixth Amendment applies at any "critical stage" of the prosecution "where counsel's absence might derogate from the accused's right to a fair trial." The Court held, to this end, that line-ups conducted after defendants are formally charged are critical stages, due to the potential for substantial prejudice to defendants if law enforcement officials were to use suggestive procedures.

Not all identification procedures qualify for Sixth Amendment protection, however. In *United States v. Ash*, 413 U.S. 300 (1973), the U.S. Supreme Court held that the right to counsel does not extend to photographic arrays since there is no face-to-face confrontation between the witness and the defendant. The function of counsel, the justices reasoned, is to aid the accused "in coping with legal problems or assisting in meeting his adversary." Since the accused is not present at a photo identification, these concerns do not come into play. Moreover, the use of a static medium created, the Court opined, "substantially fewer possibilities of impermissible suggestion."

> **QUESTION 1. Stainless steal.** Tamara and Trent awoke in the middle of the night when they heard noises downstairs in their home. They tip-toed down the staircase and peered around the corner toward the dining room. There, they saw a man placing their wedding silver in a bag. After watching him for about thirty seconds, the couple became frightened and quietly went back upstairs. When they heard the man leave, Trent telephoned the police immediately, recounting the events and describing the burglar.

---

1. In Chapter 21, Section D, we discussed the "testimonial" requirement of the Fifth Amendment *Miranda* doctrine in the custodial interrogation context.

> Two miles from the house, Officer Rick arrested Bradley, who fit the description provided by Trent. Unaware of the arrest, Tamara came to the police station the following morning for an update from Officer Rick. Coincidentally, Bradley was in an interrogation room at the time. Rick asked Tamara to wait and arranged clandestinely for Bradley to walk past Tamara at close range. When he did so, she shrieked, "That's the man!"
>
> Later that day, after Bradley's arraignment, Trent came to the police station, and Rick showed him forty photographs from which Trent positively identified Bradley as the burglar. Bradley moves to exclude Tamara and Trent's identifications under the Fifth and Sixth Amendments. He will succeed in proving a constitutional violation as to:
>
> **A.** Both identifications.
> **B.** Tamara's identification only.
> **C.** Trent's identification only.
> **D.** Neither identification.

ANALYSIS. This problem requires us to determine whether Bradley had the right to counsel for either the show-up at the station house or the photographic array that followed. We can start by eliminating the Fifth Amendment challenge. The *Wade* Court specified that identification procedures do not implicate the privilege against self-incrimination due to their nontestimonial nature. This holding applies to all types of identifications whenever they may occur in the criminal process.

The Sixth Amendment right to counsel does apply, but *only* to line-ups and show-ups, where both the accused and the witness against him or her are physically present. Because photographic identifications involve no face-to-face confrontation, the Sixth Amendment is unavailable; therefore, Bradley did not have the right to have his attorney present when Trent identified Bradley as the burglar by picking his photograph from among the forty presented to him by Rick.

Show-ups are generally disfavored because of their highly suggestive nature. The presentation of one individual to a witness tacitly communicates that the police have "found their man," which may subconsciously convince a witness to make a positive identification, even if he or she would not have done so if presented with other choices. We will discuss these concerns in the context of due process challenges in the next section.

For Sixth Amendment purposes, the focus is not on the "quality" of the procedure but rather on its adversarial nature. Because face-to-face confrontation is an essential ingredient of a show-up, the accused has the right to have his attorney present, provided the procedure takes place after the Sixth Amendment has attached. In this instance, the station-house encounter occurs the morning *prior* to Bradley's arraignment. Thus, because formal charges have yet to be filed against Bradley, the show-up does not constitute a "critical stage" of the prosecution subject to the counsel guarantee of the Sixth Amendment.

In sum, Bradley did not have the right to have his attorney present at either the pre-arraignment show-up or the post-arraignment photographic array. The correct answer is **D**.

B.   Due Process and Identifications

In a series of cases, the U.S. Supreme Court explored the circumstances under which an identification procedure is so prejudicial to the defendant as to violate due process. In *Stovall v. Denno*, 388 U.S. 293 (1967), the witness was the victim of a stabbing to which there were no other witnesses. After doctors informed police that she might die, the officers brought the accused to her hospital room, where she made a positive identification. The U.S. Supreme Court ruled that this identification procedure was not "so unnecessarily suggestive" as to violate due process. The majority noted, in this regard, that the procedure, while highly suggestive, was not unnecessary since the victim was the lone witness to the crime and might die before an identification could take place, should it be postponed.

The emergency that renders a suggestive procedure necessary need not be as compelling as impending death. In *Simmons v. United States*, 390 U.S. 377 (1968), the U.S. Supreme Court held that showing a suspect's photograph to bank tellers following an armed robbery did not offend due process. The justices emphasized the need to use the tools at their disposal to apprehend as quickly as possible the perpetrators of this serious felony.

Even if an identification is "unnecessarily suggestive," its exclusion at trial is not inevitable. The trial judge must suppress an unnecessarily suggestive identification *only* if she finds that its introduction at trial would create a "substantial likelihood of misidentification." *Perry v. New Hampshire*, 565 U.S. 228 (2012). Reliability is the "linchpin" of this evaluation; to that end, courts must determine if the witness's ability to make an accurate identification outweighs the corrupting effect of the police misconduct. Five factors inform this reliability assessment: (1) a witness's opportunity to view the suspect; (2) her degree of attention; (3) the accuracy of her description of the suspect; (4) her level of certainty; and (5) the amount of time between the crime and the identification. *Manson v. Brathwaite*, 432 U.S. 98 (1977).

> **QUESTION 2. Magic words.** Lucinda was washing dishes in her kitchen when the room suddenly went dark and someone grabbed her from behind and threw her to the floor. Once on the floor, she turned to face her attacker. The light in the kitchen was out, but a lamp in an

adjacent bedroom illuminated the room somewhat. After threatening to kill her if she spoke, the assailant dragged Lucinda out of the house and walked her at knifepoint to a wooded area, about three blocks away, where he sexually assaulted her. It was midnight, and there was a full moon that night. She reported the crime when she returned home and told a police investigator that the assailant's height was between 5 feet 10 inches and 6 feet, that he weighed 180 to 200 pounds, that he was 16 to 18 years old, and that he had a dark-brown complexion.

In the course of the next several months, Lucinda viewed a variety of potential suspects in line-ups, show-ups, and photo arrays. She did not identify any of them as her attacker. Then, approximately 8 months after the crime, a show-up took place where police instructed the accused — who was 17 years old, 5 feet 7½ inches tall, and weighed 210 pounds — to walk past Lucinda while uttering the words "Shut up or I'll kill you," which were the words spoken by the assailant. After he did, Lucinda said she had "no doubt" that he was the man who attacked her.

The assailant moves to exclude the identification, claiming that it violated his due process rights. This claim is likely to:

A. Prevail, because the procedure was highly suggestive.
B. Prevail, because the identification took place eight months after the crime.
C. Prevail, because the police did not need to resort to a show-up.
D. Prevail, because Lucinda's description did not match the suspect.
E. Fail.

ANALYSIS. This fact pattern is based on *Neil v. Biggers*, 409 U.S. 188 (1972). In determining the admissibility of Lucinda's identification, courts use a "totality of the circumstances" test that evaluates admissibility by weighing the suggestiveness of the procedure against the reliability of the witness's identification.

As mentioned above, show-ups are the most suggestive of all identification procedures. In this case, moreover, the police did not have to resort to a show-up. They could have presented the accused in a line-up with other men who fit his description and required all of them to utter the words used by the assailant. However, the fact that a procedure is "unnecessarily suggestive" is insufficient, in and of itself, to require exclusion. If the identification is reliable — meaning that it is based on the witness's recollection from the crime scene — then due process is satisfied, notwithstanding the inherent suggestiveness and bias of the procedure itself.

Turning, then, to the reliability factors identified by the Court in *Brathwaite*, the assailant will focus on the eight-month gap between the crime and the identification, the lack of full light on the night of the crime, and the discrepancies between his physical characteristics and Lucinda's description. The prosecution will emphasize Lucinda's opportunity to view the suspect directly, both in the home and during the assault, and will note that the locations were partially lit by a lamp and the full moon, respectively. Lucinda's description, while imperfect, contained only minor discrepancies — for example, one-half inch in height and ten pounds in weight. It is possible, moreover, that the assailant had gained ten pounds and grown one-half inch in the eight months that had passed since the crime took place.

Most significantly, Lucinda identified the perpetrator immediately and was absolutely certain of the identification. She had seen many potential suspects in prior months and had not identified any as her attacker, indicating she had a clear sense of what he looked and sounded like. Together with her specific and generally accurate description and her opportunity during the crime to view her attacker face-to-face at close range in partial light in two locations, the due process challenge will fail.

B, **C**, and **D** identify considerations favorable to the defendant. No individual factor is dispositive, however, in the U.S. Supreme Court's totality-of-the-circumstances approach. **C** seems the most compelling of the three, since, unlike *Stovall* and *Simmons*, the police in *Biggers* acknowledged that using a less suggestive procedure — for example, a line-up — would not have impeded the investigation.

However, as the Court reiterated recently in *Perry*, unnecessary suggestiveness does not mandate exclusion where strong indicia of reliability are present. Thus, although the use of a single photograph in *Brathwaite* was highly suggestive, its introduction at trial was appropriate since the attendant circumstances underscored the accuracy of the witness's identification of the defendant; the reliability of the identification outweighed its corrupting effect. **A**, therefore, is wrong.

E is the correct answer.

C. Remedial Considerations

Sections A and B described the Sixth Amendment and Fourteenth Amendment due process requirements for pretrial identifications. We now turn to the effect of a finding of unconstitutionality on a witness's subsequent ability to identify the defendant at trial. As we will see, the inadmissibility of a pretrial identification does not necessarily preclude a later in-court identification of the accused by the same witness.

Turning first to the Sixth Amendment, *Wade* permits a witness who identified the defendant in an uncounseled, pretrial identification to identify the same defendant in court if the government can prove by clear and convincing evidence that the in-court identification is based on observations of the suspect other than in the tainted procedure. The U.S. Supreme Court lists a number of factors that may be used to make this showing, including the witness's opportunity to observe the criminal act, the accuracy of the witness's description of the accused, any failure on the part of the witness to identify the accused beforehand, and the lapse of time between the offense and the tainted identification.

In the due process context, *Simmons* noted that an in-court identification is inadmissible if the prior unconstitutional procedure was "so impermissibly suggestive" as to give rise to a "very substantial likelihood of irreparable misidentification." While the addition of the words "very" and "irreparable" make this standard slightly more rigorous, it is very similar to that applied to the pretrial procedure itself. See Section B, *supra*. As such, it is theoretically possible that a pretrial identification could introduce a "substantial likelihood of misidentification" but not a "*very* substantial likelihood of *irreparable* misidentification." Generally speaking, however, if there are insufficient indicia of reliability to overcome a due process challenge to a highly suggestive pretrial procedure, it is unlikely that a court would permit identification at trial by the same witness.

QUESTION 3. Thief encounter.   One afternoon, Sebastian was shopping at Swank, an upscale jewelry store. As he was admiring the Rolex watches, he heard the store alarm go off and, looking up, saw a man running out of the store, clutching a diamond necklace. Asked for a description by the police, Sebastian reported that the man was Caucasian; twenty-five to thirty years old; about six feet tall; had short, light brown hair; and was wearing a bomber jacket. Having seen the thief at an angle as he fled the store, Sebastian could not provide any further detail.

The following morning, the police arrested Kenny for stealing a diamond ring from a jewelry store around the corner from Swank. Kenny is white, thirty-two years old, five feet, ten inches tall, and has sandy-brown hair. He was arraigned on formal charges that afternoon and assigned a public defender to represent him. Because he could not make bail, he was remanded to state custody pending trial.

The following day, Officer Marlene called Sebastian and asked him to stop by the police station after work. When he arrived, Marlene asked Sebastian to view a line-up and tell her if he recognized any of the men as the thief from Swank. Because Marlene did not notify Kenny's attorney about the line-up, he was not present during it. The line-up consisted of Kenny and four other men. Three were African-American; the fourth was Caucasian, six-foot, two inches in height, thirty-nine years old, with short black hair. The Caucasian and one other man wore a sweatshirt, while Kenny and the remaining two wore bomber jackets. Sebastian told Marlene that Kenny "has to be the thief, since it couldn't possibly be any of the other men in the group." Marlene thanked him and, after

Sebastian left, she called Kenny's attorney and reported that an eyewitness to the theft from Swank positively identified his client as the thief.

The attorney succeeds in having Sebastian's line-up identification suppressed on both Sixth Amendment and due process grounds. If Sebastian identified Kenny at trial as the man who stole the diamond necklace from Swank, this would:

A. Violate Kenny's Sixth Amendment and Fourteenth Amendment due process rights.
B. Violate Kenny's Fourteenth Amendment due process rights only.
C. Violate Kenny's Sixth Amendment rights only.
D. Be constitutional.

ANALYSIS. To determine the correct answer, we should evaluate the constitutional provisions separately since, on their face, the Sixth Amendment and due process standards for admissibility are different. As we will see, however, the distinctions are less significant substantively than one might suspect at first blush.

When a pretrial identification procedure violates the Sixth Amendment, as this one did, an in-court identification is permissible only if the prosecution clearly and convincingly demonstrates that the witness remembers the defendant from the crime scene and not from the tainted line-up or show-up. To make this showing, the government must proffer evidence that supports the witness's familiarity with the accused before the tainted identification took place.

We will start with Sebastian's description of the thief to the police. The information he provided is fairly superficial and could describe countless men. Because Sebastian had only a fleeting look at the thief, he is unable to provide anything more specific. His description is fairly precise as to height and hair color but, again, if we consider "about six feet" to mean anywhere from five feet, ten inches to six feet, two inches, many men would fall within the range. Likewise, brown is the most common hair color for young men. Sebastian provides a five-year range as to age; anything more precise would be surprising since he only caught a quick glimpse of the thief from the side.

Marlene's characterization of Sebastian's identification as "positive" is also somewhat disingenuous. His comment suggests that he chose Kenny only because the other men were clearly not the thief. Marlene does not further explore the degree of Sebastian's certainty. In sum, then, Sebastian had very limited visual exposure to the thief; provided only a general description of him, which does not entirely correspond to Kenny; and made only one previous identification of Kenny that, based on Sebastian's contemporaneous comment, lacks reliability. This cannot provide the kind of clear and convincing evidence necessary to allow an in-court identification.

Turning to due process, it is not surprising that the trial court would find the line-up unconstitutional. First, it contains no one who resembles Kenny at all. Only one other man is white, and he is much older than Kenny and has black hair. In addition, Kenny is wearing the type of jacket Sebastian described, but the other white man is not. Two of the remaining three men have jackets similar to Kenny's but they are African-American, which would eliminate them at the outset. There was, moreover, no emergency afoot that would justify the use of such a biased procedure. Clearly, then, the line-up was "unnecessarily suggestive" so as to create a "substantial likelihood" of mistaken identification. As such, the identification is excluded unless the surrounding circumstances indicate that it is sufficiently reliable to outweigh its inherent suggestiveness. As our Sixth Amendment discussion demonstrated, the necessary indicia of reliability were decidedly lacking here.

Because the line-up identification violates due process, Sebastian can identify Kenny as the thief at trial only if the line-up did not create a "*very* substantial likelihood of *irreparable* misidentification" (italics added). There is no basis for making such a finding here. Viewed as a whole, in fact, the evidence strongly suggests that such a likelihood exists: In an egregiously biased line-up, Sebastian made an identification of questionable certainty that followed his brief and fleeting exposure to the thief at the crime scene, which produced a general, and not wholly accurate, description.

Based on the foregoing, the prosecution will be unable to meet the standards for the admissibility of an in-court identification under either the Sixth Amendment or the Due Process Clause of the Fourteenth Amendment.

The correct answer is **A**.

D.   The Closer

QUESTION 4. **Ignorance of the lawn is no excuse.**   As she looked out her living-room window, Mary Ellen saw a man forcing her neighbor, Fran, at gunpoint into a car parked on the street in front of Fran's house. When Officer Fernando arrived, Mary Ellen described the assailant as light-skinned, medium-height, heavy-set, forty-ish, with close-cropped hair, a goatee, and wearing an earring in his left ear. Asked if she had ever seen him before, she said she didn't think so, but she remembered seeing a man mowing Fran's lawn a couple weeks back who looked similar.

After finding out that Quick Green Lawn Service mowed Fran's lawn weekly, Fernando called the owner who reported that he had one employee, Terence, who might fit the description, but he wasn't sure which lawns he had mowed recently. Terence is a bald, 5′ 9″, 190-pound ex-con, 35 years old, with pale skin, facial hair, and earrings in both ears. Terence denied having ever mowed Fran's lawn, but, after a co-worker disputed this claim, Fernando arrested Terence.

Fernando asked Mary Ellen to come to the station house for a line-up after Terence's arraignment the following day. As she entered the station, Mary Ellen saw a police officer bring Terence into the precinct in handcuffs, and Terence saw Mary Ellen. Thirty minutes later, Mary Ellen viewed a line-up with Terence and three other men, all of whom had features similar to Terence's. She first identified another man as the kidnapper but, as Fernando thanked her for coming in, she abruptly changed her mind and picked Terence, commenting that he was the man she had seen from her window. Fernando decided that they should wait a minute or two to see if she changed her mind again. After two minutes, he asked her again if she saw the man who kidnapped Fran, and Mary Ellen pointed to Terence. The assistant district attorney introduced Mary Ellen's station-house identification at Terence's trial. Mary Ellen also identified Terence as the kidnapper in the courtroom in front of the jury.

If Terence challenges the constitutionality of the foregoing identifications, he will succeed:

A. As to the pretrial and trial identifications.
B. As to the pretrial identification only.
C. As to the trial identification only.
D. As to neither identification.

ANALYSIS. This closer applies the Sixth Amendment and Fourteenth Amendment due process standards for the admissibility of pretrial and trial identifications. Working chronologically, we will begin with the pretrial line-up. The Sixth Amendment has attached and affords Terence the right to counsel at all "critical stages" of the prosecution. Because the line-up, which takes place after Terence's arraignment, is considered a critical stage, Fernando's placement of Terence in the line-up in the absence of his lawyer was impermissible. Therefore, Mary Ellen's identification must be excluded as violative of the Sixth Amendment.

Terence would find it much more difficult to succeed with a due process claim. Since the line-up itself was not problematic, his argument would necessarily focus on Mary Ellen's having seen him enter the station house in handcuffs shortly before the line-up took place. While this occurrence does not associate him directly with the kidnapping, as a show-up would, it unequivocally labels him as an arrestee, which may create prejudice in Mary Ellen's mind. Under *Perry* and *Brathwaite*, we must weigh the corrupting effect of this exposure against the reliability of Mary Ellen's identification. Her description of the perpetrator as a heavy-set white man with facial hair corresponds fairly well to Terence's appearance, and her age reference seems close enough (forty-ish versus thirty-five). The two discrepancies in her description concern earrings (one versus two) and hair: Terence's is nonexistent, as opposed to "close-cropped."

These irregularities are not likely to seem highly significant in court. If Terence had not shaved his head for a few days before the crime, his head would have shown some minor growth, making it appear "close-cropped." In addition, if he had had his left side turned toward Mary Ellen as he pushed Fran into the car, Mary Ellen might not have had a clear view of both ears; she could easily have failed to notice his second earring, if he was wearing it that day.

Mary Ellen also appears fairly certain of her identification of Terence in the line-up. While she does not choose him at first, she ultimately picks him with no prodding from Fernando. To test her certainty, Fernando waits two minutes after Mary Ellen changes her mind, but she confirms her choice of Terence. The reliability of Mary Ellen's identification of Terence in the line-up seems sufficient to overcome any prejudice that may have resulted from seeing him earlier entering the station house in handcuffs.

Because the line-up did not violate the Due Process Clause, we need not address the constitutionality of Mary Ellen's in-court identification in this context. Its admissibility will turn instead on whether the prosecution can overcome the Sixth Amendment taint by showing clearly and convincingly that the trial identification is based on Mary Ellen's exposure to Terence at the crime scene, not at the uncounseled line-up. For the reasons discussed above, it is likely that the prosecution will satisfy this burden. Mary Ellen had a good opportunity to view the suspect, provided a generally accurate, somewhat detailed description, and seemed reasonably certain of her choice at the line-up.

In sum, then, the pretrial line-up will be excluded under the Sixth Amendment but not under the Due Process Clause of the Fourteenth. The trial identification is admissible, however, since the prosecution will succeed in proving clearly and convincingly that it emanates from Mary Ellen's exposure to Terence at the crime scene when, looking out her living-room window, she saw him push Fran into a car.

The correct answer is **B**.

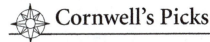# Cornwell's Picks

1. Stainless steal	**D**
2. Magic words	**E**
3. Thief encounter	**A**
4. Ignorance of the lawn is no excuse	**B**

27

Closing Closers

The reward of a thing well done, is to have done it.
—Ralph Waldo Emerson in New England Reformers

This chapter is different from the others. It includes 28 questions without introductory presentation of the black-letter case law. The questions are intended to serve two purposes. First, they review the principles and case law discussed throughout the book. Second, unlike the questions in preceding chapters, these often require consideration of multiple issues from different chapters. Because both professors and Bar examiners give questions like these, they provide a review of important cases and principles and an opportunity to see how different concepts relate to each other.

I have included complete analyses of the questions at the end of the chapter. To benefit fully from these explanations, I strongly encourage you to work through the questions fully ahead of time. If you find any ambiguities or problems, feel free to e-mail me so those issues can be addressed.

Finally, before you begin, let me offer a few suggestions you might want to consider when taking multiple-choice examinations.

1. *Read the facts carefully*. Even seemingly minor factual errors can lead students to choose the wrong answer. Make sure you take the time necessary to read the facts carefully. Before you answer the question, make sure you understand the sequence of events and what each individual named in the question did.
2. *Read each proposed answer*. It is also important to read through all proposed answers. Remember: You must choose the *best* answer. Don't stop at "A," even if you conclude that it is "plausible," because one of the other options might more fully or accurately resolve the question.
3. *Take a deep breath and relax*. Inevitably, you will find some questions to be easier and some, more difficult. If you find a question to be challenging when you first read it, don't panic. Take a deep breath and carefully reread the facts. You will find that a calm, focused demeanor pays dividends.

So, take a deep breath and begin.

QUESTION 1. Meth proof.   Officer Jim was executing a search warrant for Colleen's residence. The warrant authorized him to search "the premises at 525 Main Street, apartment 1B, for evidence pertaining to the manufacture of methamphetamine." As he was searching through Colleen's papers, Jim found floor plans, which he seized after noticing the word *LAB* written in the upper right-hand corner. If Colleen moves to suppress the floor plans, they will likely be deemed:

A. Inadmissible, because the warrant was not sufficiently particularized.
B. Inadmissible, because the warrant did not expressly authorize searching for documentary evidence.
C. Inadmissible, if the word *LAB* is later shown to refer to something other than a laboratory for the manufacture of drugs.
D. Inadmissible, if Colleen was not present during the search.
E. Admissible.

QUESTION 2. Scissor seizures (Question 1, continued).   Assume, *arguendo*, that Officer Jim's seizure of the floor plans from Colleen's residence is lawful. Upon reviewing the plans, Jim is shocked to discover that they do not depict a drug laboratory but rather the layout of a bank vault. Remembering that Colleen lives near the Langtree Avenue Bank (LAB), Jim obtains a warrant to search for "any evidence that tends to establish Colleen's participation, past or future, in bank robbery."

While he is executing the warrant, Jim finds, in Colleen's dresser drawer, a bag of hair-cutting supplies, including combs and scissors of various sizes. He notices copious amounts of dried blood on the blades of one pair of scissors and seizes them, wondering if they might be linked to the stabbing death of a woman who had lived next door. During the investigation into the woman's death, neighbors had told Jim that the victim and Colleen had hated each other and had argued constantly. As it turns out, the blood is that of the dead woman, and Colleen is charged with her murder. If Colleen moves to suppress the scissors, the scissors will likely be deemed:

A. Inadmissible, because Colleen was not a murder suspect.
B. Admissible, because scissors can be used in bank robbery.
C. Admissible, because the scissors were in plain view.
D. Admissible, because Jim's suspicions were correct.
E. Admissible, because the victim lived next door to Colleen.

QUESTION 3. Transparent behavior.   Officer Michelle watched Owen place a large, transparent bag in a receptacle located in a shed on his property. The shed was adjacent to a public sidewalk, but inside a fence enclosing Owen's front yard. Believing that the bag contained evidence that would link Owen to a crime, Michelle decided to inspect it. She reached over the fence and found the shed locked. Standing on the sidewalk, Michelle then shined her flashlight through a hole in the fence and, through an opening in the shed, saw a large, transparent bag labeled "heroin." Michelle thereafter entered the yard, broke the lock on the shed, and removed the bag from inside. Is this search permissible under the Fourth Amendment?

A. No, because Michelle had no right to visually access the shed with her flashlight.
B. No, because Michelle physically invaded the shed.
C. Yes, because the bag was transparent.
D. Yes, because Michelle had probable cause to believe the bag contained drugs.

QUESTION 4. Pocketed watch.   Jon gains entry into an exclusive art gallery by posing as a wealthy patron looking to spend freely. Once inside, he draws a pistol and forces all of the employees into a back room. Moving quickly, he steals an eight-by-eleven-inch painting worth in excess of $100,000, as well as the gallery owner's Rolex watch, which Jon stashes in the front pocket of his pants. As soon as he departs, the gallery owner calls the police, tells them what happened, and reports that the thief fled the scene in a white SUV that was heading east on Main Street. Responding to the call, Officer Yalissa soon spots the vehicle and gives chase. Upon hearing the police siren, Jon abandons the SUV and runs into a nearby preschool to hide.

Yalissa follows close behind and corners Jon inside the school lunchroom. She immediately frisks him. In his front pants pocket, she feels what she immediately recognizes to be a watch. It is later found to be the Rolex taken from the gallery owner. Finding no weapon, she then asks Jon what he did with the gun. He tells her that he stashed the weapon in a Sesame Street lunchbox on the other side of the room. Yalissa handcuffs Jon to a chair and retrieves the gun from the lunchbox.

Upon leaving the school, Yalissa secures Jon in the squad car and then searches his automobile. She finds the painting on the back seat and, proceeding to the glove box, discovers a bag of cocaine inside. She seizes both. Jon is subsequently charged with possession of cocaine and robbery. Based on the foregoing, which is Jon's STRONGEST argument?

A. The body frisk violated his Fourth Amendment rights.
B. The interrogation violated his Fifth Amendment *Miranda* rights.
C. The automobile search violated his Fourth Amendment rights.
D. The interrogation violated his Sixth Amendment right to counsel.

QUESTION 5. Pistol Pattin' Martha.   While patrolling Main Street, Officer Martha looks inside the window of Jerry's hardware store and notices a woman, Elaine, furtively placing something in her coat pocket. Elaine then hurriedly exits the store. Martha stops Elaine and asks her what she was shopping for at Jerry's and why she exited so quickly. Elaine nervously responds that she was looking for a shovel but changed her mind. Not satisfied with her answer, Martha frisks Elaine. When patting Elaine's front pants pocket, Martha feels a pistol. She removes it. When Elaine admits that it is unregistered, Martha places her under arrest for carrying an unlicensed firearm. If Elaine moves to suppress the pistol, she will likely:

A. Prevail, because Martha had no right to stop Elaine.
B. Prevail, because the stop was too lengthy.
C. Prevail, because, while the stop was lawful, Martha had no right to frisk Elaine.
D. Prevail, because, while Martha was justified in stopping and frisking Elaine, the seizure of the pistol was improper.
E. Not prevail.

QUESTION 6. Forcing the issue.   Gina was arrested for the murder of Missy. As Gina was being transported to the station house, her lawyer, Alessandro, called the station house and told the desk sergeant that he wanted to be present if Gina was interrogated. The police never informed Gina of Alessandro's call, and Gina waived her *Miranda* rights. Detective Loretta, who conducted Gina's interview, knew Gina had a clinically diagnosed paranoid personality disorder. After hearing her *Miranda* rights, Gina told Loretta that she "had to talk to her right now," without her lawyer, or else "the force" would come after her. "Hopefully," she added, "it won't make me say something that would look bad in court." Gina then executed a written *Miranda* waiver.

Starting the interrogation, Loretta falsely told Gina that a witness had seen her talking to Missy just before Missy disappeared. Gina responded by laughing, commenting that Loretta would "have to do better than that." "Maybe," Loretta speculated, "the district attorney would recommend psychiatric treatment instead of jail for you, so you could get help with your problem. I think that would be a much better place for you. I bet the prosecutor will think so, too. He's a good guy. Would you like me to talk to him about that?" Gina nodded and then began to cry uncontrollably for about five minutes. At that time, still sobbing, she told Loretta she was ready to answer more questions. She responded fully, implicating herself in Missy's murder. Which of the following is Gina's best argument to exclude her confession?

A. The failure of the police to inform her of Alessandro's call invalidated her *Miranda* waiver.

B. Her mental illness invalidated her *Miranda* waiver.

C. Loretta's lie rendered the confession involuntary under the Due Process Clause of the Fourteenth Amendment.

D. Loretta's discussion of psychiatric treatment in lieu of jail rendered the confession involuntary under the Due Process Clause of the Fourteenth Amendment.

QUESTION 7. Groovy greenhouse.   Police Officer David believed that Alison, a fifty-year-old "hippie" who lived alone in a house on Mulberry Road, was growing hallucinogenic mushrooms in her back yard. He could not see into the yard from the street, however, since Alison had erected an eight-foot fence around the area. To obtain a clear view, David decided to ask Alison's neighbor, Ted, if he could look into Alison's yard from Ted's second-floor bedroom window. Finding no one at home but the front door unlocked, David entered Ted's house, walked upstairs, and looked out the window, from which he saw mushrooms growing inside a greenhouse. He took photos of them and used that information to obtain a warrant to search Alison's back yard for "any and all instrumentalities of crime relating to the cultivation of hallucinogenic mushrooms."

When he arrived at the house later that day to execute the warrant, a neighbor who saw him knocking on the front door told him that Alison was out of town on a business trip selling "mood rings" and was not expected to return for three days. Proceeding to the back yard, David seized the mushrooms from the greenhouse but found no other incriminating information in the vicinity of the greenhouse. As he prepared to leave, he saw, through Alison's kitchen window facing the back yard, an envelope sitting on a table labeled "mushroom buyers with outstanding balances." He opened the window, seized the envelope, and left. Alison moves to suppress the mushrooms and the envelope under the Fourth Amendment. She will succeed:

A. As to both, based on David's unlawful entry into Ted's house.

B. As to both, since the warrant was insufficiently particularized.

C. As to the envelope only, since its seizure exceeded the scope of the warrant.

D. As to neither.

QUESTION 8. Access Hollyweed.   Noticing that Holly's car was weaving, Officer Kimball pulled her over on I-78 on suspicion of driving under the influence. As Kimball approached the car, he detected the odor of burnt marijuana. When Kimball asked for Holly's license and registration, she slurred out the words, "Sure, just a minute." She then started laughing in an exaggerated, inappropriate fashion while combing through papers in the glove box in search of the requested documents. Unable to find them, Holly apologized, commenting, "Sorry, man, I think I've been smoking too much weed tonight." Kimball placed Holly under arrest for driving under the influence and seated her in the back of the squad car for transportation to the station house.

Before they left, he called the station house so the desk sergeant could arrange for Holly's car to be removed from the roadside. While ordinarily the car would be taken to an impound lot on the outskirts of the city, Kimball told the sergeant to have it delivered to the station house instead. "I want to search this one myself," Kimball explained, "to make sure it gets a thorough going over. I'm gonna find that lady's stash and that's a promise." When the car arrived thirty minutes later, Kimball discovered two baggies of marijuana inside a gym bag placed on the floor behind the driver's seat. If Holly moves to suppress the marijuana, on which warrant clause exception should the prosecution rely to justify the search?

A. Automobile exception.

B. Inventory search exception.

C. *Terry* car "frisk."

D. Search incident to arrest.

QUESTION 9. Obie & the force.   Officer Nancy is a member of her police department's Organized Crime Task Force. While she has never patrolled local roads and highways, Nancy, like all officers, is authorized to enforce all state and local laws, including traffic laws. The task force is convinced that Obie is a key player in a local crime family, but they have been unable to gather enough hard evidence for a search warrant of his workplace or residence. Frustrated, Nancy hatches a plan. She follows Obie's car as it leaves home, planning to pull it over at her first opportunity, in the hope of being able to conduct a search.

Soon after Obie enters the interstate, Nancy springs into action. She pulls the car over and asks Obie for his license and registration, explaining that he was going 60 mph in a 55 mph zone. "You've got to be kiddin' me, lady," Obie exclaims, noting correctly that traffic cops in the area virtually never stop motorists unless they are travelling at least 10 mph over the limit. "You a-holes won't stop at anything will you? This is pathetic." At that point, Nancy places Obie under arrest for speeding. After handcuffing him and securing him inside the squad car, she returns to the vehicle and searches the interior cabin, finding an unregistered firearm inside the glove box. She seizes it. Viewed independently, which of the foregoing violates the Fourth Amendment?

A. The initial traffic stop.
B. The arrest.
C. The search of the vehicle.
D. Both the initial stop and the arrest.
E. The initial traffic stop, the arrest, and the search of the vehicle.

QUESTION 10. Ring-a-ding-ding.   A thief, posing as a customer, stole a $10,000 diamond bracelet and two emerald rings, each worth $3,000, from a jewelry store display case while the owner left the floor to search his stock for a special item requested by the customer/thief. The store owner gave the police a detailed description of the thief, the jewelry, and the distinctive box that housed the bracelet. Unfortunately, he did not get a clear view of the getaway car, noticing only that it was a black sedan and that the thief drove off alone. The police dispatcher immediately broadcast the preceding information to all patrol cars in the area. One hour later, Officers Kathy and Trina, who were patrolling the interstate at a location about thirty miles from the store, saw a black sedan speed by them; they immediately pulled it over.

When Kathy reached the driver's window and looked inside the car, she noticed that the driver fit the description of the thief and that a box on the back seat closely resembled the one described by the store owner. Kathy seized the box and, opening it, confirmed that it contained the stolen bracelet. She placed the driver under arrest and secured him in the squad car. Returning to the vehicle, she ordered his passenger, Lilli, out of the car and searched her person, while Trina searched the vehicle. Kathy found one of the stolen rings wrapped in a thick wad of tissue paper in Lilli's shirt pocket while, at the same time, Trina found the other ring inside Lilli's purse located on the floor behind her seat. Lilli files a motion to suppress both rings. She will:

A. Succeed as to both.
B. Succeed as to the ring found in the tissue paper only.
C. Succeed as to the ring found in her purse only.
D. Succeed as to neither.

QUESTION 11. His brother's keeper.   The police department received an anonymous letter stating that Jill was using her residence as a brothel. The letter described in detail the increased traffic into and out of the house, explaining which hours and days of the week the volume was the greatest and how long each "visitor" would remain inside. Officer Jack surveilled the home for two weeks to corroborate the information. He noticed an unusual increase in the number of male visitors at most, but not all, of the times indicated and confirmed that the visitors always stayed for one hour or less. He conveyed this information to the district attorney (DA).

The next day, the DA called Jack while he was on duty to report that she had secured a search warrant based on his information, so Jack could terminate the surveillance. As he was leaving the stakeout, Jack panicked when he saw his brother, Albert, enter Jill's house. Jack ran across the street and entered the house, running from room to room looking for Albert. Jack found Albert in a bedroom with Jill and placed her under arrest. On the way out of the house, Jack seized a book he spotted by the front door, labeled "Jill's clients." If Jill moves to suppress the book at her trial, she will:

A. Prevail, because the magistrate lacked a substantial basis for issuing the warrant.
B. Prevail, because Jack unlawfully entered her house.
C. Fail, based on the plain view doctrine.
D. Fail, based on inevitable discovery.

QUESTION 12. Doing the can-can.   Officer Jameel had probable cause to believe that Chester was storing stolen laptop computers in a number of garbage cans placed in his back yard. Accordingly, Jameel obtained a warrant to search "garbage cans located at Chester's residence at 18 Mercer Lane for stolen laptop computers." When he entered Chester's back yard to execute the warrant, Jameel found six covered garbage cans lined up next to each other. There were no barriers separating any of the cans. Inside a plastic bag in one of the cans, Jameel found four pipes with what he recognized to be marijuana residue on them. Because the property line between Chester's property and that of his neighbor,

Reggie, was unmarked, Jameel did not realize that the can with the pipes belonged to Reggie. If that can is found to be within the common curtilage of both homes, will Reggie succeed in a motion to suppress the pipes?

A. No, because Jameel reasonably believed the garbage can was on Chester's property.
B. No, because there is no protected privacy interest in garbage.
C. No, because Reggie failed to lock the garbage cans.
D. Yes.

QUESTION 13. Pipin' hot (Question 12, continued). When Reggie sees Officer Jameel searching through his garbage can, Reggie runs toward Jameel, screaming, "What do you think you're doing? Get the hell out of here!" "Stand back, mister," Jameel replies forcefully. "I have a warrant. I want you to calm down and stay where you are, got it?" After Reggie nods affirmatively, Jameel hands him the warrant and tells him to read it. Reggie does so quickly and then comments, "This warrant doesn't give you any right to search my property. Give me back my pipes." Reggie moves to suppress the statement, "Give me back my pipes" under the Fifth Amendment. Is he likely to prevail?

A. Yes, because Jameel did not obtain a valid *Miranda* waiver.
B. Yes, because Jameel ordered Reggie to remain in his presence.
C. No, because Reggie initiated the encounter.
D. No, because Reggie volunteered the information.

QUESTION 14. Made up make-up.   Marlene was indicted for consumer fraud after an undercover police operation disclosed that her company had made unsubstantiated claims about the efficacy of its wrinkle-reducing face cream. At the hearing on the indictment, Marlene was represented by her lawyer, Iris, who persuaded the judge to release Marlene on her own recognizance pending trial. After Iris left the courtroom, the assistant district attorney, Hiram, asked Marlene if she would be willing to accompany him back to the station to answer questions. She agreed to do so. Once they arrived, he read Marlene her *Miranda* rights. She acknowledged that she understood them and signed a waiver form. Asked why she believed the cream would "erase" wrinkles, she laughed and told Hiram that it didn't matter what the company claimed since "wrinkly women are gullible." Admission of Marlene's statement would violate:

A. Marlene's Fifth Amendment rights, because she had been indicted.
B. Marlene's Sixth Amendment rights, because Hiram did not tell her attorney that he wished to question her.
C. Marlene's Sixth Amendment rights, because she was represented by counsel.
D. Marlene's Sixth Amendment rights, due to inadequate waiver.
E. Neither Marlene's Fifth Amendment nor her Sixth Amendment rights.

QUESTION 15. Hook, line, and sinker.   Sonya was travelling from Washington, D.C., to New York City on a Greyhound bus. Myron and his wife, Leslie, boarded the bus in Philadelphia. Myron sat next to Leslie and across the aisle from Sonya. Myron and Sonya chatted for a while, and then Sonya fell asleep. She awoke when she felt a tug on her handbag, which was on her lap. As her eyes opened, Sonya thought she saw Myron withdraw his hand from the area near her bag as he stood up. She then noticed that her change purse, in which she had placed her diamond earrings, was missing. Convinced that Myron had furtively removed it and placed it in his suitcase in the overhead luggage area, she asked him to give it back. He claimed not to have it.

When the bus stopped to pick up passengers in Newark, N.J., Sonya got off and reported her suspicions to a police officer, Carmine, at the station. Carmine entered the bus, and Sonya led him to Myron's seat. Myron's wife told Carmine that her husband was in the restroom. Carmine reported what Sonya had told him and politely asked her permission to search the small travel suitcase bearing the couple's last name that was stowed in the overhead bin. Leslie consented, not mentioning that the suitcase was Myron's alone; hers was stored across the aisle.

Carmine did not find the change purse, but he did find a sharp, serrated knife, which he removed just as Myron returned to his seat. Myron explained that he used the knife for fishing. Carmine then frisked Myron and removed a wad of bills bound in a money clip from the inside pocket of his coat. Myron had taken the money from another sleeping passenger's purse when he went to the bathroom. It was later discovered that Myron was a convicted felon for whom possession of the knife found in his bag was unlawful. If Myron moves to suppress both the knife and the money, he will:

A. Prevail regarding the knife, based on invalid consent.
B. Prevail on the wad of bills only, as the fruit of an unlawful seizure.
C. Prevail on both the knife and the wad of bills.
D. Prevail on neither the knife nor the wad of bills.

QUESTION 16. **Slipping Mickey.**   After the store manager at Rico, an upscale department store at the mall, complained of a sharp increase in shoplifting, the local police chief told Officer Melanie to patrol the area in and around the store on foot. The next day, Melanie saw Mickey in the jewelry section of the store and became suspicious of him, since he was dressed more shabbily than most of the shoppers and was poorly groomed. She followed Mickey as he moved toward the exit and witnessed him furtively place something in his coat pocket and then leave the store hastily. Melanie ordered Mickey to stop, but he began running away from her. Melanie gave chase.

As Mickey rounded a corner at the opposite end of the mall, he lost his footing and fell. The force of the fall dislodged a small box from his pocket. The box, which had Rico's emblem on it, opened as it hit the floor, revealing a pair of diamond earrings. As Mickey picked up the earrings, Melanie told him that she would need to see the receipt for the earrings before he could go. He told her that he had left it in his car, which was parked at the other end of the mall near Rico. She then told Mickey that she would need to accompany him during the fifteen-minute walk to the car. When they reached the car, he opened the back door to retrieve the receipt from another shopping bag, and Melanie saw a marijuana cigarette in the ashtray. She seized it and arrested Mickey for possession of marijuana. Mickey moves to suppress the marijuana, claiming that it is "fruit of the poisonous tree." He will:

A. Prevail, because he was unlawfully seized when the box fell out of his pocket.
B. Prevail, because his forced detention for the purpose of answering Melanie's questions constitutes an independent Fourth Amendment violation.
C. Prevail, because by accompanying Mickey to his car Melanie committed an independent Fourth Amendment violation.
D. Prevail, because Mickey's detention violated the *Terry* doctrine's brevity requirement.
E. Not prevail.

QUESTION 17. **A whisper in the park.**   Marian was walking home from work and, since it was a pleasant evening, she decided to cross through the park. As she left the busy street, a man came up behind her and, pressing a hard object into the small of her back, whispered in her ear, "Give me your wallet if you want to live, lady!" Shaking with fear, Marian located the wallet in her purse. As she handed it to the robber, she let go before he gripped it and it fell to the ground. To retrieve it, the robber stepped in front of Marian, allowing her to get a look at him at close range. She immediately recognized him as a man she had seen loitering in the park on several occasions.

After the robber ran off, Marian left the park and found a police officer guarding a construction site across the street. She provided a detailed description of the perpetrator and the officer radioed police patrolling the park. Within an hour, park police arrested Leyton for the crime. Leyton was arraigned on felony robbery charges the next day. He pled not guilty and was remanded to custody.

While the hearing was taking place, Officer Lola brought Marian to the courthouse and had her wait outside. As Leyton was led out of the courtroom, Lola approached Rick, the assistant public defender representing him. Lola told Rick that Marian was present and asked if it was okay to conduct an identification before Leyton returned to jail. Rick agreed, but said he could not stay, since he was late to a hearing in another courtroom. Rick then shouted down the hall to the guard transporting Leyton and told him to bring Leyton over to Lola. Rick then left.

Shortly thereafter, when Leyton arrived, Lola walked him over to Marian and asked her if Leyton was the robber. Marian said she thought he was, but could only be sure if she heard his voice. Lola then asked Leyton to repeat the words spoken by the robber in the park. After he did, Marian said she was certain he was the man who had robbed her. Leyton moves to exclude both the statement and the identification itself. Based on the foregoing, which of the following claims have merit?

A. Admitting the identification would violate Leyton's Fifth Amendment *Miranda* rights.
B. Admitting the identification would violate Leyton's Sixth Amendment right to counsel.
C. Admitting the identification would violate Leyton's Fourteenth Amendment due process rights.
D. Admitting the statement would violate Leyton's Fifth Amendment *Miranda* rights and his Sixth Amendment right to counsel.
E. None of the above.

QUESTION 18. The art of deception. Nancy was indicted on drug trafficking charges and was released on her own recognizance pending trial. During this time, the son of her long-time housekeeper, Lupita, was arrested for possession of cocaine. Prosecutors told Lupita that if she helped them with Nancy they would "go easy" on her son. Lupita agreed.

Accordingly, without first obtaining a warrant, prosecutors taped a recording device to Lupita's body and instructed her to tell Nancy (falsely) that a lady named Heylia had stopped by looking for Nancy. Heylia was a well-known drug supplier whom prosecutors had been trying unsuccessfully to link to Nancy for years. Prosecutors hoped that, if she found out Heylia was looking for her, Nancy would make incriminating statements about their association.

Lupita asked Nancy if Heylia helped with her (Nancy's) business, but Nancy made no mention of any relationship between them with respect to drugs. However, when Lupita mentioned that she thought she saw Heylia's name on Nancy's e-mail when dusting Nancy's laptop computer, Nancy stated that she and Heylia had a small Internet-based business selling fake paintings that they represented to buyers as originals. Nancy is subsequently charged with consumer fraud. When Lupita disappears before the trial, the prosecutor moves the recording of Lupita's conversation with Nancy into evidence, and Nancy objects. Her objection is:

A. Valid, under the Fourth Amendment.
B. Valid, under the Sixth Amendment.
C. Valid, under the Fourth and Sixth Amendments.
D. Invalid.

QUESTION 19. SuperSpying: No ordinary prying (Question 18, continued).   One hour after recording Nancy through Lupita's wire, the recording device malfunctioned and ceased to pick up dialogue. Doug, the officer operating the system, was stationed in a truck parked outside the residence. Not wanting to lose potentially valuable evidence, Doug grabbed the SuperSpy, a powerful new device being piloted by the police department that is capable of recording conversations from distances of up to 150 yards. SuperSpy did not pick up any additional incriminating statements from Nancy; however, when Lupita asked Nancy's nineteen-year-old son, Silas, if he knew who Heylia was, SuperSpy recorded his response that he had "bought weed" from her on several occasions to support his mother's business.

Prosecutors use this statement to amend the drug trafficking indictment against Nancy to include Silas. At the time of Silas's trial, as at his mother's, prosecutors cannot locate Lupita. With Doug on the stand, they move the SuperSpy recording into evidence, and Silas objects. The judge should:

A. Sustain the objection, under the Fourth Amendment.
B. Sustain the objection, under the Sixth Amendment.
C. Sustain the objection, under the Fourth and Sixth Amendments.
D. Overrule the objection.

QUESTION 20. Barking up the wrong trees. Officers entered a barn to execute a search warrant for "all evidence of illegal dogfighting." A dogfight was taking place at the time they entered, and Officer Rafael decided to frisk all patrons. One patron, Robert, was found to be carrying an illegal firearm inscribed with the symbol of a local street gang. Rafael seized the firearm and arrested Robert. Robert was arraigned the next morning on the unlawful firearm charge and released. Two days later, Robert walked into the station house and asked to speak to Rafael. He told Rafael that he had met with his attorney and was willing to "come clean" about the unlawful firearm possession. Rafael was pleased to talk to Robert about the gun, but he was more interested in Robert's possible involvement in a gang-related shooting than in the firearm charge.

Accordingly, after Robert signed a confession about possessing the illegal firearm and got up to leave, Rafael told him to "stay put" because he might have valuable information about "another matter." He decided not to give Robert *Miranda* rights at this point, afraid he would "lawyer up." Instead, Rafael proceeded to question Robert about his gang membership, and in the course of this questioning Robert implicated himself in the shooting. At that point, Rafael ended the interrogation and told Robert he could leave.

The next day, a fellow officer went to Robert's house and told him he needed to come back to the station house for more questioning. When Robert arrived, Rafael administered *Miranda* warnings and told Robert that he would like to continue their conversation about the shooting, adding that the statements Robert had made about it the day before were likely inadmissible. Robert waived his *Miranda* rights and, in response to Rafael's questions, provided more detail about the shooting and his role in it. In pretrial motions, the court ruled the initial frisk unconstitutional and excluded Robert's pre-*Miranda* statements implicating himself in the shooting. Robert now moves to exclude (1) his station house confession re possession of the illegal firearm, and (2) his post-*Miranda* statements to Rafael about the shooting and his role in it. He will prevail:

A. As to both.
B. As to the illegal firearm confession only.
C. As to the post-*Miranda* statements only.
D. As to neither.

QUESTION 21. Potluck. Bill and Marge are furious. They have been trying to get to sleep since 11:00 P.M. and have been unable to do so because of the loud music blaring from the Smith's house across the street. At 1:00 A.M., Bill calls the police station to complain about the disturbance. As Officer Trudy arrives at the residence to investigate, she encounters many pajama-clad, angry residents in the street complaining about the noise at the Smiths. As Trudy approached the front door, she can see people dancing inside the house about 30 feet from the door. Trudy knocks on the door, but no one answers. She then enters the house, hoping to get the residents to turn down the exceedingly loud music. Once inside, she spies the stereo system across the room. As she approaches it to turn down the volume, she spots five marijuana plants in the corner. She seizes the plants. In this jurisdiction, the playing of loud music after 10:00 P.M. is a minor misdemeanor, punishable by a fine of up to $100. Which of the following best supports Trudy's warrantless entry into the Smith's home?

A. There may have been injured people inside the home.
B. Trudy was fullfilling police officers' "community caretaking" responsibilities.
C. The playing of loud music at that hour is a low-level misdemeanor.
D. Because they were not at home, the Smiths' privacy interest in the residence was diminished.

QUESTION 22. ¡Ay caramba!   Manuel arrested seventeen-year-old Ricardo for the murder of Jaime, a rival gang member. Manuel administered *Miranda* warnings, asking, after each core warning, if Ricardo understood what he (Manuel) was saying. Ricardo said that he did. Knowing Ricardo was Spanish-speaking, Manuel, who was fully bilingual, asked if Ricardo wanted to hear the warnings in Spanish. Ricardo said no; he had "heard them before" in prior arrests. He then volunteered that he did not want to talk about "what happened."

During the thirty-minute ride to the station house, Manuel chatted with Ricardo in Spanish about general topics, unrelated to the murder. When they arrived at the police station, Manuel took Ricardo into an interrogation room and told him to "sit tight." Manuel then left the room. One hour later, Manuel returned, repeated *Miranda* rights, and asked Ricardo if he wanted to get anything "off his chest." Ricardo responded by tapping his fingers nervously on the table. "I know," Manuel continued, "that Jaime deserved it." "You're damn right," Ricardo barked. "I would do it all over again if I had to."

At trial, Ricardo took the stand in his own defense. He explained how his friends from school recruited him to join the gang and how important it is to support your gang "brothers" and to "get justice" when other gangs "cross the line." He also testified that, while he was near the place where the killing "went down," he did not participate in it.

After the jury convicted Ricardo of murder, his attorney, Toni, filed a motion for a new trial, arguing that the judge had erred in allowing Ricardo's comments to Manuel to be introduced into evidence. To support the motion, Toni attached educational testing completed when

Ricardo was fourteen that placed him in the "mild mental retardation" range. Toni also included an affidavit from an educational psychologist stating that she believed Ricardo would have difficulty understanding sentences that contain more than one concept. Based on this cognitive deficit and the fact that English was Ricardo's second language, the psychologist doubted Ricardo's ability to understand the following warning read to him by Manuel: "If you cannot afford to hire a lawyer and you want one, we will see that you have a lawyer provided to you free of charge before we ask you any questions."

Based on the foregoing, did the trial judge err in admitting the statements Ricardo made to Manuel at the station house?

A. Yes, because Ricardo could not have understood his *Miranda* rights.
B. Yes, because Manuel did not scrupulously honor Ricardo's invocation of the right to silence.
C. No, because Manuel did not coerce Ricardo.
D. No, because Ricardo's conduct indicated a desire to speak with Manuel.

QUESTION 23. **In the dog house.**   Officer Natalie has probable cause to arrest Patrick for burglary, but she has not secured an arrest warrant. As a result, Natalie surveilles Patrick's residence, waiting for him to emerge. Knowing that Patrick is quick, Natalie is taking no chances. Seated next to her in the squad car is Turbo, a K-9 officer that Natalie considers the best partner she has ever had. When Patrick finally emerges, Natalie says "sick 'em, boy." As Turbo charges toward Patrick, Patrick runs into the unlocked house of his neighbor, Katy. Natalie follows and finds Patrick hiding inside a bedroom closet with a growling Turbo outside. She calls off Turbo and arrests Patrick. On the floor of the closet next to Patrick, Natalie sees a knife in a clear, plastic bag labeled "used to kill my husband." She seizes it.

Katy is later charged with the murder of her husband and moves to suppress the knife. She will likely:

A. Prevail, because Natalie needed an arrest warrant to arrest Patrick in Katy's home.
B. Prevail, because Natalie needed an arrest warrant and a search warrant to arrest Patrick in Katy's home.
C. Lose, under the plain view doctrine.
D. Lose, based on exigent circumstances.
E. Lose, under the plain view doctrine and exigent circumstances.

QUESTION 24. **Holy guacamole!**   Tobias, a college student from Texas, spent spring break in Mexico. Because Tobias felt sick, he was driving fast to get back to his dorm as quickly as possible. Speeding down the interstate, Tobias was pulled over by Officer Campbell, a Texas state trooper. When he asked for license and registration, Campbell noticed that Tobias's stomach seemed distended and he was groaning and shifting uncomfortably in his seat. Campbell asked Tobias if he was okay, and Tobias told him that he had gotten hold of "some nasty guacamole" in Mexico and had been suffering ever since.

Having just read a news report about a rise in drug smuggling by Texas college students, Campbell doubted Tobias's story. When he remembered that stomach distension is a common side effect of swallowing cocaine-filled balloons, Campbell became even more suspicious. He ordered Tobias out of the car. As Tobias exited the vehicle, he doubled over in pain, causing a marijuana cigarette to fall out of his shirt pocket. Campbell seized it. Because the possession of any amount of marijuana is unlawful in Texas, he placed Tobias under arrest. He then searched Tobias's clothing and found no additional contraband.

Campbell told Tobias that he believed that Tobias was an alimentary canal smuggler. Tobias denied the allegation and refused to submit to an X-ray to dispel Campbell's suspicions. In response, Campbell took Tobias to the back of the police van and conduced a body cavity search, over Tobias's objections. Campbell manually extracted two cocaine-filled balloons during the search. Tobias excreted seven more several hours later while in police custody.

If Tobias challenges the body cavity search, he will:

A. Prevail, because Campbell did not have a warrant.
B. Prevail, because Campbell lacked probable cause to believe Tobias was smuggling drugs.
C. Fail, because Tobias was groaning and appeared to have a distended stomach.
D. Fail, because Campbell arrested Tobias before conducting the search.

QUESTION 25. **Guns n' roses.**   At his morning briefing to patrol officers, a Setonia police sergeant read an announcement from the district attorney's office telling the officers to be on the lookout for a black Mercedes, S-Class, with tinted windows and Setonia license plate "ROSEPETAL." According to the announcement, the district attorney had probable cause that the vehicle was linked to drug trafficking. While patrolling the interstate later that day, Officer Latisha spotted a car fitting that description. She pulled it over and searched it. She did not find any drugs, but she discovered an unregistered firearm under the passenger seat and arrested Norton, the driver, for possessing it. Latisha later learned that the district attorney had withdrawn the announcement a week ago, but the withdrawal was never entered into the computer database.

Believing Latisha violated his Fourth Amendment rights, Norton moves to suppress the firearm. In which of the following scenarios is he most likely to prevail?

A. The police department maintains its own database. The department is presently two weeks behind on data entry, since two of its six clerks responsible for data entry quit unexpectedly two weeks ago.

B. The police department maintains its own database and acknowledged last month, in response to numerous complaints, that the employees presently responsible for data entry were improperly trained and had an error rate three times that of other police departments.

C. The Administrative Office of the Courts maintains the police department's database. In a recent internal investigation, three of the six data entry specialists disclosed that updating announcements from the district attorney's office is not a priority for them. Told that this had led to errors in the past, the three chuckled and one commented "that's life."

D. Latisha knew that the announcement had been canceled, but her radar gun recorded Norton's vehicle travelling 5 mph over the posted speed limit before she pulled his car over. She arrested Norton for speeding and, as Norton sat unrestrained in the front seat of the vehicle, she searched the passenger cabin and found the firearm.

QUESTION 26. **Hot wheels.**   As Jonathan was walking down the street, Setonia Police Officer Yenis mistook him for a celebrity she adored. Wanting an autograph, she shouted: "Hold up! I am an officer of the law." Disarmed by the directive, Jonathan complied. When Yenis got closer, she realized that Jonathan was not whom she thought he was. At the same time, she noticed that he was wearing "Heelys" (sneakers with wheels), which had been outlawed in Setonia after numerous injuries attributable to them. She placed him under arrest for wearing them and searched his person, finding cocaine in his jacket pocket. When they arrived at the station house for booking, Yenis discovered that the Heelys Jonathan was wearing were not unlawful, since they had custom-designed "micro-wheels" that were smaller than those banned by the legislature. If Jonathan moves to suppress the cocaine, he will likely:

A. Prevail, since Yenis lacked the authority to stop him.

B. Prevail, because his sneakers did not violate Setonia law.

C. Prevail, because she had no reason to search his coat pocket following an arrest for violating a law pertaining to wheels on sneakers.

D. Fail, because Jonathan's perceived violation of the sneaker law attenuated any prior unconstitutional conduct by Yenis.

E. Fail, if Yenis' confusion about the lawfulness of Jonathan's sneaker-related conduct was reasonable.

QUESTION 27. Cold scone crazy. After arresting Ian for carrying an unregistered firearm, Officer Brittany is transporting him to the station house for booking. When she stops at a traffic light one block from her destination, a stranger, Tim, runs up to the car and motions for Brittany to open the car window. When she does, Tim shrieks that Ian attacked his (Tim's) wife Taylor by pushing her to the ground after Ian disliked a scone that he purchased from Taylor's restaurant café. Ian responded that Tim was "crazy" and he (Ian) had never touched Taylor. Jumping into the back seat of the police car where Ian was sitting, Tim grabbed Ian by the collar, shouting "Say you hurt her, scumbag, or I'll put these fists to good use." At that point, Ian asks Brittany to intervene. She tells him not to worry since they are very close to the police station. As Tim readies his fist for action, Ian relents and admits aggressing against Taylor for the disappointing bakery item. Ian is subsequently charged with battery. Which of the following is his best argument to secure suppression of the incriminating statement as violative of his constitutional rights?

A. Brittany failed to provide *Miranda* warnings to Ian.

B. Tim threatened Ian with physical harm.

C. Brittany allowed Tim to threaten Ian with physical harm.

D. Ian's confession is unreliable.

E. Brittany failed to lock the doors to the police car.

QUESTION 28. Smokin' him out. Though he knows the purchase of Cuban cigars is illegal, Nick's passion for them has too often gotten the better of him, leading to his arrest on several occasions in the last year. To manage his cravings, he joins a Cuban cigar support group, whose 10 members all struggle to stay on the right side of the law by discussing the pain their arrests have caused to friends and family and to sample other, albeit inferior, brands of domestic cigars. Kylie joins the group. She tells the group that she is a cop who is looking to conquer the same addiction; in fact, she is part of an undercover sting operation to find Cuban cigar purchasers.

Surveying the group, Kylie sets her sights on Nick after concluding that his resolve to stay on the straight and narrow is the weakest. As Nick gets into his car after a meeting, Kylie jumps in the passenger seat and presents an enticing proposition. She asks if he would be interested in buying 10 Cuban cigars for "a special discount price." When Nick refuses, Kylie motions to a man outside the car. As the man jumps into the back seat, Kylie explains that he is a fellow officer in her precinct who is also a Cuban cigar enthusiast. The officer, Drew, tells Nick that he can offer the cigars for half the purchase price on the street "tonight only." Kylie then grabs Nick's face and, pressing her face close to his, asks: "Are you in?" "I guess so," Nick responds and then hands Kylie money for the cigars. After he does so, Kylie places him under arrest. Nick moves to suppress the drugs. Based on which of the following is Nick most likely to succeed?

A. Kylie violated Nick's Fifth Amendment rights by not giving him *Miranda* rights before offering to sell him the cigars.
B. Kylie violated Nick's Sixth Amendment rights by questioning him outside the presence of counsel.
C. If this jurisdiction follows the majority rule, Kylie entrapped Nick.
D. If this jurisdiction follows the minority rule, Kylie entrapped Nick.

Analysis

1. Meth proof. This problem raises a number of potential Fourth Amendment challenges to Officer Jim's conduct. Let's look at each in turn.

Answer **A** posits that the warrant Jim executed was insufficiently particularized. As discussed earlier, to satisfy particularity requirements, a warrant needs to specify "the place to be searched, and the persons or things to be seized." This warrant clearly indicates the place to be searched. In fact, the U.S. Supreme Court has refused to suppress evidence on particularity grounds where the address on the warrant form was less particularized, failing, for example, to specify the apartment number in a multiunit building. *Maryland v. Garrison.*

The warrant also directs officers to seize "evidence pertaining to the use of methamphetamine." While this language gives the police access to many areas of Colleen's apartment, it does not fail on particularity grounds. It is not significantly different from the warrant at issue in the leading U.S. Supreme Court case, *Andresen v. Maryland*, which authorized a search for evidence relating to false pretenses with respect to a specific parcel of property. Because the warrant is sufficiently particular as to location and the items subject to seizure under it, **A** is wrong.

Answer **B** suggests that the seizure of the floor plans was improper because the warrant did not specify documentary evidence. This fact is beside the point, however; the warrant need not detail every item subject to seizure. It need only comply with the standards detailed above. Seen in this light, the question becomes whether the search for documentary evidence is within the scope of the warrant. Under the facts of this problem, it is. Because methamphetamine is manufactured in secret labs, Jim's discovery of floor plans with the word *lab* written in the corner justifies the seizure of the documents as potential "evidence pertaining to the use of methamphetamine."

Answer **C** purports to invalidate the seizure of the documents on a different ground: that police officers later discover that the word *lab* written on the floor plans did not, in fact, refer to a laboratory used to manufacture unlawful drugs. This reasoning cannot be correct. If it were, the validity *vel non* of any warrant would turn on what is later determined to be true, without regard to what police officers believed at the time they executed the warrant. The U.S. Supreme Court has clearly rejected this sort of *post hoc* analysis. **C** is wrong.

Answer **D** focuses on a different issue altogether: Colleen's purported absence during the execution of the warrant. This answer is a bit of a red herring, since the U.S. Supreme Court has never held that occupants must be present during the execution of a search warrant to render the search valid. **D** is wrong.

Having eliminated the four justifications for suppressing the evidence, the correct answer is **E**. The evidence is admissible.

2. Scissor seizures. This follow-up to the first problem has Officer Jim searching Colleen's residence again, this time for evidence pertaining to bank robbery. Answer **A** would exclude the scissors because, at the time Jim discovered them, he did not suspect Colleen of murder. This answer is incorrect, because the validity of the seizure is dependent not on the likelihood of Colleen's involvement in the homicide, but rather on whether the scissors were found in a location and manner consistent with the language of the warrant.

For similar reasons, answer **D** misses the mark. It would evaluate the constitutionality of Jim's conduct based on the accuracy of his suspicions. The U.S. Supreme Court has never embraced this kind of backward-looking approach to the Fourth Amendment, and with good reason. Allowing the ends to justify the means could lead police officers to engage in all sorts of misconduct based on their belief that, in the end, they will discover incriminating evidence that will justify their actions.

E focuses on the proximity of Colleen's apartment to that of the victim. It is hard to see how this would have any relevance to the seizure of the bloodstained scissors. While it might increase Jim's level of suspicion, his authority to search and seize is based exclusively on the warrant. The location of the murder victim's residence has no relevance to the warrant, which concerns a search for bank robbery evidence. **E** is, therefore, wrong.

We are left with the two best options, **B** and **C**. Both provide potentially valid justifications for the seizure of the scissors. **B** would allow the seizure because scissors could be used, presumably as a weapon, while carrying out a robbery. While this is true, it seems somewhat unlikely. Most robbers who carry weapons to perpetrate a robbery use firearms or other lethal weapons; scissor-wielding robbers are a rarity.

Accordingly, **C** is the better answer. Because evidence relating to bank robbery could be found in a dresser drawer, Jim was justified in searching there. While doing so, he came upon the scissors. He immediately noticed the presence of a large quantity of dried blood on the scissors, an amount seemingly inconsistent with any minor injury that may have occurred while cutting hair. Knowing what he did about the animosity between Colleen and the stabbing victim, Jim was justified in seizing the scissors in plain view.

3. Transparent behavior. In answering this question, it is important to isolate each issue and analyze it separately. First, any privacy expectation Owen might have in the bag he places in the shed is diminished by its transparency. Whether the bag is transparent or opaque, Owen would lose any Fourth Amendment protection in it if he were to leave it where the public could readily access it, such as at the curb. In this instance, however, he deposited it in a shed, which he subsequently locked, and which was located in a fenced-in area on his front lawn. Clearly, Owen's actions demonstrate a desire for privacy in the shed and, by extension, the bag placed within it; moreover, unlike the garbage in *Greenwood*, the bag would not be "readily accessible to animals, children, scavengers, snoops and other members of the public." In sum, then, the bag merits Fourth Amendment protection.

The implication of Fourth Amendment protection does not necessarily import, however, that Officer Michelle violated Owen's constitutional rights. If Michelle had used the information she discovered by shining the flashlight through the fence to obtain a warrant to enter the shed, she would have committed no constitutional error. Instead, she conducted a warrantless search of the bag when she entered the yard, broke the lock on the shed, and opened the bag inside. This exceeded the scope of her authority under the Fourth Amendment.

Answers **C** and **D** are incorrect, inasmuch as they find Michelle's conduct lawful. **C**'s reliance on the bag's transparency is insufficient to justify the search since, as discussed above, the bag was located in a private area. Michelle had probable cause to search the bag prior to doing so, but this is also inapposite, since the level of proof would authorize the issuance of a search warrant, not excuse compliance altogether with the warrant requirement.

A provides that Michelle had no right to use her flashlight to peer into the shed. This statement is incorrect as a matter of law. Michelle conducted this search while standing on the sidewalk. Just as the police in *Ciraolo* did not violate the defendant's rights when viewing his back yard from a position overhead that was routinely accessed by ordinary citizens, neither are Michelle's actions unlawful when she stands in a public area and peers into a closed container using unsophisticated equipment commonly owned by most individuals.

B is the correct answer. Michelle had no right to physically invade the shed. Doing so constituted a physical intrusion on a protected area and violated Owen's reasonable expectation of privacy in the shed's contents. Her conduct in this instance did not consist of mere visual access from a public area. On the contrary, she entered the curtilage of Owen's home, used force to break the lock on a closed container located within the curtilage, and, after accessing the container, conducted a further search of a separate container within.

4. Pocketed watch. This problem offers Fourth, Fifth, and Sixth Amendment options for Jon in challenging the admissibility of the weapon and the cocaine.

We can quickly eliminate **D**, since the Sixth Amendment applies *only* upon the filing of formal charges, and none have been filed as yet against Jon. By contrast, because the Fifth Amendment *Miranda* doctrine applies when police engage in custodial interrogation, it does appear relevant, since Officer Yalissa directly questions Jon about the location of the weapon and does so in a coercive atmosphere.

However, the U.S. Supreme Court has excused compliance with *Miranda* when an officer's inquiry is motivated by a concern for public safety. *Quarles.* Here, since the police know that Jon used a firearm in robbing the art gallery, it is reasonable for Yalissa to believe that he carried the pistol into the preschool and hid it somewhere in the building when Yalissa gave chase. In light of the danger a loaded firearm poses if a child finds it, the public safety exception clearly applies and excuses Yalissa's failure to give Jon *Miranda* warnings before asking where he placed the weapon. **B**, therefore, is not Jon's best defense.

A and **C** raise Fourth Amendment challenges. **A** addresses the body frisk Yalissa performs after cornering Jon in the lunchroom. This is lawful under two theories. First, her belief that he is armed and dangerous justifies the frisk under *Terry*. During the frisk, she discovers what she immediately recognizes to be a watch. Because the gallery owner reported that the robber had stolen his Rolex and placed it in his front pants pocket, Yalissa had probable cause to believe that the watch was "contraband," that is, evidence incriminating the accused. Thus, it was lawful to seize it. In addition, because she has probable cause to arrest Jon for robbery, she may search his person and clothing incident to the arrest. It does not matter that the search preceded a "formal" arrest, since the search and the arrest occurred in close temporal and spatial proximity. *Rawlings v. Kentucky.*

Challenging the automobile search is Jon's best defense. Yalissa believed that Jon had stolen a painting and a Rolex watch. Prior to searching his car, she had recovered the Rolex. It was reasonable, therefore, to believe that the painting was in the getaway car, and a warrantless search to seize it was clearly permissible. Yalissa exceeded the lawful scope of her authority, however, by searching the glove box. A painting that measures eight-by-eleven inches could not be located there, and, since she has no reason to expect to find any additional contraband in the vehicle, her search should have ended when she located the artwork. **C** is the correct answer.

5. Pistol pattin' Martha. In analyzing this problem, it is important to recognize that three "events" take place in the fact pattern—a stop, a frisk, and a seizure — and that each must be justified separately. The stop requires reasonable suspicion that Elaine was engaging in criminal activity. The facts indicate that she furtively placed something in her coat pocket, exited the store hurriedly, and appeared nervous when answering Officer Martha's questions. While these circumstances might not provide the probable cause necessary for an arrest, they are incriminating enough, when viewed collectively, to justify a brief investigative detention. **A** is wrong.

But does the length of Elaine's detention exceed the bounds of *Terry*? While the U.S. Supreme Court has not provided specific time parameters, they have held that *Terry* does not justify lengthy or intrusive detentions. In this instance, however, the questioning does not last more than a minute or two and is not occasioned by practices that have concerned the U.S. Supreme Court in the *Terry* context, such as removing suspects to a different location, particularly from their homes. **B** is wrong.

The stop "blossoms" into a frisk. While Martha may pat Elaine down, her motivation for doing so must be personal safety. If she does not reasonably believe that Elaine is armed and dangerous, the pat-down is impermissible. The lawfulness of the frisk is determined by what Martha was thinking when she executed it, *not* what she subsequently discovered. Thus, that Martha discovered Elaine was carrying a pistol is relevant only inasmuch as Martha had reason to believe Elaine was armed. Unfortunately for Martha, the facts do not suggest that she entertained this belief. She suspected merely that Elaine had shoplifted an item from a hardware store and was nervous when questioned. Absent any additional information about Elaine or any threatening behavior on her part, the frisk is invalid. **C** is correct.

Note that, if the frisk had been lawful, the seizure of the gun would have been permissible. A trained police officer could readily identify in a pat-down a firearm located in the front pocket of an individual's trousers since the contours of the weapon easily identify it as such. **D** is, therefore, twice wrong!

6. Forcing the issue. This problem revisits the standards for a valid *Miranda* waiver and for violations of the Fourteenth Amendment Due Process Clause. You are asked to identify Gina's best argument. Remember: The best argument is not necessarily a strong argument. As we will see, it might be merely the defendant's only viable option under the circumstances.

A and **B** address the sufficiency of Gina's *Miranda* waiver. To pass constitutional muster, a waiver must be "knowing, intelligent and voluntary," which means the prosecution must establish that the suspect understood her rights and the consequences of abandoning them. While additional information may have been useful to the suspect in deciding whether or not to speak to law enforcement, the failure to provide such information does not invalidate a waiver that otherwise satisfies the foregoing criteria. Thus, the desk sergeant's failure to tell his colleagues that Gina's lawyer had requested to be present during the interrogation is irrelevant, provided Gina knew what she was doing and appreciated the consequences of her actions. The facts suggest that she did. Before executing the waiver, Gina specifically referenced her right to have an attorney present and expressed concern about saying something that "would look bad in court"—that is, she worried about making incriminating statements that the prosecution could use to convict her.

Likewise, Gina's mental illness is relevant in the context of her *Miranda* waiver only if it interfered with her ability to make a voluntary and intelligent decision to speak to Officer Loretta. As discussed above, Gina's pre-waiver statements establish that she knew her rights and the consequences of relinquishing them. To be involuntary, the decision to waive must be the product of *police* coercion. While Gina reports feeling pressured to speak by an outside "force," the source of those coercive influences—whatever it may be—is not law enforcement. Therefore, for purposes of the Fifth (and Fourteenth) Amendment, Gina's mental illness does not make her conduct involuntary.

We are left, then, with due process claims based either on Loretta's false representation that a witness had identified Gina or on the suggestion that, if she cooperated, Gina might secure prosecutorial leniency from the district attorney. In determining whether there has been a violation of the Due Process Clause, we must ask whether Gina's will was overborne by the conduct of law enforcement. As such, the due process test has an important functional component that examines not only the flagrancy of any police misconduct but also the *effect* that misconduct had on the suspect.

Seen in this light, Gina cannot successfully argue that Loretta's lie violated due process since, upon hearing it, Gina laughed, chiding Loretta "to do better than that." Gina's reaction was quite different, however, when Loretta mentioned the more favorable treatment available to cooperative suspects, including the possibility that Gina could be housed in a psychiatric hospital instead of jail. Gina began to cry uncontrollably and soon thereafter implicated herself in Missy's murder. Based on this sequence of events, one may reasonably conclude that Loretta's comments influenced Gina's decision to confess. Accordingly, **D** is the best answer.

As I mentioned above, the fact that **D** is the best argument does not mean that it is a particularly strong one. Gina will argue that Loretta implicitly promised that the prosecutor would recommend that she be housed in a psychiatric facility, an assertion that constitutes pure speculation at best on Loretta's part. On the other hand, the prosecution will emphasize that Loretta promised only to speak to the prosecutor; she never told Gina that Gina would not be sent to jail or even that the prosecutor would definitely agree to the recommendation. In the end, however, notwithstanding its difficulties, **D** is the right answer because—simply put—**A**, **B**, and **C** are clearly wrong.

7. Groovy greenhouse.   In evaluating the lawfulness of Officer David's conduct, we will proceed chronologically, starting with his entry into Ted's house. For his actions to be unconstitutional, they must, as a threshold matter, violate

Alison's Fourth Amendment rights in her back yard. Because she has enclosed the yard with a tall fence, we can assume that this area qualifies as curtilage that merits constitutional protection. Much like the fences erected by the defendants in *Ciraolo*, however, the fences create a privacy expectation from street-level views only.

By looking into the yard from the neighbor's bedroom window, David is gleaning the same information available each and every day to Ted. In this regard, he is similarly situated to the police officers in *Ciraolo*, who lawfully accessed the defendants' back yard visually from a plane flying 1,000 feet overhead in publicly navigable airspace used by commercial airlines. Just as there was no reasonable privacy expectation from that vantage point in *Ciraolo*, neither does one exist from Ted's bedroom window in this case.

Unlike the officers in *Ciraolo*, David views the back yard by entering private property without the owner/occupant's consent. As such, his actions constitute a trespass that implicates *Ted*'s Fourth Amendment rights. They do not, however, violate Alison's rights. Unlike the placement of the GPS device on the defendant's car in *Jones*, there is no physical invasion of a protected area of the *defendant* here. In addition, because David saw no more than what was plainly visible to private parties, looking at Alison's yard from Ted's window did not violate Alison's expectation of privacy in the curtilage. David's conduct thus far is constitutional.

Based on the photos he takes of the mushrooms growing in the greenhouse, David obtains a warrant to search Alison's back yard for "any and all instrumentalities of crime relating to the growth of hallucinogenic mushrooms." While the first six words of the warrant may appear to create the kind of "general" warrant the Framers sought to invalidate, the magistrate references the "cultivation of hallucinogenic mushrooms" in the words that follow. *Andresen* instructs, to this end, that the inclusion of language linking boilerplate language to a specific crime cures any defect in particularity that might otherwise exist. Accordingly, this warrant satisfies particularity requirements.

On his way out of the yard, David spots through a window an envelope sitting on a table that purports to contain the name of some of Alison's "clients." He opens the window, reaches inside, and seizes the envelope. This conduct exceeds the scope of the warrant, which is limited geographically to Alison's back yard. Therefore, the seizure is permissible only if the surrounding circumstances justify the noncompliance. To this end, David might argue its admissibility based on the plain view doctrine or exigent circumstances. Unfortunately for David, neither will work.

While the label on the envelope makes the criminality of its contents immediately apparent, plain view requires additionally that the officer have lawful access to the item in question. Here, the search warrant provides the sole justification for David's presence within the curtilage of Alison's home. Because the warrant does not include the house, his entry into it is unlawful, however minimally intrusive his actions may be.

Exigent circumstances will justify a warrantless search and seizure if the prosecution can demonstrate that evidence is likely to be destroyed in the time it would take to secure a warrant. Our problem, however, contains no facts that would support such a finding. Alison lives alone and is out of town for three days on a business trip. Thus, there is little risk that someone might enter the home before David obtains a warrant to search it.

Because David violated Alison's Fourth Amendment rights by seizing the envelope without a warrant, the envelope is inadmissible against her. The mushrooms are admissible. The correct answer is **C**.

8. Access Hollyweed.   This question reviews the doctrines applicable to warrantless searches of automobiles. Finding the correct answer requires careful consideration of the circumstances necessary to invoke each exception, as well as the scope of the search it authorizes.

We can start by eliminating search incident to arrest. First, automobile searches, like searches of the arrestee, must be contemporaneous with the arrest in both time and place for this exception to apply. Officer Kimball's conduct satisfied neither requirement. His search of Holly's vehicle at the station house occurred more than thirty minutes after the roadside arrest. Thus, in *United States v. Chadwick*, the U.S. Supreme Court reasoned that, once the police have reduced an arrestee's effects to their immediate control, the authority to search incident to arrest disappears since "there is no longer any danger that the arrestee might gain access to the property to seize a weapon or destroy evidence."[1] During the thirty-minute gap between Holly's arrest at the roadside and Kimball's search of the vehicle at the station house, Holly had no opportunity to access its contents. **D** is wrong.

On its face, **C** seems to be a better answer since, when "frisking" a vehicle, an officer may lawfully look inside closed containers in the passenger cabin and can seize weapons or anything he or she immediately recognizes as contraband. However, as with body frisks, car frisks must be motivated by concern for officer safety. If this were the case, Kimball would have searched the car for weapons at the roadside, where Holly could have gained access to the vehicle and seized a weapon from inside. His decision to wait until the car was at the station house, when Holly was nowhere near it, belies any possible concern for officer safety. Moreover, our fact pattern is devoid of information suggesting that Holly was, in fact, armed and dangerous. **C** is wrong.

Inventory searches of impounded vehicles are permissible for officer safety and/or to safeguard an arrestee's belongings. The lawfulness of a specific inventory search turns on the reasonableness of a jurisdiction's regulations and

---

1. In *United States v. Edwards*, 415 U.S. 800 (1974), decided three years before *Chadwick*, the U.S. Supreme Court upheld the search of an arrestee's clothing at the station house incident to his arrest the day before. In so holding, the majority emphasized that the arrestee had carried with him to the station house the items searched for and discovered. By contrast, Holly's vehicle was left at the roadside when Kimball transported her to the station house. In addition, while *Edwards* has never been expressly overruled, its continuing vitality is open to serious question in light of *Chadwick* and the Court's reasoning in other, more recent cases.

an officer's compliance in good faith with those regulations. Here, we do not need to know the content of the applicable regulations because Kimball's conversation with the desk sergeant demonstrates that he was acting in bad faith. First, he directed that the car be delivered to the station house, a departure from standard operating procedure. Second, and most importantly, he did this so he could search the vehicle for criminal evidence, a purpose plainly at odds with the justifications underlying this exception to the warrant requirement. This attempted end-run around the Fourth Amendment fatally undermines reliance on **B**'s inventory search rationale.

The automobile exception, by contrast, fits our fact pattern nicely. It requires probable cause to believe that contraband or evidence of crime will be found in the passenger cabin or the trunk of the vehicle. Kimball smells burnt marijuana when he approaches the vehicle, which indicates that contraband is very likely to be present somewhere inside the passenger cabin. Unlike searches incident to arrest, searches conducted under the automobile exception do not need to be contemporaneous with the arrest and may occur at a different location. Therefore, because Kimball had probable cause to believe there was marijuana inside the car before he initiated the search, he had the right to search the vehicle at the station house, including a search of any closed containers inside it that might contain the contraband in question. Because marijuana could easily fit inside a gym bag, its search was lawful. **A** is the correct answer.

9. Obie & the force. This problem presents three different Fourth Amendment "events." You are asked to determine which is/are unlawful. We will consider each in chronological order, starting with the traffic stop.

Officer Nancy pulls Obie over for speeding. While he did exceed the 55 mph speed limit, he did so by only 5 mph, an amount that ordinarily would not have led local traffic cops to stop the vehicle. In essence, Obie is arguing that the highly unusual nature of the stop makes it unreasonable under the Fourth Amendment. This argument lacks merit. Reasonableness is an objective inquiry that looks to the conduct in question and asks, first and foremost, if it violates applicable law. Obie's conduct does, whether by 5 mph or by 10 and whether his particular transgression is routinely or rarely prosecuted.

Likewise, it is irrelevant that Nancy is assigned to the Organized Crime Task Force and, as a result, is not responsible for enforcing traffic laws. She has the authority to do so, and that is all that matters. The fact that the stop was pre-textual in that it was motivated by the desire to search for criminal evidence is also insufficient to prove a Fourth Amendment violation. Absent extraordinary circumstances, which are not present here, "probable cause to believe the law has been broken 'outbalances' private interest in avoiding police contact," whatever an officer's subjective intent. *Whren.*

The arrest likewise satisfies Fourth Amendment requirements. While the facts do not indicate whether applicable state law permits custodial arrests for traffic offenses, this issue has no bearing on the federal constitutional question.

If the arrest is based on probable cause, as this one was, it is reasonable under the Fourth Amendment, even if it violates state law. *Virginia v. Moore.*

After arresting Obie, Nancy searches the interior cabin of his car. Because he was a "recent occupant" of the vehicle, she may do so, under *Arizona v. Gant,* if Obie was within reaching distance of the passenger compartment at the time of the search *or* if it was reasonable to believe the vehicle contained evidence of the offense for which he was arrested. At the time of the search, Obie was handcuffed and locked inside the squad car; thus, he was not within reaching distance of the car. In addition, because he was arrested for speeding, there was no criminal evidence for which Nancy could have been searching. Thus, the search of Obie's car was unlawful.

In sum, then, the stop and the arrest were lawful under the Fourth Amendment, but the search of the vehicle was not. The correct answer is **C.**

10. Ring-a-ding-ding.   This problem reviews the scope of police authority to search automobile passengers and their effects without a warrant. Before focusing their attention on the passenger, Lilli, Officers Kathy and Trina arrest the driver for theft and secure him in the back seat of the squad car after recovering one of the three items taken from the jewelry store. Thus, they are justified in searching the automobile on two grounds: First, they may search the interior cabin of the vehicle incident to arrest under *Gant* since they have reason to believe the remaining stolen items will be found there. Second, because there is probable cause to believe that the car contains criminal evidence, they can search the entire car, including the trunk, for the evidence in question.

The officers' authority extends to closed containers in which the rings may be hidden, including passengers' effects, such as purses. While Lilli has an independent privacy interest in her purse, its placement in the thief's car diminishes that interest and makes the purse primarily an effect of the vehicle, subject to search. *Wyoming v. Houghton.* Thus, the ring found by Trina in the purse is admissible.

Analytically, the search of Lilli's person is altogether different due to Lilli's independent and heightened privacy interest in her body. Kathy can frisk Lilli if she (Kathy) fears for her safety, but there is no indication that she does, and, even if she did, a search for weapons would not justify the removal and seizure of a wad of tissue paper that neither poses a safety threat nor is immediately recognizable as contraband.

Conversely, Kathy may argue exigent circumstances, claiming Lilli will destroy criminal evidence. However, before she finds the ring in Lilli's pocket and Trina finds the other in the purse, the officers lack probable cause to believe that Lilli is involved in the theft. She was not present in the jewelry store, and the store owner stated that the thief drove away alone. Because she entered the vehicle after the crime was completed, Lilli's connection to the theft is purely speculative and does not justify an exploratory search of her body that includes removing and opening a non-dangerous item located in a shirt pocket.

Thus, and in sum, the ring wrapped in tissue paper found in Lilli's shirt pocket will be suppressed, but the ring found in her purse in the thief's automobile is admissible. The correct answer is **B**.

11. His brother's keeper. This problem underscores the importance of carefully considering all choices before arriving at an answer. As we will see, one of the four options may seem, at first blush, to be the best choice, since it reflects correct legal analysis; however, notwithstanding its facial accuracy, it is not the best choice.

We can start by eliminating **A**. The district attorney presented the magistrate with detailed information from an anonymous letter subsequently corroborated, in large part, by police surveillance. As in *Illinois v. Gates*—where police corroborated some, but not all, information contained in an anonymous letter—the totality of the evidence presented to the court allowed the magistrate to make a "common sense, practical determination" that probable cause existed. *A fortiori*, there was a substantial basis for issuing the warrant.

C would admit the evidence, based on the plain view doctrine. While the book's criminal nature is immediately apparent from its label, the plain view doctrine also requires lawful access to both the book and the place from which Jack viewed it. Because Jack viewed the book from inside the house, its seizure is invalid if he lacked proper authority to enter the residence. Thus, to fully evaluate **C**, we must first consider **B**, which would suppress the book, based on Jack's unlawful entry.

Jack entered the house to find his brother. While he presumably had probable cause at that point to believe that the residence was being operated as a brothel, he would need a warrant to enter unless circumstances justified dispensing with the requirement. They do not. Waiting for a warrant, which he knew had already been issued, would not risk the destruction of evidence, since the business was ongoing and the facts do not disclose that Jill was aware of the surveillance. Accordingly, the plain view seizure of the book was unlawful.

Notwithstanding the unlawful entry, the book is admissible if the prosecution can establish that it would have been inevitably discovered through lawful means. Here, the district attorney had obtained a search warrant for Jill's residence before Jack entered. Therefore, if Jack had simply left the stakeout, as he had planned to do, officers would have returned soon thereafter to execute the warrant and would have found the book located in plain view by the front door.

In sum, then, although Jack's seizure of the book was the fruit of his unlawful entry into Jill's residence, the book is admissible. The police would have inevitably discovered it lawfully when executing the search warrant that the court had already issued. The correct answer is **D**.

12. Doing the can-can. In this problem, Officer Jameel inadvertently exceeds the scope of the warrant, which authorizes him to search only those garbage cans located on Chester's property at 18 Mercer Lane. We must determine whether the contraband he discovers in the neighbor's garbage is nonetheless admissible.

C would admit the evidence, since the neighbor, Reggie, failed to lock the garbage cans. This choice is a bit of a red herring, since the constitutionality of Jameel's conduct does not turn on this issue; the fact that the cans are closed containers located within the curtilage of Reggie's home is sufficient to convey Fourth Amendment protection, whether or not they are locked.

Likewise, the fact that the items in question are stored in garbage cans is inapposite. *Greenwood* imports that a police search of garbage left at the curb for collection is not governed by the Fourth Amendment, since it constitutes abandoned property "readily accessible to animals, children, scavengers, snoops and other members of the public." By contrast, the pipes Jameel found were not abandoned; they were stored in a can located inside the curtilage of Reggie's home, where passersby could not readily access them. *Greenwood*, therefore, does not govern here.

Although Jameel's search of the contents of the cans invaded Reggie's Fourth Amendment rights, the evidence is admissible nonetheless if Jameel's mistake was reasonable. *Maryland v. Garrison.* While the warrant was limited to Chester's property, there was no clear demarcation indicating where his property ended and Reggie's began. In addition, the cans were grouped without regard to ownership, and the facts contain no information suggesting that the one with the pipes inside that belonged to Reggie was distinct in any way from those belonging to Chester. On balance, therefore, it was reasonable for Jameel to believe that all six cans belonged to Chester. The correct answer is **A**.

13. Pipin' hot.   The Fifth Amendment *Miranda* doctrine applies whenever police custodially interrogate a suspect. Because Officer Jameel did not obtain a valid waiver of Reggie's *Miranda* rights, Reggie's testimonial statement about his pipes will be inadmissible, if it is found to be the product of custodial interrogation.

A suspect is in custody for *Miranda* purposes if the inherently coercive, police-dominated atmosphere would have made a reasonable person believe he was not at liberty to terminate the interrogation. Applying this standard, there can be little question that the encounter between Reggie and Jameel was custodial. Jameel spoke to Reggie in a forceful manner and ordered him not to move while Reggie read the warrant.

Custody alone, however, will not trigger *Miranda*. The response must also be the product of interrogation, defined as police conduct that is "reasonably likely to elicit an incriminating response." While conduct may constitute interrogation even if it is not "punctuated by a question mark," *Rhode Island v. Innis*, it is not reasonably likely that, by handing the search warrant to Reggie, Jameel will invite Reggie's incriminating statement about the pipes. Because Reggie was upset about the search, Jameel was simply providing him with documentation explaining Jameel's presence in the area. Reggie then volunteered the information contained in his remark.

The fact that Reggie initiated the encounter is irrelevant. Under *Edwards v. Arizona*, once a suspect invokes his right to counsel, subsequent interrogation is permissible only if the suspect himself initiates it. Here, there has been no invocation.

The correct answer is **D**.

14. Made up make-up. Marlene's Fifth Amendment *Miranda* rights are implicated during all custodial interrogations, whether *after* or *before* the filing of formal charges. Here, District Attorney Hiram ensures that Marlene waives these rights before he questions her. Thus, admission of her statement would not violate the Fifth Amendment.

Marlene's Sixth Amendment rights attached when the grand jury issued its indictment. As such, she has the right to have her attorney present at all "critical stages" of the prosecution, including custodial interrogations. By the same token, she can waive her Sixth Amendment right to counsel, provided such waiver is voluntary, knowing, and intelligent. Generally speaking, *Miranda* waivers are sufficient for this purpose. The fact that Hiram waited until Iris, Marlene's attorney, had left before approaching Marlene is unavailing, since it does not undermine the voluntariness or intelligence of Marlene's decision. It would be different, for example, if Hiram had misrepresented Marlene's entitlement to assistance from Iris during questioning or if Iris had asked to be present during questioning and Hiram had failed to communicate this to Marlene. For the above reasons, Marlene's statement is admissible. The correct answer is **E**.

15. Hook, line, and sinker. This problem reviews the consent exception to the warrant requirement and the permissible scope of searches of one's person under the Fourth Amendment. Not realizing the suitcase contains only Myron's belongings, Officer Carmine requests consent from Myron's wife, Leslie, to search the suitcase. Although Leslie lacks "common authority" over the bag, her consent is still valid under the concept of "apparent authority" if Carmine reasonably believed she had authority to consent. *Illinois v. Rodriguez*. The bag was located over the seat in which the couple was sitting, and it had their last name on the identification tag attached to it. When Carmine asked Leslie's permission to search it, she freely agreed without indicating that the bag was not hers. Thus, in light of the totality of the circumstances, Carmine reasonably believed that Leslie had authority to consent.

Leslie's "apparent" authority constitutionally validates her consent, unless Carmine obtained it coercively. There is no indication that he did. While Leslie might have felt pressured by knowing that Carmine suspected Myron of criminal activity, Carmine needed to explain the basis for his request and did so politely. He also did not display a weapon or otherwise communicate through his words or actions that Leslie lacked free will to refuse the request. In sum, Leslie's consent is valid, and the knife is, therefore, admissible.

Carmine retrieved the wad of bills from Myron's coat pocket. Because he lacks probable cause to believe that Myron was hiding the change purse on his body, Carmine's sole justification for searching Myron's person is a *Terry* stop-and-frisk — that is, that finding the knife made him fear for his personal safety. However, this would only allow him to seize weapons or items the criminal nature of which was immediately apparent without physical manipulation. The wad of bills is not a weapon, nor can Carmine argue that it is criminal evidence since, at that time, he was only aware that coins and earrings were missing. The bills are inadmissible. The correct answer is **B**.

16. Slipping Mickey. Officer Melanie's seizure of contraband found in Mickey's car is justified under the plain view doctrine; thus, suppression is warranted only if the seizure is a "fruit" of *prior* unconstitutional conduct, as indicated in **A** through **D**. We will consider each in turn.

The box containing the earrings fell out of Mickey's pocket when he was running away from Melanie and fell. Under *Hodari D.*, fleeing from a police officer only constitutes a seizure when, and if, an individual is physically restrained or voluntarily submits to the officer's authority. Because neither applies to the facts in our problem, Mickey was not seized at the time he fell. **A** is incorrect.

After she sees the earrings that fell out of the box, Melanie requires Mickey to produce the receipt. This is definitely a Fourth Amendment seizure since Melanie clearly communicates that he is not "free to leave." To be lawful, she must reasonably suspect that he has engaged in criminal conduct. While flight alone is insufficient for this purpose, Melanie can point to additional factors, such as Mickey's appearance, the recent sharp rise in shoplifting, and his furtive placement of something in his jacket as he exited the store. Collectively, these facts justify a brief detention to determine if criminal activity is afoot.

To conclude the inquiry, Melanie requests proof that the earrings were purchased. Because Mickey has already attempted to flee, it is reasonable for her to accompany him to his car for this purpose. It takes several minutes to reach the car, since it is not parked close by. As a result, the detention is lengthier than most *Terry* stops. This does not violate the "brevity" requirement, however, which focuses on the diligence of an officer's efforts and considers, with respect to duration, whether the suspect is responsible for prolonging the detention. *Sharpe.* Here, Melanie resolves her concerns as expeditiously as possible. It is Mickey's flight to the opposite end of the mall to avoid speaking to Melanie that prolongs the encounter. If he had remained where he was when she approached him initially, his car would have been nearby and the investigation into his activity in the store would have concluded much more quickly.

Because Melanie's conduct before arriving at Mickey's car did not constitute an unlawful seizure under the Fourth Amendment, the discovery and subsequent seizure of the marijuana in plain view was not "fruit of the poisonous tree." The correct answer is **E**.

17. A whisper in the park. This problem reviews the case law on identifications in the Fifth, Sixth, and Fourteenth Amendment contexts. I will address each in turn.

The Fifth Amendment *Miranda* doctrine applies to "testimonial" responses obtained during custodial interrogation. The U.S. Supreme Court has held, in this regard, that requiring a defendant to recite certain words in a pretrial identification procedure is insufficiently "testimonial" to implicate the privilege against self-incrimination. Therefore, requiring Leyton to utter the words spoken by the robber did not violate *Miranda*.

A pretrial identification violates due process if it is "so unnecessarily suggestive" as to create a "substantial likelihood of misidentification." *Perry v. New Hampshire*. However, even if an identification is unnecessarily suggestive, it is admissible if the surrounding circumstances indicate that it is reliable. *Manson v. Brathwaite*. The one-on-one identification that took place at the courthouse was undoubtedly highly suggestive. It was, in addition, unnecessary, since there was no emergency that required Lola to conduct a courthouse show-up. For example, police could have arranged instead for a line-up conducted at the station house at some other time.

Nonetheless, because of its reliability, admission of the show-up would not violate Leyton's due process rights. Marian provided a detailed description of the robber, based on her opportunity to see him at close range at the crime scene and on several previous occasions when he was loitering in the park. Moreover, after Leyton uttered the words spoken by the robber, she was "certain" he was the perpetrator. Collectively, these considerations overcome the constitutional infirmity inherent in the show-up so as to allow its introduction into evidence.

The show-up takes place after Leyton's arraignment. Therefore, his Sixth Amendment rights have attached and afford him the right to have his attorney, Rick, present at the identification. While Rick allows the show-up to take place outside his presence, he does not have the authority to waive his client's rights. Rick did not consult with Leyton, who is being led back to jail by a guard during Rick's conversation with Lola. Based on the sequence of events, Leyton might logically have concluded that he does not have the right to have his attorney with him. At any rate, the lack of communication between Rick and Leyton precludes any finding that Leyton intentionally relinquished his Sixth Amendment right to counsel. Based on the foregoing, the correct answer is **B**.

18. The art of deception. Lupita, acting as a government agent, attempts to elicit statements from Nancy that will link Nancy to Heylia, a known drug supplier. The conversations are recorded using a "wire" taped to Lupita's body. Although ordinarily police must obtain a warrant to eavesdrop on private conversations, they need not do so if one of the two parties consents to having the government listen to and record the conversation. Thus, Lupita's agreement to wear the wire extinguishes any Fourth Amendment claim Nancy might have.

Nancy was indicted before Lupita questioned her; therefore, Nancy's Sixth Amendment rights had attached and forbade interrogation by the prosecutor or his agent outside the presence of counsel. *Massiah.* Because Lupita's question about Heylia helping with Nancy's business clearly constituted interrogation under the Sixth Amendment "deliberate elicitation" standard, any statements Nancy made in response about drug trafficking would have been inadmissible. Instead, Nancy's incriminating statement concerns wholly unrelated criminal activity that sounds in consumer fraud. Because the Sixth Amendment is "offense-specific," it provides no protection for this uncharged criminal activity. *Maine v. Moulton.* As a result, this statement is fully admissible. Based on the foregoing, the correct answer is **D**.

19. SuperSpying: No ordinary prying.   Whereas Nancy was recorded using a wire taped to Lupita's body, Silas was recorded by SuperSpy, a new piece of police-department equipment. *Kyllo* prohibits police use of technological devices not in general public use that reveal "intimate details" of the home without physical intrusion. SuperSpy is such a device. It is a recently introduced technological innovation that has the ability to eavesdrop on private communications that are constitutionally protected since they take place inside the home. These conversations, moreover, could not otherwise be heard unless the listener was physically present inside the residence. As such, introduction of Silas's statement would violate his Fourth Amendment rights.

The Sixth Amendment right to counsel prohibits uncounseled interrogation that takes place after formal charging. Unlike Nancy, at the time he incriminates himself, Silas faces no criminal charges. Thus, the Sixth Amendment imposes no restriction on the subject matter of any questions Lupita asks Silas, and anything he says is admissible against him. (And, remember, the *Miranda* doctrine is inapplicable as well when the suspect does not know he is being questioned by a law enforcement officer or his agent.)

In sum, then, while admitting the recorded statement would not violate the Sixth Amendment, it is subject to exclusion under the Fourth Amendment, based on the unlawful use of SuperSpy. The correct answer is **A**.

20. Barking up the wrong trees.   This problem revisits the "attenuation" doctrine, which provides an exception to evidentiary exclusion. Because Officer Rafael discovered the illegal firearm during an unlawful frisk, Robert's arrest violated the Fourth Amendment. Robert contends that his subsequent confession is, therefore, inadmissible as "fruit of the poisonous tree." His argument lacks merit.

The taint from an unlawful arrest can be purged through factors such as the passage of time and intervening events and circumstances. *Wong Sun*; *Brown.* Here, the confession took place three days after the arrest, during which time Robert was free on bail and consulted with his attorney. Moreover, he went to the station house voluntarily and told Rafael he wanted to "come clean." Finally, the facts do not indicate any improper motivation or malice on Rafael's part in conducting the frisk, nor was it carried out in a flagrant or punitive fashion. Viewed together, these factors demonstrate that Robert's station-house confession was the product of his free will, not of the prior unlawful arrest. The confession is admissible.

As Robert gets up to leave, Rafael orders him to remain and proceeds to question him about a gang-related shooting in which he believes Robert participated. Rafael intentionally fails to provide *Miranda* warnings, and Robert incriminates himself. Before resuming the interrogation the following day, Rafael administers the warnings and, before asking any questions, tells Robert that his previous statements about the shooting were probably inadmissible. Robert subsequently waives his *Miranda* rights and provides a second, more complete confession.

The court is not likely to exclude Robert's subsequent incriminating statements. In obtaining the first confession, Rafael did not use "inherently coercive police tactics or methods offensive to due process." *Elstad*. In addition, while the *Miranda* violation was intentional, the substantial break in time between the two statements and Rafael's explanation of the probable inadmissibility of the first confession purges the taint of initial Fifth Amendment violation. *Seibert*.

Based on the foregoing, Robert's incriminating statements as to both the illegal firearm and the shooting are admissible. The correct answer is **D**.

21. Potluck.   This problem explores the emergency-aid application of exigent circumstances. Essentially, Officer Trudy enters the Smith's home to abate a nuisance. Is the concept of community "safety" sufficiently elastic to cover this action? While a controversial notion, various courts have held that the "community caretaking" function of law enforcement officers is broad enough to encompass the type of danger posed by playing loud music late at night — especially where, as here, police officers try to contact occupants to resolve the problem before their unconsented entry.

D is off-base. The Fourth Amendment expressly protects individuals from unreasonable searches of their homes. One does not need to be inside his or her home to realize the full benefit of this constitutional guarantee. Thus, the fact that the Smiths are not present when Trudy knocks on their door does not diminish their privacy interest in the home so as to permit the officer's warrantless entry.

A is also incorrect. The fact that loud music is blaring inside the house does not suggest, in and of itself, that anyone inside is injured. Moreover, before she enters the house, Trudy see occupants dancing with no indication of any present distress. Be careful not to indulge in unsubstantiated speculation by reading information into the fact pattern that is not there. For example, do not reason that it is possible that the Smiths are playing loud music to mask the sound of gunshots, which could mean that someone might be injured inside. If you cannot point to concrete facts to back up your theory, let it go. Bill and Marge's complaint did not refer to any violent activity, nor did Trudy encounter anything that would have raised her suspicions, such as blood trickling down the sidewalk.

The gravity of the underlying offense is a relevant consideration in determining whether exigent circumstances justify a warrantless entry into a residence. *Welsh v. Wisconsin*. As such, the fact that the playing of loud music is a criminal misdemeanor, as opposed to civil infraction, is helpful to Trudy. It is insufficient in and of itself, however, to justify her conduct, especially where, as here, the misconduct is quite minor, punishable by no more than a $100 fine. Otherwise, an officer's belief that a suspect committed any criminal offense, no matter how insignificant, would overcome individuals' express Fourth Amendment protection in their houses, which is surely not the case. **C** is wrong.

B, therefore, is the best answer. While the public nuisance at issue here does not fit neatly within any of the traditional categories of exigency, *United States v. Rohrig*, 98 F.3d 1506 (6th Cir. 1996), on which this problem is based, held that the warrantless entry was a reasonable exercise of an officer's "community caretaking" function. Where, as here, waiting for a warrant subjects neighbors to a "continuing and noxious disturbance for an extended period of time," entering the residence for the purpose of abating the nuisance was appropriate, the court reasoned, to preserve a "peaceful community."

22. ¡Ay caramba!   This problem reviews several *Miranda* issues. The first concerns Ricardo's ability to understand his rights. He faces two potential challenges in this regard: his cognitive limitations and his facility with English. The latter is easily dismissed. Ricardo is sufficiently fluent that he turns down Manuel's offer to provide the warnings in Spanish. He also testifies in English at his trial and is able to express himself clearly and cogently.

His intellectual deficits are of greater concern. In this regard, these facts mirror those of *Commonwealth v. Johnson*, 354 A.2d 886 (Pa. 1976). As with Johnson, educational testing placed Ricardo in the "mild mental retardation" range and a psychologist concluded that he would have difficulty understanding sentences with more than one concept. On the other hand, because the testing took place three years ago when Ricardo was only fourteen, intellectual development and maturation may have improved his cognitive capacity. His trial testimony suggested that it had, in that he seemed able to grasp multiple concepts, despite the psychologist's claims to the contrary. Finally, Ricardo's prior arrests had acquainted him with *Miranda* rights. As in *Johnson*, these considerations, viewed collectively, adequately support the suspect's understanding of *Miranda*'s core protections.

When he is arrested, Ricardo invokes a limited waiver of his right to remain silent by refusing to talk about "what happened." He subsequently incriminates himself at the station house when Manuel remarks that "Jaime deserved it." Ricardo's statements are admissible, because Manuel "scrupulously honored" his right to remain silent under *Michigan v. Mosley*. First, Manuel did not comment until ninety minutes after Ricardo's invocation and did so in a location different than that of the invocation. He also administered a fresh set of *Miranda* warnings and did not overtly pressure Ricardo in any way. In fact, during the first thirty minutes after Ricardo expressed his unwillingness to discuss the murder, he and Manuel chatted amiably about other topics in the squad car.

That Manuel did not coerce Ricardo is insufficient to establish a *Miranda* waiver. Under *Berghuis v. Thompson*, a suspect who has had the opportunity to assert his *Miranda* rights waives his right to remain silent by making an "uncoerced" statement to the police. The correct answer is **D**.

23. In the dog house.   In this problem, Officer Natalie discovered the knife Katy used to kill her husband on the floor of a closet in Katy's bedroom. Natalie entered the bedroom when searching for Patrick. Patrick, Katy's neighbor, ran into her house when fleeing from Turbo, a police dog that was chasing him, after Natalie gave Turbo the command "sick 'em, boy."

Natalie had the authority to arrest Patrick without a warrant in public. Thus, if he fled into a residence, she could enter that residence in "hot pursuit" without a warrant to find him. In this instance, however, she never told Patrick he was under arrest; instead, she commanded a large dog to run toward him. Understandably, Patrick feared for his safety and tried to protect himself by running into Katy's house. Natalie's pursuit of him there led to her discovery of the knife.

Based on the foregoing, the knife is not admissible against Katy. Natalie acted unlawfully by threatening Patrick's physical well-being. As such, her subsequent pursuit of Patrick inside Katy's home and the resultant discovery of the murder weapon are "fruit of the poisonous tree." Because officers ordinarily need both an arrest warrant and a search warrant to enter the home of a third party to search for an arrestee, the correct answer is **B**.

24. Holy guacamole!   In asking whether the body cavity search is constitutional, this problem addresses "higher-level" invasions of bodily privacy. Campbell searches the body cavity of Tobias, a Texas college student who has just returned from spring break in Mexico. Campbell believes he will find cocaine-filled balloons that Tobias swallowed in an effort to smuggle them into the United States. Campbell's suspicions are informed by Tobias's obvious physical discomfort, his distended stomach, the discovery of a marijuana cigarette, and a report of an increase in drug smuggling by Texas college students.

Campbell had the right to order Tobias out of the car. *Pennsylvania v. Mimms*. Thus, the dislodging of the marijuana cigarette that occurs when Tobias exits raises no constitutional flag and, because the contraband is in plain view, its seizure by Campbell is lawful. Campbell's subsequent arrest of Tobias is also lawful, since possession of any amount of marijuana is a crime in Texas. Campbell's search of Tobias's clothing, which turns up nothing, is also lawful incident to arrest.

When Tobias refuses to consent to an X-ray, Campbell conducts an involuntary body cavity search. While the body cavity is an area within Tobias's "immediate control," it is far more invasive than the searches incident to arrest contemplated by *Robinson.* Accordingly, a warrant is necessary to justify this procedure and can be obtained either by Campbell or other law enforcement personnel.

Significantly, in upholding warrantless strip searches of inmates in 2012 in *Florence v. Board of Chosen Freeholders*, the U.S. Supreme Court emphasized the correctional context of the policy at issue as applied, in that case, to individuals housed in the general population of the prison. Thus, *Florence* provides no support for the body cavity search under the altogether different circumstances of this problem. The correct answer is **A**.

25. Guns n' roses.   Officer Latisha pulls over Norton's car and searches it pursuant to an announcement from the district attorney's office that the vehicle was linked to drug trafficking. The announcement had been withdrawn a week earlier; therefore, the search based on it was in error. You are asked to identify Norton's strongest argument for exclusion of the unregistered firearm found in the search.

In **D**, Latisha is aware of the announcement's cancellation but pulls Norton over for speeding and subsequently searches his vehicle. The traffic stop is perfectly lawful based on the reading on the radar gun, and it does not matter if the stop was pretextual. *Whren.* Officers have plenary authority, in their discretion, to make custodial arrests under the Fourth Amendment, so the arrest for speeding is lawful. *Atwater.* Latisha had the right to search the passenger cabin of the vehicle incident to the arrest, since Norton was unsecured at the time of the search. *Belton*; *Gant.* Thus, the discovery and seizure of the firearm are lawful. **D** is wrong.

The U.S. Supreme Court has declined to apply the exclusionary rule to errors by non-police personnel, reasoning that doing so fails to deter future police misconduct. Accordingly, **C** is incorrect, even though the court employees' comments and demeanor suggest reckless conduct, at the very least. *Arizona v. Evans.*

In **A** and **B**, the error takes place at the hands of police employees. *Herring* specifies that, for the exclusionary rule to apply, the error must be at least *grossly* negligent. In **A**, the delay in entering the data is the result of the unexpected loss of one-third of the relevant workforce two weeks earlier. While perhaps the department should have sought to hire replacement workers, its malfeasance is nowhere as egregious as in **B**, where it disregarded information, obtained a month ago, that its employees responsible for data entry were improperly trained and had an unacceptably high error rate greatly in excess of that of other police departments. Under these circumstances, their conduct was at least grossly negligent, if not reckless. **B** is the correct answer.

26. Hot wheels.   This problem blends various Fourth Amendment concepts in a challenging way. To disentangle the issues, it is helpful to start at the beginning of the fact pattern. Yenis stops Jonathan because she mistakenly believes he is a celebrity and wants his autograph. This is an invalid ground for detention and, as such, violates Jonathan's Fourth Amendment rights, since he submitted to her show of authority. Upon realizing her mistake, Yenis concludes that Jonathan is violating Setonia's ban on Wheelys. His subsequent arrest for that misconduct turns up cocaine in his coat pocket. Yenis later discovers that Jonathan did not, in fact, violate the Wheelys prohibition due to the small size of his custom-designed wheels.

Answer **B** would uphold Jonathan's challenge since his conduct was, in fact, lawful. Though this is true, *Heien* (see Chapter 14, part D) teaches that reasonable mistakes of law will insulate otherwise unconstitutional errors; therefore, **E** is a better answer than **B**. Because officers have plenary authority to search an arrestee's person and his clothing incident to arrest, **C** is likewise wrong.

Even if Yenis' mistake of law concerning the sneakers was reasonable, she lacked the reasonable suspicion necessary to order Jonathan to stop in the first instance. She had no evidence whatsoever that he was engaging in criminal conduct; she merely wanted his autograph. By submitting to Yenis' show of authority, Jonathan was unlawfully seized, and this taints the arrest that follows. Yenis may argue that the reasonably mistaken discovery of the sneaker violation "attenuates" the unconstitutional stop that precedes it, but this argument is likely to fail. First, the two events were extremely temporally proximate, since one followed directly on the heels of the other. Second, the violation of Jonathan's Fourth Amendment rights in stopping him was purposeful and flagrant; no reasonably trained officer could have believed that it was lawful. Finally, the intervening event — discovery of the sneaker infraction — was based on a mistake of law. By contrast, in *Strieff* (see Chapter 18, part D), the intervening event — an arrest warrant — was both valid and preexisting.

For the foregoing reasons, the best answer is **A**.

27. Cold scone Crazy. To choose the best answer, it is important to remember that you are asked to identify the argument that is strongest with respect to Ian's constitutional rights. For the constitution to apply, the conduct in question must be undertaken by a government official or someone acting at the behest of that official. Officer Brittany is a government actor; Tim is not. **B**, therefore, is wrong. Since Tim is a private actor, the fact that he threatened Ian is of no constitutional significance. Likewise, the fact that a confession may be unreliable is irrelevant to its constitutional sufficiency; the rules of evidence are the appropriate forum for such claims. See *Colorado v. Connelly*, Chapter 20, part C. **D**, accordingly, is wrong.

A, C, and **E** all focus on Brittany's conduct. **A** incorrectly focuses on her failure to provide *Miranda* warnings to Ian. Remember: *Miranda* only applies in the context of custodial interrogation, and Brittany did not question Ian. **E** addresses her failure to lock the doors to the police car thereby allowing Tim to enter. While this was an exercise of poor judgment on Brittany's part, it does not mandate suppression of Ian's confession at the hands of Tim, especially where there is no indication that her oversight was designed to undermine Ian's constitutional rights.

The remaining choice, C, is the best answer. In the face of Ian's pleas for protection from Tim's aggression, Brittany stood by and allowed Tim to threaten Ian's physical well-being. As such, this situation evokes that of *Payne v. Arkansas* and *Arizona v. Fulminante* — see Chapter 20, part A — where the Court found that the refusal of law enforcement officers to intervene to protect individuals from credible threats of violence overbore the defendants' free will, thereby rendering their confessions inadmissible.

28. Smokin' him out.   This problem combines the constitutional standards surrounding confessions with the criminal law defense of entrapment. Starting with the Fifth Amendment, answer **A** incorrectly posits that Nick's failure to provide *Miranda* warnings should lead to suppression of the contraband. Even if Kylie's questioning of Nick constituted custodial interrogation, the drugs themselves would not be subject to suppression because they are a "physical fruit" and Nick was not subject to actual coercion by Kylie or Drew. See *Patane*. **B**, which argues for suppression under the Sixth Amendment, is likewise incorrect. The Sixth Amendment applies only to charged offenses and Nick has not been charged with any offense related to this transaction. The fact that he has been charged with previous similar offenses is inapposite.

C and **D** reference entrapment under the majority and minority approaches. The majority approach focuses on the defendant's predisposition to commit the crime in question. At first blush, this seems an attractive choice, since these facts are similar in certain respects to those of *Sherman v. United States*, where government agents unlawfully badgered a recovering drug addict into purchasing drugs through a drug rehabilitation center where the defendant was endeavoring to stay sober. See Chapter 19, part A. That case is distinguishable, however, in important respects. First, and most importantly, *Sherman's* prior convictions were quite old, whereas Nick's are fairly recent. This alone is strong evidence of predisposition. In addition, in *Sherman*, government agents were successful only after repeated attempts over a three-month period; here, Nick purchased the cigars the same day they were offered to him.

In contrast to the majority test, the minority approach to entrapment focuses on the conduct of law enforcement, not the defendant's predisposition. Under his test, entrapment occurs when government agents' overzealousness leads individuals to commit crimes who would otherwise have acted lawfully. Here, Kylie infiltrated a support group of people trying to overcome the urge to purchase Cuban cigars, sought out the person she believed was struggling the most, and, aided by Drew, pressured Nick to give in to his urges by offering the cigars at greatly reduced cost. This government overreach makes **D** the best answer.

Congratulations! You have done it and should feel rewarded for your efforts. I hope you have found this book helpful. I enjoyed writing it for you.

✦ Cornwell's Picks

1.	Meth proof	E
2.	Scissor seizures	C
3.	Transparent behavior	B
4.	Pocketed watch	C
5.	Pistol pattin' Martha	C
6.	Forcing the issue	D
7.	Groovy greenhouse	C
8.	Access Hollyweed	A
9.	Obie & the force	C
10.	Ring-a-ding-ding	B
11.	His brother's keeper	D
12.	Doing the can-can	A
13.	Pipin' hot	D
14.	Made up make-up	E
15.	Hook, line, and sinker	B
16.	Slipping Mickey	E
17.	A whisper in the park	B
18.	The art of deception	D
19.	SuperSpying: No ordinary prying	A
20.	Barking up the wrong trees	D
21.	Potluck	B
22.	¡Ay caramba!	D
23.	In the dog house	B
24.	Holy guacamole!	A
25.	Guns n' roses	B
26.	Hot wheels	A
27.	Cold scone crazy	C
28.	Smokin' him out	D

Table of Cases[1]

---

[1] This index lists the page on which a case is introduced and any reference to that case in subsequent chapters. Multiple references within the same chapter are included only where a case is cited for more than one principle of law.

Index